RESCUE THE PERISHI

# Rescue the Perishing

## Eleanor Rathbone and the Refugees

SUSAN COHEN



VALLENTINE MITCHELL
LONDON • PORTLAND, OR

*First published in 2010 by Vallentine Mitchell*

Middlesex House,
29/45 High Street, Edgware,
Middlesex HAB 7UU, UK

920 NE 58th Avenue, Suite 300
Portland, Oregon,
97213-3786 USA

www.vmbooks.com



British Library Cataloguing in Publication Data

Cohen, Susan, 1950-
Rescue the perishing : Eleanor Rathbone and the refugees.
1. Rathbone, Eleanor F. (Eleanor Florence), 1872-1946.
2. World War, 1939-1945—Jews—Rescue. 3. World War, 1939-1945—Refugees—Services for. 4. Jewish refugees—Services for—History—20th century. 5. Women social reformers—Great Britain—Biography. 6. Social reformers—Great Britain—Biography. 7. Women politicians—Great Britain—Biography. 8. Politicians—Great Britain—Biography.
I. Title
362.8'7525'092-dc22

ISBN 978 0 85303 778 1 (cloth)
ISBN 978 0 85303 779 8 (paper)

Library of Congress Cataloging-in-Publication Data
has been applied for



Printed in Great Britain by the MPG Books Group, Bodmin and King's Lynn

# Contents

# Illustrations

26. Page 1 of *Rescue the Perishing* (Victor Gollancz, 1943). Courtesy of The Wiener Library, London.
27. The National Committee for Rescue from Nazi Terror: Ten-Point Programme, January 1944. Courtesy of Imperial War Museum, London.
28. The National Committee for Rescue from Nazi Terror: Lists of members and application form. Courtesy of Imperial War Museum, London.
29. Dedication ceremony of the Eleanor Rathbone School at Magdiel, 19 October 1949, with Bertha Schoolman speaking. Courtesy of Hadassah Archives at the American Jewish Historical Society, New York.
30. The Eleanor Rathbone Building, Magdiel, Israel, 19 October 1949. Youth Aliyah Collection at the American Jewish Historical Society. Reproduced courtesy of Central Zionist Archives, Jerusalem. Israel.

For plate 5, every effort has been made to obtain permission to reproduce this photo, and the author will rectify any omission if further information on the copyright holder is received.

For plates 23, 27 and 28, every effort has been made to trace copyright holders and the author and the Imperial War Museum would be grateful for any information which might help to trace those whose identities or addresses are not currently known.

# Foreword

The title 'MP for Refugees' reveals so much about Eleanor Rathbone. It was, of course, an unofficial label given to her by her friends within and outside the refugee community. Yet the title was totally fitting to describe both her work and her constituency from the 1930s until her death in 1946. Eleanor Rathbone, an Independent MP for the Combined Universities, continued her wide range of political activities reflecting her reforming zeal during the Nazi era. But it was the dispossessed, and especially those fleeing from or attempting to escape fascist persecution, who most relied on her humanitarian energy during those traumatic years. In short, no other Member of Parliament devoted so much time and over such a long period to the refugee cause as did Eleanor Rathbone. Why, then, has Rathbone's refugee work been so neglected? This lacuna is even more surprising given the increasing scholarly and popular interest in this leading and pioneer woman parliamentarian in recent years.[1]

The explanation, I would suggest, lies at a general level and does not relate to Eleanor Rathbone specifically: that is, refugees have tended to be neglected and marginalized in many different ways. They are often treated, as anthropologist Liisa Malkki suggests, as 'people who do not fit'. Following the work of Mary Douglas on the concept of 'dirt', Malkki argues that they represent 'matter out of place'.ii Put simply, refugees disturb the expected equilibrium – they are not easily imagined within the idea of the nation state and are, increasingly, in the form of the legal classification 'asylum seekers', kept out of its borders. They are even difficult to subsume within the broad umbrella of the category 'migrant', their narratives of persecution rendering them awkward and uncomfortable to consider.

This unease extends to those who have helped or attempted to help refugees at different times and in different places. It is not always clear, for example, what would be the motivations for supporting what Michael Marrus has dubbed 'the unwanted'?iii Certainly, as Susan Cohen illustrates in the Introduction to her remarkable work, those who have studied Eleanor Rathbone in recent years, often interpreting her activities through a feminist perspective, have had particular difficulty in explaining why the MP devoted so much time in the last years of her parliamentary career to the refugee cause. And rather than confront this increasingly important aspect of her work, such scholars have often avoided it all together or treated it as an unusual aberration, or even less convincingly, as an indication of the loss of focus of her direction on the women's cause.

One of the great achievements of Susan Cohen's study is that it shows that the roots of Eleanor Rathbone's refugee work were deep and went back much further than the Nazi era: they were, argues Cohen, part and parcel of her wider humanitarian mission. Here one might go further. Whilst Eleanor Rathbone clearly *was* exceptional in the energy and vision she devoted to the refugee cause, she was not alone. Indeed, the absence of reference to refugee work in the historical record, relating to Britain in the twentieth century but also to other places and other times, reflects not its non-existence, but the failure of historians and others to deem it worthy of attention either as a subject in itself or in relation to other campaigning issues.iv It is to be hoped, therefore, that Susan Cohen's immaculate research will not only rescue from partial oblivion Eleanor Rathbone's refugee work, but will also stimulate others to locate those whom she worked alongside or were her predecessors and successors in fighting for the cause of the persecuted.

Eleanor Rathbone would not have welcomed an account of her refugee work that was aimed at promoting her as a heroine. Indeed, she took every effort to destroy any personal records that might have shed further light on her motivations for this and her other humanitarian campaigning – it has taken remarkable, detective-style research by Susan Cohen to piece the story together from archives in the public and private realm and from many different collections and countries. The tendency, especially in relation to the Holocaust, to create plaster saints in the form of rescuers, most famously in the case of Oskar Schindler, relates to the desire to make the event a modern morality play with the righteous gentiles providing a redemptive ending and as a foil to the evil perpetrators. Susan Cohen avoids such moralizing within this study of Eleanor Rathbone. It is not that the author does not have an admiration for the determination of her subject matter, but that the emphasis is on contextualization – the background to her work and where/how/when it was carried out.

Rathbone is not easy to categorize. She was not, as Victor Gollancz, her fellow campaigner on behalf of Jewish refugees, pointed out in an obituary in the journal of the Association of Jewish Refugees, what might be termed a philosemite. She did not see the Jews as having a special mission, as did some Protestants and religion played perhaps only an indirect spur to her overall work. Gollancz was perhaps being a little unfair when he stated boldly that 'she didn't particularly like Jews', but the point he was making was to emphasize the importance of what she did for Jewish refugees and for the Jewish cause more generally in these desperate years.v It was simply that the Jews were people in need that prompted Eleanor Rathbone to take action. And whilst she did not put her life directly at risk as was the case with rescuers of Jews on the continent during the Second World War, it is undoubtedly the case that she added great stress, frustration and anxiety to her life by recognizing the horrors experienced by European Jewry and then in failing to convince the British government to do something about it. In the end, it cost her faith in British, or more specifically English, decency facing the reality that her government was so unmoved by her pleas to help.

*Rescue the Perishing*, named after Rathbone's powerful call to do something to stop the slaughter of European Jewry, is thus the sort of study we need of those that campaigned against injustice and for the vulnerable in society – in this case, refugees from Nazism. In a world in which politicians and the media play so much heed to those who are hostile to newcomers, a study that explores the world of those whose responses to refugees were motivated by humanitarianism is not just needed as a historical correction – it is a necessary political intervention in the broadest possible sense.

Professor Tony Kushner
Parkes Institute for the Study of Jewish/non-Jewish Relations
University of Southampton

## NOTES

1. At a popular level, see, for example, Philip Carter, 'Women First', *BBC History Magazine*, 10, 3 (March 2009), p.55.
2. Liisa Malkki, 'National Geographic: The Rooting of Peoples and the Territorialization of National Identity among Scholars and Refugees', *Cultural Anthropology*, 7, 1 (February 1992), p.34.
3. Michael Marrus, *The Unwanted: European Refugees in the Twentieth Century* (Oxford: Oxford University Press, 1985).
4. More generally on this point see Tony Kushner, *Remembering Refugees: Then and Now* (Manchester: Manchester University Press, 2006).
5. Victor Gollancz, obituary of Eleanor Rathbone in *AJR Information*, 2 (February 1946).

# Preface

I've been asked many times what made me take such an interest in Eleanor Rathbone and decide to research and write about her refugee work. My first introduction to her was in the 1970s when I was taking a sociology course at my local college and discovered that she was the person responsible for the introduction, in 1946, of the Family Allowance that I, and thousands of mothers, collected every week from the Post Office. I was eternally grateful to this unknown woman for the regular sum of money that was specifically for me and my children. Little did I know that her life would have such an impact on mine some two decades later, but for very different reasons. My re-acquaintance with this remarkable woman occurred, again by accident rather than design, when, in the late 1990s, I was considering options for my doctoral thesis. Whilst looking for a neglected aspect of Anglo-Jewish history to research, I came across the dedication in Tony Kushner's book, *The Holocaust and the Liberal Imagination*, in which he paid tribute to Eleanor Rathbone as the person 'who knew, cared and acted'.[1] What, I asked myself, had she cared about so much that warranted such sincere sentiments? I also wondered if there was room for further investigation to be undertaken into these unidentified activities? The answer to the latter question was a resounding 'yes', for the actions which Tony Kushner alluded to in his poignant comments, and which also answered my first question, were Eleanor Rathbone's campaigning activities on behalf of Europe's Jewish refugees and her commitment to the refugee question during the Nazi era. This aspect of her life and work, which began in 1933 and continued until her death in 1946, had, as I discovered, been neglected or misunderstood by historians, and had evaded serious historical research. I feel privileged to have been able to redress this imbalance and to be the author of a book that, at last, fully acknowledges Eleanor Rathbone's unique humanitarianism and her contribution to the welfare and rescue of refugees during the Nazi period.

I wish to express my gratitude to a number of people who have had such faith in my ability to complete my doctoral thesis and subsequently write this book. My special thanks go to my supervisor, Tony Kushner, for all his encouragement and wise counsel. David Cesarani provided valuable support in the early stages of my research and my friend, Clive Fleay, generously spared time to read and comment on drafts of certain chapters, for which I am very grateful. I gratefully acknowledge the financial assistance that I received when working on my doctoral thesis from the Eleanor Rathbone Charitable Trust, and the exceptional grant they made for microfilming purposes.

I have very many people and institutions to thank for their assistance. These include: the BBC Written Archives Centre, Birmingham University Library, the Board of Deputies of British Jews, the Bodleian Library, the British Library, Cambridge University Library, Churchill Archives Centre, Cambridge, Contemporary Medical Archives at the Wellcome Library for the History and Understanding of Medicine, the Imperial War Museum, Institute of Education, University of London, John Rylands Library at the University of Manchester, Lambeth Palace Library, Lancashire Record Office, the London School of Economics and Political Science, the library of the Religious Society of Friends, London, the Modern Records Centre, University of Warwick, the National Archives, Kew, the Parkes Library at the University of Southampton, the Parliamentary Archives, Somerville College, Oxford, St Antony's College, Oxford, Trinity College, Cambridge, the library of the University of Hull, the library of the University of Reading, the Women's Library, London Guildhall University, the Sydney Jones Library of the University of Liverpool, the Wiener Library; in Israel the Central Zionist Archives, the Social Work library at the Hebrew University, Mount Scopus, the Weizmann Institute of Science and Yad Vashem Institute Archives; in Switzerland, the International Committee of the Red Cross, Geneva, and in the United States, Ball State University Archives and Special Collections, the Beinecke Library, the Center for Jewish History at the American Jewish Historical Society, Hadassah Archives, New York, the library of the Leo Baeck Institute New York, Yale University and the Franklin Delano Roosevelt Presidential Library, New York State.

I am very grateful to Ms Val Traylen of the National Archives, without whose help I would not have had access to 'closed' Home Office case files, and to Adrian Allan, archivist at University of Liverpool, for his insight into the Rathbone family, and his introduction to the late Lady Margaret Simey. I am also very appreciative of the time that people spared to share their memories of Eleanor with me. Their names appear in the list of interviews at the end of the book.

Last but not least, a special thank you must go to my family and friends for believing that I would finish this book, which is dedicated to my late parents, Edith and Sam Balcombe.

NOTES

1. Tony Kushner, *The Holocaust and the Liberal Imagination: A Social and Cultural History* (Oxford: Blackwell, 1994).

# Abbreviations

| | |
|---|---|
| APAG | All-Party Parliamentary Action Group |
| BBC | British Broadcasting Corporation |
| BCC | Basque Children's Committee |
| BCIWF | British Committee for Indian Women's Franchise |
| BCRC | British Committee for Refugees from Czechoslovakia |
| BDBJ | Board of Deputies of British Jews Bermuda Report 'Report to the Governments of the United States and the United Kingdom from their delegates to the Conference on the Refugee Problem held at Bermuda, April 19–29, 1943.' 29 April 1943, NA FO 371/36725, W6711/6711/48 |
| BL | British Library |
| BLPES | British Library of Political and Economic Science, London School of Economics |
| BOD | Bodleian Library, Oxford |
| CAC | Churchill Archives Centre, Cambridge University |
| CCR | Central Committee for Refugees |
| CIL | Committee For Intellectual Liberty |
| COS | Charity Organisation Society |
| CO | Colonial Office |
| CRTF | Czech Refugee Trust Fund |
| CUL | Cambridge University Library |
| CZA | Central Zionist Archives, Jerusalem |
| FEC | Family Endowment Committee |
| FO | Foreign Office |
| *Hansard* HC | House of Commons Debates |
| HO | Home Office |
| ICG | India Conciliation Group |
| IGCR | Intergovernmental Committee on Refugees |
| ILP | Independent Labour Party |
| IWM | Imperial War Museum |
| IWSA | International Woman Suffrage Alliance |
| JWERA | Jewish Women's Equal Rights Association |

| | |
|---|---|
| JA | Jewish Agency |
| JRL | John Rylands Library, University of Manchester |
| KM | Katherine Mayo Papers, Beinecke Library Yale University |
| LCRS | Liverpool Central Relief Society |
| LMA | London Metropolitan Archive |
| LN | League of Nations |
| LNU | League of Nations Union |
| LPL | Lambeth Palace Library |
| LVWS | Liverpool Victoria Women's Settlement |
| LWCA | Liverpool Women's Citizen's Association |
| LWIC | Liverpool Women's Industrial Council |
| LWSS | Liverpool Women's Suffrage Society |
| MRC | Modern Records Centre, University of Warwick |
| NA | National Archives |
| NBKR | Papers of Philip Noel Baker |
| NCFS | National Committee of the Friends of Spain |
| NCRNT | National Committee for Rescue from Nazi Terror |
| NJCSR | National Joint Committee for Spanish Relief |
| NUSEC | National Union of Societies for Equal Citizenship |
| NUWSS | National Union of Women's Suffrage Societies |
| OIOC | Oriental and India Office Collection, British Library |
| PA | Parliamentary Archives |
| PCO | Passport Control Officer |
| PCR | Parliamentary Committee on Refugees |
| PJWERA | Palestine Jewish Women's Equal Rights Association |
| RP | Rathbone Papers |
| SPSL | Society for the Protection of Science and Learning |
| SSFA | Soldiers and Sailors Family Association |
| UE | University of Edinburgh Library |
| ULL | Special Collections and Archives, Sydney Jones Library, University of Liverpool |
| USL | Parkes Library, Special Collections, University of Southampton |
| WCC | War Cabinet Committee on the Reception and Accommodation of Jewish Refugees |
| WHI | Graham White Papers, Parliamentary Archives |
| WIA | Women's India Association |
| WJC | World Jewish Congress |
| WL | Women's Library, London Guildhall University |

| | |
|---|---|
| WRB | War Refugee Board Papers, Franklin D. Roosevelt Library, New York. |
| WSPU | Women's Social and Political Union |

# PART I

# Introduction

Eleanor Rathbone, Independent MP for the Combined Universities, had a varied career during her lifetime and made significant and unique contributions to many aspects of life in Britain. The first indication that she would become the staunchest of British Gentile supporters of Jewish refugees occurred following Hitler's accession to power in Germany in January 1933. On 13 April 1933 she made a prophetic speech in the House of Commons warning of the dangers heralded by the new Nazi government, its leadership and party. As the threat to the Jews of Europe grew, so her commitment to their rescue and welfare increased exponentially, and remained undiminished until her death in 1946. This devotion may have only consumed some 20 per cent of her working life, during which time she gained renown as a feminist, suffragist, philanthropist, social reformer, campaigner for family allowances, pacificist and MP, but it was far greater in terms of the impact that her humanitarian activism had on the recipients of her help. Her colleagues and friends held her in great esteem, as did the refugees whom she sought to help, and many of them felt that they owed their lives to her. But even though in her lifetime she earned the honorary title 'MP for refugees', and was considered to be foremost amongst the British refugee activists, her involvement with the refugee cause has subsequently been overlooked in many quarters, and diminished or marginalized in others. Explaining how and why her commitment to the refugee question has been neglected is complex, and has as much to do with a prevailing but ill-conceived perception of Eleanor as first and foremost a feminist who was dedicated exclusively to the women's cause, as it does with the failure of those researching the response of the democracies to the Holocaust to give greater attention to refugee-related issues and the work of refugee activists. What is undoubtedly clear is that Eleanor's refugee work was not aimed specifically at women, and nor should it be considered an inexplicable aberration in the career of a woman whose earlier campaigns were often, but not exclusively, related to women's issues. Nor, as this book argues, was her engagement with the welfare and rescue of refugees disconnected from her earlier activities.

The purpose of this book is therefore to put the record straight by critically examining Eleanor's involvement with the refugee question within the context of her life, her work, especially in the international field, and times. Only then can her contribution be fully understood and appreciated, and her place in history as a humanitarian activist secured. Key questions that are addressed are what impelled Eleanor Rathbone to take up the refugee cause, and how it fitted in with the rest of her life. Was she, as both Mary Stocks and Susan Pedersen consider, a feminist whose overriding interest in female-related causes was coincidentally replaced by a concern for refugees, as the impetus went out of first-wave feminism in the early 1930s? Or was she, as I believe, first and foremost a humanitarian activist who, throughout her working life, responded to the needs of the under-represented and vulnerable in society, both at home and abroad, regardless of their gender, religion or race? What emerges from this study is a realization that the various causes she championed were not mutually exclusive, but were linked by a common theme of helping others less fortunate than herself. The driving forces were a complex weave of nature and nurture in which inherited and inculcated traits, religious influence and philosophical teachings all had their part to play.

Looking back at the attention paid to Eleanor's refugee work in the various accounts of her life, there have been two full-length biographical records written about her. The first, by Mary Stocks, appeared in 1949, just three years after her death.[1] Evaluating the life of a close friend and colleague was certainly an onerous task, and even though it was generally accepted at the time that the author had 'austere respect for factual truth,' the result was not as 'broad in scope, objective and critical' an account of Eleanor's public activities as claimed.[2]

Importantly, this book failed to provide any sort of insightful comprehensive account of Eleanor's work for Jews fleeing Nazi persecution from 1933 onwards, even though it was such a significant aspect of her career. Of course Mary Stocks was hindered to some extent by the lack of evidence available to her. Masses of material was lost when Eleanor's London office was bombed during war-time raids, besides which she requested that all her personal correspondence and diaries, along with those of her companion, Elizabeth Macadam, be destroyed after their deaths. Nor did Mary Stocks have access to official Home Office, Foreign Office, Cabinet and Treasury papers in the National Archive, closed at the time under official rules, which subsequently shed enormous light on the relationship between Eleanor and the government. Many of the latter lost opportunities, and more besides, were available to Eleanor's most recent biographer, Susan Pedersen, whose memoir was published in 2004, but she did not, by her own admission, undertake a detailed a study of Eleanor's refugee work as such. Rather she marginalized it, and produced a work that has reinforced the view of Eleanor as, primarily, a feminist at the expense of a full understanding of her humanitarian activism.[3] A third short study by the feminist historian Johanna Alberti is based on the erroneous assumption that Eleanor's work can be neatly categorized as gendered and non-gendered, and whilst the author has conceded that there was a shift of focus in Eleanor's commitments in the 1930s, she has not offered any reasons for this change in direction.[4] Instead she chose to pay far less attention to her subject's career after 1933, thereby diminishing the significance of her campaigning activities during this period. By writing through the prism of feminism, Johanna Alberti has produced a rather crude and reductive picture of Eleanor's work and ideas that lacks objectivity and balance. In defence of Johanna Alberti, Susan Pedersen maintains the fault is due to the author's reliance upon Eleanor's published writings as source material. It is true that less material was printed on the refugee issue than on, for example, Eleanor's long-running campaign for family allowances, but her political career was well documented in published sources including *Hansard*, and these could have been used in conjunction with material in the National Archives as well as the considerable body of less accessible extant archive material scattered in small pockets across many collections.

Given that there is a major repository of Eleanor's papers at the University of Liverpool, there would seem, at first glance, to be no shortage of primary source material readily available to the researcher. However, documents relating to refugee issues are particularly badly represented in the collection, a factor that has undoubtedly contributed towards the limited interest in this subject. In researching this book, innumerable collections, private and public, national and international, were examined to enable a detailed picture of Eleanor's campaigning activities to be compiled and considered within the wider context of her life's work. The fact that correspondence to her was inevitably in English – even when the author was Czech, as in the case of Mme Plaminkova – serves as a reminder that Eleanor was English-speaking and working in an English-speaking environment. This explains the absence of sources in other languages. As far as possible, previously neglected unpublished sources have been utilized, as exemplified in respect of her communications with the War Refugee Board, Arthur Koestler, Doreen Warriner, Chaim Weizmann, Esther Simpson and Dr Schwarzbart in the 1940s. Privileged access to certain collections, including Victor Cazalet's diaries, certain closed files of the Board of Deputies of British Jews (BDBJ),[5] and numerous closed Home Office files relating to refugees with whom she was personally involved, have proved invaluable. Cazalet's diaries provided a very personal glimpse of Eleanor's dedication to the refugee cause, whilst the BDBJ papers yielded an important source of information about refugee committee meetings and her relationship with the Anglo-Jewish community. Home Office files concerning individual internment cases were of special significance, not only because they helped establish the extent of Eleanor's personal involvement, but because no researcher has ever been granted access to them before. It should be explained that the Home Office routinely created a file for every immigrant who had contact with the Aliens Department. Following standard practice, the Home Office periodically destroyed case files no longer required for official purposes, setting aside for transfer to the National Archive only a small number of representative or historically significant cases. This process was halted in the mid-1990s and all surviving files opened before 1948 were individually reviewed. All those relating to individuals who arrived before 1948 and subsequently applied for naturalisation have been preserved within Home Office files HO 405. In addition a relatively small number of non-naturalisation cases were selected, including those that contained transcripts of internment tribunal hearings or appeals against internment, which are to be found in HO 382. The files in HO 405 are closed as a block for 100 years, but the Home Office policy is to review the closure of individual files on request, with special access arrangements for academic researchers. Identifying cases proved especially difficult, and was achieved by crossmatching refugee names that appeared in a variety of Eleanor's correspondence with Home Office lists. This could not have been achieved without the generous cooperation of Home Office and National Archive officials.[6]

Extensive use has been made of House of Commons daily *Hansard* papers, and Home, Colonial and Foreign Office files in the National Archives. The latter proved to be crucial in establishing the nature of the relationship between Eleanor and government officials, thus highlighting the obstacles that she encountered in her battle on behalf of refugees seeking rescue and refuge. They also provided many documents and references relating to the Parliamentary Committee on Refugees (PCR) established by her in December 1938. Assessing the scope and value of her activities within the PCR was vital, and proved challenging, for there is no single collection of papers, but a fragmented mosaic of correspondence, reports, memos and minutes scattered within a wide range of personal and official archives. A small and incomplete collection of material was donated by Vera Craig, one of Eleanor's wartime PCR secretaries, to the Parliamentary Archives, but it was within this same repository that the papers of Graham White, Member of Parliament and PCR member, proved to be an especially rich and unexpected resource. Interviews with people who had come into contact with Eleanor in the course of her refugee work added a personal dimension to this research, and, as in the case of, for example, Arieh Handler and Nicholas Winton, served as poignant reminders of her sometimes eccentric character. More forthcoming as far as the PCR was concerned was correspondence between Eleanor and Esther Simpson, secretary of the Society for the Protection of Science and Learning, which was helpful in providing information about the collaboration between the two organizations in handling individual interned alien cases. By piecing all of this evidence together it has been possible to produce a detailed chronological examination of the work of the organization during the Second World War, and enabled an assessment of Eleanor's activities and role within it to be made. Much the same applies to the National Committee for Rescue from Nazi Terror (NCRNT) which she was instrumental in establishing in 1942/43, for again, primary source material was found within a wide range of collections.

It has also been suggested that Eleanor lacked the enthusiasm to pursue feminist goals after 1933[7] and that the new campaigns she championed – including her refugee work – were a convenient replacement for gendered activities.[8] Following on from this is the claim that by involving herself in non-gendered campaigns, Eleanor was being disloyal to the feminist movement. These arguments do not hold up when the decline and change in the nature of feminist activism by the 1930s is taken into account, and when the fact that she maintained an active interest in many of her earlier feminist and gendered activities, especially the fight for a family allowance to be paid to mothers, is considered. As Susan Pedersen has suggested, the greater crisis in international affairs may have diverted Eleanor from feminist issues,[9] but this is a view also based on a gendered perspective, and confirms the problem that many gender-biased historians have in reconciling Eleanor's female-related campaigning with her later parliamentary activities and non-gendered refugee interests.

Setting aside the failure of gender-biased writers to properly address Eleanor's refugee work, numerous biographical pictures of her are too fleeting in their reference to this important aspect of her life's work. *The Dictionary of National Biography* summarized these aspects of her career as the 'polemical phase of her concern with foreign affairs ... accompanied by untiring efforts on behalf of refugees both before and during the war of 1939–45'. Pedersen's more recently compiled entry in the *Oxford Dictionary of National Biography* improves on its predecessor, but, like her biography of Eleanor, still fails to pay sufficient attention to her refugee work. Even less generous is *Chambers Biographical Dictionary of Women*, which merely notes that she took a stand against the appeasement of Hitler, and worked vigorously 'in the service of refugees'.[10] Yet another biographical reference is succinct in its conclusion that she 'supported an aggressive opposition to Hitler.'[11] Brian Harrison, in his exploratory chapter on Eleanor, provides a more global picture of her political career, but has again examined it through a narrow range of primary sources. Furthermore, he has also failed to explore in any significant detail her commitment to refugee issues. Only Harrison and Sybil Oldfield, whose recent chronological overview of Eleanor's life has captured the essence and extent of her commitment to the rescue of the perishing, have commended her for her outstanding record as a humanitarian activist.[12]

What of historians undertaking refugee studies and the way in which her activism has been marginalized? At a general level, refugee-related issues and the work of refugee activists has never been a very popular subject so that little attention has been given to these areas by those researching the response of the democracies to the Holocaust. More specifically, the major problem is that most researchers in this field have considered Eleanor Rathbone's involvement to be an episode in, rather than a concomitant part of her life's work. So, like those with a gender bias, they have failed to appreciate the connections between her refugee work and the various other strands of her multifarious career. The leading scholarly monographs have made short shrift of Eleanor's refugee work within comprehensive studies of the broader subject of British policy towards the Jews. Examples include A.J. Sherman's monograph, *Island Refuge: Britain and Refugees from the Third Reich 1933–39*, originally published in 1973. This study, which is largely devoted to pre-war policy development and Britain's involvement in international discussions of the refugee question, includes a few references to Eleanor, mostly in connection with her campaign for Czech refugees. Michael Marrus's *The Unwanted: European Refugees and the Twentieth Century*, published in 1985, makes passing reference to her Twelve-Point Plan for rescue in a section devoted to rescue efforts after late 1942. Others include Louise London's comprehensive study of British policy towards Jews, *Whitehall and the Jews, 1933–1948: British Immigration Policy and the Holocaust*, which appeared in 2000. London does little more than give a flavour of Eleanor's involvement in the Czech refugee question and a mention of her and her organization, the NCRNT.[13]

The exceptions of note include David Cesarani in his article, 'Mad Dogs and Englishmen: Towards a Taxonomy of Rescuers in a Bystander Country – Britain 1933–45' published in 2000, which includes a brief study of her role during the Holocaust. Eleanor's commitment to the refugee cause has also received greater attention from

Tony Kushner in *The Holocaust and the Liberal Imagination: A Social and Cultural History*, published in 1994, and *Refugees in an Age of Genocide: Global, National and Local Perspectives during the Twentieth Century*, co-written with Katherine Knox in 1999. There is also Aimée Bunting's short review of the NCRNT, and Pamela Shatzkes's references to and assessment of Eleanor in her 2002 book, *Holocaust and Rescue: Impotent or Indifferent? Anglo-Jewry 1938–1945*.[14]

Describing Eleanor as a humanitarian activist, and examining what motivated her actions, clearly warrants some exploration. The *Oxford English Dictionary* locates the derivation of 'humanitarian' to the early nineteenth century, when it was first used in a religious context as 'one who affirms the humanity but denies the divinity of Christ'. Such people are described as philanthropists who advocate or practice humanity or humane action, devoting themselves to the welfare of mankind at large.[15] Minear and Weiss have concluded that, historically, such people characteristically involved themselves in saving others from life-threatening situations, attempted to rescue helpless civilians in imminent danger, or tried to prevent mass suffering.[16] Eleanor can clearly be identified within these descriptions, for her rescue work, especially after late 1942 through the auspices of her NCRNT, was explicitly about saving the lives of Jews threatened with annihilation. Her view of Christianity was, in part, defined by doubt and she was certainly sceptical about the divinity of Christ, evident in the instructions she wrote for her funeral:

> My own feeling is that whether the soul survives the body – and of that I am not sure – my body is not me and of no more importance than a cast-off garment. Do not take this to mean that I am un-Christian. I do not think I am. But Christianity seems to me a guide for life, but is rather vague about the after-life of individuals.[17]

With an overt lack of concern for dissenting voices within the political machinery, she repeatedly and vociferously demanded that the British government take steps to intercede in the human catastrophe, using every means at her disposal. The apparent lack of compassion which the government displayed towards Jews in particular acted as a catalyst, and impelled Eleanor to pursue her campaign with added vigour, for her ideological belief in Victorian liberalism and national and personal responsibility was severely challenged. Her philanthropic gestures were legendary, even though she did, to a certain extent, adhere to the Victorian idea of the 'deserving' and 'undeserving'. The fact that political imperatives and gains outweighed moral considerations in the minds of the British government was something that Eleanor was never able to accept. Whilst she was, as Tony Kushner has suggested, an 'exceptional individual', willing and able to rebel against convention and defy the received wisdom of the time, it was this very individualism that marked her out as an outsider.[18]

The latter question, as to what compelled Eleanor to become a humanitarian activist, is complex. Nature certainly had a part to play, for the twin ideals of personal service and responsible citizenship, and her belief in the concepts of liberty and freedom, were deeply rooted within her psyche. But nurture developed, honed and influenced these attributes, especially during her years at university. She was undoubtedly devoted to the welfare of others, a commitment that was founded in selflessness, characteristic of the altruistic personality conceived by Auguste Comte almost two centuries earlier.[19] Every campaign Eleanor fought was undertaken to improve the human condition, whether it was conducted from inside or outside the framework of governmental authority. However, unlike the rescuers of Jews in Nazi Europe whom S. and P. Oliner studied, she was never, as far as we know, in the position of risking her life in the course of her activities, although it is hard to imagine that she would not have done so had the opportunity arisen. For this reason she can never be included in the list of Righteous Gentiles at the Yad Vashem Holocaust memorial.

That she was able to pursue a course of humanitarian activism owed much to her position within society, for she had privileged access to governmental circles, the media and the intelligentsia. She had the added benefit of financial independence, and continually channelled resources into supporting her campaigns, and especially to the running costs of the PCR. But the fact remains that, as Tony Kushner has pointed out in respect of refugees, she chose to ally herself to the fate of people with whom she had no bond in terms of ethnicity, religion or nationality. Instead, what bound them was a common humanity. Whilst she may have lacked the ties Tony Kushner has cited, Eleanor came to identify closely with the Jews, and in admiring them for their cultural, philosophical and religious contributions to society, viewed them as deserving of help.[20] According to Victor Gollancz, her fellow refugee activist, left-wing publisher and founder of the Left Book Club, Jewish refugees were 'the greatest sufferers, the most grievously oppressed: and to succour the suffering and oppressed was something more than the motive of her life – it *was* her life'.[21] No less important was her personal conscience and profound belief in her own responsibility, and that of the British nation, to alleviate the suffering of European Jews – men, women and children – who, through no fault of their own, had been singled out by Hitler for annihilation.

Eleanor herself was modest about her achievements, and did not consider her actions to be exceptional in any way. As Margaret Simey and Mary Stocks confirmed, she never sought public recognition for her work, nor would she accept any commendation.[22] She would have undoubtedly disapproved of anyone writing about her life and work, so that researching, evaluating and documenting her activities is somewhat paradoxical. However, her humanitarian activities, and especially those that took her into the international arena and laid the foundations for her refugee work, deserve greater attention, for they are an integral part of the jigsaw, and shed light on the progression of her commitment to the needs of others. Caring for and about those fleeing tyranny was of far greater significance than has, up until now, been acknowledged, and was a concomitant part of the broad scope of her life's work.

## NOTES

1. M. Stocks, *Eleanor Rathbone. A Biography* (London: Victor Gollancz, 1949).
2. A view expressed by S. Simon in 1950 and reasserted by Brian Harrison in 1987. See S. Simon, 'Two Women', *Universities Quarterly*, 4, 2 (Feb 1950), pp.184–91, and B. Harrison, *Prudent Revolutionaries. Portraits of British Feminists Between the Wars* (Oxford: Oxford University Press, 1987), p.101.
3. S. Pedersen, *Eleanor Rathbone and the Politics of Conscience* (London: Yale University Press, 2004), pp.441–2, n.43.
4. J. Alberti, *Eleanor Rathbone* (London: Sage, 1996).
5. My thanks to Sandra Clark, administrator for the BDBJ, for allowing me access to certain closed files.
6. I am indebted to Ms Val Traylen of the National Archives for alerting Professor Kushner to the survival of these files, and locating 'names' on my behalf. My thanks also to Mr Stewart Mead, at the Home Office, for allowing me access to individual files.
7. S. Jeffreys, *The Spinster and Her Enemies: Feminism and Sexuality 1890–1930* (London: Pandora, 1985), p.153.
8. S. Pedersen, 'Eleanor Rathbone 1871–1946. The Victorian Family under the Daughter's Eye', in S. Pedersen and P. Mandler (eds), *After the Victorians. Private Conscience and Public Duty in Modern Britain* (London: Routledge, 1994), p.118.
9. Ibid., p.118.
10. L.G. Wickham Legg and E.T. Williams (eds), *Dictionary of National Biography* (London: Oxford University Press, 1950), pp.711–13; S. Pedersen, 'Rathbone, E.F. (1872–1946)', in C. Matthew and B. Harrison (eds), *Oxford Dictionary of National Biography* (Oxford: Oxford University Press, 2004), Article 35678: M. Parry (ed.), *Chambers Biographical Dictionary of Women* (Edinburgh: Chambers, 1996), p.547.
11. A. Crawford *et al.*, *The Europa Biographical Dictionary of British Women* (London: Europa, 1983), pp.338–9.
12. Harrison, *Prudent Revolutionaries*, pp.99–124. S. Oldfield, *Women Humanitarians. A Biographical Dictionary of British Women Active between 1900 and 1950* (London: Continuum, 2001), pp.190–2.
13. A.J. Sherman, *Island Refuge: Britain and Refugees from the Third Reich, 1933–39*, 2nd edn (Ilford: Frank Cass, 1994); M. Marrus, *The Unwanted: European Refugees and the Twentieth Century* (New York and Oxford: Oxford University Press, 1985); L. London, *Whitehall and the Jews, 1933–1948. British Immigration Policy and the Holocaust* (Cambridge: Cambridge University Press, 2000).
14. D. Cesarani, 'Mad Dogs and Englishmen: Towards a Taxonomy of Rescuers in a Bystander Country – Britain 1933–45', *The Journal of Holocaust Education*, 9, 2 and 3 (2000), pp.34–6; T. Kushner, *The Holocaust and the Liberal Imagination: A Social and Cultural*

*History* (Oxford: Blackwell, 1994); T. Kushner and K. Knox, *Refugees in an Age of Genocide: Global, National and Local Perspectives during the Twentieth Century* (London: Frank Cass, 1999); A. Bunting, 'Representing Rescue: The National Committee for Rescue from Nazi Terror, the British and the Rescue of Jews from Nazism', *The Journal of Holocaust Education*, 9, 1 (2000), pp.65–84; P. Shatzkes, *Holocaust and Rescue: Impotent or Indifferent Anglo-Jewry 1938–1945* (Basingstoke: Palgrave, 2002).

15. *Oxford English Dictionary*, 2nd edn (Oxford: Clarendon Press, 1989), p.475.
16. L. Minear and T. Weiss, *Mercy Under Fire: War and the Global Humanitarian Community* (Boulder, CO and Oxford: Westview, 1995), p.18.
17. Stocks, *Rathbone*, p.34.
18. Kushner, *Holocaust and the Liberal Imagination*, pp.45–6, 273.
19. Credited to August Comte almost two centuries ago, the word 'altruism' derived from the Latin *alter*, meaning 'other', as cited in S. and P. Oliner, *The Altruistic Personality: Rescuers of Jews in Nazi Europe* (New York: Free Press; London: Collier Macmillan, 1988), p.4.
20. Kushner, *Holocaust and the Liberal Imagination*, p.45.
21. V. Gollancz, 'Eleanor Rathbone', *AJR Information* (February 1946), p.13.
22. Stocks, *Rathbone*, pp.194–5, p.266. See also M. Simey, *Eleanor Rathbone 1872–1946, A Centenary Tribute* (Liverpool: University of Liverpool, 1974). In April 1943, Winston Churchill confirmed that he was very willing to consider Rathbone's name when forming his proposals for the next Honours list. See letter of Winston Churchill to Violet Markham, 20 April 1943, CHAR/20/93B/149, CAC.

# 1

# *A Life in the Making*

What follows is not a full biography of Eleanor Rathbone, but rather a snapshot of her life up until 1933. I make no apology for this. I never set out to write about her life in detail, but I did intend to put the pieces of her background together so that her commitment to the refugee question, which has been so shamefully neglected, could be seen within the context of her heritage and upbringing. Only then could I hope to explain the process by which she became a lifelong humanitarian activist and the 'MP for refugees', and demonstrate how this significant final phase of her activities fitted into the wider context of her life and career, much of which involved her in issues concerning women.

Eleanor Florence Rathbone's family history, influences and advantages formed the core of her life, and were instrumental in creating one of the twentieth century's outstanding humanitarian activists. No one, least of all Eleanor, could have imagined that during her lifetime her achievements would include being a pioneering Oxford University student, a first-wave feminist, a suffragist, city councillor, biographer, social investigator and reformer, welfare worker, Justice of the Peace, Member of Parliament, pacificist and finally, from 1933 until her death in 1946, the champion of refugees fleeing Nazi Europe.

London, Liverpool and Oxford were the three cities that had the greatest impact on her life. London was her birthplace and the city in which she ultimately lived and worked, Liverpool abounded with familial connections and the social influences which shaped her character, and Oxford, with its late-Victorian intellectual milieu, nurtured the philosopher in her and left a powerful impression on her future actions and deeds. At the time of Eleanor's birth, 12 May 1872, her father, William Rathbone VI (1819–1902) was Liberal MP for Liverpool, and whenever the House was in session, as it was in spring 1872, he, his second wife, Emily Acheson Lyle, and their family took up residence in their London home at 14 Princes Gardens, Kensington. But the main focus of family life was always 'Greenbank' in Liverpool for it was there that Eleanor and her siblings, eleven in all, spent their childhood years and enjoyed the security and comfort which her father's position provided.[1]

His prosperity, which derived from his success as a merchant, was matched by a set of high moral principles combined with an acute awareness of his obligation to others less fortunate than himself.[2] Such attributes were not uncommon, as exemplified by William Gladstone, four times prime minister between 1868 and 1894, for he too was born in Liverpool, the son of a successful merchant whose evangelical religious philosophy included constant and spontaneous acts of charity. In William Rathbone's case, he was following a family tradition stretching back over six generations, and one that had only been able to develop because of the unique nature of Liverpool, which, like other cities including Norwich and Carlisle, took a laissez-faire attitude towards religion. The Rathbones belonged to the Quaker (Society of Friends) fellowship, and, in common with other Nonconformists, had found a safe haven in Liverpool. There, everyone, regardless of creed, was free to pursue their business interests and build thriving dynasties without compromising their beliefs or straying from their ideals and principles.

Liverpool's economic success was due largely to its position as a slave-trading port, and afforded the dissenting entrepreneur unrivalled opportunities which were denied them elsewhere.[3] For in most other parts of the country legal religious discrimination largely excluded them from the main current of English life, including admission to Oxford and Cambridge universities. Nonconformity effectively forced followers into socially stigmatized pursuits such as commerce and trade. This was how Eleanor's Quaker antecedent, William Rathbone II (1696–1746), came to move to the growing port of Liverpool from his native Gawsworth, near Macclesfield, and where his son, William III (1726–1789), established the ship-owning business on which the family fortune was founded. But they also followed the maxim 'what ought to be done, could be done' which was passed down through the generations, and had its foundation in their religious beliefs. The Quakers considered the ultimate authority came from within rather than from the Bible, and that the 'inner light' or the 'Christ within' promoted an ethos of personal responsibility for oneself and one's actions. So it was that generations of Rathbones undertook acts of practical philanthropy whereby each member determined, in their own way and as a reflection of their own particular interest and the needs of the time, to improve the health and welfare of those less fortunate than themselves.[4] For William Rathbone III this took the form of abolitionist activities, and he was one of the first members of the Liverpool branch of the Society for the Abolition of the African Slave Trade. His was a brave stand, for the slave trade was considered to be the foundation of prosperity in Liverpool at the time. Not only was his business endangered, but his fellow traders reproached him for threatening their wealth, leaving him vulnerable to mob violence.

Eleanor's great, great grandfather, William Rathbone IV (1757–1809), was an educated man with a deep thirst for knowledge and an interest in the same Scottish school of philosophy which was later to influence her own philosophical studies. He always put principle before popularity, and in common with other family members, insisted upon conducting trade according to certain ethical standards. Following in his father's footsteps, he embraced the abolitionist cause, a stance that, once again, met with the opprobrium of those on the Liverpool Exchange. As 'a champion of lost causes', another characteristic which Eleanor was to inherit, he sought to help the aged and infirm and repress the growth of pauperism by promoting improvements in the administration of the Old Poor Law. Whilst he spent much of his large fortune on releasing poor and respectable debtors from jail, more than a century later Eleanor chose to devote substantial amounts of her money to various aspects of the refugee cause. There was a fundamental difference between this William and his father for when it came to religion, he was unwilling to accept the religious intolerance exercised by the Quakers, and his personal campaign for religious freedom led to his exclusion from the Society.

A generation later, the name of William Rathbone V (1787–1868) became a household word in Liverpool. The concerns that this popular man championed were legion and diverse, but they all reflected the family tradition of social consciousness and moral integrity. He continued to fight against slavery, even suspending the cotton trade between the Rathbone company and America for a period in the 1850s. A Nonconformist like his father, he could not abide religious intolerance, and lent his support to the cause of Roman Catholic emancipation. He also took a strong stand against bribery and other forms of corruption in municipal elections. His interests in political, parliamentary and municipal reform reflected the shift of the real centre of national interest in the first half of the nineteenth century. At a local level, he and his wife involved themselves in the move to improve elementary education, whilst Mrs Rathbone's charitable efforts were largely responsible for the establishment of the first public baths in Liverpool. In the customary Rathbone tradition, this William Rathbone never sought credit for his work.

Like his predecessors, Eleanor's father, William VI, was a well-educated man but he was not a scholar. Early on in his adult life he had made up his mind to divide his time between the family business interests and public service, in the knowledge that financial success would enable him to engage in practical philanthropic and social work. Such issues were at the forefront of the hearts and minds of very many people for this was the era of a general preoccupation, both local and national, with the so-called 'condition of the people' debate. Interest and concern over the extent and nature of poverty in mid-Victorian Britain had been fuelled by a deluge of literature that included the results of various surveys and investigations, as well as social commentaries and studies. These focused variously on specific or general aspects of working-class life, and upon the quantitative as well as the qualitative reality of poverty. There was no better example than the seventeen-volume study undertaken by the shipowner Charles Booth, William's own pupil and fellow Liverpudlian. Booth's *Life and Labour of the People of London*, finally published between 1892 and 1903, was indeed pioneering for it not only investigated the extent of poverty, but also attempted to define its nature and analyze its causes. Another more specific driving force came from the corridors of academia, for Oxford University had amongst its fellows and tutors the renowned philosopher T.H. Green (1837–1882) whose influential school of thought encouraged undergraduates to devote considerable attention to social problems. The thread of the Rathbone family was evident here, for decades earlier Eleanor's great-great-grandfather had found direction from the philosophy of Green's predecessors, and she was subsequently heavily influenced by his ideology whilst at Somerville College.[5]

There was plenty of scope for William Rathbone's philanthropic work in mid-nineteenth-century Liverpool: the chronic and self-perpetuating poverty of the mass of the population was palpable and it was well nigh impossible for these people to improve their standard of living. Eleanor's father became directly aware of the lack of medical care available to the sick poor as an indirect consequence of his own wife's illness, and this prompted him to pilot a scheme of home nursing for them in Liverpool. Applying his customary methodological and organized approach, techniques which Charles Booth had utilized in his pioneering survey and which Eleanor later emulated, his experiment proved highly successful. It was soon extended and led to the foundation, in 1887, of Queen Victoria's Jubilee Institute for Nurses, the first and most enduring national organization to provide home nursing for the sick poor in Britain. His interest in the health care of the poor also led to his close involvement in the reform of workhouse nursing, and to very close ties with the huge local workhouse at Brownlow Hill, which had an official capacity for 3,000 inmates. This poverty-stricken area of the city was, by 1875, also home to some 3,000 Jewish immigrants who had settled themselves in the area, and for this reason was known as the 'Brownlow Hill Ghetto'. Jewish immigrants had been a prominent feature of Liverpool life during the last decades of the nineteenth century, for Merseyside, in common with other port cities, had become the destination of thousands of Russian Jews who were fleeing the pogroms of Eastern Europe after 1882. Eleanor's father was also a renowned advocate of the Liverpool Board of Guardians for the Relief of the Jewish Poor, established in May 1876, which operated on the same lines as the Charity Organization Society (COS) which he so admired. The Board offered financial support to those deemed, after thorough investigation, to be 'deserving', while taking steps to discourage the settlement in Liverpool of 'casual beggars' and the permanent dependence of the resident poor on communal charity.[6] Such charitable organizations earned the Jewish community a reputation for their independence and self-reliance. On the negative side, the absence of 'immigrant work' – furniture-making, tailoring and the sweated trades – and a serious glut in the local labour market during the 1890s, precipitated an anti-alien campaign by the Liverpool Trades Council in 1890/91, mirroring campaigns in other areas of the country where immigrants had taken root.

There was also an inextricable link between religious nonconformity and active concern with social problems, which had a moral dimension at this time. In Liverpool this had been exemplified by, for example, Josephine Butler's vigorous campaign against the 1860s Contagious Diseases Acts, which brought prostitution into the public eye. Charles Booth had turned his attention to the 1889 dock strike in London whilst others concerned themselves with the moral and social implications of overcrowded urban dwellings. This was the Liverpool and the social and welfare issues which William Rathbone wanted to concentrate on, but his political status as a Liberal MP, from 1868, forced him to focus on other concerns including the reform of local government, bankruptcy reforms, licensing, commercial law and Home Rule. There was one notable exception which was to Eleanor's great advantage and that was his enduring interest, passed down through the generations, in the extension of education, and in particular, his active support of higher education for women, for without this she may never have been able to attend university.

Only in 1895, having retired from politics, was he able to devote himself to the social and welfare issues that were of lifelong concern to him. Besides rationalizing the existing Liverpool Central Relief Society (LCRS) to the benefit of those in receipt of poor relief, William Rathbone believed that Liverpool's poverty would never be eradicated unless an alternative was found to the casual labour system. To this end he, and subsequently Eleanor, applied themselves to the problem faced by the Liverpool dock and railway workers in an effort to force change.

This background to Eleanor's life was certainly varied and by all accounts her childhood was happy and stable, but sometimes a little lonely. She grew up in an atmosphere of comfort where there was never any question of scrimping, saving, or shortages, but it was always made clear that the material wealth enjoyed by the family was a privilege and not a right. Even as a small girl her father instilled in her a respect for the power of money, for in his view luxury spending and self-indulgence weakened the character, whereas frugal living and philanthropy strengthened it.

As 'sweet' as she appeared on the surface, Eleanor's true character was far more complex: wilful and independent of spirit, she had strong likes and dislikes, and could be very troublesome when she chose to be, a trait that was especially evident in the case of her schooling. Matters were not helped by the way family life was structured, for the year was divided between London and Liverpool, interspersed with regular summer holidays in Scotland and elsewhere, which was hardly conducive to the routine of a formal education (see Plate 1). Apart from a brief spell at Kensington High School, she received most of her schooling from a series of tutors and governesses, many of whom possessed dubious qualifications, and most of whom the stubborn young girl disliked. The one exception was a German lady, Marianne Muller, whom, according to her friend, Margery Fry, she loved and admired. There were other informal but influential fonts of knowledge, and besides that which her parents passed on, there were innumerable interesting and intellectually stimulating people who visited their home and with whom Eleanor regularly mixed. This social circle embraced 'the leading disciples of Gladstonian Liberalism' and the 'pioneer thinkers of this age of administrative bricklaying', and they undoubtedly enhanced the mentally energizing atmosphere of the London house.[7]

As for religion, the prevailing atmosphere at 'Greenbank' was, unsurprisingly, Nonconformist, and William Rathbone VI's doctrinal views were, as Eleanor later wrote, best described as those of the school of Unitarianism, but she was still able to detect elements of the Rathbone Quaker heritage. Each member of the family was at liberty to practise their faith as they saw fit, perpetuating the Rathbone tradition, firmly established by William IV, of religious freedom. So, whilst her father attended the Unitarian chapel and her mother the Anglican church, Eleanor never professed an adherence to any theological creed. As a young girl she occasionally attended a Quaker meeting, but soon gave up on them, ostensibly turning her back on formal religion.

Eleanor may have tried the patience of her many teachers over the years, but this never quenched her insatiable thirst for knowledge or her determination to learn. By the time she was 19, she had managed to persuade her parents to allow her to be tutored in the classics, an activity which was quite out of keeping for a young Victorian woman. Had her parents thought about the long-term effect of this dip in academic waters, her mother Emily would almost certainly have taken a firm stand against it. However, they seem not to have considered the consequences and allowed their daughter to have her way. Eleanor's choice of Janet Case as her tutor was inspirational: not only was she a talented educator with a passionate interest in philosophy and Greek literature, but she was also an ardent feminist and a graduate of Girton College, Cambridge. Case quickly established herself as a role model for Eleanor, for she found the picture that her tutor painted of academic life and learning irresistible, fuelling her resolve to study philosophy at university. This was easier said than done and for months Eleanor harboured a secret desire to attend Newnham College, Cambridge, but when she eventually broached the subject with her parents, her mother raised serious objections. As far as she was concerned, education for women was a pursuit that was entirely incompatible with marriage, and even though neither she nor William Rathbone ever doubted Eleanor's lack of interest in being a wife, her mother was not willing to concede without a fight.[8] Her father was a different matter, for he had a positive attitude towards the higher education of women, and was unlikely to have objected to his daughter's plans to attend university. Any reservations that he had were more to do with the universities themselves, and probably harked back to Oxford and Cambridge's historic exclusion of Nonconformists.

A long struggle ensued before the matter of university was resolved, causing great anguish to both Eleanor and her mother. Emily was in fact attempting to control her daughter's future, which she wanted to contain within the domestic and conventional female sphere. Eleanor, meanwhile, was struggling with the dilemma of trying, albeit reluctantly, to be a dutiful daughter without relinquishing her passionate desire to study. The strain on the young woman's mental health was so severe that eventually her father intervened, imploring her to make up her own mind about her future. For, as he wrote, if she continued to hesitate she would end up with 'a very unhappy wasted life'.[9] He also made it clear that he and his wife would accept any decision she made. A compromise was finally reached whereby Emily Rathbone managed to retain a vestige of authority: it was agreed that Eleanor could attend university, but at her mother's insistence Newnham was dismissed as a possibility. The place on offer was Somerville, Oxford, which was then a hall of residence with a strict regime of rules and regulations, and a warden who could be trusted to keep a watchful eye on the young woman. But as luck would have it, Somerville became a college in 1893, the same year that Eleanor arrived, so she was truly a pioneer of the new establishment.

By going to Somerville Eleanor opened a new and exciting chapter in her life and although it certainly loosened her ties with home, it also exacerbated the worsening relationship with her mother, who now had no control over her daughter's destiny. Conversely, the young woman became even more in her father's mould, and it was his authority which predominated and exerted the most enduring influence on her. It was he who brought her up to respect others and to recognize the value of every individual, regardless of their class, sex or creed, and it was these tenets that remained constant and which informed her philosophy on life (see Plate 3).

The Eleanor Rathbone who entered Somerville in 1893 to study Litterae Humaniores, or Greats, was amongst the vanguard of young women to attend the University and benefit from the enlightened ideas of Oxford dons T.H. Green and his protégé, Professor Edward Caird, the master of Balliol. Both men, whose teachings were to influence Eleanor, had a generous belief in the intellectual capacity of women, and had spearheaded the campaign for their admission to Oxford. However, had another radical reform not taken place, with the removal of restrictions on the admission of Nonconformists to both Oxford and Cambridge in 1871 she, like her male predecessors, would still have been excluded. Although she and her contemporaries were amongst the pioneering women at Oxford, the concessions ended there for women students, for they were still restricted from being members of the University and were not permitted to graduate. And up until 1893, the year that Eleanor entered, women still had to have a chaperone at all lectures.

Her pursuit of scholarship was far from easy. Greats was the body of study which included grammar, rhetoric, logic, rudimentary mathematics, Greek, Latin, some religious matter, ancient history, moral and political philosophy as well as study of the history of philosophy, but her earlier peripatetic education had not equipped her with a sound foundation in the classics. She remedied these deficiencies through a combination of extra-curricular tuition and, characteristically, hard work and determination. Even though she was never considered to be a very great scholar, Eleanor's tutors at Oxford recognized her to be a talented student whose work was always first class.[10] But this was not reflected in her Finals results, for, as her tutor in Aristotle, Charles Canaan predicted, the pressure of 'schools' (exams) was too great for her.[11] Her handwriting was indecipherable and the examiners insisted that she return to Oxford to dictate her scripts to a typist before they could be assessed. This was humiliating enough, and gaining a second-class degree was a huge disappointment, for up until then Eleanor had been considering an academic future, perhaps eventually becoming principal of Somerville. A poor result put an end to this ambition, and the reality was that her sex barred her from the careers she and her fellow feminists aspired to, with the door to politics, and most other public offices, firmly shut. There was also the sense that she had failed the college and the feminist movement. But ultimately, Eleanor's paper qualification was of no significance, for once she had resolved what to do with her future, it was the profound and enduring influences of her immersion in the philosophical milieu of Oxford which had the greatest impact.

The first of these influences was located within the realm of academia itself. The main focus of Eleanor's studies at Somerville was upon the fundamental problems of human life and existence, the self-same questions to which her father directed his philanthropic work. Noted by her tutors for her 'considerable powers of independent thought'[12] she soon earned the title of 'Philosopher'.[13] Through the teachings of Caird, her tutor in moral philosophy, she encountered the prevailing Oxford ideology of Green. As Mrs Humphrey Ward later described, Green was 'preoccupied ... with the need of leading "a useful life"', a concern which was exemplified by his interest in the contemporary debate about the 'condition of the people' – temperance, housing, wages, electoral reform – in fact social reform in general.[14] His challenge to liberal orthodoxies included the proposal that an increase in state intervention in the lives of individuals (in, for example, education) could give them greater freedom rather than less. That Eleanor came under Caird's wing at this time was fortuitous, for he was personally involved in improving the condition of women's education at Oxford, and took the unusual step of admitting women students to his lectures, and, even more radically, accepted essays from them in philosophy.

Whilst Caird shared Green's beliefs, he interpreted the doctrine in his own way, and during his years as professor of moral philosophy at Glasgow University became a key figure in the drive to relate the subject more closely to real life. At Oxford, the thesis of personal service and citizenship, whereby the actions of the individual rather than abstract institutions would create a better society, was central to his teaching of ethical idealism. Caird's personal contribution was his active involvement in the settlement movement. The paradigm for settlements, which were a product of Green's influence on social thinking of the period, was Toynbee Hall in London's East End, founded by Samuel Barnett and sponsored by Oxford University. There, graduates and undergraduates bridged the gap between rich and poor by living, for varying periods of time, cheek by jowl with the working classes, and from this position they were able to involve themselves and ostensibly effect improvements in the local social, educational, charitable and governmental structure. As far as Caird was concerned these institutions were one of the chief means of closing the gap that existed between different classes, and he viewed settlements as efficient centres of social work on modern lines. His ideals and enthusiasm in this respect undoubtedly influenced Eleanor's own developing interest in social problems, and were, at least in part, responsible for her future involvement with the Liverpool Victoria Women's Settlement (LVWS). Nor was she the only one of Caird's students to be influenced in this way, for William Beveridge, with whom Eleanor was later to become involved politically over the introduction of family allowances, was at one time equally involved in the settlement movement. Further links came in 1933 when Beveridge instigated the founding of the Academic Assistance Council (later the Society for the Protection of Science and Learning) to meet the special needs of academic refugees from Nazi Germany, and again in 1943 when he became a member of Eleanor's National Committee for Rescue from Nazi Terror (NCRNT).

Despite Johanna Alberti's claim to the contrary, there is plenty of evidence to establish direct links between the philosophical influences that Eleanor encountered at Oxford, and the philanthropic practice that she later engaged in.[15] She was in fact one of the stream of ex-pupils that Green's school sent out into public life who 'carried with them the conviction that philosophy and particularly that which they had learned at Oxford, was an important thing and that their vocation was to put it into practice'.[16]

Whilst the academic atmosphere of Oxford provided a climate in which Eleanor's own brand of late-Victorian idealism could develop, she was also exposed to the intellectual milieu of her fellow female students. Contrary to her father's biased view of Oxford as a mentally and morally enervating place, she found the atmosphere energizing and emancipating. There were new, lasting and influential friendships made with Ethel Maude Samson (later White), Rose Graham, Lettice Ilbert, Margery Fry, Helen Darbishire, Lucy Papworth, Barbara Bradby (later Hammond) and Hilda Oakeley, all of whom went on to pursue a variety of careers in the spheres of public service, welfare work and humanitarian causes as well as academia. The subsequent achievements of these pioneering women were formidable: Maude Samson became a stalwart of feminism and socialism, whilst Rose Graham gained renown as an historian and archaeologist.[17] Lettice Ilbert, who married H.L. Fisher, a young New College, Oxford don, held the post of tutor in modern history at St Hugh's College, Oxford from 1902 to 1913 and was chair of the National Council for the Care of the Unmarried Mother and her Child from 1918 to 1949. Margery Fry, who remained a lifelong friend of Eleanor's, contributed to public service in innumerable ways, including her work with the Quaker War Victims Relief Mission and her campaign for penal reform. Besides this, in common with Helen Darbishire, a leading literary scholar, she held the post of principal of Somerville. Lucy Papworth entered Somerville in 1893, the same year as Eleanor, and became a social activist and social investigator. During her thirteen-year tenure as general secretary of the Women's Industrial Council, the organization established in 1894 to 'watch over women engaged in trades and all industrial matters which concern women', she was closely involved with a widely publicized enquiry into married women's work.[18] Barbara Bradby and Hilda Oakeley also maintained their friendship with Rathbone: the former became an historical writer in collaboration with her husband whilst Hilda Oakeley earned a reputation as a philosopher, and was also the first female warden of the Passmore Edwards Settlement in St Pancras, London between 1914 and 1921.

The person whom these and other Somerville students encountered was an attractive, well-mannered young woman of middle height whose clear, smooth complexion, soft dark hair and splendid eyes were often remarked upon. So too was her behaviour, for in contrast to her serious and studious side, there was the vague, and absent-minded persona, whose rare capacity for mental concentration often made her distinctly unapproachable.[19] Never one for frivolity, her ideal reading had a definite intellectual element, for, according to her friends, 'she found pleasure in reading Blue Books even when she lay in bed'.[20] Nor did clothes and fashion hold any interest for her, and her mode of dress, which was inevitably black, remained firmly fixed in the Edwardian era, creating the impression of a formidable blue-stocking. Her appearance was often smart but this was an accidental achievement which owed more to the intervention of the female members of her family, and later her companion, Elizabeth Macadam, than it did to her own care and attention (see Plate 2).

Leisure was always important to Eleanor, but she had no taste for sports or activities that required any degree of manual dexterity or physical strength, both qualities that she lacked. Instead, she derived great pleasure from domestic and foreign travel, walking, boating, cycling and later motoring. The only area in which she could ever be accused of self-indulgence was where her smoking habit was concerned. She was already a veteran smoker by the time she went to Oxford in 1893 and despite the unfashionable and scandalous nature of the custom, could never be persuaded to give it up. Her niece, Noreen, was sure that Eleanor's smoking both affected her health and contributed towards the heart attack which killed her.[21]

University gave Eleanor so many opportunities to develop, but one in particular stood her in good stead, for she was to gain renown for the oratorical skills that she honed at Oxford. Her distinct and pleasant voice belied a robust personality and she was driven by an emotional energy that infused her speeches with passion. Whilst all the causes she was later to champion, both inside and outside of parliament, benefited from the depth and persistence of her arguments, this was especially true where the refugee issue was concerned. It also gained her a reputation as a formidable adversary. As a novice debater at Somerville, she took part in the women's inter-collegiate debates, but early on she and a few fellow students established a small, select and secret college society for more intimate discussions. Called the 'APs', short for Associated Prigs, their remit was to discuss 'things in general', but the society was characterized from the outset by the high moral earnestness of its members and the concern which they all showed for the moral issues of the day. Eleanor was launched on her debating career at the third meeting of the APs, even though the subject she introduced, the Elberfeld System of Poor Law Administration, was neither philosophical nor original.[22] Rather, it rehearsed her father's interest in a system that had led him to help establish the LCRS in 1863. Subsequent topics were more profound: luxury, Plato and the position of women in the Republic, Benjamin Kidd's *Social Evolution* (1894), freewill and the evolution of morals.[23]

Whilst immersed in the intellectual climate of Somerville, Eleanor's passion for, and commitment to the emergent feminist movement grew and was, according to her friend Hilda Oakeley, infectious. This affiliation was somewhat surprising for, apart from the growing popularity of feminist activities amongst young women of her class, Eleanor differed in that she never articulated any animosity towards men, nor had she, or any other Rathbone woman, ever been treated unequally at home because of their sex. She was, however, aware of the complacency of Liverpool society towards two local women social reformers, Josephine Butler and Mary Macaulay (later Mrs Charles Booth), and may, as has been suggested, have been fired by resentment of their treatment.[24] Eleanor was certainly inspired by the pursuit of equality for women but saw emancipation as the means to an end, which was the 'right to exercise the full responsibilities of citizenship', as promoted by Green and Caird's ideology. There was a connection between Eleanor's feminism and the prevailing Oxford ideology, but Eleanor's years at Oxford did not, as Johanna Alberti has suggested, foster her feminism rather than her intellect.[25] The evidence of her tutors confirms beyond any doubt that it was her intellect and not her feminism which was stimulated and invigorated by her environment: it was this newly discovered state of mind which provided a setting within which she was able to test out new ideas and thoughts, including her interest in the women's cause. Eleanor and her female Oxford contemporaries were, after all, amongst the vanguard of women enjoying the fruits of educational emancipation, so it was not surprising that many of them should have taken an active interest in the wider 'equality' debate.

Even beyond the female enclave of Somerville, Eleanor's new acquaintances were invariably women. Although the Victorian notion of separate spheres, public and private, male and female, was beginning to be eroded, as exemplified by the admission of women to university, many aspects of segregation still prevailed in the last quarter of the nineteenth century. Social contact between the sexes, either formally or informally, was still rare and actively discouraged, and the men whom she did meet, like Oliver (later Sir Oliver) Lodge, whom she knew through her brother, were either male relatives and their friends, or her tutors.

Oxford completed, Eleanor returned to Liverpool in 1896, and settled back into family life at 'Greenbank' where her financial and social position were such that she was unencumbered by household or employment demands. Never one to indulge in idleness, and like many other women of her class, she soon found an outlet for her zeal and energy through her involvement with a number of local philanthropic agencies. Collectively, the experience she gained from these voluntary posts served as an apprenticeship in the principles and practice of social investigation and reform. What set her apart from her female contemporaries was the way she donned the Rathbone family mantle of philanthropy, which in preceding generations had passed almost automatically through the male lineage. Her brothers were somewhat of a disappointment to her father, for none were inclined to follow in his footsteps, but his favoured daughter more than compensated for their failures.

Besides this, her father's religiosity had a direct effect on the way her own religious views developed. Eleanor had long ago given up on religion, and Margery Fry, whose family were also Quakers, later recalled how she and Eleanor followed the fashion and went to New College Chapel, Oxford, whilst they were at Somerville, but remarked that their visit was motivated more by an interest in the architecture and the music than in the famous preacher.[26] Religious belief did present Eleanor with a philosophical dilemma, which she discussed in depth with her friend, Oliver Lodge. She eventually came around to his way of thinking, developing a scepticism about religious faith which enabled her to believe that a person's worth was vested in their moral life, rather than in their spiritual beliefs. Leaving instructions for her funeral, she explained her views on her beliefs and the hereafter:

> My own feeling is that whether the soul survives the body – and of that I am not sure – my body is not me and of no more importance than a cast-off garment. Do not take this to mean that I am un-Christian. I do not think I am. But Christianity seems to me a guide for life, but is rather vague about the after-life of individuals. [27]

Her guiding principle was rooted in a profound sense of responsibility to relieve individual human distress rather than the hope of gaining heaven: humanitarianism unfettered by concerns for race, class or religious prejudice informed the causes she championed, and nowhere was this of greater import than in connection with her later work with Jewish refugees.

Eleanor took her first tentative steps as a humanitarian activist in 1897, putting into practice the ideology of Green and Caird, when she became simultaneously a manager of Granby Street Council School, honorary secretary of the Liverpool Women's Industrial Council (LWIC) and a visitor for the LCRS, which her father had helped to reorganize. It remains unclear exactly what her responsibilities were as a manager of Granby Street Council School, but as honorary secretary of the LWIC she would have been involved in publicizing the exploitation of women workers, a position that was consistent with her feminist sympathies. Her work as a visitor brought her into direct contact with the 'extremely peculiar constitution of the Liverpool population' that she had described to the APs at Somerville.[28] Now she saw for herself the deprivation suffered by the families of the unskilled casual dock and railway labourers, and the consequences of the irregular and poorly paid nature of their employment. The report that she subsequently presented to her father in early 1897 made depressing reading. Even his determined efforts at reorganizing the way the LCRS dispensed charity had been ineffectual, for not only had the organization failed to bring about any permanent material improvement in the lives of the poor, but Eleanor was of the opinion that it was also responsible for causing some permanent harm.

In identifying the main cause of the problem, Eleanor singled out the visitors themselves, described by her as mainly 'lower middle-class people, very willing and interested, but not highly educated and quite untrained'.[29] They were, in her view, ineffective and gullible, and made a mockery of the principles of the COS. Founded in 1869 as the Society for Organising Charitable Relief and Repressing Mendacity, their remit was to organize and coordinate charitable activity rather than give relief. Casework was the central feature and applicants were subjected to rigorous investigation to ascertain whether they 'deserved' help. Only then were they directed to the appropriate charity, or to the Poor Law. The rationale of the COS was this: if aid was given indiscriminately then the poor would be deprived of their self-respect and sense of responsibility. It was assumed that those who failed to satisfy the investigators, the so-called 'undeserving' poor, would, in the face of pauperism and the workhouse, see the error of their ways and seek work. Eleanor was, at this time, a strong defender of the principles of the COS and accepted the notion that the 'deserving' poor could be redeemed and made into 'respectable citizens' through the work of the organization.[30] However it was not long before she abandoned their dogma, and was amongst the vanguard of those promoting the idea of state intervention in the relief of poverty, a proposal that was taken up by William Beveridge within a decade. The recommendations which she presented to her father were based on her belief that matters would only improve if the quality of the visitors was raised, a goal which was achievable if they were given professional training. The concept of a specific course for people undertaking social work was highly innovative but was an idea which she developed and subsequently put into practice when she became involved with the LVWS.

Having completed this first report on the dispensing of charitable relief in Liverpool, Eleanor looked to her father again for inspiration. Her next project was what she called her 'little Dock Labour Enquiry' in which she investigated and made suggestions for reform of the casual labour system and its concomitant under-employment at the Liverpool Docks.[31] At this point she turned her back on the principles of the COS which she had earlier defended, and in stark contrast applied techniques which emulated those of her father's protégé, Charles Booth, citing his work within her own. Methodical analysis of the facts was now preceded by observation and the acquisition of detailed background knowledge. She never anticipated that her father would respond positively to her conclusions, which included the suggestion that a change be made in the way payment was made to the workers, but her proposals were, once again, ahead of their time. The results of the dock labour enquiry represented Eleanor's first important piece of social research, but were not published until 1903, the year following her father's death.

Her first-hand contact with Liverpool's poor clearly alerted her to the burden that was placed on the social structure of the city by the numbers of illiterate migrants, immigrants and trans-migrants who continued to seek work in the city, despite the miserable prospects for employment. There were undoubtedly Jews amongst the city's poor, and it is hard to imagine that she was unaware of their presence and of the attitudes, negative and positive, towards them. The extent to which these experiences affected Eleanor's admiration for the Jews, her repudiation of anti-Semitism and determined stand against anti-alien immigration policies in the 1930s and 1940s is unquantifiable, but was a part of her background which cannot be ignored in the broad scheme of her development.[32]

Eleanor's correspondence with Hilda Oakeley, with whom she had apparently been contemplating a joint philosophical project on the problem of personality, reveals the extent to which this period of her life was one of maturation and psychological challenge as she struggled to reconcile her own privileged position with the magnitude of poverty that surrounded her. As she made clear in a letter to her friend, dated around 1900, she realized that her conscience would not permit her the luxury of further theoretical study. Rather, as the following extract shows, she saw her future in terms of practical philanthropy that was informed by the philosophical ideology she had acquired at Oxford:

> When one is young and a newcomer in the world, one looks at it in a detached way, wondering why the inhabitants take themselves and their trivial affairs so seriously, and finding one's chief interest outside it. But by degrees one warms to one's fellow mortals, and the danger becomes that one should lose the power of detaching oneself to the extent necessary for serving it effectively. Of course, this does not mean that one almost inevitably has one's sense of proportion spoiled – and in a world where everyone was as well off as oneself, the utilitarian spirit might be a thing to fight against. But in *such* a world with all its wrongs shouting in one's ears and every miserable face claiming kinship, how can one be *sorry* that it is no longer easy to shut one's ears and revel in thought for thought's sake.[33]

Her consciousness had been raised by her first-hand experiences in Liverpool, and her perception of the poor changed so that she now saw them as victims of circumstances beyond their control, and as real human beings who led unhappy lives. As the standard-bearer of the next Rathbone generation, she now sought, like her predecessors, to establish her particular interests within the field of practical philanthropy, with regard to the needs of the time. What is highly significant is that no one cause was to engage her continuously throughout her life, for she was always alert to any 'unsuspected obligation', the unplanned-for injustice that she felt compelled to investigate. The death of her father in 1902 was a bitter blow for Eleanor, and was a turning point in her life, signalling both the end of her so-called apprenticeship and the beginning of her role of leadership in Liverpool civic affairs. But before she embarked upon this new path, she was asked to compile a biography of her father, an undertaking that was both challenging and emotionally charged.[34] For, as Mary Stocks, Eleanor's friend and first biographer, has commented, Eleanor's affectionate memoir highlights, perhaps unwittingly, the parallels between William and his daughter, and the extent to which she was 'the outcome and the natural continuation of the [Rathbone] lives that had gone before'. He was clearly her mentor and she his successor, but her friend and pupil Margaret Simey concluded that despite this inheritance, Eleanor may well have floundered without the support of equally committed people of calibre from within Liverpool University, with whom William Rathbone had been closely associated.

Broadly speaking, the three areas of social work that she had already been introduced to, namely the relief of poverty, education and women's issues, still occupied her mind and actions after her father's death, but in more diverse and industrious ways. Her determination to bring about change made her receptive to new causes, each one leading her on to even greater responsibilities and opportunities. It is important to bear in mind that the causes Eleanor championed, be they feminist, female-related issues or humanitarian activities, were not mutually exclusive. Rather they were, as Margaret Simey described, 'an integral part of an overall process'. They also provided a climate in which she was able to cultivate her own ideology on social policy, against a background of political and economic change. At the root of all her campaigns, along with their concomitant proposals for reform, was the inspiration Eleanor drew from her conviction that 'dignity was the right of every human being and the fight to ensure it was the reason for their existence'.[35]

None of Eleanor's investigations were undertaken in a vacuum, for studies of poverty, both quantitative and qualitative, were constantly being pursued by innumerable male and female social investigators across the country. Her next survey, *How the Casual Labourer Lives*, ably demonstrated this, and, by her own admission, owed much to the pioneering work of Rowntree in York, for it included amongst its stated aims the intention of providing Liverpool with 'a companion picture to Mr. B.S. Rowntree's study of the diet of labourer families in York'.[36] It was also a natural progression from her dock labour investigation. The report, which highlighted the problem faced by the wives of casual workers and the responsibility which they bore for housekeeping on an irregular wage, was a collaborative undertaking, involving amongst other voluntary bodies, the LWIC and the LVWS, of which Eleanor was now honorary secretary.

It is evident from the way in which her interests developed at this time that, against a background of concern for the poor, Eleanor was particularly aware of, and disturbed by certain specific hardships suffered by the women amongst them. Her sense of injustice was particularly aroused by the inequality of wages paid to both sexes doing the same work. Thus for a while she turned her attention to the relationship between men's and women's labour, publishing a paper on the subject, *The Problem of Women's Wages*, in 1912.[37] Once again, her interest and activities echoed a national anxiety, and this topical issue remained active for decades to come. Like most of the studies that Eleanor undertook before the First World War her report, *The Condition of Widows under the Poor Law in Liverpool*, published in 1913 under the auspices of the LWIC, was a local case study of a nationwide issue. Here she drew attention to the financial hardship suffered by widows with young children, who fell outside the net of any state provision. Despite the introduction of some welfare reforms by the Liberal government in 1911, neither the Insurance Act, with its limited provision for the unemployed and sick wage earners, nor the Old Age Pensions Act (of which Booth was an early champion), addressed or even acknowledged the plight of widowed mothers. Eleanor's assessment, which advocated a state-aided scheme of payment, was of great significance, for it established the idea of the economics of motherhood. Eleanor's argument, that motherhood was a service to the community and should be recognized as such by way of a state-paid allowance, became fundamental to her long-running campaign for a family allowance to be paid to mothers. Like so many other issues with which she involved herself, she was influenced to a certain degree by contemporary investigators. In the case of both the family allowance and her study of the casual labourer, she acknowledged the effect that Rowntree's study of York had exerted over her. For, as she stated in the introduction to her book *The Disinherited Family*, first published in 1924, 'I do not forget the work of Mr Seebohm Rowntree and of the sociologists and labour leaders who have followed him in pleading for the claim of the wage-earner to a "living wage" based on the needs of the family'.[38]

Alongside the social investigation and reports that Eleanor produced in the years following the death of her father in 1902 was her increasing involvement with the LVWS. The Liverpool settlement, which was founded in 1897, was pioneering in that it was run by women for women. In other respects it mirrored similar establishments elsewhere in the country, in that it was a practical exercise of the prevalent ideology of active citizenship and personal service, as promoted by the Oxford philosophers, Green and Caird. The stated aims and scope of the fledging LVWS were somewhat vague, 'the primary idea of a settlement is to plant in a centre of vice, squalor and misery, a little oasis of education, refinement and sympathy, to try (to use a Scriptural phrase) to introduce the little leaven which in time – a very long time, of course – may help to leaven the whole lump'[39] and the early years were fraught with problems. Liverpool society was sceptical about the venture on the grounds that it was not a conventional form of charitable effort. It also disapproved of the women involved with it, in the same way as they had censured Josephine Butler and Mary Macaulay for their earlier work. Discontinuity of leadership had an equally adverse affect on the work being undertaken, and was only resolved with the appointment, in late 1902, of Elizabeth Macadam as the paid warden. Macadam's outstanding qualification was the fact that she had trained as a social worker, and had experience in settlement work.[40] At the time of Elizabeth Macadam's appointment, Eleanor, who shared the new warden's belief in the professionalization of social work, was already active as a voluntary visitor for the LVWS. The two women had an immediate rapport and the working relationship that resulted, led, in 1905, to the foundations of the School of Social Studies and Training for Social Work in Liverpool.

The techniques of casework were exacting, and emphasized the importance of the collection and analysis of information, practices in which Eleanor was well versed. Besides lecturing on civic administration, she was a major fund-raiser. Seen in the wider context, like so many other issues she was then involved with, the local nature of the training scheme had much wider, national implications. At a personal level, her involvement in the provision of opportunities for training in social work was another aspect of her commitment to improving the status of women.

The suffrage movement was at the heart of the struggle for equality for women and Eleanor, whose fierce commitment to feminism had developed during her Somerville days, expressed this practically by becoming a non-militant suffragist. In her view, the achievement of the vote for women would not be an end in itself, but represented the means to an end, that being greater power over government decisions. She talked of suffrage 'with an ardour approaching importunity'[41] and was clearly an eminently suitable candidate for the post of parliamentary secretary to the non-militant Liverpool Women's Suffrage Society (LWSS), which she accepted in 1897. The LWSS rejected violence and law-breaking, whether national or regional, in favour of a parliamentary approach to achieving the vote, which probably contributed to Mary Stocks' view that 'the public was scarcely awake to it as a practical political issue'.[42] This was in stark contrast to the newly formed militant pressure group, the Women's Social and Political Union, founded in 1903 by Emmeline Pankhurst and her elder daughter, Christabel. The Pankhursts were audacious in their belief that militancy would succeed where thirty-six years of campaigning by more experienced and well-connected suffragists had failed, and in 1905 changed the face of the campaign with their violence and political agitation, awakening the public to their demands. As far as Eleanor was concerned, this new phase brought with it an increase in her own responsibilities within the local organization, as she and her colleagues pursued all the avenues open to non-militant, law-abiding political agitators. But in typical Rathbone fashion, she did not confine her energies to one area, and alongside campaigning for the franchise for women, she sought other channels through which women could achieve greater social and economic freedom. This fact explains why Mary Stocks was able to assert that, at this time, Eleanor was more widely known 'as an expert on social problems and local government than as a prominent speaker or agitator for the suffrage cause'.[43]

Indeed, it was to the sphere of local government, on which she lectured at the LVWS, that she next turned her attention. Encouraged by the success of her cousin Margaret Ashton, who was elected the first woman member of Manchester City Council in 1908, Eleanor replicated this 'first' by winning a seat as an independent councillor on Liverpool City Council in 1909. This appointment opened the way for her to achieve change in a more visible and tangible way, and in the years leading up to the First World War her social work activities in Liverpool were diverse and numerous. By now Eleanor had gathered an army of fellow workers around her, always ready to assist in whatever activity she undertook. She also had the practical and philosophical support of a number of important people from within Liverpool University, who were equally committed to solving the city's problems. As with her earlier social investigations, the issues that she became involved with were to have far-reaching consequences. In 1909 municipal housing administration – a non-gendered humanitarian rather than a feminist issue – became a priority, preparing her for her post-war preoccupation with the legislative aspects of this problem. Her active role in the establishment of the Liverpool University School of Social Science was a natural progression from her involvement with the training scheme in social work at the LVWS. Similarly, the establishment of the Liverpool Women's Citizen's Association (LWCA) in 1913, which was Eleanor's personal inspiration, emanated from the LWSS, and was a splendid example of her capacity for original thought. The organization supported the 'votes for women' campaign, but its main intention was to educate them as citizens through lectures and discussions. In respect of its educative capacity, the LWCA was a vehicle through which Eleanor could disseminate the philosophical teachings she had absorbed at Oxford. Once again, what began as a local initiative soon became a national network, with the Liverpool model being recreated, post-war, up and down the country.

The pace of Eleanor's pre-war humanitarian and feminist activities and achievements were marred somewhat by her resignation, in April 1914, from the executive of the National Union of Women's Suffrage Societies (NUWSS). The dispute over policy which precipitated this action – she had mobilized opposition to the Union's affiliation with the Labour Party – revealed a hitherto undisclosed vulnerability in her character, for she became obsessed by the belief, which was totally unfounded, that people thought she had been disloyal or had been involved in some sort of conspiracy. The heat quickly went out of this incident, aided on Eleanor's part by a retreat to the Lake District with Elizabeth Macadam, and within a year she was back within the Union fold, thus enabling her to further her feminist career.[44]

Before this, however, other more pressing matters came to the fore as a result of the outbreak of the First World War in August 1914. The war created urgent social problems nationwide, for as the mobilization of reservists progressed according to plan it became apparent that no attention had been given to their dependants, nor had any financial provision been made for them. Existing rules for the payment of allowances meant that few families were actually eligible, so that vast numbers of women and children, with no other means of support, faced immediate and lasting destitution. One voluntary organization, the Soldiers and Sailors Family Association (SSFA) was singled out as being appropriate for administering war relief, but most branches were unprepared for a crisis of such magnitude. In Liverpool Eleanor was invited to take over the local SSFA branch and develop its operation, a job that she tackled skilfully and with urgency. Her ability to fire others with her enthusiasm came to the fore once again, and she was able to muster the support of nearly 1,000 voluntary workers, including colleagues, friends and family. From March 1915, the separation allowance was being paid weekly, in advance, directly to mothers through the nationwide network of the Post Office.

The conditions of war not only hastened the state payment of allowances to married women, but the call for women to do 'men's work', precipitated by wartime dislocation to the labour force, strengthened the case for equal pay for equal work. For Eleanor, her involvement with the SSFA served to highlight the peacetime status quo whereby most married women were financially dependent upon their husbands. Thus, by accident rather than design, the crisis provided her with the empirical evidence she needed to support her argument for a family allowance that was paid to women, a proposal that had been fermenting since the publication, in 1913, of her report, *The Condition of Widows under the Poor Law in Liverpool*. Following the inclusion of two papers on the subject of separation allowances in the feminist publication, *Common Cause*,[45] Eleanor argued her case for the endowment of motherhood, which was ideologically both feminist and humanitarian, in her article, 'The Remuneration of Women's Services', published in 1917.[46]

By now Eleanor's views on the dispensing of financial assistance to the needy had undergone a sea change, and she accepted that, in stark contrast to the COS ideology, statutory state intervention in the lives of the poor was both desirable and necessary. This shift may have come about partly as a result of her professional contact with Elizabeth Macadam, who had already studied child poverty prior to her friend's study of casual labour. Both women shared a horror of 'haphazard philanthropy', and Elizabeth wrote of the need for co-operation between voluntary and government services.[47] So, after outlining her analysis of the topical and highly politicized 'living wage' debate, defined by Snowden in 1913 as 'a wage which will allow the worker to maintain his working powers in the highest state of efficiency, to properly fulfil all his duties as a citizen, and to support his family in decency and health',[48] Eleanor linked this to her argument for the continuation, post-war, of a state allowance paid directly to mothers. This was on the lines of the wartime separation allowance that she had been involved with administering in Liverpool. Eleanor's concept of a family allowance as a universal right was based on her view that there should be special recognition for women as mothers, which, by definition, put a value on their contribution.

There was certainly no consensus amongst feminists for her proposals, and this dissent caused a schism within the movement. Advocates of 'equal rights' opposed Eleanor's case on the grounds that any demands based on the special needs of women would diminish their quest for equal rights with men, especially within employment. Undeterred by such disagreement, Eleanor took the first tangible step in her long-running campaign to promote the economics of motherhood by establishing her Family Endowment Committee (FEC) in 1917. The group included two former colleagues from the NWSS executive committee, Kathleen Courtney and Maude Royden. Maude Royden subsequently worked alongside Eleanor with her Indian women's campaign in 1934, and, more pertinent to her subsequent involvement in refugee issues, became a lay preacher in the 1930s and was outspoken in her condemnation of anti-Semitism and the persecution of Jews in Nazi Germany.[49] The FEC presented its first report,

'Equal Pay and the Family: A Proposal for the National Endowment of Motherhood', written jointly by Eleanor, Mary Stocks, Maude Royden, Kathleen Courtney, the Radical Liberal Emile Burns, H.N. Brailsford and Elinor Burns, in 1918. This reinforced Eleanor's already published argument that women would never achieve equal pay while a man's wage was meant to support a family, and therefore the state payment of an allowance to mothers and equal pay for women working outside of the home were two sides of the same coin.

It is worth noting that Susan Pedersen has described how, by launching the family endowment battle in 1917, Eleanor 'opened a new chapter in her life, one marked by information-gathering, lobbying and endless expert testimony'.[50] But Eleanor was basically and consistently a humanitarian activist, and this was not so much a new chapter as a change of direction, which came about because of prevailing circumstances. For, as new humanitarian crises presented themselves in the ensuing years, so her priorities altered, culminating in her almost exclusive devotion to the refugee question from 1933 onwards. Nor were the skills that Susan Pedersen has identified confined to the years after 1917, for Eleanor had already utilized these in various other contexts, even at university, and continued to do so throughout her career.

It was around this time that Eleanor made a major decision in her personal circumstances, for in 1919 she set up home with her companion, Elizabeth Macadam, in her newly acquired house in Tufton Street, London. Their cohabitation has fuelled speculation about the nature of their friendship, and led at least one feminist historian to assume that it had a sexual dimension.[51] David Cesarani is also inclined to believe that Eleanor was probably 'homosexual' and that in some way this 'encouraged an identification with persecuted outsiders and engendered an appreciation of tolerant societies in which diversity, of all types, was regarded as non-threatening'.[52] Both are speculative assessments that are not borne out by any concrete evidence. It was not uncommon in the Edwardian period for a highly educated, financially independent woman in the public sphere to live with another female, as this arrangement enabled both to pursue their diverse activities, supported by an understanding companion, without the complications of marriage. Eleanor herself had an 'imperturbable unconcern with sex',[53] not unusual for a woman brought up in the Victorian period for whom the whole question of sexual relationships was veiled behind a culture of privacy and reserve. Even though it is possible that this atmosphere enabled Eleanor and Elizabeth to share an intimate relationship behind closed doors, a number of people who knew Eleanor firmly refuted this idea. Her niece, Noreen Rathbone, herself a lesbian, was categorical on this matter,[54] as were Vera Schaerli and Helga Wolff, wartime colleagues in the refugee cause, and Joan Gibson, one of her wartime secretaries.[55] They all confirmed Noreen Rathbone's assessment of her aunt's attitude towards sex, for they described her as being extremely prudish, and of adhering to a very strict Victorian moral code which would never have countenanced or even considered such a liaison. Moreover, these women went so far as to say that they thought Eleanor would have been disgusted by the very thought of it. The two women's personalities certainly complemented one another, for Eleanor's demeanour, so often distracted and absent-minded, was balanced by Macadam's organizational skills. Indeed Eleanor was far more dependent on her friend than she cared to admit. In the final analysis, the question of her sexuality is less important than the fact that Eleanor possessed emotional forces which were 'conserved to add depth and passion to the intellectual drive with which she served the causes of humanity'.[56]

Content in her partnership with her like-minded friend, Elizabeth, Eleanor continued to pursue the campaign for family allowances, of which she was the initiator and leading propagandist, whilst characteristically pursuing many other causes. Her interests were not exclusively female-related or feminist but reflected her humanitarianism and sense of social responsibility. For example, in the aftermath of the First World War, and in her capacity as a councillor on Liverpool City Council, she responded to the urgent social problems in the city by zealously renewing her work to ameliorate the acute housing situation, due mostly to the large numbers of Irish Catholic dock labourers, in Granby. But she also remained involved with feminist issues, and in 1919 stood for and gained presidency of the National Union of Societies for Equal Citizenship (NUSEC), as the NUWSS became in 1919, described by Pedersen as 'the headquarters of the movement'.[57] The battle for votes for women was partially won on 21 November 1919, when the Parliament (Qualification of Women) Bill received the royal assent and extended the franchise to women over thirty, even though this meant that only 40 per cent were able to vote, and many of the younger militant women were still excluded. The passing of the Sex Disqualification (Removal) Act in the same year ostensibly allowed women to 'assume or carry on any civil profession or vocation', putting the future of feminism in jeopardy, and requiring its urgent revitalization if it was to survive. Under Eleanor's somewhat controversial ten-year leadership of NUSEC, her ideas on 'New Feminism' evolved. Not only did these not meet with universal approval, but by 1921 Eleanor had to admit that the whole women's movement had lost its popular appeal. She continued to try and revive flagging interest in the movement through NUSEC, alongside carving her own niche within the newly opened political sphere, for she anticipated that an official position would give her greater and more powerful opportunities to effect social and political change. She was already a member of the Liverpool War Pensions Committee when, in 1920, she became a Justice of the Peace for the county of Lancashire. But greater political status and a more powerful platform were essential if her campaign for family endowment was to become a reality, and it was with this in mind that Eleanor made her first attempt, in 1922, to gain a seat in parliament. Her failure to win East Toxteth, Liverpool was due in part to her election appeal for endowment being pitched against Liverpool's notorious popular Toryism, and she determined never to contest a Liverpool seat again.

Her family endowment campaign gained momentum in 1924, with the publication of her book, *The Disinherited Family*. Described by Mary Stocks as 'one of the finest examples of polemical economic literature ever written',[58] the work was a detailed and well-argued analysis of Eleanor's case for the introduction of a state allowance to be paid to mothers, and gained her wide acclaim. Despite the book's influence, it also contained more than a hint of the popular contemporary eugenicist thought, arguments that Eleanor would have found hard to ignore. The ideology of Social Darwinism and the debate over eugenics in the early 1900s had been fuelled by revelations of the poor physical condition of troops in the Boer War. Public concerns over the health and efficiency of the population were allied to fears over the declining birth rate, and provided the eugenics movement, headed by Sir Francis Galton and Karl Pearson, with a receptive audience and congenial political climate. Whilst the eugenicists were disseminating an ideological belief in 'survival of the fittest' and a superior Anglo-Saxon race, Eleanor had launched her battle for the state endowment of motherhood. There were times during this long-running campaign when she was blatant in her reiteration of eugenicist rhetoric. An early example, in 1917, occurred when she wrote of her worry that whilst the upper and middle classes were practising birth control and restricting their family size, the impoverished lower classes were 'multiplying as freely as ever' but producing children whose health was poor. The result, she concluded, was that 'we are as a nation, recruiting the national stock from those who have sunk into the lowest strata because they are physically, mentally or morally degenerate'.[59] Similarly, *The Disinherited Family* was peppered with references to the 'bad habits' of the poor. Like many social investigators of the period who categorized the poor as 'deserving' or 'undeserving', Eleanor adopted discriminatory terms such as 'the cream' and 'the dregs' to distinguish between groups of working-class people.[60] She could find no better way to describe the homes of the very poor other than as 'slums', but at the same time apologized for using such 'an odious but expressive nickname'.[61] Contrasted with derogatory remarks such as these were the more frequent discourses in which she was clearly very sympathetic towards the plight of the poor, and where she was firmly at odds with eugenicist doctrine. She was, for example, adamant in her belief that environmental and not genetic factors accounted for working-class behaviour and habits, and that financial pressures were the major problem. Her solution was, through her proposed family endowment scheme, to raise the standard of living for the poor by providing mothers with 'the material means for healthy living'.[62] This would enable them to have 'an orderly and self-respecting living' which was 'the best cure for indiscriminate and dysgenic breeding'.[63] Her address to the Eugenics Society in 1924 on the subject of family endowment and population was intended to allay the fears of its members, who argued that a family allowance would encourage poor mothers to have even more offspring, so increasing the number of genetically unfit children.[64]

Another aspect of early 1900s eugenicist thought that Eleanor could not fail to have noticed was their concern with race issues, the biological consequences of immigration, and their attitude towards Jews, especially those from Eastern Europe. The extent of this position, which manifested itself as anti-Semitism, continues to be the subject of academic debate: Geoffrey Searle has maintained that the majority of eugenicists viewed Jews as the very model of what they sought to establish, 'a closely knit community which had identified religion with a sense of racial destiny and which invested its customary sexual and hygienic regulations with all the weight of religious authority',[65] and that anti-Semitism was apparent in only a handful of followers of the movement in Britain, who called for the exclusion of Jews from the country. However, Dan Stone, in his 2002 study of eugenics in Edwardian and interwar Britain, takes issue with Searle's view, and has argued that anti-Semitism was far more prevalent than previously acknowledged, and includes plenty of evidence in support of his counter-claim. For him, eugenics was not some kind of 'free-wheeling amorphous project, but was an aspect of generally-held ideas about social reform ... (that) ... pervaded social and cultural life in this period'.[66]

Eleanor did not articulate her opinions about Jews until the 1930s, when she openly applauded them, often from the political platform of the House of Commons, for their values and ethics. Less publicly, at a meeting of the Union of Jewish Women which she attended in 1934, she raised the issue of eugenics when she spoke of the 'danger of excessive "racialism"' and of how she was inclined to believe that 'in the long run mongrel races are the best and that there is very great danger from too much in-breeding'.[67]

The conclusion that should be drawn from this brief analysis of Eleanor's links with the eugenics movement is that she flirted with their ideology for purely opportunistic reasons, her aim being to gather together as large a base of support as possible for her family endowment scheme. Like many from her background, she adopted a 'soft' version of mainly positive eugenics, and to do this she adjusted her writing and speeches to suit her audience, harnessing some of their arguments, specifically on population, to suit her own purposes.[68] Her views on the subject were confused and often inconsistent, suggesting a lack of commitment to the movement. She was never party to any sort of anti-Semitism and her subsequent campaigns for the rights of women in India, Kenya and Palestine were inconsistent with racist ideology. However, she was fiercely nationalistic, and often paternalistic, as exemplified in her notorious and ill-conceived dealings with Indian women in the 1930s, when she was totally unable to understand Indian nationalist aspirations (see Plate 4).

Coincidental to the publication, in 1924, of *The Disinherited Family*, Eleanor was invited by the Independent Labour Party (ILP) to present her case for family endowment at their summer conference,[69] which led to them asking the Labour Party to place family allowances on the legislative agenda. Then, in 1926, the Labour Party and the Trades Union Congress Joint Committee on the Living Wage was established to look into the whole ILP proposal. Eleanor was amongst those who, optimistically, gave evidence to the committee in 1928, only to be totally dispirited when eventually, in May 1930, both the Trades Union Congress and the Labour Party rejected the idea of a family allowance, and did not discuss the proposal again until the Second World War. Eleanor pursued her goal for a family allowance for a further two decades, although by the end of the 1930s the proposition had been revived in official circles and moved forward by its own momentum. She, in turn, had shifted her attention to wider international issues.

There were a number of interrelated factors that persuaded her to seek election to parliament again in 1929. As far as Mary Stocks was concerned, it was a decision stimulated by her preoccupation with Indian affairs.[70] Another view is that she was driven by the need to represent women in the House, where so many questions relating to women were being aired.[71] What mattered was Eleanor's determination to remain independent of any political party doctrine, and to this end she stood as an independent candidate for the Combined English Universities – Birmingham, Bristol, Durham, Leeds, Liverpool, Manchester, Reading and Sheffield – in the 1929, so-called Flapper Election.[72] Of the sixty-nine women candidates, fourteen were returned, including Eleanor, whose success at the poll surpassed even her own expectations. Her contemporaries included Nancy, Lady Astor, Ellen Wilkinson and Katherine, Duchess of Atholl, all of whom were subsequently involved in her refugee campaigning activities.

Having achieved this major goal, Eleanor was now ready to use her newly acquired status as an MP as the springboard for her campaigning activities. When she entered parliament she had already achieved a reputation in the world of feminism and social economics, but her new position gained her wider recognition within the national and international political arena. As a female politician she commanded both respect and fear from those she encountered. Not that this was ever going to be easy, for despite all the advantages which she had – the support of Elizabeth Macadam, who relieved her of mundane day-to-day tasks and put order into her otherwise somewhat disorganized lifestyle, a secretary and office, money, brains and brawn – she was still a woman in a male-dominated culture. The House of Commons was essentially a man's world in which the hours and facilities were arranged for the benefit of the male majority, and where the minority of recently admitted women members were tolerated, but often segregated. Whereas some women MPs were ill suited to the combative, assertive and essentially quarrelsome, adversarial arrangement of the House, Eleanor appeared to thrive in this environment.[73] This was not entirely surprising, for her academic and philosophical training at Oxford and experience of debating with the Somerville APs proved to be an excellent training ground, and she found the House responsive to a reasoned approach. She had the added benefit of being able to recall the political experiences of her late father, with whom she had shared such an intimate relationship. Nor was she daunted by her minority position, even though she, in common with other women MPs, was subject to prejudice and anti-feminist remarks. This was exemplified, for example, in 1942, when Mr Andrew MacLaren, the Independent Labour MP for Burslem, commented, in Eleanor's brief absence from the House, 'I see that she is not present now. What a pity. I wish she had stayed. For years she has wasted her life advocating family allowances. I suppose that is a good enough substitute for the absence of a family.'[74] She had no interest in impressing her political colleagues by following fashion or dressing in a particularly feminine way, even if this was expected of female MPs. It was Eleanor's style, consistency, well-informed and rational argument, and her ability to hone her political skills, which enabled her to survive and to move on to fight humanitarian causes at home and abroad. Gaining a seat in parliament was most definitely a watershed in her career: it gave her the most powerful platform from which to campaign for government action, and it is hard to see how she could have been as successful and influential as she was had she not become an MP. The significance of her position became apparent as she became involved with international humanitarian issues, the first of these being in Imperial India.

NOTES

1. For the first biography, see M. Stocks, *Eleanor Rathbone. A Biography* (London: Victor Gollancz, 1949). For the most insightful account of Rathbone's early years, S. Pedersen, *Eleanor Rathbone and the Politics of Conscience* (London: Yale University Press, 2004).
2. L. Nottingham, *Rathbone Brothers: From Merchant to Banker 1742–1992* (London: Rathbone Brothers, 1992).
3. For a description of Liverpool at this time, see M. Simey, *Charity Rediscovered: A Study of Philanthropic Effort in Nineteenth-Century Liverpool* (Liverpool: Liverpool University Press, 1992).
4. W. Rathbone, *Social Duties: Considered in Reference to the Organization of Effort in Works of Benevolence and Public Utility: By a Man of Business* (London, Cambridge (printed) 1867). E.F. Rathbone, (EFR) *William Rathbone: A Memoir* (London: Macmillan, 1905).
5. J. Lewis, 'Eleanor Rathbone 1872–1946', in P. Barker (ed.), *Founders of the Welfare State* (London: Heinemann, 1984), p.83.
6. B. Williams, 'History of Liverpool's Jewish Community'. Paper presented to Manchester Jewish Museum, June 1987.
7. Stocks, *Rathbone*, p.27.
8. Demographically, Rathbone's chances of marriage would have been slim, for the excess of females to males was estimated, by 1913, at 1,200,000 in England and Wales, 18,887,000 females outnumbering 17,687,000 males. See D. Read, *Edwardian England 1901–15. Society and Politics* (London: Harrap, 1972), p.209.
9. Letter of William Rathbone to EFR, 6 September 1893, RP IX.4 (188), ULL.
10. See, for example, entries for Summer Term 1894, Summer and Michaelmas Terms 1895 for EFR, Reports of Collections, Somerville Hall 1891, pp.186–7. Somerville College Archives.
11. Report of Mr Cannan, Summer Term 1896, Reports of Collections, Somerville Hall 1891, pp.186–7. Somerville College Archives.
12. Report of Mr Ritchie, Lent Term 1894, Reports of Collections, Somerville Hall 1891, pp.186–7. Somerville College Archives.
13. Lucy Kempson to Stocks, 8 May 1947, RP XIV.4 (40), ULL.
14. As cited in M. Richter, *The Politics of Conscience. T.H. Green and his Age* (London: Weidenfeld and Nicolson, 1964), p.146.
15. J. Alberti, *Eleanor Rathbone* (London: Sage, 1996), p.18.
16. R.G. Collingwood, *An Autobiography* (London: Oxford University Press, 1939), p.17.
17. V. Brittain, *The Women at Oxford* (London: Harrap, 1960), p.96.
18. C. Black (ed.), *Married Women's Work* (London: Virago, 1983 reprint of 1915 edition), p.iii.
19. As noted in Letter of Margery Fry to Dorothy Scott, 4 September 1898, private collection.
20. E.V. Isaacs, *For the Record. The Memoirs of Eva, Marchioness of Reading* (London: privately published by Hutchinson Benham, 1972), pp.185–6.
21. Author's telephone interview with Noreen Rathbone, 21 November 2000.
22. Minute Book of the APs, 18 February 1894. Somerville College Archives.
23. Minute Book of the APs, Somerville College Archives.
24. M. Simey, *The Disinherited Society. A Personal View of Social Responsibility in Liverpool during the Twentieth Century* (Liverpool: Liverpool University Press, 1996), p.31.
25. Alberti, *Rathbone*, p.18.
26. E.H. Jones, *Margery Fry: The Essential Amateur* (Oxford: Oxford University Press, 1966), p.41.
27. Stocks, *Rathbone*, p.34.
28. Stocks, *Rathbone*, p.50.
29. Stocks, *Rathbone*, p.51.
30. See Letter of EFR to Hilda Oakeley, c.1901, RP XIV.6.6, ULL.

31. E.F. Rathbone, *Report on the Results of a Special Inquiry into the Conditions of Labour at the Liverpool Docks* (Liverpool: Liverpool Economic and Statistical Society. Transactions, etc. Session 1903/04).
32. See, for example, Letter of EFR to Shertok, 27 October 1934, Weizmann Archives.
33. Pedersen, *Politics of Conscience*, pp.62–3.
34. Letter of EFR to Oakeley, c.1901, RP XIV.6.6, ULL.
35. Simey, *Rathbone*, pp.13, 15.
36. E.F. Rathbone, *How the Casual Labourer Lives: Report of the Liverpool Joint Research Committee on the Domestic Condition and Expenditure of the Families of Certain Liverpool Labourers* (Liverpool, 1909), p.vi. See also B.S. Rowntree, *Poverty: A Study of Town Life* (London: Macmillan, 1901).
37. E.F. Rathbone, *The Problem of Women's Wages: An Enquiry into the Causes of the Inferiority of Women's Wages to Men's* (Liverpool: Northern Publishing Co., 1912). This was first presented as a paper in 1902 to the Liverpool Economic and Statistical Society.
38. E.F. Rathbone, *The Disinherited Family: A Plea for the Endowment of the Family* (London: Edward Arnold, 1924).
39. Cited in Simey, *Charity Rediscovered*, p.131.
40. E. Macadam, *The Equipment of the Social Worker* (London: George Allen and Unwin, 1925).
41. Stocks, *Rathbone*, p.64.
42. Ibid., pp.63–4.
43. Ibid., pp.65–7.
44. B. Harrison, *Prudent Revolutionaries: Portraits of British Feminists between the Wars* (Oxford: Clarendon Press, 1987), p.103.
45. E.F. Rathbone, 'Separation Allowances', *Common Cause*, 25 February 1916, pp.611–12; 17 March 1916, pp.648–9.
46. E.F. Rathbone, 'The Remuneration of Women's Services', *Economic Journal*, 27, 105 (March 1917), pp.55–68.
47. Pedersen, 'Eleanor Rathbone 1871–1946', pp.116–17.
48. P. Snowden, *The Living Wage* (London: Hodder and Stoughton, 1912).
49. 'Jews and Christians'. Lesson given by Dr Maude Royden, Guildhouse, London, 18 October 1936.
50. Pedersen, *Politics of Conscience*, p.153.
51. S. Jeffreys, *The Spinster and her Enemies: Feminism and Sexuality 1890–1930* (London: Pandora, 1985), p.153.
52. D. Cesarani, 'Mad Dogs and Englishmen: Towards a Taxonomy of Rescuers in a Bystander Country – Britain 1933–45', *The Journal of Holocaust Education*, 9, 2 and 3 (2000), pp.51–2.
53. Stocks, *Rathbone*, p.48.
54. Author's telephone interview with Noreen Rathbone, 21 November 2000.
55. Author's interview with Vera Schaerli, 22 February 2000. Author's interview with Joan Gibson, 31 March 2000.
56. Author's telephone interview with Noreen Rathbone, 21 November 2000, and also Stocks, *Rathbone*, p.48.
57. Pedersen, *Politics of Conscience*, p.177.
58. Stocks, *Rathbone*, p.96.
59. E.F. Rathbone, 'The Remuneration of Women's Services', *Economic Journal*, 27, 105 (March 1917), p.66.
60. Rathbone, *Disinherited Family*, pp.318–19.
61. E.F. Rathbone, *The Ethics and Economics of Family Endowment* (London: Epworth Press, 1927), p.110.
62. Ibid., p.124.
63. Ibid., p.321.
64. E.F. Rathbone, 'Family Endowment in its Bearing on the Question of Population', Speech delivered by Eleanor Rathbone to a meeting of the Eugenics Society, 12 November 1924.
65. G. Searle, *Eugenics and Politics in Britain, 1910–1914* (Leyden: Noordhoff International Publishing, 1976), p.41.
66. D. Stone, *Breeding Superman: Nietzsche, Race and Eugenics in Edwardian and Interwar Britain* (Liverpool: Liverpool University Press, 2002), pp.112–13.
67. Report of the general meeting of the Union of Jewish Women, 19 February 1934. Union of Jewish Women Papers, MS 129/AJ161/16/4, Parkes Library, Special Collections,

University of Southampton (USL).
68. Rathbone, 'Family Endowment in its Bearing on the Question of Population', 12 November 1924.
69. Sidney M. Potter, 'The ILP Summer School', *New Leader*, 8, 8 (22 August 1924), pp.37–42.
70. Stocks, *Rathbone*, p.129.
71. Pedersen, *Politics of Conscience*, p.219.
72. P. Brookes, *Women at Westminster: An Account of Women in the British Parliament 1918–1966* (London: Peter Davies, 1967), p.71ff.
73. Ibid., pp.83–4.
74. *Hansard* HC, vol. 380, col. 1876, 23 June 1942.

# 2

# *India and Other Imperial Concerns*

Eleanor's championing of humanitarian causes in India, Kenya and Africa marked a turning point in the focus of her work, and paved the way for her later devotion to the refugee question. It is not hard to see why she came to be involved with these issues, for as the imperatives of one humanitarian cause diminished, so she embarked on an even more challenging campaign. At home, interest in the feminist movement was losing ground and this change coincided with her acquiring knowledge of cultural practices that, from her Western viewpoint, were inhumane and evil. Though geographically distant, these events were taking place in countries with which Britain still had powerful colonial, imperial and foreign policy links, and her status as an MP after 1929 gave her a powerful platform from which to campaign. Thus Indian, Kenyan and African causes overtook female-related issues at home, and these were, in turn, superseded by the urgent need of refugees, mainly Jews, fleeing Nazi-occupied Europe and the threat of extermination. Susan Pedersen's description of Eleanor's belief in a 'hierarchy of challenges and crimes'[1] is very appropriate, for the victims of Nazi oppression presented her with the ultimate campaign in her long career as an activist, and the crimes that were being committed by the Nazi regime were the greatest atrocity perpetrated against humanity in the twentieth century.

Her first venture was an entanglement in the battle against the custom of child marriage in India, which although gender-related by virtue of girls suffering as a result of this practice, had wider implications. This was a legislative and traditional matter within what was, ostensibly, a foreign country, albeit an imperial one. Her sense of right and wrong, and conviction that she, as a British citizen, had a duty to try and change a practice that was deeply entrenched within a foreign society, was a belief that motivated her to react similarly elsewhere in the international arena. As far as Eleanor was concerned, this was an 'unsuspected obligation' to which she was compelled and conditioned to respond. An unforeseen outcome of her involvement in matters outside of her personal experience was the challenge to her attitudes towards race and culture, which emerged as a result of her involvement with Indian issues. She certainly experienced problems in her relationship with the 'Indian woman question', these being compounded by her unshakeable belief that the colonial government, and British women in particular, had a major part to play in improving the condition of Indian women. Not all Indian women shared this view, for many of them perceived Eleanor's assumption of responsibility as patronizing and condescending, and as yet more imperialist interference. They certainly did not take kindly to her 'mother knows best' attitude.[2] Nor were they enamoured of the tactics that she adopted, for although these had been tried and tested at home, they proved inappropriate in the very different circumstances of an international campaign.

The religious practice of child marriage had a complex history that Eleanor described later in her 1934 publication, *Child Marriage: The Indian Minotaur*.[3] It was not uncommon for girls as young as 6 years old to be married to boys or men much older than themselves. Indians who defended the religious tradition explained this as the first marriage, with the consummation ceremony or *garbhadhan* delayed until puberty. In practice there had been cases of very young girls being forced into pre-puberty sex, with disastrous effects on their psychological and physical health. In the 1880s the issue of child marriage became the subject of renewed debate, and once again met with opposition from some Indian nationalists who strongly objected to government interference in what they considered a private, religious issue.

It was Behramji M. Malabari, a journalist and social reformer from Bombay, who was responsible for putting the debate on the feminist agenda. He was a member of the minority Parsi (or Parsee) community of Indians, many of whom were well-educated Anglophiles, and in the 1890s he extended his Indian propaganda campaign against the practice to Britain. His tactics included lobbying government, writing lengthy descriptive articles for *The Times*, and mustering the support of feminists. This combined crusade resulted, in 1891, in the British government amending the Indian Penal Code of 1860, and raising the age of consent for sexual intercourse from 10 to 12 years. Despite this, the status quo remained the same and the difficulties of enforcement persisted: for example, girls forced into illegal acts could never find anyone willing to support their case, evidenced by the lack of any convictions for another thirty years. Interest in the age of marriage and age of consent was renewed in the 1920s, largely due to a conference held by the League of Nations in 1921, convened to debate the traffic in women and girls for immoral purposes.[4] But although the League of Nations recommended that the minimum age for consent be raised to 21, other interested parties, including private individuals and the colonial administration, intervened and hindered progress. The introduction, in 1927, of the

Sarda Hindu Child Marriage Bill seemed destined for greater success, and led to the appointment of a select committee, known as the Joshi Committee after the chairman, Sir Morophant Visavanath Joshi, to assess public opinion.

At this time Britain's imperial policy towards India was undergoing momentous change. The declaration made in 1917 by Edwin Montagu, secretary of state for India, that the British government intended to include more Indians in the governing process, theoretically paved the way for self-governing institutions in India. The British government still held the reins of power, via the Government of India Act of 1919, which dictated the speed and nature of political change. But the slow pace of reform inflamed nationalism across India. During the 1920s violent outbreaks between Hindus and Moslems resulted in the death of more than 450 people with a further 5,000 injured, whilst strikes at steel works and on the railways caused widespread disruption and in November 1927, the outgoing Conservative government announced its intention to convene the already agreed statutory Simon Commission, named after its chairman, Sir John Simon, and with whom Eleanor had many confrontations in the late 1930s when he was chancellor of the Exchequer, nearly two years ahead of schedule.

It was against this background that Eleanor became engaged in the child-marriage debate in Britain in 1927, but like so many of the issues with which she became involved during her life, her commitment to improving the status, health and education of Indian women occurred by accident rather than design. The impetus came from her reading, during the summer holidays of 1927, of *Mother India*, written by Katherine Mayo, an American journalist with a reputation for sensationalist writing.[5] The content of Mayo's book, with its vivid and lurid descriptions of human suffering, especially where child brides were concerned, shocked Eleanor, who abhorred cruelty in any form. Mayo's motives for writing the book, which was certainly a direct attack upon Indians and their customs, are uncertain. She maintained in a letter to Eleanor that the book was never meant to be 'a rounded picture of India' but was written 'for her own people as a practical contribution on certain definite points only'.[6] More recent research has argued that Mayo was encouraged to write her book by the British government's propaganda machine[7] as a way of reinforcing the imperialist view that Indians were not ready 'to hold the reins of Government'.[8] Whatever the reasons, the polemical nature of the book, which was published within days of the Sarda (Child Marriage Restraint) Act being announced, ensured that it became the centre of an unprecedented international controversy, with Eleanor, unwittingly, at the heart of the argument in Britain.

Her reaction to *Mother India* was clearly motivated by her concern for the welfare of others, and in mid-1927 she made an unequivocal and immediate decision to help Indian women and children, launching herself into this new campaign with her customary fervour and enthusiasm. By the time that the storm broke over the book in November 1927, she had already planned the first stage of her campaign, which was to confirm the veracity of Mayo's claims. Eleanor gradually established a rapport with the author, first through correspondence and later with personal meetings, which included inviting Mayo to her London home for dinner in the spring of 1928.[9] The episode that unfolded proved quite disastrous, and there is little doubt that Eleanor was guilty of many mistakes in her Indian campaign. Praising Mayo for drawing her attention, and that of the world, to the evils perpetrated on young girls in India[10] was underhand and not strictly true for as she admitted in 1931, she had actually acquired some information on the tradition whilst representing the International Women's Suffrage Association on the Child Welfare Committee of the League of Nations years earlier.[11] Ingratiating herself with Mayo was foolish for it gave the erroneous impression that she was sympathetic to Mayo's anti-independence views.[12] And urging Mayo to produce a cheaper edition of *Mother India* for distribution to members of the Labour Party as a way of deterring them from blithely promoting self-government in India,[13] did little to dispel this notion.[14] In fact these moves added fuel to the fire of those who thought she opposed political autonomy for India. This was clearly not the case, for not only had Eleanor been brought up in a family who traditionally had faith in political self-determination, but she had also fought passionately for the political self-determination of women. She was an active supporter of the Indian nationalist demand for autonomy, but her ineptitude and failure to grasp the complexities of Indian affairs resulted in many aspersions being cast upon her character and beliefs.

Alongside her personal contact with Mayo, Eleanor utilized her position as president of the National Union of Societies for Equal Citizenship (NUSEC) and convened a conference at Caxton Hall, London in November 1927, at which the issues raised in *Mother India* were to be discussed. Even though she did, as Mayo predicted, find it hard to get 'frank and fearless speakers to testify'[15] and confessed to being 'very dissatisfied' with the meeting because 'there were far too many set speakers',[16] two major decisions were made at the conference. The Women of India Survey was set up to establish the exact nature of Indian women's conditions, and it was proposed that a booklet be published which would 'present in a convenient form to British readers the main facts concerning women in India and the various reformative activities at work'.[17] Eleanor was more than happy to endorse Lord Lytton's resolution that emphasized the accountability of British women for Indian social problems, for it reflected her own commitment to responsible citizenship.

Coincidentally, the Simon Commission was just beginning its own survey of India, examining the workings of the new political reforms in preparation for the introduction of a new India Act. The shortcomings of the commission soon became obvious, for not only was it deficient in Indian personnel, a fact which owed much to the unanimous support from the major political parties in Britain who wanted an 'all-white' group, but it also lacked female representatives. Eleanor, through NUSEC, was amongst those who urged Simon to appoint two women as technical advisors to act as 'assessors' and to give the commission 'some continuous link with that part of India hidden behind the veil', but these representations came to nothing and the situation remained unchanged in May 1928.[18]

It was a momentous occasion when, on 6 July 1928, the Representation of the People (Equal Franchise) Bill gained royal assent and NUSEC's most significant goal of women's suffrage was achieved; Eleanor was quick to seize the opportunity of voicing her own thoughts on the future of the women's movement, and her commitment to Indian women, in an article the following week in *Women's Leader*, the official organ of NUSEC. She was in no doubt as to her patriotic duty when she wrote:

> Some of us are imperialists; some of us are not. But so long as imperialism is an inescapable fact, its responsibilities are also an inescapable fact, and these, for the women of this country, include the welfare of all those women in India and the East whose wrongs, as compared to the worst wrongs of our past, are as scorpions to whips.[19]

Juxtaposed against this was her gradual realization that the goals she sought to achieve, especially in connection with India, could be best effected from inside the political machine. It was this that contributed towards her decision to seek election to parliament in 1929.

The questionnaires from the Women in India survey had begun to filter through to India at around this time, and Eleanor became aware of a deep and growing resentment towards her, which she had not anticipated. First, it never occurred to her that Indian women would not share her albeit well-intentioned assumption of responsibility. Nor had she considered that the excessively British nature of the conference initiative might upset the very Indians whom she sought to help. But when social, educational and women's organizations in India became aware of NUSEC's activities, their reaction was passionate: foreign interference in Indian social and cultural issues was intolerable and above all, they were suspicious of Eleanor and her motives. Their mistrust of her was reinforced by her apparent alliance with Mayo. A further crucial mistake was to deny Indian women any involvement in a campaign that was of such relevance to them, and which ignored their own independent investigations. There was little excuse for these failings, other than lack of forethought, for there were other British women's organizations, including the British Commonwealth League, the Women's International League for Peace and Freedom and the International Alliance for Suffrage and Equal Citizenship already working in conjunction with their Indian counterparts to promote social change. Over and above this, Eleanor had a very narrow view of India, which, until her visit there in 1932, excluded any interest in the 'rich, many-sided personality' of the country itself.[20]

What is certain is that she made grave errors of judgement in her handling of Indian affairs, and her lack of tact, which the *Indian Daily Mail* remarked upon in their report of the 1929 NUSEC conference, combined with her condescending attitude, was palpable.[21] The damage was nevertheless done, and despite Eleanor's efforts at re-establishing her credibility – she subsequently entertained six influential Indian women, including Lady Tata and Mrs Sen, at home for an informal discussion – they clung to their resentment of her and continued to mistrust her motives. Eleanor apparently found it very difficult to come to terms with these personal rebuffs, and they certainly highlighted flaws in her character which she had either been unaware of, or had avoided confronting. With hindsight, some of these failings can be seen as a reflection of the strongly Victorian and Edwardian imperialist society in which she lived. She never considered that Indian feminists might, because of their culture, have a different agenda to their Western counterparts, and this was a shortsighted mistake for someone of her intellect.

Within a few months of Eleanor entering parliament, NUSEC sponsored a further meeting at Caxton Hall, London. The Conference on Women in India, which met in October 1929, was projected as 'a gathering of British women's organisations interested in social reform to which Indian women would be invited, but only as advisers'.[22] Eleanor, who chaired the event, presumed that the leading Indian women whom she knew had accepted these terms of reference. However, her complacency was shattered once proceedings got underway, for her assessment proved to be wrong and the conference turned into an acrimonious affair. Representatives from the Indian women's organizations felt they were being patronized, and were championed on this occasion by Mrs Dhanvanthi Rama Rau. Mrs Rau was also a member of all three Indian women's associations, the Women's India Association (WIA), the National Council of Women in India and the All-India Women's Conference (AIWC), and had excellent credentials, being the wife of an Indian official stationed in London who was appointed financial adviser to the Simon Commission in 1928/29. Her personal offer of service to the conference had already been ignored, and she verbally attacked Eleanor, disputing 'the right of British women to arrange a conference on Indian social evils in London, where all the speakers were British and many had never even visited India'.[23] Eleanor was outraged by what she considered Mrs Rau's audacity, and ungraciously curtailed her speech. The Indian contingent were also incensed by the effrontery of her provocatively entitled article, 'Has Katherine Mayo Slandered "Mother India"?', in which she set out her conclusions on Mayo's book.[24] This was like a red rag to a bull, and not surprisingly engendered more mistrust and animosity. As far as Eleanor was concerned, the outcome of the conference, which ended very abruptly, was most unsatisfactory, for the delegates refused to pass the resolutions that her committee had framed. From Mrs Rau's perspective, her stance at the conference enabled her to build close ties with British women's organizations, and ultimately she and Eleanor reached an understanding of sorts and were able to communicate with one another in a civil manner.

In the aftermath of the meeting, the Indian press accused Eleanor of sharing Mayo's political views, and of advocating an end to political moves towards self-government until the 'evil practices', which she wrote about in her *Hibbert Journal* article, were removed. In London, *The Times* published an accusatory letter in a similar vein, signed by seven Indian and seven European women, including her major conference opponent, Mrs Rau.[25] Eleanor was quite unable to resist writing the last word, and having drafted a letter of reply for publication in the paper, she sought the support of, amongst others, her fellow MP, Ellen Wilkinson. On this occasion Wilkinson refused to undersign the letter, exhibiting a sensitivity to British interference in Indian cultural affairs that Eleanor lacked.

Eleanor was not against Indian political self-determination, but she seemed unable to comprehend the difficulty of fighting for social reform against the volatile political background in India. In this respect she was not alone, for Eva Hubback, her friend and NUSEC's parliamentary secretary, had previously stated that 'British women were not interested in the "political situation" but simply wanted to "help" Indian women'.[26] Such statements lend some credence to the argument that British feminists nurtured a sense of national and racial superiority, viewing their

Indian counterparts as the 'White Women's Burden' and were almost obliged to respond.[27] The obverse of this was Mrs Rau's reference to the assumption that the 'eradication of social evils in Indian society was the responsibility of the British, "the White Man's Burden"'.[28] Ultimately, although Eleanor did certainly try to assume responsibility for Indian women, she clearly saw herself acting as a responsible citizen, as 'one human being sympathising with another'.[29]

Probably the only good thing that resulted from the second NUSEC conference was the advice that Eleanor received from Lady Hartog. The latter had spent many years in India with her husband, Sir Philip, whilst he was vice chancellor of Dacca University, and her personal experiences enabled her to identify and empathize with Eleanor's strengths and weaknesses, applauding her motives but criticizing her incompetence. She could see that the only way forward for the Women of India Survey was for Eleanor to disassociate herself from the editorship, advice that she took.[30] When *The Key of Progress: A Survey of the Status and Conditions of Women in India* was published in 1930, Eleanor's name was tucked away in the index, and there was no reference to Mayo at all. A further suggestion that Eleanor acted upon came from an Indian lady, Sri Maya Devi, who wrote to her in 1929 to try and explain why Indian women so resented the interference of British women. Devi urged her to 'make a political visit to India and meet the different schools of thought to which a number of highly educated and cultured ladies belong'[31] so that she might better understand their point of view (see Plate 5).

The opportunity for such a journey did not present itself until late 1931, but the timing then was fortuitous as far as Eleanor was concerned, for it coincided with the visit being made by the Lothian Franchise Committee commissioned by the second Round Table Conference of India. Meanwhile, other Indian matters took precedence. The Sarda Act was approved by the Legislative Assembly on 1 October 1929, but was not set to come into effect until 1 April 1930. Eleanor doubted the adequacy of law alone: the colonial government had to be persuaded, by Britain, to implement the existing measures, the British and Indian public needed educating on the subject, and Indians needed persuading that an even more stringent law was required if girls and young women in India were to be adequately protected.[32] Eleanor directed her parliamentary offensive at William Wedgwood Benn, the secretary of state for India, bombarding him, and subsequently his successor, Sir Samuel Hoare, with questions, letters and memoranda. His intransigence, or what she politely called his 'vague assurances of sympathy', only strengthened her resolve. Then, as later during her campaign for refugees fleeing Nazi and fascist terror in

Europe, she was tenacious and channelled an enormous amount of energy into her work.

Yet another disturbing cultural practice came to Eleanor's attention in 1929, that of ritual female circumcision, as practised by the Kikuyu tribe in Kenya, and brought her into an unlikely alliance with fellow MP, Katherine Stewart Murray, Duchess of Atholl.[33] The two were complete opposites for Atholl was a former anti-suffragist, a staunch Conservative as well as being a determined opponent of Indian nationalism. But what united the two women was an abhorrence of cruelty, and it was inevitable, given Eleanor's stand against the issues raised in *Mother India*, that when Atholl initiated the all-party Committee for the Protection of Coloured Women in the Colonies, she should invite her fellow MP to join. Under the chairmanship of the Josiah Wedgwood, Labour MP for Newcastle-under-Lyme, a former resident magistrate in South Africa and a future working partner of Eleanor's on refugee matters, the committee gathered evidence. This must have been a very distressing time for all concerned, but it was especially so for Eleanor: not only was she attempting to deal with the fallout from the second NUSEC conference, but she was now confronted by disturbing and painful descriptions of female mutilation, carried out in the name of a rite of passage. As if this was not enough, more upsetting news reached her from abroad concerning the practice of bride sale and the state of maternity conditions in East and South Africa. The former, which relied upon the native assumption that women were a commodity to be bought and sold, clearly flouted the terms of the Geneva Convention of 1925 and was vividly described in a series of articles in the *Women's Leader* by Miss Nina Boyle, an old campaigner of the militant suffrage movement. The latter was reminiscent of Mayo's descriptions of childbirth in *Mother India*. Both issues added greatly to the volume of evidence that Eleanor was accumulating but she was, characteristically, indefatigable and undeterred by the ever-increasing workload.

When the House met in December 1929 to discuss the exploitation of coloured races, Atholl bravely tackled the issue of female circumcision with Eleanor, rising to her defence in the face of a hostile interjection from James Maxton, Independent Labour MP for Glasgow Bridgeton. This marked the start of a campaign in which Eleanor utilized her renowned 'walls of Jericho' technique, whereby she hammered away at an issue to achieve even a small concession in the belief that any gain was better than none and that a small gain opened the door to larger ones. Whilst the committee continued its investigations, Eleanor found herself supporting or making parliamentary representation for a number of other organizations concerned with humanitarian issues. As far as her success in effecting cultural reform in Africa was concerned, the problems that she and others encountered mirrored some of those which dogged her Indian causes, specifically the difficulty of an imperial country attempting to confront the cultural values of its colonized peoples.

In India itself, the political situation had become extremely volatile. By the time the report of the Simon Commission appeared in 1930, it was clear that their findings, which indicated a gradual handing-over of power to India, were already obsolete. Nationalist disorder was widespread with articulate Indians clamouring for immediate self-government, juxtaposed against communal disorder resulting from Moslem-Hindu hostility. The Labour government, under Ramsay MacDonald, passed the problems of the future government of India on to a Round Table Conference, which was held in three sessions, the first in London on 12 November 1930, the last on 17 November 1932, before the conference was finally adjourned on 24 December of that year. Of the ninety members, only two women, the Muslim noblewoman, Begum Jahan Ara Shah Nawaz, and the Indian feminist, Mrs Subbarayan, were included as part of the Indian contingent, but members of the WIA were furious because of the arbitrary nature of this selection. Whether Nawaz was included because she was attending the conference as private secretary to her father, Sir Muhammad Shafi, or because, as has been asserted, she had a close relationship with Eleanor, is debatable.[34] Subbarayan, who was well known to British feminists, and was a student at Somerville in 1912, had been in correspondence with Eleanor from 1929 onwards, and in confidential letters had accused the WIA of being 'the puppet of Congress'.[35] In response, Eleanor, who considered Subbarayan to be 'a tame Indian woman', shared her correspondent's views on the Indian franchise.[36]

Not only was Eleanor satisfied by the fact that there were two 'friendly' women representatives, but she was delighted by the overwhelming view of the delegates that the British parliamentary system of government should prevail. This provided her with the opportunity, already articulated, of widening the scope of her Indian campaign to include women's suffrage. To this end, and prior to the commencement of Round Table proceedings, Eleanor produced a 'Memorandum on certain questions affecting the status and welfare of Indian women in the future constitution of India, addressed to the Indian Round Table Conference', which was signed by a group of people experienced in Indian and British political affairs, including the women MPs Lady Astor, Edith Picton-Turbervill, Lady Cynthia Mosley and Megan Lloyd George.[37] The difference now was that, in contrast to the early days of her Indian campaigning, she kept very much in the background, restricting her activities to 'supplying the motive force or driving the engine'.[38]

Concurrent with the situation in India was the political instability in Britain, where the depression of the early 1930s, which reverberated across Europe, had forced up the numbers of unemployed to two and a half million in December 1930. This placed an intolerable burden upon the national unemployment insurance fund, and drained the gold reserve. The financial crisis resulted in the downfall of the Labour government in August 1931, and the emergency appointment of a National government. The general election of 1931 returned a National government which was to remain in power until 1940, after the outbreak of the Second World War. Fifteen women MPs were returned to the House, thirteen Conservative, one Liberal and one Independent – Eleanor Rathbone – an increase of just one over the previous election. The new government heralded cabinet changes that would affect her current and future campaigning. Sir Herbert Samuel became home secretary, and Sir John Simon replaced Arthur Henderson as foreign secretary.

With an elected National government now in place, the Round Table Conference continued its deliberations over India. As a part of the investigations, the delegates appointed a Franchise Committee, chaired by Lord Lothian, and in late 1931 he planned a fact-finding tour of India. Eleanor was somewhat disappointed that she was not one of the two women selected as members of the so-called Lothian Committee, but she decided in spite of this that the time was right for her to make a long overdue visit to India. Her trip, which Devi had urged her to take some three years before, coincided with that of the Lothian Committee, and gave her the chance to discuss the plight of Indian women with the members in advance of their enquiries. It also gave her an insight into the way in which special ordinances sharply restricted free speech in the country.[39] Amongst those whom she met en route was Mr N.M. Joshi, an influential Indian and member of the Servants of India Society: Joshi subsequently enlisted Eleanor's help in pressuring the British government to accept the Das Amendment Bill, which sought alterations to the Sarda (Child Marriage Restraint) Act. Eleanor agreed to assist Joshi, but, acting more prudently than at the outset of her Indian campaign, insisted that her name 'be kept entirely out of it'.[40] The Bill was finally enacted in 1938, a small measure of triumph for Eleanor who had, as feminist historians acknowledge, played an important role in securing legislation, even though she was unable to render it effective.

Once in India Eleanor was able, through her many contacts, to meet and try to influence people who were giving testimony to the

Lothian Committee. Friends, family and colleagues got news of her progress via the circular letters that she sent home.[41] As far as she was concerned, her campaign to ensure the franchise was extended to as many Indian women as possible was fairly successful, but the outcome was a matter of grave dissatisfaction to many Indian women. For, whilst Eleanor argued that 'we are so used here to working to get what we can and making it the basis for more, that we can only go on that method and hope for the best',[42] Indian women's groups generally called for equality and no special privileges for women, and specifically for full adult suffrage in any new constitution. Ultimately, Eleanor and the Indian women she sought to help were outraged by the result, for there was a gradual diminution in the proportion of men to women voters from 1:2 in the Simon Report, 1:45 in the Franchise Commission Report, culminating in a further reduction of 1:7 in the White Paper of 1933.

At that time Eleanor was able to claim in the House of Commons that for the past four years she had 'lived almost night and day' with the question of the position of women under the new Indian Constitution.[43] Nor was she about to give up her fight. Her response to the White Paper was twofold. She instigated and coordinated the compilation of an angry letter to *The Times* and then, by way of a challenge to the British government, moved for the establishment of a Joint Select Committee to examine the franchise proposals.[44] The resulting organization, the British Committee for Indian Women's Franchise, of which Eleanor was chairman, swung into action in June 1933 and worked almost continuously until December 1934. In that same year Eleanor published her book, *Child Marriage: The Indian Minotaur*, an outspoken study that, as she stated, had two purposes. The first was to promote 'more effective action', the second to act as 'a warning of the frightful risks to which we are exposing Indian women if we give them in the new Indian constitution no better means of self-protection than they have had in the past, during the years of our dominion'.[45] Implicit within these assertions was Eleanor's desire to sever any link between herself and Mayo, for by attacking the British government's apathetic and intransigent attitude towards child-marriage legislation, she could not be accused of being against Indian independence. Her letter to Begum Jahan Ara Shah Nawaz, her acquaintance and representative at the Round Table Conference, set out to put the record straight:

> I felt I had to write it, because the reply I received from Sir Samuel Hoare to the last of the thirteen questions amounted to this: that the Governments both Central and Local could do nothing in the matter, not even undertake the education of public opinion as to the

> provisions of the Act and the necessity for them. Frankly I cannot let it go at that. The unnecessary sufferings and deaths of these young wives and widows have become a continuous nightmare to me.[46]

A number of Indian feminists were asked for their opinion of the book and its proposals, which was generally considered to be 'helpful, fair and forcibly written'.[47] Nevertheless, Eleanor was still berated for failing to comprehend the impossibility of enforcing the 1929 legislation, especially in rural areas. It is hard to believe that after all her years of work on Indian matters, and having acquired so much first-hand knowledge from her visit to the country, that she was still as naïve about the practicalities of enforcement as her Indian critics made out. A more credible answer is that she was still being driven by her 'obligation' to help Indian women, but sought to draw greater attention to the overall situation regarding child marriage: specific problems relating to, for example, rural areas, were perfectly valid but could not be resolved until the main issues were addressed satisfactorily. As a way of maintaining progress on this front, Eleanor offered to subsidize the salary of an AIWC worker who would organize a single-issue campaign on child marriage, but was rebuffed. This refusal highlighted the divergence of Indian opinion in accepting foreign aid, which was bound up within the complex relationship between imperialist Britain and its colony, India. Rajkumari Amrit Kaur, the AIWC president, insisted that the association should undertake this work themselves but Lakshmi Menon, a young Indian lawyer, disagreed, arguing on behalf of herself and others that they could see no reason to discriminate between Eleanor's offer and the financial assistance being accepted from abroad in the aftermath of the recent earthquake in Bihar.[48]

Even whilst preoccupied with Indian issues, Eleanor pursued various domestic campaigns, many of which had no feminist or female-specific connection. This shift away from gendered causes was not surprising, for the 1930s were a lean time for the feminist movement in Britain. More political emphasis was put upon the poverty of children, which fitted in well with Eleanor's continuing fight for a family allowance. Social and economic reforms and civil-rights issues, all of which were humanitarian concerns, featured in her maiden speech in the House. And her enduring involvement in municipal-housing matters in Liverpool motivated her to argue for an amendment to the Greenwood Act, which was concerned with rent subsidies, a campaign which she pursued, successfully, with the support of Sir Ernest Simon (later Lord Simon of Wythenshawe) during the two years 1930/31.

Eleanor kept in touch with Indian affairs until about 1935, mainly through contacts with friends in the country. But before then, other more pressing campaigns came to the fore, so that by 1938 she was able to confess that she was 'absorbed in other perplexing questions in the international sphere'.[49] This was a typical understatement, which gave no indication of the extent and nature of her involvement in the rescue of refugees from Fascist and Nazi Europe. The last notable contact that Eleanor had with India was in 1941, and the timing of her powerful 'open letter to some Indian friends' was crucial for it was written in 'the aftermath of the highly destructive Battle of Britain'.[50] The purpose of the letter was twofold: Eleanor was able to articulate her fears for Britain's survival in the war against Hitler, appealing to India to join Britain in the fight against the common enemy. And she was also able to express her deep concern for the deadlock over the constitutional issue in that country.[51] The cooperation, and tacit approval of Mr Leopold Amery, the secretary of state for India, ensured that Reuters transmitted the letter to the Indian press and that the imprisoned Pandit Jawaharlal Nehru received a copy. Thus began an exchange of lively letters between Eleanor and Nehru in which the former criticized India's non-involvement in the war, and the latter berated Eleanor and the British government for imagining that India would give up its struggle for independence 'to fight for and in the name of an Empire which has crushed us and which we have been combating in our own peaceful way all our lives'.[52] Eleanor had also to contend with the criticism of people like Carl Heath, a colleague of Agatha Harrison, the secretary of the India Conciliation Group, a liaison group founded by members of the Society of Friends during the second Round Table Conference. Heath lamented that British people like her

> believe that if *they* do things for India which *they* think are good for India, they deserve to be met with thankfulness. They dislike the idea that this well-wishing towards India should be regarded as imperialism and resented as it certainly is ... they seem unable to realise how baffling and infuriating insistent paternalism is to grown-up India.[53]

She clearly did have problems in her relationship with India and its people, and even after years of involvement with the child-marriage issue and enfranchisement for women, was unable to see that, as Heath remarked, her actions were still considered imperialist. She failed to comprehend that Indian feminists came from a different background and had a different agenda to their British counterparts, and that tactics which worked well at home were unsuited to an another culture. Even though Eleanor was undoubtedly motivated by humanitarian concerns, she would have been wiser not to have become involved in

Indian affairs, given her lack of understanding of, and empathy with, the people and their society.

Her failure to acknowledge Indian women's organizations, or to recognize the continuing work they did for social and political change, did little to enhance the image she wished to promote as a friend and ally. Attempting to change the religious and cultural practices of a country that she did not visit until late 1931, and of which she had only limited theoretical knowledge, was, in hindsight, foolhardy, with the *Indian Daily Mail* accusing her of a 'lack of imagination and knowledge of Indian people'.[54] In this latter respect, she could be seen to fit Burton's description of 'British feminists' who believed, albeit erroneously, that 'their common gender gave them an understanding of Indian women which transcended national and racial boundaries',[55] but it is fair to say that it was not necessary to be a feminist to hold such beliefs. For behind Eleanor's campaign was more than a hint of the notion of British superiority, and of national responsibility towards a society that was perceived as less civilized, and in need of educating. These same beliefs informed Eleanor's next humanitarian campaign in Palestine.

NOTES

1. S. Pedersen, *Eleanor Rathbone and the Politics of Conscience* (London: Yale University Press, 2004), p.327.
2. A. Burton, *Burdens of History. British Feminists, Indian Women and Imperial Culture 1865–1915* (Chapel Hill, NC and London: University of North Carolina, 1994), p.203.
3. E.F. Rathbone, *Child Marriage: The Indian Minotaur. An Object Lesson from the Past to the Future* (London: George Allen and Unwin, 1934), pp.17–21.
4. B. Ramusack, 'Women's Organizations and Social Change: The Age of Marriage Issue in India', in N. Black and A.B. Cottrell, *Women and World Change: Equity Issues in Development* (Beverly Hills, CA and London: Sage, 1981), pp.200–1.
5. K. Mayo, *Mother India* (New York: Harcourt, Brace, 1927).
6. Letter from Miss Mayo to EFR, n.d., Sorabji Papers, MSS Eur.F.165, folio 161, 8. Oriental and India Office Collection, British Library (OIOC, BL).
7. For details of correspondence between Mayo and members of the India Office in 1925 which confirm that she was encouraged by a government official to include the subject of child marriage as the central theme of her book, see K. Mayo (edited with an introduction by M. Sinha), *Selections from Mother India* (Ann Arbor: University of Michigan Press, 2000), p.25.
8. Mayo, *Mother India* (1927), p.32.
9. Letter of EFR to K. Mayo, 1 May 1928, folio 345, Series 1, Box 6 (46), Katherine Mayo Papers, Beinecke Library Yale University (KM).
10. Letter of EFR to K. Mayo, n.d. but circa 1929, folio 345, Series 1, Box 11, KM.
11. *Hansard* HC, vol. 254, col. 2369, 9 July 1931.
12. M. Sinha, 'Reading Mother India: Empire, Nation and the Female Voice', *Journal of Women's History*, 6, 2 (Summer 1994), pp.29–31.
13. Letter of EFR to K. Mayo, 24 August 1927, folio 345, Series 1, Box 5, Folder 37, KM.
14. It later transpired that an anonymous individual had already anticipated the propaganda value of the book and had arranged for a copy to be distributed to every MP. See Letter of

Lady Lytton to *The Times*, 14 January 1928, and Report in the *New York Times*, 14 January 1928, p.6 as cited in Mayo, *Mother India* (2000), p.37, n.90.

15. Letter from K. Mayo to EFR, n.d. but pre-21 November 1927, Sorabji Papers, MSS Eur.F.165/161, OIOC, BL.
16. Letter of EFR to Elena Rathbone, 25 November 1927, Sorabji Papers, MSS Eur. F.165/161, OIOC, BL.
17. A. Caton, *The Key of Progress: A Survey of the Status and Conditions of Women in India* (Oxford: Oxford University Press, 1930), p.v.
18. M. Stocks, *Eleanor Rathbone: A Biography* (London: Victor Gollancz, 1949), p.135. The Women's India Association also exerted pressure. See G. Forbes, *Women in Modern India* (Cambridge: Cambridge University Press, 1996), p.106.
19. *Women's Leader*, 13 July 1928.
20. Stocks, *Rathbone*, p.140.
21. *Indian Daily Mail*, 23 October 1929, John Simon Papers, MSS Eur. F77/86, OIOC, BL.
22. A. Basu and B. Ray, *Women's Struggle: History of the All Indian Women's Conference 1927–1990* (New Delhi: Manohar, 1990), pp.138–9.
23. D.R. Rau, *An Inheritance: The Memories of Dhanvanthi Ramu Rau* (London: Heinemann, 1977), pp.170–1.
24. E.F. Rathbone, 'Has Katherine Mayo Slandered "Mother India"?' *Hibbert Journal*, 27, 2 (January 1929), pp.193–214.
25. Letter signed by D.R. Rau, Hannah Sen *et al.*, 'Women in India', *The Times*, 22 October 1929.
26. As cited in Sinha, 'Reading Mother India', p.30.
27. For this and for British feminism maturing in an age of empire, see A. Burton, 'The White Woman's Burden. British Feminists and the Indian Woman, 1865–1915', *Women's Studies International Forum*, 13, 4 (1990), pp.295–308.
28. Rau, *An Inheritance*, p.170.
29. *Spectator*, 6 April 1934.
30. Stocks, *Rathbone*, p.140 and see Letter of EFR to Lady Hartog, 20 May 1930, Box 5, Folder 4, Rathbone Papers, Women's Library, London Guildhall University (WL).
31. Stocks, *Rathbone*, p.138.
32. B. Ramusack, 'Cultural Missionaries, Maternal Imperialists, Feminist Allies: British Women Activists in India 1865–1945', *Women's Studies International Forum*, 13, 4 (1990), p.315.
33. For Eleanor's involvement in this issue, see S. Pedersen, 'National Bodies, Unspeakable Acts: The Sexual Politics of Colonial Policy-making', *Journal of Modern History*, 63 (1991), pp.647–80.
34. C. Candy, 'Competing Transnational Representations of the 1930s Indian Franchise Question', in I. Fletcher, L. Mayhall and P. Levine (eds), *Women's Suffrage in the British Empire. Citizenship, Nation and Race* (London: Routledge, 2000), pp.191–206.
35. Letters of EFR and Mrs Radhabai Subbarayan, 20 November 1930–31 December 1936, and especially Letter of Subbarayan to EFR, 24 April 1931, all Box 93, Folder 5, Rathbone Papers, WL.
36. M. Sinha, 'Suffragism and Internationalism: The Enfranchisement of British and Indian Women under an Imperial State', in Fletcher *et al.*, *Women's Suffrage*, pp.224–39.
37. For biographical details of these and other women politicians see S. Oldfield, *Women Humanitarians. A Biographical Dictionary of British Women Active between 1900–1950* (London: Continuum, 2001).
38. Stocks, *Rathbone*, p.150.
39. As noted in B. Ramusack, 'Catalysts or Helpers? British Feminists, Indian Women's Rights and Indian Independence', in G. Minault (ed.), *The Extended Family: Women and Political Participation in India and Pakistan* (Delhi: Chanakya Publications, 1981), p.130.
40. Letter of EFR to Joshi, 23 January 1934, Folder 8, Rathbone Papers, WL.
41. EFR, Circular letters, January–February 1932, RP XIV.1, University of Liverpool Library (henceforth ULL).
42. Letter of EFR to Rajkumari Amrit Kaur, 9 January 1932, Box 93, Folder 12, Rathbone Papers, WL.
43. Stocks, *Rathbone*, p.163.
44. *The Times*, 25 March 1933.
45. Letters of EFR to Muthulakshmi Reddi, Shareefah Hamid Ali and Raj-Kumari Amrit Kaur, 29 February 1934, Box 93, Folder 9, Rathbone Papers, WL. Letter of EFR to Menon, 29

February 1934, Box 93, Folder 14, 30, Rathbone Papers, WL. Rathbone, *Child Marriage*, p.13.

46. Letter of EFR to Nawaz, 29 February 1934, Box 93, Folder 12, Rathbone Papers, WL.
47. This description was given by Shareefah Hamid Ali, first chair of the AIWC committee on child marriage in a letter to EFR in 1934. See Letter of Ali to EFR, 8 August 1934, Box 93, Folder 12, Rathbone Papers, WL.
48. Letter of Menon to EFR, 13 September 1934, Box 93, Folder 14, Rathbone Papers, WL.
49. Letter of EFR to Mrs Copeland, 24 June 1938, Box 93, Folder 16, Rathbone Papers, WL.
50. Ramusack, 'Catalysts or Helpers?', p.123.
51. This letter, dated May 1941, in Stocks, *Rathbone*, pp.337–41. See also Pedersen, *Politics of Conscience*, pp.323–6.
52. Letter of Jawaharlal Nehru to EFR, 22 June 1941, reprinted in Stocks, *Rathbone*, p.345.
53. Letter of Carl Heath to EFR, 17 September 1941, Box 47, Agatha Harrison – India Conciliation Group, Library of the Religious Society of Friends, London.
54. *Indian Daily Mail*, 23 October 1929, John Simon Papers, MSS Eur. F77/86, OIOC, BL.
55. Burton, 'The White Woman's Burden', p.303.

# 3

# *Humanitarian Causes in Palestine*

It was not entirely surprising that Eleanor should have become concerned about humanitarian issues in Palestine, for following her forays into India and Africa, this was another territory effectively under British colonial rule. Another common thread was the causes that she championed there, which included improving the position of women within the spheres of child marriage, votes for women, immigration, education and welfare provision, reflecting those she had associated herself with in India. Even though all these were perceived as feminist concerns they were also humanitarian matters, and as Eleanor viewed it, were wrongs that had to be set right. For underlying everything was her unconscious and previously unchallenged belief in the duty of care and authority that she considered she owed members of the colonial empire, just as she had in connection with her Indian campaigning.[1] Ultimately, her feminism and humanitarianism were not totally incompatible. For even though she clearly preferred Jews and Judaism to Arabs and Islam, the former being more 'advanced' in her view, she nevertheless championed causes in Palestine regardless of race, religion and gender.

What was very different was the impetus for Eleanor's involvement in Palestine, and her personal attitude towards the country and its people. Whereas India had presented her with alien religious and cultural practices in a vast and inhospitable geographical location, Palestine was smaller and in closer proximity to Britain and, even for a non-practising Christian like Eleanor, was identifiable by familiar biblical connections and similarities in religion and culture. Thus she, like other British visitors, developed an affinity and empathy with Palestine that was absent in her dealings with India. Furthermore, her relationship with this Middle Eastern territory, which lasted from 1933 until her death in 1946, evolved into a fervent belief in and affiliation with Zionism. Nor can her involvement with humanitarian issues in Palestine, and the effect that her association with the country had on her subsequent work on behalf of Jews fleeing Nazi and fascist Europe, some of them to Palestine, be ignored, for they are inextricably linked.

By the time that Eleanor became involved with Palestine, Britain had occupied the territory since 1917, but it was not a British colony in the usual sense, and was unique in many respects.[2] The Balfour Declaration, issued by the British foreign secretary on 2 November 1917, had set out Britain's intention to establish a 'National Home' for the Jews there, and had also promised self-determination for the Arab population. Until self-government could be assumed, Palestine was to be governed under a Mandate of the League of Nations. The British government had decided that rather than introducing new laws, existing Ottoman (Turkish) practice should prevail, with amendments grafted on, as and where necessary. Nor, according to Tom Segev, was the government interested in imposing British values or identity upon the colony. The reasoning behind this was, apparently, to prevent 'a grave injustice' whereby local traditions were destroyed and the biblical heritage lost.[3] Whilst Norman Bentwich, who became a prominent figure in Anglo-Jewish refugee work, writing in 1932, considered the resulting Palestine law book to be 'a remarkable example of the combination of tradition with creation', more recent historians of the period are generally agreed that the policy was misguided and resulted in a legislative muddle, with the Arab press speaking derisively of the 'Law Factory' to describe the multitude of annual ordinances passed by the British.[4]

Eleanor's introduction to Palestinian affairs was far less dramatic than in the Indian case, for this time there was no polemical book to spur her into action, but rather a letter from Margery Corbett Ashby, a fellow feminist and subsequently co-member of the Friendly (later Refugee) Aliens Protection Committee and the Committee for Development of Refugee Industries. Ashby wrote from Geneva in February 1933 whilst on League of Nations business, alerting Eleanor to proposed legislative change in Palestine, which, if implemented, threatened existing progress toward female equality in the territory. The plan was to give the high commissioner, General Sir Arthur Wauchope, the power to decide whether women might vote or stand for election in municipal elections. Whilst Ashby recognized that the government was aiming to 'maintain the delicate balance between the Jewish, Arab and Christian communities',[5] she argued that the change would not serve the best interests of the community: not only would it remove rights which some women already had but it also meant adopting the social standards of the least developed section of the Palestinian community. Besides this, she pointed out, there was no precedent in any British colony for such action, citing Rhodesia, Turkey and India where women still had the vote as examples of colonies where 'there were racial groups'.[6] As a way of mustering support, Ashby circulated Eleanor's letter to a number of other British feminist organizations, including the British Commonwealth League, the Open Door Council and St Joan's Social and Political Alliance, all of whom expressed their concern, and offered to liaise with her. The position of the women's franchise in Palestine was complex, as Eleanor was to discover, due in part to the Ottoman heritage. It was further complicated as there was no consensus amongst the different religious groups of women as to whether they should have the right to vote. The progress of women's groups in Palestine bore little resemblance to that in Britain, as Millicent Fawcett, Eleanor's fellow suffragist campaigner, commented after her visit to Palestine in 1921, on behalf of the International Women's Suffrage Alliance. She concluded that whilst the women of the Palestine Jewish Women's Equal Rights Association (PJWERA) were 'progressive',[7] their Moslem contemporaries were, as she described, 'unorganized, inarticulate (and) little-educated'.[8]

In the 1930s the situation had barely altered. As far as Palestinian Moslem Arab women were concerned,[9] their culture and tradition denied them any involvement in public affairs: added to this was the fact that their political status was hardly better than that of men, many of whom were also denied the right to vote. Thus the newly emergent Palestinian women's movement was devoted to the establishment of a sovereign nation state in British Mandate Palestine, and adhered to the belief that equality for women would inevitably evolve from nationhood.[10] The women of the Yishuv (the Jewish settlement in Palestine) were more politically active than their Arab counterparts, even though their society was in itself highly divided, with differences between the Sephardi community, the Ashkenazi Haredi (the ultra-Orthodox), the orthodox Zionists and the non-religious Zionists. The PJWERA comprised women from all sectors of the community, including the centre and right-wing sectors, known as the civic sectors, and women workers. A non-political national women's organization, their slogan was 'one constitution and the same law for men and women',[11] the achievement of equal rights for women being a major concern between 1919 and 1926. Legislation introduced in June 1922 had provided women who owned property, and by definition, paid taxes, the right to vote in local council elections, a law which enfranchised women in the Jewish cities of Petach Tikva and Tel Aviv. But in cities with mixed Arab and Jewish populations, namely Jerusalem, Haifa, Tiberias and Safat, Moslem law prevailed and women were denied the right to vote. The promulgation of the Municipal Franchise Ordinance of 1926 had extended the range of male electors eligible to vote, seen by some as an improvement in franchise eligibility,[12] but it categorically excluded women. This led the PJWERA to agitate vociferously for women's suffrage for both Arab and Jewish women, an unsatisfactory campaign due to the lack of support from the Arabs.[13] The

1933 proposal, which Eleanor was alerted to, would give the high commissioner discretion as to which, if any, women should be allowed to vote, and was, as Dr Rosa Welt-Straus, a reputable medical doctor and president of the PJWERA, told Eleanor, anathema to the Jewish women's organizations. There was, she stressed, a wealth of difference between Jewish communities giving rights to their women to vote and this being left to the mercy of the high commissioner.[14] If invoked, the 1933 proposal would, the Association asserted, destroy 'all that Hebrew women had achieved in the area of civil and political life by a snap of the fingers'.[15]

Eleanor's reaction to Ashby's communication was predictable. She wasted no time in writing to Sir Phillip Cunliffe-Lister, the secretary of state for the colonies, noting that she considered the situation to be 'so serious' and was certain it would 'cause so much indignation among women's societies' in Britain.[16] Included in this letter was a copy of her proposed parliamentary question, and a request for a meeting with him so she could discuss additional information that she had received from Ashby and Dr Welt-Straus. Interestingly, and in contrast to her position with India, Eleanor not only freely admitted to her lack of personal knowledge concerning the powers of the government in this matter, but she also sought his advice.[17] It appears, however, that the meeting never took place: the additional information was sent to Cunliffe-Lister in a subsequent letter, to which Eleanor received a lengthy written response. Outside of Parliament, she responded to offers of support from Ashby's contacts, including the British Commonwealth League, St Joan's Social and Political Alliance and the Open Door Council,[18] urging them, and others, to 'send a letter or resolution of remonstrance to the Colonial Secretary' on the basis that 'the more fuss we make about this the better'.[19] As far as support for the British campaign from within Palestine was concerned, Ashby had hoped that Miss Nixon, chief female welfare officer for the government of Palestine, would support them, but was dismayed to report that Nixon had become 'more and more official and anti-feminist'.[20] What became of a questionnaire sent out by the British government, and which Ashby hoped to gain sight of, remains unclear.[21]

When Eleanor raised the issue of the proposed Municipal Franchise Ordinance and its effect on women's suffrage in Palestine in the House, she was far from happy with the answers she received. The British government was, according to Cunliffe-Lister, adamant that 'no general right of voting and membership at municipal elections has ever been granted to Jewish women in Palestine' and that the only voting rights that Jewish women had enjoyed, in accordance with the Local Councils Ordinance of 1921, were confined to committees of local Jewish communities and the Jewish Assembly.[22] But as Eleanor persistently noted, the latter ordinance was about to be superseded by the new Municipal Franchise Ordinance, with all its restrictions, and the status of Jewish women was, indeed, about to be diminished. What she wanted was for legislative changes to be made that would 'raise Arab women to the level of Jewish women, rather than debasing Jewish women to the level of Arab women'.[23]

In spite of Eleanor's intervention, the Municipal Corporations Ordinance was enacted on 12 January 1934. However, two Labour MPs, Mr Rhys Davies, Eleanor's most bitter family endowment opponent, and Colonel Josiah Wedgwood, her future fellow refugee activist who had visited Palestine in late 1933 and early 1934, would not let the matter rest, and as the *New Judea* reported in March 1934, continued to raise questions concerning the disenfranchisement of women in Palestine in the House of Commons for some months. By then, however, Eleanor had another burning issue to champion in the Middle East, namely the practice of child marriage.

It was a letter from Dr Welt-Straus, in June 1933, which alerted Eleanor to paragraph 182 of the Criminal Code Bill, 1933, published in the *Official Palestine Gazette* on 5 June 1933, along with the Mandatory government's plans to amend the law by setting the minimum legal age for female marriage at 13.[24] Although, as Eleanor discovered, child marriage was less prevalent in Palestine than in India, girls as young as 10 or 11, from Arab, Jewish and Christian communities, were being married off to men much older than themselves, with the same type of disastrous physical and mental results as Mayo had exposed. The PJWERA had been pressing the mandatory government to end the 'social evil' almost since their inception in 1919. They had sent memoranda to the government offices in Jerusalem in 1928, 1930 and 1932, and the 1930 Arab Congress of Women in Damascus had moved for the practice to be made illegal.[25] But, as Dr Welt-Straus outlined to Eleanor, in line with established practice, the British government were reluctant to tamper with Ottoman law or interfere with cultural traditions, even though they had admitted, in 1930, that there were 'evils attendant upon the system of child marriage'.[26] In the wake of this admission, an attempt was made in late 1930 to raise public awareness. This took the form of an unattributed article published in the *Palestine Bulletin*. The author warned the government that it would be better to 'do what it could to remedy a real evil' before someone produced a *Mother Palestine* exposé following the example of Mayo's *Mother India*. For, as anyone who had knowledge of the subject knew, 'child marriage both takes its toll of human lives and carries with it the usual train of misery'.[27]

There was the added problem of accurate demographic information for there was no consistent system of birth or marriage registration and doctors could not be trusted to correctly certify a bride's age. The 1931 census did shed some new light on the problem of child marriage but, with the exception of the Moslem community, the data was far from complete or reliable.[28] Above all, the British government tried to avoid situations that would leave them open to criticism or attack. They were also mindful of the need to preserve the precarious balance between the different religious communities. Just as they used these as excuses for avoiding the franchise issue, so they invoked them in respect of the child marriage issue. In an effort to please everyone, and with age at marriage being the only common denominator amongst the diverse communities of Palestine, the proposal was to set a minimum number of years attained, 13, before a girl could be betrothed. However, there were provisos attached, which allowed for marriage at a younger age if the girl had reached puberty, if her family consented, or if it could be proved that no physical effects would follow consummation. It was these provisos that critics like the PJWERA knew would render the legislation wide open to abuse. As far as Dr Welt-Straus was concerned, the empirical evidence that she had gathered left her in no doubt that young girls suffered considerable mental and physical damage as a result of premature marriage. Nor would this, given the revelations concerning the practice in India, have surprised Eleanor. Besides this, there was no consensus as to when puberty was reached: Dr Welt-Straus's evidence put this at between 14 and 15 for Arab girls, whereas Miss Freda White of the LNU considered it to be earlier.

To those who maintained that child marriage was not very prevalent in Palestine, Dr Welt-Straus argued that 'few cases reach the public press, almost all are transacted and remain in the privacy of the family and religious courts'.[29] Miss Nixon was certainly able to substantiate the continuing practice, for she had worked in close contact with a number of medical and law enforcement officers in Hebron, and had reported back on the cruelty inflicted on young girls, many younger than 12, by their husbands. Whilst the Moslem authorities stated that a girl should be 16 before she was married, Nixon affirmed that 'such rules are dead letter in the Hebron district and also in many other villages in Palestine'.[30]

As Dr Welt-Straus hoped, Eleanor responded immediately to her call for support, for she considered the matter to be a humanitarian concern and very serious indeed. Eleanor's initial contact with Colonial Office officials were strictly off-the-record, and she made it clear to Dr Welt-Straus that nothing she reported could be quoted, printed or discussed. Dr Welt-Straus's claim that the age of consent had been fixed in Palestine by the Amendment Law of 1926 at the age of 16 was challenged by Eleanor's contact, who requested authority for her assertion, and concluded that it probably alluded to age of consent outside of marriage. In any event, the official made the government position clear that 'the law covering Mandates prohibits interference with local laws' and that to do so would offend the religious communities.[31] It was also asserted that 'child marriage was not of frequent occurrence in Palestine, and was at any rate tending gradually to disappear', a claim which Dr Welt-Straus had already answered.[32] Eleanor's next move was to raise the issue in Parliament. She wanted to know if Cunliffe-Lister had had his attention drawn to the Criminal Code Bill, 1933 and did he have any idea of the level of opposition in Palestine to this proposal? What did he intend to do about it? Would he enable a committee to be established which would assess the medical and social effects upon young girls? And would he furnish the House with a return showing the minimum age of consent (inside and outside of marriage) in all the colonies under his jurisdiction?[33]

Matters moved slowly and Eleanor did not receive a reply to the 'return' question until January 1934: the government had indeed conducted enquiries and compiled a return which Mr Lee, of the Colonial Office, suggested she examine before asking to move for the return in the House, in case there were any minor amendments to be made.[34] What she did ask for was supplementary information on other Moslem, non-colonial countries including Turkey and Egypt, to establish whether they had made better progress than countries under British rule.[35] The implication here was clear: she wanted facts that would highlight the extent to which the colonial government, she believed, was hindering the progress of 'backward' races. In fact she already knew what the information would show, for Dr Welt-Straus had furnished her with details of the strict laws in force in Egypt and Turkey the year before. The 1926 law in Egypt had set the minimum age at 16 for women and in Turkey, Article 88 of the Civil Code set the age of marriage at 18 for men and 17 for women, clear enough evidence that more could be done by the British government if it had the will.[36] Whether this additional information was forthcoming is uncertain, but Eleanor was under pressure from Dr Welt-Straus in Palestine, to 'raise the question again in Parliament' for, as she wrote, 'the time is short [and] the case is urgent'.[37] In the interim period she, characteristically, set about gaining facts about Palestine for herself, for, as she freely admitted, she lacked knowledge of the country, its people and its customs. It is evident from Freda White that the information she was given was not always objective, being biased by either pro-Arab or pro-Jewish feeling. In fact, Eleanor remarked of her subsequent visit to

Palestine that she was 'hearing Arab *versus* Jew questions from every possible angle'.[38] White was keen to defend child marriage, assuring Eleanor that Arab girls did mature at an earlier age than their Western counterparts, and that it was essential to link the age of marriage to puberty to avoid even greater immorality. Arab families would never tolerate an unchaste daughter and their custom demanded that she be punished by death.[39] Her assertion, that she had never come across any Arab girl under the age of 17 who was married, was clearly at odds with the evidence collected by Dr Welt-Straus. White's pro-Arab feeling was confirmed by her claim that 'Jewish inspired agitation against the ordinance' and 'the action of Jewish feminists may have the effect of rousing Arab defence of the ordinance',[40] whilst some leading figures in the British government, including David Lloyd George, who lent their names to an organization which defended Arab child marriages, warned Eleanor that 'protests against the practice (of child marriage) were part of the Zionist movement's plot to take over the country'.[41]

Ultimately, the protracted efforts of the PJWERA, Eleanor and others, to have the minimum age of marriage for girls in Palestine raised to 16 failed, for in August 1934, Cunliffe-Lister confirmed, much to the satisfaction of Lord Lugard,[42] that 'with the consent of the heads of the religious communities in Palestine' the minimum age had been set at 14.[43] In the light of Dr Welt-Straus's data, this was only a marginal improvement, but while Wauchope was still expressing concern over child marriage six months later, he was also cautiously optimistic when he stated,

> I think that I may claim to have made an appreciable advance in the provisions of the new Criminal Code, especially as those provisions have the whole-hearted support of all the Religious Heads. At least the law will not be a dead letter and to that extent progress in this important direction is assured, while there is nothing to prevent us from attempting a further step forward as soon as we can.[44]

Eleanor, meanwhile, had finally decided to undertake her own fact-finding tour of Palestine, and the summer recess of 1934 provided the perfect opportunity for a visit which she had been considering since the summer of 1933.[45] On hearing of Eleanor's impending visit to the Holy Land, Millicent Fawcett told her that the best handbook she could take was the Bible, which amused Macadam, who accompanied her friend. She recorded that Eleanor took this advice literally, ignoring the implied religious connections, and used it literally as a guidebook.[46] The trip not only had the blessing of the Colonial Office, but they also provided Eleanor with a number of useful official introductions.[47] Two agencies provided the women with help and advice. For Arab conditions, Eleanor had the services of Miss Nixon, who, despite Margaret Corbett Ashby's earlier reservations, proved cooperative. She took the two women on visits to Arab schools – and to the totally independent high school at Bir Zeit, established and run by Miss Nahiba Naser, a Christian Arab from an influential family, and an activist on behalf of Palestinian Arab women.[48] In the villages they were entertained most hospitably by the sheikhs. They were also permitted, albeit reluctantly, a glimpse of the contrasting village life of the womenfolk and children, which left Eleanor with abiding images of poverty and squalor.

Whilst some influential Arab men whom she met urged her to press the mandatory government to increase educational opportunities for men and women, her meeting with the Grand Mufti, Amin Eff: el Husseini, the most powerful Arab in Palestine, was far less harmonious. In an encounter that was similar to her disastrous Indian debacle, Eleanor mistakenly, or naively perhaps, assumed that he would be objective about a local social phenomenon. She attempted to discuss recent statistics with him, which highlighted a predominance of males amongst the Arab population, evidence that she translated as indicating a lack of value in female life, and a concomitant neglect in the care of baby girls such as she had come across in India. This accusation inflamed the Grand Mufti, who could not be placated by Nixon's attempts at a more reasonable interpretation of his guest's patronizing remarks, and he immediately ended the meeting. A later explanation of what the Grand Mufti claimed was an anomaly in the census return – according to him no high-class Arab would want to tell a young male enumerator how many daughters he had – only served to confirm Eleanor's inference, that many Arabs considered women to be second-class citizens.

Eleanor's investigations into Jewish conditions were greatly assisted by the Jewish Agency, which had been founded at the same time as the Mandate. The organization was accepted by the British government as the official body under the Mandate, with which it was supposed to confer over all questions affecting the establishment of a National Home. The two British ladies were put under the care of a Miss Goldie Myerson [*sic*] whose name, as Elizabeth Macadam made a point of mentioning, had been 'conspicuous in United Nations negotiations'.[49] Nixon later remarked that Eleanor's 'clear brain and direct character' made it easier 'for her to meet the clever Jewish leaders on equal terms'.[50] What really impressed Eleanor were the Jewish colonies 'with their curious experiments in collective organisations (which) seem to me to be the most interesting and hopeful things I have seen in years'.[51] She was equally struck by the achievements of the settlers, and admired the way in which they were making progress in education, agriculture, business and the professions.

Despite Eleanor's often repeated assertion that Jews and Arabs were equal, she nevertheless favoured the former, and considered them more advanced, trustworthy and entrepreneurial. What is quite shocking is the extent of Eleanor's racist attitude towards Arabs. Whilst being driven to Jaffa and Tel Aviv by Nixon, Eleanor asked 'in a quiet and meditative voice' whether it would matter 'to the progress of civilisation if all the Arabs were drowned in the Mediterranean,' a suggestion which totally shocked Nixon. Eleanor reluctantly agreed with her host that the Arabs had, in the past, made valuable contributions to the world, but by then she had revealed her true colours.[52] Despite this, she was concerned about the way in which Jewish advances were widening the cultural gap between the Arabs and themselves, and which became an issue that she would raise on her return home. Since the aim of the trip was to learn and to observe, Eleanor did not undertake many public engagements.[53] Apart from addressing the Jewish Palestine Association of University Women, she did present one notable speech to the PJWERA in Jerusalem on 8 October 1934.[54] The subject matter, the women's movement in England and the Dominions, was perhaps less significant than the palpable effect which the audience's generous reception had on Eleanor. In sharp contrast to the animosity that accompanied her discussions with Indian audiences, she was fired with enthusiasm,[55] and revealed that her interest in Zionism had been influenced by her reading of Arnold Toynbee's *A Study of History*, with its emphasis on examining why some great civilizations developed whilst others decayed. The philosopher in her was evident when she wrote about pondering on the Zionist experiment: was this the 'first day's progress of a new civilization'? Were there identifiable elements to it, how much did it owe to Western and Eastern European ideals, and would it be corrupted by these other cultures? A parallel can be drawn here between Eleanor's ideas of Empire, with Britain as a civilizing force in 'backward' regions, and the Jews in Palestine performing a similar role in respect of the Arabs. Beyond this, and much to Elizabeth Macadam's amazement, Eleanor confessed that 'If I believed in the reincarnation of souls and could choose the place of my next incarnation, I am not sure that I should not choose to be a Jew in Palestine'.[56] Above all, she hoped that if Jewish and Arab women could learn to work together it might 'make just that difference to the future without which the great and wonderful experiment of a National Home may be a failure, or at best, a partical [*sic*] and dearly bought success.'[57]

These remarks provide an early glimpse of Eleanor's curiosity about Zionism, and confirm that this visit to Palestine was the catalyst for what developed into a commitment to the Zionist aim 'to create a home for the Jewish people in Palestine, secured by public law'.[58] This took on a special resonance especially after 1943, when refugees fleeing Nazi-occupied Europe were seeking safe havens abroad. Her emerging interest was certainly evident to the Zionist leader, Chaim Weizmann, for in correspondence sent in November 1934, after her return home, she was described as a useful ally for the Zionist cause, who could be used to promote Zionism 'later on'.[59] That her dedication grew was reasserted by Victor Gollancz, left-wing publisher, founder of the Left Book Club and fellow refugee activist, to whom she later confessed that she would have been especially satisfied 'to be chosen as one of the British members of the Enquiry Commission'. And one of her unachieved projects was to write a pamphlet on the lines of 'A Gentile's Plea for Zionism'.[60] More numerous were the private invitations which Eleanor accepted during this visit, and no person impressed her more than the ageing Henrietta Szold, social worker and reformer who had trained in the US in COS methods. Szold had become responsible, albeit inadvertently, in December 1933, for organizing, through the newly founded Children and Youth Aliyah, the rescue and transfer of children from Nazi Germany to Palestine.[61] There is no doubt that Eleanor's meeting with Szold had a profound effect on her, for her humanitarian work with refugees had a special resonance for her own devotion to this cause in the ensuing years.[62] And by way of a tribute, her humanitarianism and role as a refugee activist was remembered after her death with the establishment of the Eleanor Rathbone Memorial School in Magdiel, near Tel Aviv, in 1949. Immediately upon her return to Britain, and in typical fashion, Eleanor set her campaigning wheels in motion. First she reported her findings to the Colonial Office. Her 'brief but emphatic' memorandum landed on the official desk on 5 November 1934, and became the forerunner of numerous communications, official and unofficial, which passed between her, Wauchope and Cunliffe-Lister.[63] Child marriage, the education of Arab girls and the lack of women doctors all received Eleanor's scrutiny. In respect of the former, and since the exact terms of the enactment of the Criminal Code had, apparently, still to be finally decided, she hoped that her report would influence the government's decision. The prevalence and 'disgusting cruelties' of child marriage, especially in Hebron, were expounded, and Eleanor invoked the Sarda Act as an example of how transparent defects in legislation left it wide open to abuse. If the law failed, as she predicted, discredit would be heaped on the 'sincerity of the British authorities in their desire for social reform'. Eleanor also called for a compulsory system of registration of marriage to aid the effectiveness of legislation. So great were her concerns over the new amendment that she concluded it would be far better to 'abandon the whole enactment than to include the proviso'. Of considerable concern too was the poor education that Arab girls received, and she lamented the attitude of the government, who blamed the problem on the lack of trained women teachers. In respect of the medical care that was available to Arab women, Eleanor found it hard to credit that 'in a predominantly Moslem country where in the towns a large proportion of poor women are still heavily veiled' there were no women doctors whatever employed in government service either in hospital or in district work.[64]

A lengthy response was forthcoming in January 1935, with the caveat that Wauchope's 'composite memorandum', which included references to new provisions, was not yet public knowledge and should be treated in confidence.[65] He did not take issue with Eleanor on her comments on certain social and educational problems in Palestine but instead noted that they had 'long engaged his attention': his proposals were the outcome of consultation 'with the Directors of Medical Services and Education' (in Palestine) and were allowed for within his budget estimates for the following year. The government planned for the provision of six new village schools to remedy, in part, the problem of inadequate facilities, particularly in rural areas. The establishment of a rural training centre for women teachers would, in the longer term, help rectify the staff shortages. Provision was also to be made within the budget for the appointment of two women doctors from England, who would be replaced by two Palestinian women who it was anticipated would be undertaking medical training in Beirut.[66]

The British government's announcement of its intention to set up a Royal Commission of Inquiry on Palestine, known as the Peel Commission, named after Lord Peel, the former secretary of state for India, once again aroused Eleanor's consciousness. The remit of the commission was to investigate the Arab Revolt of 1936, an uprising which Shepherd suggests was as much against the British as it was against the Jews.[67] The causes of the revolt, launched in the aftermath of the murder of two Jews by Arabs and the reprisal killing of two Arabs by Jews in mid-April 1936, were very complex, but were intimately bound up within the issues of the national rights of Arabs. The latter situation had been exacerbated by the surge in immigration of Jews from Germany into Palestine in 1935 and the sale of Arab Palestinian land to Jews.[68] Besides drafting in a military force to protect the authority of the mandatory government, the Peel Commission was to attempt to resolve the issues. Eleanor, who still had a keen interest in improving the rights of Arab girls and women, especially in the areas of child marriage, health issues and education, saw the commission as a vehicle for improving their status, in much the same way as she had viewed the Simon Commission in respect of India.[69] Once again, the thrust of her campaign was for female representation on the commission, and she fought for this both inside and outside the House, directing her action at William Ormsby-Gore, the secretary of state for the colonies. Ormsby-Gore became the recipient of innumerable official and private letters, the first of which appeared immediately following the commission announcement in the House. Eleanor forewarned him that she intended to have 'someone else' table a question in the House on the matter of female representation, and that this person was a man. This, she explained, was to ensure 'that this question should not be regarded merely as a bit of feminism'. In interpreting this latter statement, Eleanor was aware of the prejudice that many male Members of Parliament harboured against feminist issues, and no doubt hoped that a man putting forward the question would add gravitas to it. She certainly considered it to be a matter of humanitarian concern, and was motivated, as always, by her desire to right what she perceived as an injustice. It is also worth reflecting on the fact that by the mid-1930s the mounting crisis in international affairs overshadowed most other concerns, thus reducing the significance of them. Bearing in mind that the commission was likely to focus its attention on 'Arab grievances concerning Jewish immigration' she was convinced that 'the woman's side of the immigration question should get some attention'. After all, as she pointed out, there had been complaints about insufficient quotas of women allowed entry in certain categories and also about marriages of convenience.[70] It was Mr Lovat-Fraser, the MP for Lichfield, who put Eleanor's question to the secretary of state on 30 June 1936, asking 'Whether, in view of the special needs and disabilities of women, especially Arab women, in Palestine, and the importance of paying attention to those needs in considering all questions bearing on the future administration of the country, he will include in the proposed Royal Commission women qualified to ensure fulfilment of this purpose?'[71]

Ormsby-Gore's negative reply must have dismayed Eleanor but she can hardly have been surprised by it, given the resistance she had met in regard to a similar request vis-à-vis India. Not only did he believe that the appointment of a woman would be incompatible with Arab sensitivities, and thus impede the work of the commission, but he had also been advised, by Wauchope, that devout Moslems, and possibly some orthodox Jews, would refuse to appear before a commission that included women.[72] This infuriated Eleanor and she challenged Ormsby-Gore's rationale, arguing that she had been reliably informed by two of the Arab leaders who had addressed a meeting in the House of Commons, and by Arab and Jewish ladies attending the International Conference on Social Work that his contentions were spurious – they all maintained that the presence of women on the commission would not give such offence to Arab opinion as to impede the work of the body.[73] Even if Ormsby-Gore's argument was true, the matter could easily be overcome, as Miss Pye, vice-chairman of the Women's International League for Peace and Freedom (WIL), pointed out; all that was needed was for a woman appointee to hear evidence separately from the men, and vice versa.[74] Eleanor's suspicion, that there was 'a good deal of prejudice among those whom Ormsby-Gore consulted',[75] was a fair assessment according to Miss Emery, an Englishwoman with seventeen years of teaching experience in Jerusalem and Haifa. She not only challenged the secretary of state's views concerning a woman on the commission, but maintained that his advisers were indeed 'all elderly and willing to believe anything'. There was also her rather daring suggestion of a compromise if the government were 'too hidebound to appoint a woman on the Commission' that 'perhaps one or two chosen fair-minded women could go unofficially'.[76]

At this point, Emery's views on the Arab–Jewish conflict were opposed to Eleanor's, for in attempting to answer her supplementary question as to whether it was 'an index of the fitness of the Arabs for self-government that they would not appear before a Commission which included a woman?'[77] She took a very strong pro-Arab line, which did not endear her to Eleanor. The very notion that the government should yield to 'organized terrorism' by putting a halt to immigration, as Emery suggested, was anathema to Eleanor, and was quite evident in the tone of her reply and her pointed refusal to discuss the subject.[78] More constructive support came from women's organizations and politicians at home. The WIL,[79] the Women's Freedom League, and the British Commonwealth League all fought the case,[80] as did the MPs Mr George Lansbury (Bow and Bromley), Major Milner and Colonels Cazalet and Wedgwood, who badgered Ormsby-Gore to include a woman on the Peel Commission.[81]

When the composition of the Peel Commission was finally announced on 29 July 1936 there was considerable consternation in Parliament, especially from Eleanor and her supporters.[82] Not only were there no members of the House of Commons included, but the chairman, Lord Peel, was accused by Wedgwood of being 'strikingly pro-Moslem'. Once again, Eleanor raised the issue of a woman member, suggesting that he 'at least undertake to appoint a woman as technical expert ... so that half of the Palestinian population may not be left wholly out of account?'[83] In the aftermath she wrote again to

Ormsby-Gore, almost pleading with him to give further consideration to her suggestion that he appoint two women technical experts. 'Without them one is bound to fear that the Commission will represent just the limitations of the colonial people on the spot and share all their prejudices' she wrote.[84] At the same time she put forward the name of Miss Margery Fry, her friend and fellow Somervillian, as a person who was eminently qualified for the job. Miss Fry was, by then, former principal of Somerville and former honorary secretary of the Howard League for Penal Reform and had an impeccable CV that Eleanor sent Ormsby-Gore.[85] By early August 1936 it was clear that Ormsby-Gore was not going to adopt any of Eleanor's suggestions, and he left it to a secretary to inform her of his decision. The only hope left open was Ormsby-Gore's remark, communicated to Eleanor in a private letter, that he had 'no doubt that the Commission would welcome any authoritative expression of the women's point of view in these matters, if it should be thought to differ from that presented other wise to the Commission'.[86] This prompted Eleanor to contemplate offering to give evidence herself, an idea that it must be assumed she dropped.[87]

It is difficult to quantify the effectiveness of her activities in Palestine, but to claim, as Segev has done, that Eleanor's intervention in respect of child marriage had little effect,[88] misses an important point. Whilst she may have failed to persuade the government to change the legislation, something she was still trying to do in 1936, it is significant that she was a thorn in the side of government, persistently cajoling and pressurizing them, and could always be relied upon to support unpopular causes. Her success in respect of the franchise for women was bound to be limited, given the attitude of the Arab population and their overriding concern for nationalism. The question of immigration into Palestine was to occupy Eleanor's mind a good deal over the ensuing years, especially when it came to finding a haven for Jewish refugees fleeing Nazi persecution. Bentwich, writing eighteen years after Eleanor's death, praised her for giving her 'heart and brain' to two aspects of the Jewish problem, one of these being 'the opening of the doors of Palestine. In her capacity as head of an all-party Palestine committee, she and her co-members aimed to keep the British government faithful to their promises about the Jewish Home'.[89] Palestine was indeed intimately linked with Hitler's regime: the planned national homeland attracted increasing numbers of Jewish immigrants as the repression in Germany and elsewhere intensified, exacerbating tension between Arabs and Jews within the colony.

It was a source of great disappointment to Eleanor that she was not invited to participate in any of the commissions on Palestine. However, from the time of her introduction to issues in Palestine, and her subsequent visit to the country, she became a firm friend of the Jewish people, and an ardent Zionist. These factors were to prove crucial in the coming years as she involved herself in the rescue of refugees from Nazi and fascist Europe. But in the interim there was her engagement with international events and foreign affairs in the 1930s, as Britain moved closer to war.

## NOTES

1. Sherman describes this same attitude being adopted in respect of Britain and Palestine. See A.J. Sherman, *Mandate Days: British Lives in Palestine 1918–1948* (London: Thames and Hudson, 1997).
2. For recent scholarship on British rule in Palestine see N. Shepherd, *Ploughing Sand: British Rule in Palestine 1917–1948* (London: John Murray, 1999) and T. Segev, *One Palestine, Complete: Jews and Arabs under the British Mandate* (London: Little, Brown, 2000).
3. Segev, *One Palestine, Complete*, pp.167–9.
4. N. Bentwich, *England in Palestine* (London: Kegan Paul, 1932), p.278. For a more recent assessment see Shepherd, *Ploughing Sand*, pp.74–5.
5. Letter of Ashby to EFR, 10 February 1933, RP XIV.2.5 (21), ULL.
6. Ibid. See Letter of Ashby to EFR, 14 March 1933, RP XIV.2.5 (16), ULL.
7. R. Abrams, '"Pioneering Representations of the Hebrew People". Campaigns of the Palestinian Jewish Women's Equal Rights Association, 1918–1948', in I. Fletcher, L. Mayhall and P. Levine (eds), *Women's Suffrage in the British Empire: Citizenship, Nation and Race* (London: Routledge, 2000), pp.121–5.
8. M. Fawcett, 'A Glimpse of Egypt and a Journey Through Palestine', *Jus Suffragii*, 15, 9 (June 1921) as cited in L. Rupp, *Worlds of Women: The Making of an International Women's Movement* (Princeton, NJ and Chichester: Princeton University Press, 1997), p.58.
9. E. Fleischmann, 'Nation, Tradition and Rights: The Indigenous Feminism of the Palestinian Women's Movement, 1929–1948', in Fletcher *et al.*, *Women's Suffrage*, p.151, n.14: 'during the mandate period use of the word "Palestinian" to denote only Palestinian Arabs is somewhat problematic considering that Jews in Palestine sometimes referred to themselves as "Palestinian". However, by and large, it was the Arabs who demonstrated an attachment to the concept of "Palestine", whereas the Jews identified more with the Hebrew term Eretz Israel, "the land of Israel", a biblical term.'
10. Ibid., p.139.
11. H. Herzog, 'The Fringes of the Margin: Women's Organizations in the Civic Sector of the Yishuv', in D. Bernstein (ed.), *Pioneers and Homemakers: Jewish Women in pre-State Israel* (Albany, NY: State University of New York, 1992), pp.286–9.
12. A. Hyamson, *Palestine under the Mandate 1920–1948* (London: Methuen, 1950), pp.102–3.
13. Azaryahu, *Union of Hebrew Women*, p.37.
14. Letter of Welt-Straus to Ashby, 28 February 1933, RP XIV.2.5 (12), ULL.
15. Azaryahu, *Union of Hebrew Women*, p.37.
16. Letter of EFR to Cunliffe-Lister, 15 February 1933, RP XIV.2.5 (1), ULL.
17. Letter of EFR to Cunliffe-Lister, 20 February 1933, RP XIV.2.5 (6), ULL.
18. Letter of the BCL to EFR, 27 April 1933, RP XIV.2.5 (20), ULL. Letters between Florence Barry (secretary of St Joan's Social and Political Alliance) and EFR, 13 and 14 February 1933, RP XIV.2.5 (1/2), ULL. Letters between Elizabeth Abbott (chairman of the Open Door Council) and EFR, 2 and 11 April 1933, RP XIV.2.5 (18/19), ULL.
19. Letter of EFR to Florence Barry, 15 February 1933, RP XIV.2.5 (2), ULL.
20. Letter of Ashby to EFR, 13 February 1933, RP XIV.2.5 (7), ULL.
21. Ibid.
22. Letter of Cunliffe-Lister to EFR, 21 February 1933, RP XIV.2.5 (8), ULL.
23. Letter of EFR to Cunliffe-Lister, 28 February 1933, RP XIV.2.5 (11), ULL.
24. Letter of Welt-Straus to EFR, 21 June 1933, RP XIV.2.5 (23), ULL.

25. Letter of PJWERA to chief secretary, Government Offices, Jerusalem, 9 May 1932, RP XIV.2.5 (24), ULL.
26. Letter of acting chief secretary, Government Offices, Jerusalem to Welt-Straus, 19 March 1930, RP XIV.2.5 (32), ULL.
27. Published in *Palestine Bulletin*, 18 November 1930, RP XIV.2.5 (23), ULL.
28. M. Simoni, '"Germs Know No Racial Lines". Health Policies in British Palestine (1930–1939)', PhD diss., University of London, 2001, p.172.
29. Letter of Welt-Straus to EFR, 21 June 1933, RP XIV.2.5 (23), ULL.
30. 'Child Marriage in Palestine'. Memorandum by Miss Margaret Nixon, 12 February 1933, ISA J202/35 as cited in Simoni, '"Germs Know No Racial Lines"', p.173.
31. Letter of EFR to Welt-Straus, 29 June 1933, RP XIV.2.5 (25), ULL.
32. Stocks, *Rathbone*, p.210.
33. *Hansard* HC, vol. 280, cols 1068–9, 12 July 1933.
34. Letter of Lee to EFR, 25 January 1934, RP XIV.2.5 (36), ULL.
35. Letter of EFR to Lee, 16 February 1934, RP XIV.2.5 (37), ULL.
36. Letter of Welt-Straus to EFR, 7 July 1933, RP XIV.2.5 (32), ULL.
37. Letter of Welt-Straus to EFR, 8 July 1934, RP XIV.2.5 (39), ULL.
38. Postcard written by EFR from Palestine, n.d., RP XIV.2.5 (46), ULL.
39. ISA, J202/35, Memorandum of Eric J. Mills, 20 February 1933, as cited in Simoni, '"Germs Know No Racial Lines"', p.176, n.52.
40. Letter of Freda White to EFR, 6 July 1933, RP XIV.2.5 (33), ULL.
41. Segev, *One Palestine, Complete*, p.168.
42. *The New Judea*, 1 June 1934, p.6.
43. Letter of Cunliffe-Lister to EFR, 30 August 1934, RP XIV.2.5 (41), ULL.
44. Letter of Wauchope to Cunliffe-Lister, 15 January 1935, NA CO 733 (37332/34), ULL.
45. Letter of Welt-Straus to EFR, 7 July 1933, RP XIV.2.5 (32), ULL.
46. Notes made by E. Macadam of visit to Palestine, RP XIV.2.5 (45), ULL.
47. Letter of EFR to Williams, Colonial Office, 1 September 1934, RP XIV.2.5 (42) 211. A number of letters written in September 1934, and pertaining to Eleanor's visit, are noted as having been 'destroyed under Statute'. See NA CO 793/21/317, (37332).
48. I.M. Okkenhaug, 'The Quality of Heroic Living, of High Endeavour and Adventure. Anglican Mission, Women and Education in Palestine 1888–1948', D.Art. diss., University of Bergen, 1999. 'The two Naser ladies' are mentioned in letter of EFR to Nixon, 17 July 1936, RP XIV.2.5 (53), ULL.
49. Notes made by E. Macadam of visit to Palestine, 1934, RP XIV.2.5 (45), ULL.
50. Letter of Nixon to Stocks, 30 July 1948, RP XIV.6.14, ULL.
51. Letter of EFR to Shertok, 27 October 1934, Weizmann Archives, Jerusalem.
52. Letter of Nixon to Stocks, 5 August 1948, RP XIV.6.14, ULL.
53. *Palestine Post*, 30 September 1934, p.5.
54. *Palestine Post*, 9 October 1934, p.5.
55. The *Palestine Post* confirmed the PJWERA's gratitude to Miss Rathbone 'for her interpolation in Parliament on the questions of child marriage and women franchise in Municipal Elections in Palestine'. *Palestine Post*, 30 September 1934, p.5.
56. This is what Eleanor wrote in the draft of a speech to be given in Palestine. See Draft of speech, n.d., RP XIV.2.5 (44), ULL. However, in notes made by E. Macadam on a trip to Palestine this claim is stated thus: 'if she had not been born an English woman she would wish to have been born a Jew', RP XIV.2.5 (45), ULL.
57. E.F. Rathbone, Draft of speech given to the ERA, 8 October 1934, RP XIV.2.5 (44), ULL.
58. B. Tuchman, *Bible and Sword: England and Palestine from the Bronze Age to Balfour* (London: Phoenix, 2001), p.289.
59. Letter of Jewish Agency, London to Chaim Weizmann, 16 November 1934, Weizmann Archives, Jerusalem.
60. Presumably she was referring to the Anglo-American Committee of Enquiry into the Palestine Question, proposed by Britain in 1945. Victor Gollancz, 'Eleanor Rathbone', *AJR Information*, February 1946, p.13.
61. Notes made by E. Macadam on trip to Palestine, RP XIV.2.5 (45), ULL.
62. This speech was given to the PJWERA in Jerusalem on 8 October 1934. E.F. Rathbone, 'The Women's Movement: At Home and In the British Commonwealth', typed with handwritten notes, RP XIV.2.5 (44), ULL.
63. Stocks, *Rathbone*, p.215.

64. Notes by EFR, November 1934, RP XIV.2.5 (47), ULL.
65. Letter of Cunliffe-Lister to EFR, 15 January 1935, RP XIV.2.5 (48), ULL. This letter followed correspondence that passed between Wauchope and Cunliffe-Lister. See Letter of Wauchope to Cunliffe-Lister, 3 January 1935 and Letter of Cunliffe-Lister to Wauchope, 15 January 1935, NA CO 733 (37332/34).
66. Letter of Wauchope to Cunliffe-Lister, 3 January 1935, NA CO 733 (37332/34).
67. Shepherd, *Ploughing Sand*, p.117.
68. R. Zweig, *Britain and Palestine during the Second World War* (Woodbridge: Boydell for the Royal Historical Society, 1986), p.2. See also Stocks, *Rathbone*, p.218.
69. Okkenhaug, 'The Quality of Heroic Living', p.18.
70. Letter of EFR to W. Ormsby-Gore, 19 June 1936, RP XIV.2.5 (50), ULL.
71. *Hansard* HC vol. 314, col. 236, 30 June 1936.
72. Ibid.
73. Letter of EFR to W. Ormsby-Gore, 17 July 1936, RP XIV.2.5 (52), ULL. In a subsequent letter Eleanor included copies of letters in a similar vein that she had received from Miss Nasir, the head of Beir Zeit school (visited in 1934) ULL. She also included extracts from Emery's letter about Ormsby-Gore's advisers. Letter of EFR to Ormsby-Gore, 24 July 1936, RP XIV.2.5 (64), ULL.
74. Letter of Miss Pye to EFR, 23 July 1936, RP XIV.2.5 (54), ULL.
75. Letter of EFR to Nixon, 17 July 1936, RP XIV.2.5 (53), ULL.
76. Letter of Emery to EFR, 22 July 1936, RP XIV.2.5 (55), ULL.
77. *Hansard* HC, vol. 315, col. 425, 22 July 1936.
78. Reply of EFR to Emery, 6 August 1936, RP XIV.2.5 (59), ULL.
79. Letter of WIL to EFR, 29 July 1936, RP XIV.2.5 (60), ULL; Letter of WIL to Ormsby-Gore, 30 July 1936, RP XIV.2.5 (61), ULL; Letter of WIL to EFR, 6 August 1936, RP XIV.2.5 (62), ULL.
80. Articles were sent to the *Manchester Guardian*, the *Chronicle* and the *Herald*. Letter of Miss Pye to EFR, 23 July 1936, RP XIV.2.5 (54), ULL.
81. *Hansard* HC, vol. 315, cols 1511–16, 29 July 1936.
82. Ibid.
83. *Hansard* HC, vol. 315, col. 1513, 29 July 1936.
84. Letter of EFR to Ormsby-Gore, 30 July 1936, RP XIV.2.5 (56), ULL.
85. Ibid.
86. Letter of E. Boyd to EFR, 1 August 1936, RP XIV.2.5 (57), ULL.
87. Letter of EFR to the WIL, 5 August 1936, RP XIV.2.5 (58), ULL.
88. Segev's conclusion is based on reference to just two letters in the Rathbone Papers and pays no heed to other historical or contemporary sources.
89. N. Bentwich, *My 77 Years: An Account of my Life and Times 1883–1960* (London: Routledge and Kegan Paul, 1962), pp.146–7.

1. Eleanor, with her family on holiday in Scotland, 1892. Back row, left to right: William, Emily, Eleanor. Front row, left to right: Evie, Frank (with Nancy), Hugh (with Reynolds), Elsie. Courtesy of University of Liverpool Library.

2. Eleanor as a young woman. Courtesy of University of Liverpool Library.

EDITOR - M. CORVIN -
PUBLISHED IN "Y" CAMP
2d

NR. 1

16. AUG. 1941

## CAMPSPEAKER'S GREETINGS:

After this Camp has gone through its first three months it starts a Camp-Paper. As its editor was very successful with his Hutchinson Camp News, and knowing how much we old "Onchanese" liked our "Onchan Pioneer" I feel sure our "Camp Tribune" will flourish for as long as a common fate will keep us within our Camp's boundaries. We internees have lived very different lives, are of different creeds and upbringing, even from various native countries. Nevertheless, these 15 months of internment we have lived through, brought home to us much we now have in common. Ans one thing most of us feel in unison is our hope to be released out of even the nicest possible internment and to do our share in the common cause. May the Camp Tribune help to make this known to the outside world whilst helping to shorten the time of waiting for us in the Camp.

Walter JACHMANN

---

2

MARRIED ALIENS INTERNMENT CAMP    Port St. Mary. I.o.M.
4th August, 1941.

Miss Eleanor Rathbone, M.P., London, S.W.

Dear Madam,

When recently you called on our camp, the first British Married aliens internment camp, I had the privilige of being allowed to draw your attention to several points which, in our view, might lead to further our cases for release or to improve our conditions while still kept in internment. You kindly allowed us, the Camp's Council, to repeat some of these points in writing.

Before doing so, however, I should like to take this first opportunity of expressing on behalf of all my fellow internees our gratitude for having been transferred to this camp and re-united with our families and for the most satisfactory living conditions as far as the billeting, freedom of movement, food etc. goes, for the kind understanding and assistance which we are receiving f om the Commandant and his staff.

I should, therefore, be grateful if my following remarks were not taken as mere criticism but as an expression of good will to assist the authorities in running our camp.

Release The majority of us went through a second or even third Tribunal and were classified "C". They have made applications or had them made from outside and although authorization for their release may arrive daily they very often do not know whether their application for release has arrived and is receiving attention. It would be greatly appreciated if the system of confirming a plications from the side of the Home Office which, we understand, was accepted a few months ago, could be put into force without much further delay.

There are a n mber of people who were interned some time prior to the general round up of "C" cases. They still do not know what their present classification is nor whether they will be given the chance of defending themselves against accusations of which they are often not aware.

Other internees have had their Douglas Tribunal and were c assified "B" or "A". Only when questioned were they able to gather what seems to be against them. In most cases they are certain to be able to clear up any doubts as to their loyalty or good conduct, personal or in business. They do not know, however, how to proceed and they regard it as a special ha dship not to have known of the authorities' suspicions before they have had to appear before the Tribunal.

Occupation Some sixty of the total of approximately 150 men are going on farm work outside the Camp every day. A small number of men find occupation inside the Camp as school teachers or in the administration. All the others and most of the women are left without money-producing occupation and it is felt that, as in other camps, some industries could successfully be started, useful to the war effort and solving the problem afore mentioned. May I venture to suggest that the Manx Government be approached with a view to appoint one responsible person to deal with this important question, im ortant because there are so many willing hands in the Camp, idle at present, and we hope that our readiness to help as farm workers will lead to further assistance by the Manx Government.

Welfare We feel that the problem of the "semi-destitutes" is a most urgent one. These are the internees who are still left with a few pounds on their accounts, and who, owing to this fact, cannot at present be registered as destitutes and thus benefit from the facilities granted by the welfare. Before their internment they had their occupation, entered obligations and will, when released, have to face liabilities which they will be unable to meet at once in any way. They are made to pay part of their medicine bills, certain necessary dental treatment, shoe re airs, clothing repairs etc. Although an effort is being made to keep such expenses at a minimum, they strike us as extremely hard. We understand that the dentists' charges are regulated by the minimum charges fixed by the Dental Board. There is however this discrepancy between the wages of 1/7d per day for a farm worker and the cost of 7/6d for a tooth filling. While at the first mentioned figure the

- fact -

---

-3-

fact of our being kept here without cost to us is fully accounted for not so however at the latter figure where it seems forgotten that our earnings are not the minimum earn ngs of any free labourer. We should be grateful if the position in regard to these "semi-d stitutes" could be reviewed.

War-Risk-Insurance We want to express our gratitude for the assistance promised in regard to the War-Risk-Insurance question and hope that soon the internees in the I.O.M. owning chattels on the mainland, will be treated equally to those interned in Great Britain.

We are convinced th t you will do your best to assist us in the matters afore mentioned, and we are, dear Madam,

Yours very respectfully,
For the internees of the married Aliens Camp,
Camp Speaker.

14. *Camp Tribune*, 16 August 1941. Letter to Miss Eleanor Rathbone, 4 August 1941, pp.1, 2, 3. Manx Ref. Section B115/13xf(7). Courtesy of Manx National Heritage Library

# 4

# *Foreign Policy and Collective Security*

The inter-war years were a crucial period in Eleanor's life, for her involvement with foreign policy issues, and the response of the British government to events abroad, challenged her deeply rooted sense of Britishness and her concept of right and wrong, and shaped the remainder of her career. These years brought her face-to-face with the humanitarian crises that developed in Europe, involving her in activities which were directly related to the rescue of refugees, and thus setting the scene for her subsequent campaigns on behalf of Jews fleeing Nazi persecution.

Eleanor's entanglement with international affairs and the collective security debate developed against a background of interrelated world events. Central to her political philosophy was her commitment to the ideology of collective security[1] and progressive international disarmament, actively promoted by the League of Nations from its early days. Following a preparatory commission in 1925 to investigate the ways in which disarmament could be achieved, the Disarmament (Geneva) Conference finally opened in Geneva in February 1932, but its progress was threatened as a result of the Japanese advance into Manchuria (which comprised the three provinces of North East China) in the winter of 1931. US Secretary of State Henry Stimson (1867–1950) responded by urging President Hoover, unsuccessfully, to impose an economic boycott on Japan.[2] The British government distanced itself from the conflict on the grounds that the dispute was between two independent countries, and refused to intervene, a reaction that not only brought the effectiveness of the League of Nations machinery into question but also rendered its future uncertain.

The combined failure of Stimson's efforts, the USA's subsequent isolationist stand, and most particularly the announcement by Sir John Simon, the foreign secretary, in February 1933 that His Majesty's Government did not intend to take any action against Japan, despite the country having been denounced as an aggressor by the League of Nations Assembly, caused consternation in the House of Commons. The Geneva conference was still under way when Adolf Hitler came to power in Germany on 30 January 1933, and within a month it was evident that the country, admitted to the League of Nations in 1925 under the terms of the Treaty of Locarno, was preparing to rearm. When challenged at Geneva, Germany argued that if world disarmament, to the German level, was not accomplished, then it had the right to rearm and achieve military equality. Deadlock ensued and the disarmament conference was abruptly adjourned in June 1933. When it reconvened in October 1933, Germany withdrew from the talks and from the League, Japan also leaving the League in the same year.

Hopes of international disarmament continued to fade during 1934, whilst another international disaster was looming as Italy threatened to attack Abyssinia. Sir Samuel Hoare, the new foreign secretary, was responsible for handling this impending crisis and his famous declaration at Geneva on 11 September 1935, in which he claimed to embrace the obligations of the League of Nations, was encouraging. Public optimism was, however, short-lived, for Benito Mussolini's attack on Abyssinia a month later, on 3 October 1935, put Hoare's recent endorsement of League policy to the test. The 'steady and collective resistance' of which Hoare had so recently boasted lasted a mere three months. Economic sanctions imposed on Italy's supply of oil were ineffectual, and there were critics at home who believed that Hoare's measures were designed merely as a vote catcher.[3] Such cynicism was not without foundation, for when Stanley Baldwin, who had succeeded Ramsay MacDonald as prime minister in June 1935, decided to call a general election in November 1935, his government was able to present a seemingly flawless foreign policy. They claimed in the election manifesto that 'The League of Nations will remain, as heretofore, the keystone of British foreign policy'.[4] Meanwhile, Hoare entered into discussions with Monsieur Laval, the French prime minister. The Hoare-Laval Plan, as it came to be known, was intended to end the war in Abyssinia by endorsing the transfer of the fertile Ethiopian plains to the aggressor, Italy. The betrayal of Abyssinia through these proposals caused such a public outcry in Britain, that, as Eleanor later described, the government were compelled 'temporarily to reverse engines, even at the cost of losing one of its ablest and most influential Ministers'.[5]

Hoare's short tenure as foreign secretary ended abruptly with his resignation on 19 December 1935, but the Abyssinian crisis was far from over. In June 1936, Britain abandoned existing sanctions, leaving the way open for Mussolini to continue his war. Abyssinia's fate was officially confirmed in April 1938, when Neville Chamberlain, who had replaced Baldwin as prime minister on 31 May 1937, finalized an agreement with the Italian dictator that recognized Italy's conquest of the country. Meanwhile, there were separate conflicts simmering in Europe. The first of these occurred in Spain, when, in July 1936, the Popular Front government, which had been democratically elected in February that year, faced a *pronunciamiento*[6] by army officers, including General Franco. This rebellion marked the opening phase of the Spanish Civil War between the Republic, proclaimed in April 1931 with the fall of the monarchy, and the insurgent Nationalists. Whilst a detailed examination of the Spanish conflict is beyond the scope of this book, it can be said that it differed from the Abyssinian crisis in that there was no clear aggressor and victim, and there was a less obvious argument between right and wrong. The Spanish Civil War also posed a less complicated case in respect of League obligations, for as far as the British public were initially concerned, it was seen as an essentially Spanish problem, possibly because no vital national interests were apparently at stake. However, as the war progressed, so too did a humanitarian catastrophe which evoked an unprecedented response in Britain, embracing people of all classes. In a surge of practical support, citizens went to fight as volunteers whilst others organized food supplies, medical support and the evacuation of refugee children from Bilbao in the Basque country, humanitarian activities with which Eleanor became involved. These campaigns also gave rise to a deluge of rallies, committees, pamphlets, debates and books: many of the latter were published by the Left Book Club, founded by Victor Gollancz (who subsequently worked closely with Eleanor on the refugee question) in June 1936 (see Plate 19).

Against the background of civil war in Spain another, not wholly unexpected, international crisis was unfolding in Europe. As part of his programme of territorial expansion, Hitler marched his troops into Austria in March 1938, annexing it to Germany. Czechoslovakia was next in line for assault. Britain now faced a dilemma: should Hitler be allowed to take the territory by aggressive action, thus destroying the country and allowing the dictator free reign to expand to the east and south? Or should Britain support the French guarantee of Czechoslovakia and prevent the German domination of Europe?[7] A fundamental difference of opinion between the prime minister, who wanted to enter into talks immediately, and the foreign secretary, Anthony Eden, who refused to support a decision, resulted in the latter's resignation on 20 February 1938. Months of debate at home and abroad ensued, with Britain and France exerting pressure on the Czech government to make concessions and so avoid war. Both states made it clear to Hitler that if he ignored the negotiations and invaded Czechoslovakia they would be forced to fight. At a special Executive Committee meeting held on 23 September 1938, the League of Nations Union bitterly opposed the proposal to permit territorial concessions to Germany, berating His Majesty's Government for discrediting the country without securing peace.[8] Despite such protestations, a settlement was reached with the signing, by Chamberlain, Mussolini, Édouard Daladier and Hitler, of the Munich agreement on 29 September 1938, when Germany was granted the strategic Sudeten northern frontiers of the Czechoslovak Republic. In return, Hitler made a promise, empty as it transpired, not to attack the rest of the Republic, and to keep the peace in the future.

Eleanor's vision of the route to peace included wholeheartedly supporting the League of Nations Union (LNU) and their promotion of progressive international disarmament as an element of collective security during the 1920s and up until 1933,[9] and she agreed, for a time at least, with the process of appeasement. The LNU, of which she was an active member, had been created in Britain in October 1918 to act as a pressure group, exerting influence over British government foreign policy-making, as well as promoting and supporting the work of the League itself. Just how influential the LNU proved to be is debatable, but it was, for a time, the largest peace association in the world, with a membership that peaked in 1931 at 406,868, only to decline to 46,607 by 1945.[10]

Eleanor's commitment to collective security was as a 'pacificist', a term coined by A.J.P. Taylor, that is to say she wanted peace, but not at any price, in contrast to the pacifist, absolutist view, which opposed all forcible resistance to aggression.[11] The proponents of the pacifist movement, which she expounded in her book, *War Can be Averted*, were, in Eleanor's opinion, a 'queerly assorted group' whose political and religious rejection of collective security would, she feared, result in a major war. She certainly believed, naively as it turned out, that disarmament was possible and that it would result in an enduring world peace. This was a view that was endorsed during a visit she made to Berlin in the summer of 1929, in the brief period between gaining her seat in Parliament and the opening of the new session in the October. Although she was there primarily on official business, to lead the British delegation to the triennial conference of the International Women's Suffrage Alliance, she made good use of her free time, sightseeing and socializing. She mixed with ordinary German people whom she found to be 'liberal, feminist, pacific and lavishly hospitable'.[12] She was impressed by the palpable measure of goodwill towards England, and of the progress towards European pacification and prosperity that she identified. Conversely, she was acutely aware of how inhibited the Italian delegates were, and of the control which Mussolini, the Italian fascist dictator, exerted over their every move. Mary Stocks expressed the view that, in 1929, Mussolini was not regarded as a world menace, and that Germany was, at that time, enjoying 'a passing prosperity on the crest of the inter-war boom which deflationary finance had denied to Great Britain'.[13] It was in fact the last occasion on which Eleanor made a relatively untroubled trip to Europe, and would no doubt have been recalled by her many times over the next decade when her illusions of peace were shattered, and she was absorbed in her work for Jewish refugees fleeing Nazi-occupied Europe.

Eleanor's confidence in the possibility of universal harmony and the false sense of security that this trip may have induced, was shattered as a result of the Japanese invasion of Manchuria in the winter of 1931, and advocacy of disarmament was replaced by pressure on the League of Nations to adopt a tough foreign policy. More than anything she was shocked by the response of the British government to this act of aggression, and it had a profound effect on her thoughts, actions and deeds. It precipitated what Mary Stocks described as Eleanor's 'intellectual pilgrimage',[14] and was indeed a turning point in Eleanor's life. For not only did her views on the achievement of world peace undergo a process of re-evaluation, but she also became cynical and deeply critical of the government. Even though she found it very painful to accuse them of being cowardly and dishonourable in their foreign policy, and to blame politicians for the lack of understanding of cause and effect that they displayed, Eleanor was never afraid to speak her mind, especially when matters of principle were concerned. Thus she now embarked upon a multi-faceted campaign that greatly increased her political profile.

The action she pursued was typically relentless: at every available opportunity she put down questions on a wide range of armament-related topics, including savings to be made by disarmament,[15] the private manufacture of and trade in arms,[16] air limitation contention,[17]air defence,[18] exports of materials used in the production of arms,[19] arms exports,[20] and economic sanctions,[21] including discouraging British tourists from visiting Germany.[22] For example, on 27 June 1932, she raised the question of His Majesty's Government policy towards disarmament and how it differed from President Hoover's proposals, only to be told, by Sir John Simon, that the government was aware of the importance of the proposals and that they were receiving immediate consideration.[23] Still pursuing the matter, she prepared an address for the 12 July 1932, only to be refused leave to give it by the Speaker and Deputy-Speaker, on the grounds that the Geneva Conference was apparently not for discussion. This infuriated her for she protested that the Lord President of the Council had evidently proposed a debate on the subject some days previously.[24] Her anger was fuelled further when Mr Geoffrey le M. Mander, MP for Wolverhampton East, was allowed to discuss Geneva unhindered. Undaunted, she proceeded to compare the Geneva conference to a game of chess, whereas Lausanne, convened to discuss the payment of reparations, which was being freely discussed, was more like a game of football.[25] Eleanor's major concern was not that the government had failed to treat seriously the matter of multilateral disarmament, but rather the way in which they failed to regard armaments as potential instruments of deterrence to aggressors. What, she asked, was the use of agreeing in principle with US ideas concerning the reduction in the numbers of capital ships, if the government proceeded to disagree with the practical application of those plans in nearly every particular?[26] Outside of the House she wrote letters to the press, canvassed colleagues and lent support to many committees. The attitude of the foreign secretary, Sir John Simon, towards Japanese aggression, and the apparent ease with which Britain could retreat from the League Covenant seriously disturbed Eleanor. Her distrust of the government's foreign policy grew as it appeared that they seemed bent on ignoring what seemed obvious to her: an accumulation of similar retreats would result in international anarchy.[27]

The opportunity for voicing her very real concerns came on 13 April 1933, during the course of the foreign affairs debate on the Easter adjournment. She delivered an awesome and prophetic speech, for which she was long remembered, in which she vociferously denounced the newly elected German chancellor, and warned the House of Commons of 'the re-emergence of an evil spirit (in Germany) which bodes very ill for the peace and freedom of the world'.[28] She also used this speech to urge the government and the League of Nations to satisfy themselves, and reassure the country, that Germany was not violating Article 162 of the Treaty of Versailles which forbade or limited them rearming. In truth, as Brigadier-General Spiers stated subsequently in the debate, Germany had already violated the terms of the Treaty by making enormous additions to their police forces.[29] Nothing could be worse than sanctioning any measure of German rearmament, for, as she wrote to the *Manchester Guardian* shortly afterwards, she believed that 'the chief and ultimate aim of Nazi policy is revenge and military aggrandisement abroad'.[30] The unanimous all-party support that her parliamentary speech had attracted was regrettably short-lived, and it was not long before she became aggrieved that many ministers of state were prepared to grant concessions to Hitler's regime, thus giving the dictatorship a foothold in Europe. To her astonishment they were also quite happy to continue entertaining the German ambassador at Carlton House Terrace, London.

By 1934, with the hopes of disarmament evidently failing, Eleanor turned her attention towards actively promoting the application of carefully planned and supervised economic sanctions as an additional aspect of collective security. She was on her feet again during the

Whitsuntide debate on foreign affairs on 18 May 1934, urging Parliament and the press to treat the matter of economic sanctions seriously. These were, as she reminded her audience, represented in Article 16 of the League Covenant, a fact that seemed to be overlooked. She considered sanctions and disarmament to be 'kindred subjects' and saw the former to be a potential method of dealing with 'would-be aggressors or violators of international covenants'.[31] In view of the failure of the Disarmament Conference, the failure of the League of Nations in the Sino-Manchurian dispute and the move towards rearmament and isolationism, she urged the government to adopt a set of 'articulated measures' before the ultimate recourse was made to war. As to the viability of such measures, she invoked the authority of Sir Arthur Salter, the chief financial adviser to the League of Nations, who, in 1919, had stated that careful preparation was needed in advance of the introduction of sanctions if they were to work.[32] She foresaw the impending collapse of the Disarmament Conference having a most negative effect on public opinion, and considered preparation for the introduction of economic sanctions as the next logical step in the peacekeeping programme. But the government, and Stanley Baldwin in particular, took a different view. Baldwin told the Commons that 'there was no such thing as a sanction that will work that does not mean war'.[33]

Like a dog with a bone, Eleanor continued to harangue government in Parliament, to plan economic sanctions alongside supporting the Peace Ballot campaign, as well as writing letters to the press.[34] Anthony Eden would not accept her premise that 'other forms of collective security' could not be relied upon, only going as far as conceding that sanctions had been considered.[35] On the matter of publicity, she confided in Viscount Cecil that, despite the extensive LNU network and the immense output of literature she thought that the executive 'were not always in touch with the value of general propaganda, and consequently when the time comes for putting pressure on governments the pressure has still to be created'. What other reason could there be, she asked, for the government's 'apparent ignoring of the economic sanctions problem compared with the volume of popular support for the Air Force idea' that Lord Davies was boosting?[36]

The future of Abyssinia soon overtook other concerns, for whilst Hoare's famous, or as Eleanor termed it, infamous declaration at Geneva on 11 September 1935 concerning the country's fate inspired her with great confidence, her optimism was short-lived. Much to her horror, the Hoare-Laval plan to settle the war by the division of Abyssinia received the approval of the British cabinet. With the country's fate still in the balance in April 1936, Eleanor's deeply ingrained sense of morality, her fear of war and her belief in the inherent powers of collective security were all passionately expressed in the *Manchester Guardian*.[37] The League of Nations was due to hold a vital meeting the following month and she believed this would be the last chance to save Abyssinia. She pleaded for Britain, and the government, to face up to their responsibilities and to persist in efforts to avert abandonment of the country. Juxtaposed against this she articulated her sense of shame at 'the intolerable disgrace of betrayal', especially by Eden, who was still making idle promises and prevaricating about the imposition of sanctions.[38] In the meantime she had plenty of evidence of German rearmament, supplied by Churchill[39] and other informants,[40] which she broadcast in the press.[41] And as part of a plan to maximize the government's embarrassment over Abyssinia, she joined Sylvia Pankhurst's party, along with fellow refugee activists, Philip Noel-Baker and Norman Angel, in welcoming the exiled Emperor, Haile Selassie, to Britain in June 1936. Later in the year she was urging Churchill to lead 'a really big campaign in favour of collective security' – he preferred the phrase 'combined defensive strength' – certain that his qualities of leadership would be very influential.[42]

The fate of Abyssinia, which had been occupied since late 1936, and the British government's subsequent abandonment of the country to Mussolini in April 1938, had a profound effect on Eleanor's hitherto intense loyalty to, and national pride in Britain: tolerance and decency were characteristics that she ascribed to her country, and she expected the government to act honourably. Whether this was misplaced trust or naivety on her part, she was nevertheless shaken to the core, so much so that when Abyssinia's fate had been sealed, she was convinced that it 'was unlikely that anything could happen to make us feel more ashamed or more wounded in our racial pride than we did already. But we were mistaken; there was worse to follow.'[43] Eleanor's choice of words is interesting, for there was a certain irony in her using a race discourse to articulate her sense of pride in national identity, for it suggests that she was not without racial prejudice, and nor was she totally immune to eugenicist ideology. And her prophecy of 'worse to follow' was correct, for as Mary Stocks later recalled, there was Spain.

The government adoption of, and adherence to, a policy of non-intervention in the Spanish Civil War, was, as far as Eleanor was concerned, another example of Britain abdicating its moral responsibilities. The government line, that this was the only way to prevent the war in Spain becoming a general war, did not persuade her. Rather, she argued, it would be highly inadvisable to let Spain fall into Franco's, and by implication, Hitler and Mussolini's hands. Her view was that a general war was unlikely unless the two dictators had already decided on conflict and were looking for an excuse. The other scenario was that if Franco's success was so important to fascist dictators, they would risk war rather than see him defeated.

At the heart of Eleanor's reaction to Britain's response to events in Spain was her profound belief in peace, liberty and democracy. Every action and statement she made on foreign policy was carefully considered and contributed to the pro-Republican, pro-collective security and anti-non-intervention campaign that sought to safeguard these fundamental rights.[44] Within the House, she took every opportunity of expressing her dismay at the way in which the government was portraying the situation in Spain, and refusing to abandon non-intervention in favour of collective security.[45] Outside the House, her attack was multi-faceted. When the LNU General Council met in June 1937 Eleanor implored delegates to do more than pass a resolution on the Spanish situation, which had, by then, developed from a civil war into flagrant aggression and terrorism.[46] There were also the numerous pro-Republican committees with which she became associated, including the Bristol Committee for Defence of Spanish Democracy of which she was a vice-president, the National Joint Committee for Spanish Relief (NJCSR) formed in November 1936 to co-ordinate the work of the many 'Aid Spain' bodies, and the National Committee of the Friends of Spain (NCFS). When the NCFS was wound up, Wilfrid Roberts, Liberal MP for North Cumberland, who later became honorary treasurer and a vice-president of Eleanor's refugee group, the NCRNT, set up the all-party Parliamentary Committee for Spain (PCS) in January 1937.[47] The function of the PCS was to prime MPs with information, and of the thirteen members, five, significantly, were women – Eleanor, Katherine, Duchess of Atholl, Megan Lloyd George, Edith Summerskill and Ellen Wilkinson (see Plate 6). An important platform was the Committee of Enquiry into Breaches of International Law Relating to the Intervention in Spain, set up by the Communist party in August 1936. The inclusion of Eleanor and Professor J.B. Trend was a clever move on the part of the committee, since both were Independent pro-Republicans, and added balance, weight and influence. The members sought to influence public opinion away from non-intervention by providing evidence from witnesses of the way in which the policy was severely disadvantaging the Republicans. One of these witnesses was Arthur Koestler, the Hungarian-born refugee who was working in Spain as a correspondent for the London *News Chronicle*,[48] and with whom Eleanor later worked on the refugee issue (see Plate 7).

Beyond this political involvement, there was a far more personal and humanitarian aspect to Eleanor's engagement with Spain which involved her in the rescue of refugees, and which had important implications for her future campaigns on behalf of Jews fleeing Nazi persecution.

Her abhorrence of hardship and cruelty had already been demonstrated in the work she had undertaken for women in India, Africa and Palestine, but now she was involved with the saving of lives, which she considered to be 'a labour of love'. She found it much more satisfying to be doing something constructive rather than 'hurling invective week by week against a wall of unresponsive Front-bench faces'.[49] A fact-finding tour of war-ravaged Spain in April 1937, in the company of her left-wing MP colleague, Ellen Wilkinson, the Duchess of Atholl and Dame Rachel Crowdy, alerted Eleanor to the overwhelming Republican need for arms, equipment and medical supplies and she also saw the devastation caused by German planes. Her response was to become a member of the Spanish Medical Aid Committee, created in July 1936 and a sponsor, alongside the Duchess of Atholl, of the fund-raising International Brigades' Dependants and Wounded Aid Committee, established in June 1937.

More specifically she became chairman of the British Committee for Refugees from Spain, a sub-committee set up by the NJC, to deal with International Brigaders who were held in camps in France. This, in turn, brought her into working contact again with the Duchess of Atholl and Wilfrid Roberts on the Basque Children's Committee (BCC). The committee was set up in the spring of 1937 specifically to take responsibility for the care of children rescued from war-torn Spain, and was a cause that became very dear to Eleanor's heart. The removal of some 4,000 children from the combat zone in 1937 to the safety of Britain, albeit temporarily, was a logistical and political challenge which Eleanor and her colleagues worked tirelessly to achieve. It was no easy task to persuade the government to allow even this relatively small number of refugees into the country, and was only accomplished by the NJC promising to assume responsibility for their selection, care and evacuation.[50] What cannot be ignored here are the direct comparisons with the limited numbers of Jewish refugees whom the government allowed to enter Britain from 1933 until the outbreak of the Second World War. During that time, the Jewish refugee organizations assumed total financial responsibility for such people, ensuring their safety whilst avoiding any drain on the public purse.

The full story of the evacuation of children from the Basque country has been explored elsewhere but what was significant from Eleanor's point of view were the implications that the campaign had for her later refugee work. These were two-fold. She learnt the value of intense public pressure and of imaginative and brave individuals who would stop at nothing to achieve their goal of rescuing people from war-torn countries. Pedersen has also stated that Eleanor discovered that, even though the British public might have appeared reluctant to welcome refugees into the country, they were magnanimous in their generosity once they had arrived.[51] This may well have been the case in respect of children from Spain, whose stay was, from the outset, intended to be limited, although only half were repatriated by 1939, and hundreds remained in Britain permanently. It was also valid in regard to Jewish children who arrived on the Kindertransport in 1938 and 1939, for by August 1939, 9,354 children, the majority of whom were Jewish, had been rescued from Germany by the Kindertransport, 7,800 of them arriving in the United Kingdom between January and August of that year.[52] However, when it came to adult Jewish refugees from Eastern Europe, their 'foreignness' made them far less attractive and appealing, and they were perceived in some circles as posing a threat to the fabric of society, and were not welcomed with such open arms.

Eleanor's disenchantment with the British government's negative attitude towards humanitarian relief continued, and was not enhanced by the change in leadership when Neville Chamberlain replaced Baldwin as prime minister on 31 May 1937. Eleanor's opinion of Chamberlain was partly informed by his physical appearance: her comments about the shape of his head, 'narrow, suggesting a narrow mind' were a reminder of her tenuous involvement with the eugenics movement and race science, and she was convinced that this change in leadership would have disastrous results.[53] He was certainly not the strong leader whom she had hoped for, nor did she anticipate that he would be able to avert war.

More refugee-related appeals followed, this time in respect of naval activities and the government's refusal to protect ships taking refugees from Bilbao in May 1937. Eleanor made an appeal to Clement Attlee, the leader of the opposition, to debate the situation in the House,[54] and sent a stream of condemnatory letters to Eden, Cranborne and Sir Duff Cooper.[55] She was subsequently incensed by Duff Cooper's statement in the Commons on 22 July 1937, and his refusal to countenance rescuing or feeding starving women and children in northern Spain. Either action would, he claimed, constitute military assistance and breach non-intervention. How, she later wrote to Lord Lytton in a passionate display of humanity, could it a be a breach of non-intervention or neutrality for British merchant or war ships 'to pick up drowning men, women or children, or those clinging to rafts, even within territorial waters?'[56]

An ongoing aspect of the Spanish conflict that concerned Eleanor was the paucity of published information broadcast in Britain, even in 'the Liberal and Labour Press'.[57] She accepted that the situation was partly due to the lack of correspondents in Spain, and also to the loss of public interest since the Bilbao crisis, and she made strenuous efforts to right the situation. Of her sources in Spain, Commander Pursey, the NJCSR representative in Santander, kept her well informed of events, especially during July 1937, when the farce of the naval blockade of Bilbao was being played out.[58] The systematic bombing of Basque towns by German aircraft and the evidence of Italian troops in Spain prompted her to ask Eden, in the House, whether 'the government would secure the appointment of an international commission to check on, and act as a check on further breaches of non-intervention'.[59] She made no bones about challenging Eden in the House over the Non-Intervention Agreement, although he thought it, and by implication the Committee, was a 'leaky dam', but he maintained, 'Better a leaky dam than no dam at all'. As far as Eleanor was concerned the Committee was disastrously ineffective, and the Non-Intervention Agreement itself was an exercise in 'shutting the stable door after most of the horses had been stolen'.[60] When she addressed the International Peace Conference (IPC) at Caxton Hall in October 1937 the government's defeatist attitude led her to describe their behaviour as 'ignoble at best'. By then her faith in the Peace Movement was severely diminished for, as she wrote, it was not 'that it has abandoned hope, but that it behaves as though it had years ahead of it to realise its hope'.[61]

By 1938 the Spanish Republicans' position had deteriorated and the insurgent forces were on the verge of entering Barcelona, when Eleanor received information from the Council of Action for Peace and Reconstruction (whose parliamentary group she belonged to)[62] and from the Dean of Canterbury, confirming that German bombers were being sent out to Spain.[63] This precipitated a series of parliamentary questions that reflected her concern about the implications this would have for the refugee mission, due to the bombing of British ships.[64] She was incensed when it became clear that, despite the gravity of the situation, and the loss of life – the bombing killed twenty-seven men, injured thirty-seven and caused great damage to the ships – the government was doing nothing other than 'send verbal protests of the kind that General Franco invariably disregards'.[65] Personally, she had absolutely no faith in anything that Franco said,[66] and had no hesitation in making her views known via the press, in published letters to the editors of a number of papers, including the *Manchester Guardian*, *Birmingham Post*, *Yorkshire Post* and *Liverpool Daily Post*.[67] She also urged the National Union of Seamen to organize a delegation to meet with the prime minister.[68]

The refugee issue in Spain was still burning in 1939, with Eleanor pressing the government to send more food, medical and nursing personnel, medicine and camp equipment; she was also asking why it was that the Red Cross had not acted to help with the 'deplorable lack of medical necessaries and personnel'.[69] Her loss of faith in the ability of the medical agency was obvious when she asked, 'What is the Red Cross for if it is never on the spot?'[70] Where the welfare of Spanish refugees was concerned, secrecy was sometimes of paramount importance. As late as 1941, whilst deeply immersed in the Jewish refugee crisis, she sought the help of R.A. Butler, then parliamentary undersecretary at the Foreign Office, to ensure the safety of 140 of the most important Republican figures who had escaped from Spain. Six hundred pounds in sterling was needed to secure their admission to Argentina, but Foreign Office support was required before the money could be released from NJCSR funds.[71]

Eleanor was, as Mary Stocks remarked, 'living night and day' with foreign affairs for, alongside Spain, there was the grave political situation unfolding in Eastern Europe in late 1936, the outcome of which was to profoundly effect Eleanor's future campaigning.[72] The 'Little Entente', comprising the small countries of Romania, Yugoslavia and Czechoslovakia, faced a potential threat of invasion by Germany, but had inadequate defences to deal with such incursions, and Eleanor believed that Czechoslovakia would become the first victim. The fact that even intelligent people in Britain knew so little about the country and its precarious geopolitical position shocked her,[73] precipitating a concerted effort on her part to raise public awareness and mobilize support for the country. To further this campaign, she joined Katherine, Duchess of Atholl and Lady Layton, on a three-week, Foreign Office–approved (but unofficial) visit to the Balkans in February 1937 (see Plate 8).[74] The trip was gruelling but successful, in that the women met a wide section of the public as well as government officials in Prague, Budapest and Belgrade.[75] Eleanor made some interesting assessments of those she met, describing the British legations as 'very aloof from democratic sections of opinion' and the chargé d'affaires in Prague 'completely pro-Henlein'.[76] On her return, she was vocal in the House of Commons, asking 'whether it would be decent to abandon this country, the last free enlightened democracy left in Central Europe? Also, would it be safe?', reminding MPs of Bismarck's dictum that 'He who is master of Bohemia is master of Europe'.[77]

The trip also brought her into renewed contact with her friend, Mme Frantiska Plaminkova, a Czech feminist and member of the Senate of the Czechoslovak Republic. Eager to raise the profile of Czechoslovakia at home, Eleanor warned Mme Plaminkova how difficult it was to make the British public 'recognise their duty and responsibility towards Czechoslovakia as it was not easy as people know so little about the country,' sentiments with which Plaminkova did not disagree.[78]

More pertinent in view of her subsequent activities on behalf of

Jewish refugees was her opinion of the British ambassador in Bucharest, whom she described as 'strongly anti-Semite'[79], which did not bode well for Jews who were attempting to flee the country. It also highlighted Eleanor's own awareness of the prevailing negative attitude towards Jews, which she certainly did not share. On the contrary, she was full of admiration for them, and took great pleasure in a visit she made to the School for Jewish Girls run by a Christian Mission to the Jews in Bucharest.[80] Miss Gedge, former warden of the University Settlement for Women at Bombay, was with her on this visit, and recalled how Eleanor spoke to the children at prayers and said 'what a pleasure it was to her to meet Rumanian Jews', adding that many of her best friends were Jewish.[81] The latter comment warrants brief attention, for it was so often added as a defensive rider by people who were making attacks on Jews or their behaviour. But in Eleanor's case it was of course true.

Even more revealing were the comments she made in a letter sent to Miss Boyd, the school's headmistress, on her return home:

> They (the pupils) will know that in our Parliament some of the most honoured and useful members belong to the Jewish community, which also includes some of my most intimate friends. But I feel that my little visit to your school helped to bring home to me how much the presence of members of the Jewish community in every country, makes a link which should help to bind these countries together and is a constant reminder of all we owe the Jewish race.[82]

It is surprising, given the significance of this letter in terms of Eleanor's opinion of Jews and her future commitment to saving them from Nazi persecution, that there does not appear to be any reference to it in Susan Pedersen's biography of her. In Eleanor's view, articulated in 1945, but equally valid in 1937, the debt that society owed the Jews extended from providing the basis of Christianity, through to their contributions in medicine, literature and philosophy, which were all of incalculable value to mankind.[83] Nor was it entirely surprising that she should admit to having Jews amongst her most intimate friends – Eva Hubback and Victor Gollancz, for example, to say nothing of friends amongst the wider Jewish community through her connections with the Board of Deputies of British Jews. Besides this there were Jewish colleagues in Parliament, including Sidney Silverman, Leslie Hore-Belisha and Daniel Lipson. There is no doubt that she had a strong identification with Jews, through familiar biblical connections and similarities in religion and culture, and she much admired their values and ethics. Neither was this the first time that Eleanor had paid tribute to the

Jews: besides her passionate and prophetic speech in the House of Commons in 1933, when Hitler came to power,[84] she had reiterated her praise when she visited Palestine in February 1934.[85] Such overt empathy cannot be disassociated from her admiration of and affiliation to Zionism, which was also articulated in 1934, nor, more importantly, from her subsequent humanitarian work for Jewish refugees fleeing Fascist and Nazi Europe.

The most significant result of Eleanor's visit to the Balkans was to confirm her worst fear, that Czechoslovakia was in imminent danger of a German attack, and that the resulting conflict would be 'another Spain'.[86] Thus she was eager to put her signature to a letter to *The Times* on 10 March 1937, in which Germany's propaganda campaign against Czechoslovakia was denounced. Besides this, she included warnings about the dangers of the fascist powers in every speech she gave.[87] Nor was it surprising that she should agree, in January 1937, to become a member of the Committee For Intellectual Liberty, a pressure group formed to counter the fascist threat.[88]

In notes she made for a speech at the IPC conference to be held at Caxton Hall, London on 22 October 1937 she warned that 'Unless some great change happens [of] which at present there seems no sign, the other European democracies (excluding France) appear destined to fall, one by one, either as victims of armed aggression, or because they have not waited to be attacked but have put themselves under the sheltering wing of one or other of the great totalitarian powers'.[89] As the downward spiral in foreign affairs continued into 1938, Eleanor presented her views on Eden's resignation as foreign secretary in an address to the Manchester Union Convocation. She was convinced that he was right to insist that formal talks should be preceded by some indication of Mussolini's good faith, and that Italy was a question of principle, not a matter of debate.[90] By way of support, which he greatly appreciated, she wrote to him on 24 February letting him know the extent to which her constituents backed him: 'I have received more telegrams and letters in the time urging me to oppose the government's policy and support you – and none in the contrary sense – than I have ever received on any one subject during the eight years I have been in Parliament, except in protest against the Hoare-Laval proposals.'[91] She warned the Left Book Club Protest Meeting held at Queen's Hall, London on 1 March 1938, that Hitler and Mussolini would take full advantage of Eden's resignation to disseminate the claim that they were responsible for dislodging a British foreign secretary – it would also confirm their impression that they could coerce Great Britain to give them something for nothing.[92] Germany marched into Austria on 12 March 1938, and Eleanor's attacks in the House continued unabated.

Notes that she made for the foreign affairs debate on 24 March 1938 confirmed her unequivocal condemnation of the government's 'litany of failure'. She wrote prophetically that 'Whatever form the subjugation of Czechoslovakia takes it will lead to hegemony of Germany over Europe'.[93] In speeches made to various LNU and IPC meetings, she described April 1938 as 'the blackest month since 1914'.[94] Lord Halifax, the foreign secretary, was still pursuing a policy of appeasement with Hitler, and when the House adjourned for the summer vacation in July 1938, Eleanor gave a lengthy and carefully considered view of the dire state of foreign affairs. There were, in her view, 'no signs of real appeasement. After every fresh concession the arrogance of the aggressive powers becomes more marked and more openly expressed ... We go away in deep anxiety, wondering how many passes the Prime Minister will have sold before we return'.[95] And days before the Munich agreement was signed on 29 September, sealing Czechoslovakia's fate, she declared at a meeting of the Cambridge Peace Council that 'there (must) be no more concessions ... Hitler's terms are not only [those] of a bully, but a sadist who is determined to torture those he has vanquished'.[96]

Eleanor most definitely did not breathe a sigh of relief after Munich, for she knew instinctively that the agreement only offered a temporary respite from war, and had not averted it. Appeasement was in her opinion, 'a clever plan of selling your friends to buy off your enemies – which has the danger that a time comes when you have no friends left, and then you find you need them, and then it is too late to buy them back'.[97] Whilst on 30 September 1938 Chamberlain was hailed in London as 'the angel of peace with honour',[98] Eleanor later spoke of the 'angel of death'.[99]

At a personal level the inter-war period was a crucial phase in Eleanor's life, for world events paved the way for her campaigning work on behalf of refugees fleeing Nazi and fascist terror in Europe. Given this significance, it is all the more surprising that so little attention has been paid by historians to her thoughts, actions and deeds during this time. Once again, this raises the question of feminist or gender interest, or the lack of interest in an area of Eleanor's life that has no obvious connection with women's rights, and where her commitments were not specifically gender orientated. As ever, at the heart of all Eleanor's activities was her fervent desire to speak out for and defend those who had no voice, regardless of creed, culture or religion. Philosophically she was a 'pacificist' so that when it became clear that collective security, in which she put so much faith as a means of averting war, was no longer a realistic aim, she was willing to modify her views and support a tough government stand against aggressors. This was also a period during which Eleanor's patriotism and pride in Britain were severely tested, bringing her into direct conflict with the government. The global events outlined in this chapter forced her to conclude that they had dealt with foreign policy matters – Japan, Italy, Abyssinia, Austria, and Czechoslovakia – in a cowardly and dishonourable way. She did not reach this opinion in haste, but suffered much soul searching and anguish in the process, but it hardened her indomitable resolve to right the wrongs of the world. The failure of Britain to live up to the ideals of honour which she so valued and which she ascribed to her country was a huge blow to her. Although Johanna Alberti claims that 'her shame for her own country was transformed after 1939 into a passionate moral pride, declaring "Britain has expiated her sin"',[100] this statement fails to take account of Eleanor's disillusionment with government over its attitude towards refugees fleeing persecution in Nazi Germany from 1933 onwards.

The majority of the refugees whose cause she was to champion were Jews, and her guiding principle, ingrained through her upbringing and university education, was the duty of personal service. Her opinion of the Jewish race developed during this time, and although her trip to Palestine in 1933 confirmed her as a Gentile Zionist, further encounters in Prague in 1939 reaffirmed her admiration for the Jewish race. By March 1939 Eleanor was overwhelmed with 'the mass of urgent work arising out of recent events'. In her annual address to her constituents, she confirmed that 'the League [of Nations] as an instrument of collective security has been shelved: even its humanitarian activities curtailed'.[101] Conversely, her humanitarian activities were accelerating at an unprecedented rate and her work for refugees was to consume her for the rest of her life.

NOTES

1. The term was coined in the 1930s, whereas previously the terms 'pooled security' and 'collective defence' had been in use. See D. Birn, *The League of Nations Union 1918–1945* (Oxford: Clarendon Press, 1981), p.131. My thanks to Clive Fleay for this reference.
2. E.F. Rathbone, *War Can Be Averted* (London: Gollancz, 1938), pp.27–32.
3. Rathbone, *War Can Be Averted*, p.46.
4. N. Thompson, *The Anti-Appeasers: Conservative Opposition to Appeasement in the 1930s* (Oxford: Clarendon Press, 1971), p.77.
5. Rathbone, *War Can Be Averted*, p.23.
6. There is no equivalent term in English, though 'coup' is perhaps the closest word. My thanks to Clive Fleay for this information.
7. This is, of necessity, a simplified overview of the very complex events of 1938.
8. LNU Executive Committee Minutes, Special Meeting, 23 September 1938, BLPES.
9. Stocks is quite clear in her assertion that in 1929 Eleanor was 'an ardent advocate of progressive international disarmament'. Yet Harrison maintains that Eleanor opposed disarmament. M. Stocks, *Eleanor Rathbone: A Biography* (London: Gollancz, 1949), p.222, and B. Harrison, *Prudent Revolutionaries: Portraits of British Feminists between the Wars* (Oxford: Clarendon Press, 1987), p.114.

10. For the debate on the LNU see D. Birn, 'The League of Nations Union and Collective Security', *Journal of Contemporary History*, IX (3 July 1974), pp.133ff. For membership, see M. Ceadel, *Semi-Detached Idealists: The British Peace Movement and International Relations 1854–1945* (Oxford: Oxford University Press, 2000).
11. A.J.P. Taylor, *The Trouble Makers: Dissent over Foreign Policy, 1792–1939* (Harmondsworth: Penguin, 1957), p.51n.
12. Stocks, *Rathbone*, pp.130–1.
13. Stocks, *Rathbone*, p.131.
14. Ibid.
15. *Hansard* HC, vol. 268, col. 1265, 13 July 1932; vol. 273, cols 182–4, 13 December 1932; vol. 274, col. 1025, 15 February 1933; vol. 275, col. 159, 13 March 1933; vol. 277, cols 515–6, 1 May 1933.
16. See, for example, *Hansard* HC, vol. 293, col. 1300, 1331, 8 November 1934; vol. 298, cols 2126–8, 7 March 1935; vol. 300, cols 796–7, 8 April 1935; vol. 301, col. 689, 3 May 1935.
17. *Hansard* HC, vol. 289, col. 1434, 14 May 1934.
18. *Hansard* HC, vol. 299, col. 23, 11 March 1935.
19. *Hansard* HC, vol. 283 cols 671–2, 28 November 1933.
20. *Hansard* HC, vol. 304, col. 734, 15 July 1935.
21. *Hansard* HC, vol. 289, cols 2074–82, 18 May 1934; vol. 299, cols 7–8, 11 March 1935; vol. 304, col. 2306, 29 July 1935.
22. Letter of EFR to the editor, *The Times*, 11 August 1933, RP XIV.2.6 (5), ULL.
23. *Hansard* HC, vol. 267, cols 1459–60, 27 June 1932.
24. *Hansard* HC, vol. 268, col. 1252, 12 July 1932.
25. The Lausanne Conference ended on 9 July 1932.
26. *Hansard* HC, vol. 268, col. 1252, 12 July 1932, RP XIV.3 (8), ULL.
27. Stocks, *Rathbone*, p.223.
28. *Hansard* HC, vol. 276, col. 2761, 13 April 1933.
29. *Hansard* HC, vol. 276, cols 2763, 2778, 13 April 1933.
30. E.F. Rathbone, 'Democracy's Fight for Life', Letter to the editor, *Manchester Guardian*, 15 May 1933.
31. E.F. Rathbone, Draft of House of Commons speech on economic sanctions, not given, 13 July 1934, RP XIV.3 (17), ULL.
32. *Hansard* HC, vol. 289, cols 2078–82, 18 May 1934.
33. *Hansard* HC, vol. 289, col. 2139, 18 May 1934.
34. One such letter to the *Manchester Guardian* is referred to in Letter of Cecil to EFR, 27 April 1935, Cecil of Chelwood Papers, Add MSS 51141, folio 266, BL.
35. *Hansard* HC, vol. 299, cols 7–8, 11 March 1935.
36. Letter of EFR to Cecil, 3 May 1935, Cecil of Chelwood Papers, Add MSS 51141, folios 267/8, BL.
37. Letters of EFR to the editor, *Manchester Guardian*, 28 March 1936, pp.7, 9; 9 April 1936, p.20. For replies see Letter of R. Toynbee, *Manchester Guardian*, 31 March 1936, p.20 and Letter of EFR to Toynbee, *Manchester Guardian*, 2 April 1936, p.20. Letter of C. Padel, *Manchester Guardian*, 1 April 1936, p.20. Letter of H. Sand, *Manchester Guardian*, 2 April 1936, p.20.
38. Letter of EFR to the editor, *Manchester Guardian*, 29 April 1936, p.20.
39. Letter of EFR to Winston Churchill, 17 April 1936, CHAR/2/266/A, CAC.
40. Letter of T. Plaut to EFR, 17 April 1936, CHAR/2/274/16–17, CAC.
41. E.F. Rathbone, 'British Public Opinion and the Crisis', *Manchester Guardian*, 28 March 1936, p.7.
42. Letter of EFR to Winston Churchill, 8 November 1936, CHAR/2/260/109–11 and Letter of Winston Churchill to Lady Houston, 18 November 1936, CHAR/2/260/115, CAC.
43. Rathbone, *War Can Be Averted*, p.42.
44. S. Pedersen, *Eleanor Rathbone and the Politics of Conscience* (London: Yale University Press, 2004), pp.279–80.
45. *Hansard* HC, vol. 326, cols 1896–1900, 19 July 1937; vol. 337, cols 1371–6, 23 June 1938; vol. 338, cols 3015–21, 26 July 1938.
46. Report by L. Aldous, *Headway* (July 1937), p.129.
47. S. Bruley, 'Women Against War and Fascism: Communism, Feminism and the People's Front', in J. Fyrth (ed.), *Britain, Fascism and the Popular Front* (London: Laurence and Wishart, 1985), p.145.

48. For Koestler's role, see D. Cesarani, *Arthur Koestler: The Homeless Mind* (London: Heinemann, 1999), pp.118–35.
49. Stocks, *Rathbone*, p.244.
50. For these negotiations, see NA FO 371/21370/W9147, W9446, W9496 and W9705.
51. Pedersen, *Politics of Conscience*, p.287.
52. Movement for the Care of Children from Germany: First Annual Report, 1938–1939, NA HO 213/302.
53. Stocks, *Rathbone*, pp.244–6.
54. RP XIV.2.13 (26), ULL.
55. Letters of EFR to Eden, Lord Cranborne and Duff Cooper, 7 July 1937, NA FO 371/23.
56. Letter of EFR to Lytton, 27 October 1937, RP XIV.2.13 (33), ULL. Duff Cooper's contentions were challenged on grounds provided by the legal firm, Elwell and Binford Hole, who said he had been poorly advised. He was the only Cabinet minister to resign over Munich. RP XIV.2.13 (34), ULL.
57. Letter of EFR to unknown recipient, 22 July 1937, RP XIV.2.11 (8), ULL.
58. See collection of letters and telegrams between Eleanor and Pursey in RP XIV.2.11 (9–12), ULL, mostly dated July 1937.
59. *Hansard* HC, vol. 324, col. 991, 2 June 1937.
60. Rathbone, *War Can Be Averted*, p.56.
61. Notes for speech, 22 October 1937, RP XIV.3 (43), ULL.
62. Pedersen, *Politics of Conscience*, p.278.
63. Letter dated 4 April 1938, RP XIV.2.13 (37), also Letter of Dean of Canterbury to EFR, 14 April 1938, RP XIV.2.13 (38), ULL.
64. *Hansard* HC vol. 332, cols 1953–7, 9 March 1938. *Hansard* HC, vol. 47, col. 1616, 18 May 1938.
65. E.F. Rathbone, 'British Shipping and the Spanish War: The Government's Attitude', *Liverpool Daily Post*, 21 May 1938, p.5.
66. Letter of EFR to R.A. Butler, 16 April 1938, RP XIV.2.13 (38), ULL.
67. E.F. Rathbone, 'The Bombing of British Ships: Does the Government Intend to Act?', *Manchester Guardian*, 14 June 1938, p.22; *Birmingham Post*, 14 June 1938, p.5; *Yorkshire Post*, 14 June 1938, p.8; 'British Shipping and the Spanish War. The Government's Attitude', *Liverpool Daily Post*, 21 May 1938, p.5, and Rathbone, 'British Shipping and Spain: Miss Eleanor's Reply', 11 June 1938, p.5.
68. Letter of EFR to the National Union of Seamen, 14 June 1938, RP XIV.2.14 (89), ULL.
69. *Hansard* HC, vol. 343, cols 1347–9, 13 February 1939.
70. Ibid.
71. Letter of R.A. Butler, 21 January 1941, RAB 912/51, Trinity College Library, Cambridge University.
72. Stocks, *Rathbone*, p.246.
73. She reached this conclusion having addressed six meetings in late October 1936, attended by LNU members, university graduates and others. See Memo of EFR, 3 November 1936, Rathbone File, 910, BBC Written Archives Centre. There is a possibility, unconfirmed, but suggested in another memo in this file, that William Wedgwood Benn gave a report on Czechoslovakia in November 1936.
74. RP XIV.2.9 (22), ULL.The archive for EFR's Balkan Tour in 1937 is contained in RP XIV.2.9 (1–56), ULL.
75. RP XIV.2.9 (19), ULL.
76. Henlein was the self-appointed leader of the Sudeten-Deutsch Partei. See Rathbone, *War Can Be Averted*, pp.94–7.
77. *Hansard* HC, vol. 321, col. 3120, 25 March 1937.
78. Letter of EFR to Mme Frantiska Plaminkova, 5 March 1937, RP XIV.2.9 (37), ULL, and Letter of Mme Frantiska Plaminkova to EFR, 23 March 1937, RP XIV.2.9 (8), ULL.
79. Letter of EFR to Winston Churchill, 18 April 1938, CHAR/2/374/66, CAC.
80. Letter of EFR to Miss Boyd, 3 March 1937, RP XIV.2.9 (44), ULL.
81. Note of Miss Evelyn Gedge, 13 February 1937, RP XIV.2.9 (31), ULL.
82. Letter of EFR to Miss Boyd, 3 March 1937, RP XIV.2.9 (44), ULL.
83. *Hansard* HC, vol. 413, cols 364–5, 20 August 1945.
84. *Hansard* HC, vol. 276, cols 2761, 2763, 13 April 1933.
85. Report of the General Meeting of the Union of Jewish Women, 19 February 1934, UJW Papers, MS 129/AJ161/16/4, USL.

86. WG/LON/4, William Gillies Papers, Labour History Archive, JRL.
87. For example, *Hansard* HC, vol. 321, cols 3119–22, 25 March 1937; E.F. Rathbone, Notes for Summer Adjournment Debate, 30 July 1937, RP XIV.3 (42), ULL. E.F. Rathbone, Notes for Debate on Foreign Affairs, 21 December 1937, RP XIV.3 (45), ULL.
88. Letter of Hon. Sec to EFR, 9 January 1937, Add 9369, B1/90, CUL.
89. E.F. Rathbone, Notes for speech at IPC conference, Caxton Hall, 22 October 1937, RP XIV.3 (43), ULL.
90. Meeting of 25 February 1938, RP XIV.3 (47), ULL.
91. Letter of EFR to Eden, 24 February 1938, and reply of Eden to EFR, 2 March 1938, RP XIV.6.12, ULL.
92. Meeting held 1 March 1938, RP XIV.3 (49), ULL.
93. RP XIV.3 (51), ULL.
94. LNU meetings, Warrington and Chester; IPC meeting, Leeds, RP XIV.3 (53), ULL.
95. E.F. Rathbone, Notes for Foreign Affairs Debate, 26 July 1938, RP XIV.3 (56), ULL. Also Stocks, *Rathbone*, pp.246–7.
96. E.F. Rathbone, Notes for speech, 26 September 1938, RP XIV.3 (57), ULL.
97. Address of EFR to the University of Manchester graduates, 24 February 1939, and 'A Common Front Would Save the Day', *Manchester Guardian*, 25 February 1939, p.18.
98. Stocks, *Rathbone*, p.259.
99. E.F. Rathbone, Notes for meetings on 1, 2 and 3 April 1939, RP XIV.3 (53), ULL.
100. J. Alberti, *Eleanor Rathbone* (London: Sage, 1996), p.130.
101. E.F. Rathbone, Letter to the Graduate Electors of the Combined English Universities, March 1939, RP XIV.3 (3), ULL.

# PART II

# 5

# *A Humanitarian Disaster Looms: The Czech Refugee Crisis*

Eleanor's concern for refugees, and most specifically Jews fleeing Nazi Europe, developed from 1933 and endured right up until her death in 1946. March 1933 was a defining moment and heralded a remarkable period in her life, for she shifted the focus of her earlier campaigning away from the domestic, social and welfare issues which had, up until then, engaged so much of her time, and consolidated her involvement with foreign affairs. This had begun with her campaigning on behalf of Indian women from 1927, as a newly appointed MP in 1929 championing certain rights for African women, followed by her involvement with women's franchise issues in Palestine. This coincided with Adolf Hitler's accession to power as chancellor of the German Republic on 30 January 1933 and was the point at which her dedication to relieving human suffering crystallized, and when humanitarianism, in its broadest sense, became of paramount importance to her. Throughout the thirteen years that followed she never wavered from her ideological belief in national and personal responsibility, but juxtaposed against this was her growing commitment to Zionism and its ideals, Jews and the Jewish cause.

The reasons why Eleanor embraced the cause of Jewish refugees so passionately are complex and a combination of interrelated factors. There seems little doubt that she was motivated by her identification with Jews. The roots of this included her admiration for their many attributes, including their idealism, values, cultural and societal contributions. There was also her empathy with them as 'Europeans', for they were people with whom she could identify and even consider as kin. And despite being a non-practising Christian, she recognized familiar biblical connections and similarities in religion and culture. Transcending this was the fact that the Jews of Europe were, without doubt, the most vulnerable and helpless victims of an evil regime. Their helplessness resonated with the Victorian ideology of the 'deserving' and the 'undeserving', only now it was Jews who were in need of help rather than the worthy poor. Beliefs such as these would, to an extent, explain why Eleanor did not support the cause of other minority groups such as gypsies, who, despite being singled out by the

Nazi regime as undesirable, had not made their mark on society in a similar fashion as had the Jews. Her vociferous calls for Britain to take responsibility for populations not tied to it by political obligation or control, and for there to be a comprehensive effort to save the Jews, was bound up with both her notions of collective and individual responsibility. Her conscience impelled her to try and mitigate the evils being meted out to Europe's Jews, and to save as many as possible from annihilation. As she often pointed out, other individuals, as well as the government, shared this responsibility, but their failure or reluctance to respond did not absolve her from acting: rather it impelled her to campaign even harder. There was also her humanitarianism, which transcended political boundaries. Beyond all this her actions were certainly underpinned by the philosophical idealism she had absorbed from her family upbringing and tradition, and imbibed from her Oxford tutors.

As Britain moved closer to war, Eleanor's devotion to the twin aims of the welfare and rescue of refugees became of paramount importance, with the two often running concurrently. But the focus of her activities did alter over this period: during the latter part of 1941 there was a change in Nazi policy, with 'emigration', which had been seen by the regime as a solution to the 'Jewish question' halted, and an exterminatory programme fully implemented. It was at this point that Eleanor shifted her campaigning efforts towards the rescue of people rather than dealing with the welfare of those already in Britain.

The first public pronouncement of Eleanor's concern for the future of European Jewry came in a bold statement she made in the House of Commons on 13 April 1933 when she confronted the threat of Nazism to democracy and the lives of the Jews of Europe at that time. As the first woman MP to speak out against Hitler's newly appointed regime, the warnings she articulated were prescient:

> A spirit has come over Germany. One speaker called it a new spirit, but I would rather call it a re-emergence of an evil spirit which bodes very ill for the peace and freedom of the world ... there is one dreadful fact beyond doubt, that is that the (Herr Hitler's [*sic*]) party ... is now in uncontrolled power in Germany and is inflicting cruelties and crushing disabilities on large numbers of law-abiding peaceful citizens, whose only offence is that they belong to a particular race or religion or profess certain political beliefs ... Herr Hitler and his colleagues have let the world see plainly their feelings which they cherish about questions of blood and race.[1]

Eleanor was clearly aware that, in Germany, cumulative and increasingly draconian legislation and strategies intended to disenfranchise and dispossess Jews were being implemented, and that many perceptive German Jews, who feared for their future, had begun to seek safe havens abroad.[2] Nor did she have any doubt about the implications of Nazi policy, with its major theme of anti-Semitism, but she was deeply concerned to see how her country would respond to the threat.

Amongst the wider public, knowledge of the early atrocities aimed at German Jewry received fair coverage in papers such as *The Times*, the *Manchester Guardian* and *The Daily Telegraph*. But as Eleanor observed in a letter to the *Manchester Guardian*, the paper that was particularly supportive of her views:

> Unfortunately, everybody does not, although everybody should, read the '*Manchester Guardian*'. The little that appears on the subject in most journals is insufficient to bring home to their readers the real significance of these events. The general public, jaded with horrors and pre-occupied with its own distresses, only knows vaguely that the German government is persecuting the German Jews, feels sorry about it, and turns to its own affairs.[3]

In her customary determined way, she continued to protest and, within months, was using the columns of *The Times* to argue against those who were encouraging British motorists to travel to, or even pass through Germany en route to Austria.[4] Putting themselves in a position where, as tourists, they had, even for a day, to avail themselves of the protection and authority of the present government was unquestionably wrong in her view. The German government was, she declared, a diabolical and cruel regime, the enemy of freedom of speech, thought and democratic institutions, bent on aggression and conquest, and much else. She invoked the recent words of Sir Austen Chamberlain to explain the bearing these charges had on travelling in Germany: 'We stand for something in this country. Our traditions count, for our own people, for Europe and for the world. Europe is menaced and Germany is afflicted by this narrow, exclusive, aggressive spirit, by which it is a crime to be in favour of peace and a crime to be a Jew.' Such a boycott was, she believed, the only tangible way by which ordinary British citizens could demonstrate their abhorrence of the present German government, which she was sure was influenced by foreign, especially British opinion. It would also demonstrate to ordinary Germans the way in which their country was viewed as 'the leper camp of Europe, which healthy people avoid because they cannot separate the sound from the corrupted'.[5]

Coincidental to her denunciations of Nazi Germany, Eleanor

became acquainted with the women's franchise issue in Palestine, and the threat it posed to Jewish women in particular. The connection between these events might, at first sight, seem tenuous, but Eleanor's introduction to Palestine fostered a deep and lasting respect for the Jews and for Zionism, which developed and endured to the end of her life; the fact that she earned her reputation as the 'MP for refugees' had as much to do with her admiration for the Jews as it did with her humanitarianism. Nowhere was this more clearly demonstrated than in a talk she gave to the Union of Jewish Women in February 1934, shortly before her first visit to Palestine, on the subject of the German refugee problem. She spoke of 'The feeling of gratitude that we all owe to the Jewish people and the consequent desire to do reparation for the undeserved insult that they have suffered. All of us should understand what the world owes to Judaism.' Juxtaposed against this were Britain's collective imperial responsibilities, and Eleanor's view that all subjects of the Empire were bound to resent 'the arrogant and wholly unjustified racial doctrine in which these persecutions have taken their origin'.[6]

She was, meanwhile, deeply involved with the League of Nations Union and her active campaign for collective security. This affiliation afforded her the opportunity of instigating a stronger anti-German campaign than previously, this time trying to impose an economic and social boycott on the country by vigorously discouraging her fellow countrymen from visiting there.[7] Her well-meaning efforts were, however, hampered by no less than royalty, and particularly by the actions of the pro-Nazi King Edward VIII, for he took the completely opposing view by urging the British Legion to 'go to Germany and make friends with the Germans'.[8] Much to her dismay her remonstrations fell on deaf ears, and even with the support of Mr Rodgers of the British Non-Sectarian Anti-Nazi Council, she was unable to persuade any of the tourist agencies that she regularly used, even the Jewish-owned Wayfarers, which included the Workers Travel Association, Cooks and the Wayfarers Travel Agency, to stop promoting German tours.[9] Regrettably, her noble belief that the Nazi government could be induced, through a boycott, 'to give up its persecutions of Jews, by convincing them that persecution does not pay' was, with hindsight, naïve.[10] Nevertheless, her remarks provide a very strong insight into her feelings of nationalism and of British national identity, of the 'good' traditions of being English versus the 'bad' character emerging from German society. Throughout her years of campaigning for refugees she retained a fundamental belief in the innate benevolence within British society, invoking it whenever she could in support of rescue measures, always trusting others, especially those in government, to abide by the principles of responsible citizenship which she held so dearly.

International affairs continued to engage Eleanor through the mid -1930s: there was the crisis in Abyssinia, the looming civil war in Spain and, most particularly, the mounting threat to Czechoslovakia. Anticipation of the annexation of Austria, home to 180,000 Jews, precipitated the prospect of a new influx of refugees from there into Britain, especially in 1936/37, but it was the Anschluss itself in March 1938, that was a turning point in the European refugee crisis, transforming a problem into a catastrophe. The situation in Greater Germany rapidly deteriorated, and the Hitler regime unleashed an unprecedented reign of terror against Jews, characterized by anti-Semitic violence, intimidation and humiliation intended to dehumanize them. As a consequence, the refugee problem escalated exponentially, with serious repercussions being felt abroad, and certainly in Britain, as more and more desperate people sought a safe haven elsewhere. The Anglo-Jewish refugee organizations and the British government each responded in their own way. The most significant of the organizations was the Jewish Refugees Committee, established in the spring of 1933 in response to the first influx of refugees. With no idea of how many people would be seeking refuge, they had not only relieved the British government of all financial responsibility for Jewish refugees from Europe by giving an unlimited guarantee of financial support, but they had also undertaken responsibility for them. For there was always the assumption, amongst many of the Anglo-Jewish community as well as the government, that Britain was only a temporary destination, with Palestine the favoured ultimate destination. One senior official in the Foreign Office even went so far as to refer, in 1935, to Palestine as 'our contribution to the refugee problem'.[11] The Anschluss resulted in an about-turn from the Jewish Refugees Committee who were already under financial strain, for they not only decided to exclude future applicants from the general guarantee given in 1933, but they also imposed a selection process to conserve their dwindling resources.[12]

Likewise, the government restricted the means of entry into the country. The fact was that in 1938 Britain had no formal refugee policy, but rather a continuing aliens policy through the instrument of the Aliens Restriction (Amendment) Act of 1919. Alien immigration was severely restricted and there were sweeping powers in place that provided for deportation. The act had also abolished all rights of appeal to the Immigration Boards so that no trace of legal protection for refugees remained on the statute book. The government's response to the renewed fear of a flood of refugees was to tighten the controls on immigration, including making changes to the entry rules. In March 1938 a confidential Home Office memo noted that the Department of Overseas Trade and the Foreign Office were to be put on notice that a visa system was under consideration, so that they could be ready to advise on any difficulties arising. This requirement, it was noted, could be imposed by an instruction of the secretary of state under Article 1 (3) (h) of the Aliens Order 1920. The new regulation was instituted immediately and from April 1938 hopeful immigrants with German and Austrian passports could no longer travel without having acquired a British visa. This had to be applied for at the point of exit: the government justified the change on the grounds that a pre-selection policy would save refugees the disappointment of being turned away on reaching Britain.[13] But in reality the policy had more to do with regulating the flow and controlling the quality of would-be entrants. It was also seen as a way of preventing anti-alien feeling at home by avoiding the admission of so-called 'unsuitable' refugees. Shifting the problem overseas did alleviate the pressure on Home Office officials at the ports of entry, where chaos was the norm, but if it solved one problem, it effectively created others. At home it precipitated an ever-increasing burden upon staff in London, who became inundated with pleading letters, referrals and personal visits from panic-stricken relatives: abroad, the Foreign Office had to handle the pandemonium created at consular offices in Germany and Austria by the overwhelming numbers of applications for visas from desperate individuals, many of whom queued for days on end.

The Home Office soon found themselves under increasing pressure from activists, including Eleanor, who demanded that they place immigration policy and procedures on the political agenda, and adopt a more humane and generous admissions policy. Eleanor's concern about the way in which officials were handling these humanitarian issues led her to demand the creation of a more formal refugee policy-making machinery in Britain, something she described as a 'new thought-out and co-ordinated policy – national, imperial and international'.[14] The prime minister, Neville Chamberlain, gave her proposal short shrift, informing her that the government was quite satisfied with the current collaborative arrangement and were going to rely upon the recently formed Co-ordinating Committee. This committee, an umbrella group set up, with Home Office encouragement, by the main refugee bodies, provided a new vehicle for the articulation of grievances by refugee organizations, and was intended to produce constructive policy proposals.[15] Amongst the multitude of responsibilities, the voluntary organizations dealt with all correspondence from refugees, so that the government was distanced from the desperate plight of Jews abroad. It was hardly surprising that the government were so keen to make use of the new committee, for not only were they insulated from the reality of the crisis but it absolved them of any responsibility, financial or otherwise, a situation that was reinforced at the subsequent Evian Conference. One outcome of Evian, the international intergovernmental debate on places of refuge and refugee policy held in July 1938, at the behest of President Roosevelt, was the establishment of the Intergovernmental Committee on Refugees (IGCR) 'for the purpose of facilitating the emigration from Austria, and presumably from Germany, of political refugees'.[16] However, Louise London's detailed examination of the IGCR has indicated that the impact on rescue was largely negative, and even undermined other initiatives to save refugees.[17] As for Eleanor's reaction to Evian, she later wrote of Britain's 'uncompromising refusal to depart or ask other States to depart from the fatal principle laid down at the Evian Conference last July, that whatever is done (by Britain) must be limited by the capacity of the voluntary organisations to initiate, finance and carry out schemes of long-term settlement'.[18]

By early September 1938 Eleanor was writing to Henry Wickham-Steed, the journalist and political commentator, expressing her concern over the lack of initiatives being taken by the Czech Association, of which he was chair. The Association had been set up in mid-May as a centre of action and information, yet Eleanor was constantly being asked how the Czech case could best be publicized, and she was anxious to secure audiences for two speakers, Dr Ecer, the Social Democratic vice-mayor of Brio, and Mr Kosina, the international secretary of the Social Democratic Union, both of whom were due to be in Britain around 28 October. It seems that there was dissent over the original Czech Association which some thought was too far to the Left, frightening off those to the Right, and the suggestion now was that the whole body be transformed into a European Association, with subcommittees, the first of which would be a Czech Committee, with Lord Lytton as chairman. Eleanor, Noel-Baker, Wilfrid Roberts, Walter Layton and the Duchess of Atholl were amongst the members. The purpose of the committee, which was part of the original scheme, included 'disseminating correct information on Czechoslovakia and of convincing this country of its vital interest in the preservation of Czechoslovak independence'.[19] Days later Wickham-Steed sent Eleanor information about the proposed Czech weekend, which was planned for around 28 October to coincide with the twentieth anniversary of the declaration of Czech independence, and at which he was to be a principal speaker.[20] This would be just the right platform for her two speakers, but international events were destined to alter these plans, for the growth of tensions between nations was increasing.

The Munich Settlement, signed on 29 September 1938, did resolve the immediate international crisis and delayed war for the time being. However, in its wake came a human tragedy that Eleanor had envisaged. The fear of a German invasion had already precipitated a flow of refugees from the Sudeten areas, and once the region was ceded to Germany, the numbers fleeing to the provinces of Bohemia, Moravia and Slovakia increased dramatically. The Munich agreement included some complicated provision for refugees, ostensibly guaranteeing them a future in the dismembered Czechoslovakia. However, certain groups of people, notably Sudeten Germans, Communists and Jews were afforded no such protection, and these were the people who sought salvation from foreign governments. Britain's response was complicated: as a part of their responsibility for implementing the Munich Settlement, Britain was committed to ensuring that the rights of people in German-controlled areas were upheld. In practice this meant choosing Czech nationality, living in Czech areas and having personal and property rights protected. Despite the fact that the British government had maintained its refusal to provide funds to help refugees from Germany and Austria resettle, the Czechs were a different matter, and were offered financial help with their refugees to ease the economic and monetary difficulties which they faced. Consequently, on 3 October 1938, Chamberlain announced that the government would guarantee a loan of £10 million to Czechoslovakia, £4 million of which was to be given as a gift for the relief and resettlement of refugees within Czechoslovakia and overseas:

> What we feel to be required and justified now is that the action I have mentioned should be taken without any delay, first, to assist the Czechoslovak State in what must be the crisis of its difficulties. The Chancellor of the Exchequer, on behalf of the Government, has addressed a letter to the Bank of England requesting the Bank to provide the necessary credit of £10,000,000 sterling, and when the House resumes its sittings in November, Parliament will be asked to pass the necessary legislation to reimburse the Bank from the Exchequer.[21]

But Eleanor was not happy. She wrote to Noel Baker on 6 October,

> Won't you try to extract some definite answer from the Government as to what further financial help they intend giving to Czechoslovakia besides the £10,000,000 which the Prime Minister described as 'an advance ... to meet urgent needs'?

> There has been so little pressure from the Opposition and I am afraid the government may get away with little more than the first ten million and leave the rest to relief funds. Why not back up Amery's suggestion of the price of one week's war, which Arthur Salter says was £50,000,000? Do try to get some further reassurance from them.[22]

Notwithstanding the promise of funds, Eleanor had already put her name to a statement on the international situation signed by scores of others, expressing relief that they were 'spared the scourge of war' but recording their 'protest and our determination to stand in future for a policy which will not expose this country either to dishonour or to distaste'.[23] Eleanor knew that time was of the essence as far as rescue was concerned, and along with Sir John Hope-Simpson, was soon appealing to Lord Halifax and the Home Office for 2,000 visas for refugees from Czechoslovakia.[24] Attacking the refugee problem from another angle, she swallowed her pride and wrote a pleading letter to her friend Mme Plaminkova on 17 October, hoping that she might have some influence in getting the deportation of ethnic Germans halted. There was palpable outrage in Plaminkova's reply, and she could not contain her disdain for Britain's behaviour: Whose fault was it that Germany had a foothold in her country? Britain had created the problem and it was now her responsibility to provide help to the dispossessed people. Czechoslovakia had barely enough resources for its own people, and could not provide support for the thousands of German and Austrian refugees streaming into the country:

> Not lack of goodwill but of an absolute necessity Czechoslovakia cannot give hospitality to refugees. Now it is the turn of other countries to show that they are aware of the responsibility of their international decisions. Dear Miss Rathborne [*sic*], you ask me how you could help my country! The best help will be to use your influence that the loan which England promised to give to Czechoslovakia would be sufficiently great and under the conditions <u>bearable</u> to us! Of course I hope you understand that this intervention wants to be done without delay!!!![25]

Meanwhile, a new non-sectarian voluntary body, the British Committee for Refugees from Czechoslovakia (BCRC) was formed in late October 1938 to handle the allocation of all funds raised at home, as well as helping settle refugees who might arrive in the United Kingdom. There were three classes of refugee who needed to be extricated quickly – Sudeten Czechs, Sudeten Germans, numbering approximately 30,000, mostly Jews, and some five to six thousand old Reich refugees –

German and Austrians who were already living in Czechoslovakia, half of whom were Jews.[26] Eleanor established close and valuable links with the BCRC, especially with Doreen Warriner, their first representative in Prague, with her successor, Beatrice Wellington, and with Robert Stopford, who worked very closely with Doreen Warriner. Stopford was a banker by profession, and had played an important role in the decision to make government funds available to the Czechs. His recent experience of the country, as part of the failed Runciman Mission, made him an ideal, but reluctant, substitute British liaison officer in Prague, a post that he took up in October 1938, when Edward Playfair of the Treasury was taken ill. His remit was far from straightforward, for besides being responsible for supervising the expenditure of funds, he was to ensure that distribution was free of racial or political discrimination. He also was required to collect information on the refugee problem and send reports back to the Treasury and Foreign Office.[27] Stopford was a man with strong humanitarian instincts, and his work in Prague undoubtedly saved many hundreds of lives.[28] As for any financial support for the Czech refugees, both Hoare and Sir John Simon, the chancellor of the Exchequer, stuck by the official line that a 'general principle in this country [is] that the maintenance of refugees is a matter for voluntary contributions and is not an object to which it would be proper to appropriate public funds'.[29] There were in fact several voluntary funds launched for Czech refugees, including the Lord Mayor of London's Fund, and those set up by the Trades Union Congress, the Labour Party, the *News Chronicle* and *Manchester Guardian,* as well as other organizations, including dozens of ad hoc refugee aid committees all over the country. The Lord Mayor's Fund, inaugurated in September 1938 and closed in July 1939, raised £528,510, mostly from non-Jewish sources, whilst the Council for German Jewry raised in the region of £500,000 by December 1938.

As the crisis in Czechoslovakia deepened, Eleanor became more entrenched in her campaign to help the refugees in Nazi-occupied Europe. She personally convened a group of MPs who pledged to do their individual best on behalf of the country, and by the time the House resumed sitting in November 1938, the government had bowed to pressure, largely from the BCRC, and agreed to grant a single quota of special, limited-stay visas to 250 Sudeten Germans and 100 Old Reich refugees, reflecting the policy of giving priority to 'political refugees'.[30] This was not enough for Eleanor and she continued to challenge what she saw as the unnecessary rigidity and torpidity of the government in respect of immigration quotas, entry permits, financial aid as well as the Czech loan. She urged Sir Samuel Hoare, the home secretary, to consider 'very substantially increasing the number of 350 permits' to enable more of the estimated several thousand in danger of being driven back into the hands of the enemy to come to Britain. She was insistent that the government had a large measure of responsibility for the refugee situation, but could only secure Hoare's agreement to 'consider cases individually and sympathetically' (see Plate 15).[31]

Amongst her informants on the Czech situation was Miss Warriner, but she also received news from Gabriel Carritt, the son of Edgar Carritt, professor of philosophy at Oxford, whom she had sent out to Prague in early October 1938, on behalf of the National Council for Civil Liberties (NCCL).[32] According to a Special Branch report written on 5 November, Carritt was identified as the British Communist Party agent in Prague, whose principal task was to ensure that a good proportion of the refugees who were evacuated were Party members. Bruce Binfold Hole and Eleanor were, according to the chief constable, effectively in control of the NCCL refugee sub-committee, and in order to obtain permission for Carritt to go out to Prague, Hole had needed to impress upon Eleanor the need for a responsible person to be on the ground to ensure an equitable distribution of the visas, so that the majority did not go to Social Democrats. Eleanor 'fell in' with the suggestion and immediately arranged with the LNU for Carritt to go. The chief constable had good reason to believe that Eleanor knew that Hole was a member of the Communist Party – as were many of the Czech refugees that came to Britain – and there was an implied suggestion that she was acting improperly, but in the end the report was so delayed that it was deemed unnecessary to send it on to Butler, for there was no action to be taken.[33]

Another source of information was William Gillies, the secretary of the International Department of the Labour Party, who bumped into Eleanor in the Lobby of the House of Commons on the evening of 9 November, and gave her a 'very detailed and intimate description of what was happening in Prague and what was being attempted'. His view was that 'if Miss Rathbone and others make representations on the matter (of visas) to the Home Office we should encourage them rather than interfere'. Eleanor needed little encouragement, for the very next day, with Carritt back in Britain, she wrote to Butler, asking him if he could obtain leave for even temporary entry for the four men whose names she supplied and who had been identified as being in grave danger. They had, it seemed, been removed from the permit request list by either the Home Office or the Foreign Office, probably because they were thought to be Communists, but they were threatened with death or torture in a concentration camp if they could not get out of Prague and Czechoslovakia. Butler's reply, that this was a matter for the Home Office, not him, was not the end of the matter, for he did promise to have it investigated. In the interim, Eleanor, in the company of Harold Nicolson, Harold Macmillan, T.E. Harvey and Mr Henderson-Stewart, went, as a deputation, to the chancellor of the duchy of Lancaster in the hope of gaining his support for the endangered political refugees. This door was firmly closed as such matters 'were not within the purview of the IGCR'.[34]

Eleanor, Carritt, Hole and all the other campaigners must have been pleased with the outcome of this small campaign, for on 1 December, Butler was able to write to Eleanor and confirm that permission had been granted for the four named men to come to Britain for a limited period. This was an achievement, for a Foreign Office official, P.L. Rose, had questioned whether 'these people were in imminent danger?' His remarks were based on a lack of official confirmation, even though he admitted that the Foreign Office had plenty of unofficial corroboration.[35]

Outside the House, Eleanor stepped up her campaign by trying to mobilize the support of other groups whom she thought could be influential. Amongst these was the British Federation of University Women, of which she was a founder member. The Federation which had, by 1938, established their own Emergency Refugee Committee, was asked to bring pressure to bear on the prime minister, MPs and Home and Foreign Office officials to secure admission for a much larger number of refugees, 'perhaps 1,000 or 2,000' and for the government to 'give a financial grant for their maintenance'. Strong words accompanied her request:

> Remember what we owe these refugees. They are the greatest sufferers from the Agreement which Mr Chamberlain made with Herr Hitler at Munich. They are not the ordinary type of destitute alien, but men and women whose only offence is that they have been leaders in their own districts in standing up against Nazi doctrines. There is reason to believe that unless they are got out quickly, perhaps within the next fortnight or so, it may be too late. Women's organizations are accustomed to taking quick action in good causes. Hence this letter.[36]

Immediate evacuation, as Eleanor subsequently wrote, was urgent.[37]

*Kristallnacht*, the pogrom against Jews that erupted throughout Germany and Austria on the nights of 9 and 10 November 1938 elicited an immediate, but not necessarily sustained response from Britain. There were outraged public protests, and within days Neville Chamberlain told the Commons that the government would be 'taking into consideration any possible way in which we can assist these people'.[38]

But it became evident that although action was seen to be necessary, the government had no clear idea of what to do about Jews fleeing persecution.[39] The full Cabinet discussed the so-called 'Jewish Problem' and the immediate need for large-scale refuge on 16 November 1938,[40] precipitating various suggestions as to places of safety in British colonies. Countries mooted included Northern Rhodesia, British Guiana and Kenya, but very little came of these proposals.

The Home Office continued to oppose the mass immigration of refugees, and maintained its policy of pre-selection, admission being linked to employment or re-emigration. Hoare warned the House of Commons of the dangers of allowing a 'stagnant pool' of refugees to grow in the United Kingdom.[41] Only in the case of children were entry restrictions eased considerably, and the admissions procedure streamlined, with Hoare agreeing that children could enter 'without the slow procedure of passports and visas'. By August 1939, 9,354 children, the majority of whom were Jewish, had been rescued from Germany on Kindertransports, 7,800 of them arriving in the United Kingdom between January and August of that year.[42]

Eleanor recognized that the escalating refugee crisis called for a cohesive lobbying group and her initiative, the Parliamentary Committee on Refugees (PCR), established in November 1938, was a brilliant move on her part. Its all-party composition enabled MPs of all political shades to exert pressure on the government, and since the majority of its members, indeed of the government itself, were Christians, it could never justifiably be said that there was parti-pris influence from within in favour of Jews. As a direct response to the refugee crisis, its remit, which was outlined in a letter to the *Manchester Guardian* on 4 January 1939, was to act as a pressure group to 'influence the government and public opinion in favour of a generous yet carefully safeguarded refugee policy'.[43] Despite the official-sounding title, the group was entirely voluntary, and included many of Eleanor's stalwart supporters amongst its members. For example, co-founders were David Grenfell, Labour MP for Gower and her ally from the NJCSR, Sir Arthur Salter, Independent MP for the University of Oxford and her associate from the LNU, and her staunch supporter, Victor Cazalet, a member of her 1929 Committee for the Protection of Coloured Women in the Crown Colonies.[44] Cazalet, the appointed chairman, had come to admire Eleanor enormously, and was, like her, a Gentile Zionist.[45] He had been galvanized into action following a visit to Vienna in April 1938, where he witnessed the dire condition of the city's Jews.[46] Lord Marley and H. Graham White, MP for Birkenhead East, were appointed vice-chairmen, and Eleanor the honorary secretary.[47] Summing up Eleanor's pre-eminent role within the committee, Cazalet remarked, in 1942, that she was 'a saint for doing everything and paying for most things'.[48] In fact there were donations from individuals which helped supplement Eleanor's financing; these included Mr Wolf, 'a very rich Jew (in Holland) who is giving his money and time to our Refugee cause', whilst another regular contributor from the outset was Sigmund Gestetner, a successful Jewish businessman and member of the Committee for Development of Refugee Industries.[49] Eleanor's devotion to the PCR was far from exclusive, for she had many other commitments and strings to her bow. Besides her parliamentary duties, she was involved with numerous refugee-related organizations. These included her role as patron of the Youth Relief and Refugee Council[50] and her membership of the Friendly (later Refugee) Aliens Protection Committee, the Council on Aliens (COA), the Committee for Development of Refugee Industries (whose major concern was the effect of the recent government regulations on the refugee industries),[51] the Central Committee on Refugees, which dispensed government grants,[52] and the Advisory Committee of the Czech Refugee Trust. That she was able to summon up the energy for all these obligations was a reflection of her deeply rooted need to 'do what could be done' to help others: never had the need been greater, and there was an urgency about saving lives and ameliorating the harshness and injustice of internment policies that impelled her as never before.

The most pressing commitment that PCR had to deal with was the refugee crisis in Czechoslovakia, and Eleanor and Harold Nicolson were amongst a deputation of MPs who met Sir John Simon on 19 December 1938. The delegates were there pleading for more money to be given to the refugees, and made a great appeal to the chancellor. Robert Stopford, who was an accidental bystander at the meeting, witnessed the visible shock on Sir John's face when Eleanor asked him, 'would (you) rather be a rat in a trap about to be drowned in a bucket of water or a free man living in a free country?'[53] It seems that Stopford's presence gave the deputees the feeling that they were being taken seriously and indeed, when they had left, Stopford recorded how the chancellor told him that 'he was very much impressed with what they had said and felt he must ask for authority to increase the amount of the loan, and add another five hundred thousand pounds to the free gift for the refugees, if he found it necessary'.[54] But his decision was clearly not enough, for Eleanor noted that the government would only agree to make 'adequate provision in foreign exchange for all refugees from Czechoslovakia emigrating to other countries'.[55] They would not commit any financial provision to the cash-strapped voluntary organizations, and nor did they intend the Czech loan to finance the settlement of refugees in Britain, although, as Louise London has pointed out, the money came to be seen as a means to this end.[56]

Eleanor was kept well informed about the situation by her BCRC contacts, especially Doreen Warriner, who visited England in late December 1938. Miss Warriner, much of whose work was undertaken secretly, had just, at considerable risk to herself, accompanied a group of 150 women and children across the German frontier en route to rejoin their menfolk who had already been allowed into Britain.[57] She and Eleanor disagreed as to whether to press the government for another 300 visas: Miss Warriner confided in Miss Layton, the committee secretary, that Eleanor was against the idea as she felt it likely to 'spoil the larger issue', but as the larger issue – the financial agreement which was guaranteed but not finalized – was not due to be decided for at least two weeks, Miss Warriner was against any further delay.

Ten days later she wrote an impassioned letter to Eleanor, in which she recounted the desperate situation. She had applied for visas for another twelve people who had not been given expulsion orders but needed to be got out 'secretly and quickly', for if they were found out they would be 'handed in and executed'. She described the 'painful experience of visiting the camps, and the conditions in two of them, Delni Mesto and Delni Krupa, which were unbearable'. In the latter, an insanitary and rat-ridden, ruined castle with broken floors and windows, and fungus growing on the walls, four children had died of diphtheria before Christmas. It was no wonder that a local doctor called it 'a living grave'.[58] As far as Miss Warriner was concerned, the most serious issue was the small numbers on the lists. There were 5,000 people in the camps and yet the BCRC had only sanctioned 100 visas, and this was despite Gillies and Grenfell agreeing, in Eleanor's presence, to 300 visas. All concerned knew that money was not an issue, and Miss Warriner begged Eleanor to 'urge them to anticipate the final decision and grant two hundred more visas'. The question of the camp conditions worried Miss Warriner immensely, and she was determined that Eleanor should concentrate her attentions on these, rather than be too much influenced by the question of the expulsion orders.[59] Finally she pleaded, 'I hope you will come, if you cannot, do you think I should come and see your Committee? I begin to feel that someone must come here. I doubt if the Commission will see the camps.'[60]

Eleanor was unable to resist such an impassioned call, and having turned down an invitation from Jan Masaryk, the Czech diplomat, to visit Prague earlier in June 1938,[61] she now made immediate plans to visit the beleaguered city.[62] She realized that if her plea for the Czech refugees was to carry any weight, she needed to back up her case with hard, first-hand evidence.[63] Even the prophetic words of Sir Hector Hetherington, the vice-chancellor of Glasgow University, who warned that her trip would be 'a rather painful experience', did not deflect her.[64] Miss Warriner recorded how she arrived

> with that splendid energy and determination to get to the truth which inspired her work in the Parliamentary Committee. She, unlike so many who came out to Prague, did realise that the Czech Government was absolutely powerless, and that there was no protection for the refugees if Hitler really wanted them.[65]

During the course of her brief visit, which took place between 14 and 20 January 1939, Eleanor visited ten camps, having requested that she be taken to the worst of them. Her impression of the conditions was better than she had expected, although they were far from satisfactory. What bothered her was the lack of work or occupation for the men in particular, for many of the women were fully taken up with childcare. She knew that the Czechs were avid readers, so she suggested that Miss Warriner ask 'one of her rich Jewish friends' (the Jews, she was told, apparently owned most of the innumerable book shops in Prague) to give 'a handsome present of Czech and German books' to the refugees.[66] She also encountered Nicholas Winton, a young English stockbroker, whose personal crusade facilitated the rescue of hundreds of Czech children.[67] Winton recalled showing her around the camps, and was impressed by the great interest she took in the condition of the refugees. But his abiding memory was of an absent-minded lady who left her handbag behind, rather mirroring an earlier trip to Bucharest, when she mislaid her coat and umbrella.[68] Such anecdotes serve as a reminder of Eleanor's character, outwardly unworldly and forgetful, but inwardly so preoccupied with her work and innermost thoughts that she was oblivious to mundane matters. Reference to Winton and his actions also raises the question of where Eleanor fitted into the rescue of children in particular from Nazi-occupied Europe. Frank Field maintained that, in 1996 'the Holocaust Education Trust reunited some of the children whose lives she saved', implying a significant level of personal involvement.[69] However, this is an example of the uncertainty surrounding Eleanor's rescue work, and is not substantiated by evidence. Despite her close contact with innumerable people connected with Winton's rescue, including Sir Walter Layton, editor of the *Economist* from 1922 to 1938, and proprietor of the *News Chronicle*, and his sister Miss Layton, as well as Beatrice Wellington and Doreen Warriner, both refugee officers for the BCRC, she was not involved with his or their mission. Nor is there any evidence to suggest that she was directly involved with the Kindertransports, organized under the auspices of the Movement for the Care of Children from Germany (MCCG), an umbrella organization of numerous aid groups responsible for saving children from Germany and Austria.[70] Zena Herman, a member of Youth Aliyah who was present at the laying of the foundation stone at the Eleanor Rathbone House in Magdiel, near Tel Aviv, in October 1948, maintained that Eleanor 'used her own private means to extend help to all those in need, but chiefly children ... She was directly responsible for the rescue of hundreds of Jewish children', but she also asserted that Eleanor 'was the headmistress of a School for Girls in Oxford'. The latter statement was definitely not true, which throws into a question the veracity of her other claims about Eleanor's involvement in rescue.[71] Such discrepancies only serve to confuse matters. What can be said is that Eleanor was well acquainted with Sir Wyndham Deedes, another Gentile Zionist and one of the joint chairmen of the MCCG, and that she had a working relationship, through the PCR, with Wilfred Israel, scion of a wealthy Anglo-German family, who was responsible for setting up the infrastructure of this rescue scheme. One Kinder, Bertha Engelhard (later Leverton) who arrived in England in July 1939, did write to Eleanor in 1943, but this was in connection with helping her parents gain permission to enter Britain from Lisbon.[72] Nor does Eleanor's name appear on the extant list of contributors to the Central British Fund.[73] In the light of this uncertainty it would be prudent to conclude that Eleanor was probably directly or indirectly involved in helping some child refugees come to Britain, but not necessarily on the Kindertransports.

Apart from the camp visits, Eleanor made it her business to meet as many people as she could, the chief ones being Vladislav Klumpar, the Minister of Social Welfare and Health who was responsible for refugee work, and Dr Ivan Krno, the under secretary for Foreign Affairs. Besides them she met with the heads of many of the refugee groups, including Siegfried Taub, secretary general of the Sudeten-German Social Democratic Party,[74] Mr Dolling, leader of the Sudeten-German Communists, Mr Peres for the Sudeten-German Liberals, Madame Smolka, chair of the Central Committee for Reich Refugees and head of Hizem, the Jewish aid agency and Mr Rudolf Katz for the Reich Germans. Then there were the journalists: Eric Gedye for the *Daily Telegraph* and *New York Times*, John Segrue of the *News Chronicle*,[75] and Alec Dickson, who was then working freelance, to say nothing of members of the British legation, notably John Troutbeck, the First Secretary,[76] as well as Sir Ronald Macleay, the chairman of the Lord Mayor's Fund,[77] and Mr Sams, the fund's Prague representative.[78] She may also have met Miss M. Hughes, an ex-Somervillian and acquaintance of Miss Warriner, who was working with the Quakers and with refugees in Prague, whose letter reached Eleanor when she was already in the city. Miss Hughes wanted to discuss the practical difficulties of getting the refugees to England – how visas could be obtained more quickly, and how a reasonable form of (financial) guarantee could be secured for a limited period, 'as people can't undertake it for life'.[79] There can be no doubt that Eleanor's comprehension of the many nuances of the Czech refugee problem was enhanced as a result of her visit to Prague. The claim often made by British government officials, that she did not really understand the complexity of the refugee crisis, may have been repeated as a way of deflecting her persistent pressure, but if so it was a tactic which failed. But whether she was really able to understand the Czech mentality is another matter. For, as Miss Warriner wrote some years later, 'they were difficult people to know, intensely reserved, and with no capacity to put themselves over – I noticed how English visitors – Layton and Miss Rathbone for instance, did not seem to make contact with them in spite of trying to do so. They are an acquired taste.'[80] Miss Warriner also told Eleanor that time was running out for the refugees – she reckoned there were about six weeks left in which to achieve rescue, but shipping facilities for no more than 200 each week, even if visas were issued at that rate. For Eleanor's part, she thought Warriner was nervous and tired and inclined to exaggerate, but she nevertheless set about, on her return home, demanding immediate aid for the doomed Czechs.

In the 'very urgent and strictly confidential' report that she produced for the PCR on 20 January 1939, Eleanor maintained that 'no one I saw in Prague (except perhaps Sir John Maclay) shares the optimistic views that I heard expressed in London before leaving'. The fact that certain individuals, including Mr Sams and Mr Troutbeck, seemed to spend much of their time in their offices meant that they were out of touch with general feeling. She found the general attitude to be very pessimistic, and personally thought the situation was so 'menacing' that she found herself pleading with the BCRC to take 'bold action and persuade the government to agree to their taking it.' Added to this was her suggestion, boldly underlined, that 'both the British Committee and the British Government will incur a frightful responsibility if through the interminable delays, the opportunity [for rescue] is lost and these men perish'.[81] Parliamentary questions were fired in quick succession,[82] and when the Czechoslovakia (Finance Assistance) Bill was discussed in the House on 7 February 1939, she went against the tide of opinion by expressing concern that almost every speaker in the debate welcomed the Bill without criticizing the actual terms. Her doubts reflected her sense of responsibility, both personal and collective, and hinged upon whether the Bill did 'full justice to our obligations towards Czechoslovakia', and whether:

> we are really paying the debt that we owe to that people for the sacrifice that we demanded of her, a debt which we owe not only to Czecho-Slovakia [*sic*] as a State but to every one of her citizens who is now leading a shrunken life, with poorer prospects of employment and poorer social services because of the sacrifices which have been forced upon her.[83]

Two days later Eleanor was questioning Sir John Simon as to what influence Robert Stopford would have over the choice of refugees and the priority given to different individuals to benefit from the funds. How would he decide who was to receive money and could he be persuaded to give preference to people who could 'pull strings'?[84] Sir John's assurance of Stopford's ability to deal fairly was not misplaced,[85] for he was a man with strong humanitarian instincts who 'proved able to inspire trust and win friends on all sides in Czechoslovakia and became an effective advocate for refugees'.[86] He even admitted much later on that he was involved, unofficially, with illegal emigration, but kept this activity undercover, 'as it would have ruined my official work'.[87]

Eleanor's visit to Prague had an enduring and profound effect on her, and this was evident in the celebrity lecture she delivered to Sheffield University Union of Students in mid-February 1939. This was a broad-ranging, hard-hitting and critical lecture which was quite out of character for her: the traditional philosophical bias was absent and instead she addressed head-on the issue of racial persecution, reflecting her deeply seated feelings of responsibility for its victims. The most chastening feature was her conclusion that 'nearly every receiving country has raised high walls with narrow, closely guarded doors, the highest walls and narrowest doors have been around Great Britain'.[88] Equally candid was her unpalatable view of a country whose inaction diminished national self-esteem and whose generosity and hospitality was, to say the least, questionable.

As Germany stepped up the pressure on military preparations, it became clear that the Munich Settlement, ostensibly meant to maintain the peace, was worthless. Final proof came on 15 March 1939 when Hitler's troops seized Prague and occupied the rest of the Czech state. This came as no surprise to Eleanor, nor should it have surprised the British government, for warnings were apparently being given by a variety of different sources in Prague, and other capital cities, some ten days before of the likely date of invasion. In the House, the prime minister refused to be drawn on what the government did or did not know,[89] but, as Eleanor confided in Churchill, she was convinced that either the Foreign Office had ignored warnings from representatives in

Berlin and Prague of Hitler's intentions to invade around 15 March, or the representatives had failed to warn the government of the symptoms. Both she and Churchill were agreed that the government's secret service information from abroad was apparently inadequate, confirmed in Eleanor's mind by the fact that the British Legation in Prague had failed to 'pick the brains of some of the German refugees in Czech who were often well-informed'.[90]

As soon as Eleanor heard the news of the invasion she phoned Doreen Warriner in Prague and told her that anyone whom the latter recommended for a visa would receive one. But as Miss Warriner later recorded, 'The German general staff were milling around the [telephone] box ... so I felt this decision was probably too late'.[91] And her plea to Eleanor's fellow refugee activist and MP, David Grenfell, to come out to Prague urgently, as she thought he could be of service, was unsuccessful, as he was advised not to apply for a visa.[92] Mme Plaminkova, who refused to leave Czechoslovakia, was amongst one of 5,000 people arrested by the Gestapo in Prague, and was later executed by the Nazis. For Eleanor, Hitler's incursion into Czechoslovakia confirmed her worst fears and precipitated a diatribe against the government officials who, for two and a half years, had ignored her prophetic warnings.[93] In the most heated of her numerous telephone conversations with Mr Randall of the Foreign Office on 21 March 1939, she cautioned that government ambivalence was costing men, women and children their lives. Recognizing that such a desperate situation called for desperate measures, she begged him to allow the transfer of small sums of money in the diplomatic bag, and so facilitate a small rescue mission, remarking cynically that 'most of the men might have been saved if the government had been as prompt in its action in rescuing them as it has been this week in rescuing the remnant of the Czech loan'. With an added note of sarcasm, she wrote that 'this would be "irregular" and your legation at Prague may be trusted to countenance no irregularities for an object towards which they have always shown complete indifference'.[94] Her evidence for this came from her own visit to Prague weeks before, for she later confided in Winston Churchill, telling him how she had heard from everyone there 'that the British Legation was completely aloof, uninterested and unhelpful over refugee questions'. This was in contrast to how Mary Stocks recalled the situation, for she wrote of how Miss Warriner was 'working away at visas and transport arrangements with "the extremely helpful" British Consul'.[95]

Randall's minuted response demonstrated his disdain for her cause and for the refugees, and here, as on other occasions, he exhibited a defensive and narrowly nationalistic attitude in his dealings with her:

> Having consulted Treaty and Passport Control Departments I am going to try and soothe Miss Rathbone's injured feelings by conversation. She is particularly indignant because I refused to transmit English currency to Prague by the Foreign Office bag, ostensibly for British subjects but really for refugees in hiding. It is difficult to persuade people like Miss Rathbone that the consciousness of the necessity for an all-round view, and for maintaining good faith or at least good relations between us and the Germans is not cynical, inhuman indifference.[96]

His impatience with her and other activists was demonstrated in remarks he subsequently made about her staunch activist colleague, Colonel Josiah Wedgwood, and how impossible it was to keep pace with his letters, etc., for 'we already have sufficient difficulty with the recognised members of the PRC [*sic*] who are in a special category'.[97] Indeed his lack of sympathy with the plight of Jews was only matched by the zealous and ingenious way in which he tried to outmanoeuvre campaigners, Eleanor included. Randall, a Catholic convert, later defended the actions of Pope Pius XII against charges that he failed to do enough to save the Jews in *The Pope, the Jews and the Nazis* (1963), published by the Catholic Truth Society. He also expounded his own view of rescue attempts, claiming that efforts by governments 'were bound to be puny compared with the horrible reality', but, as Louise London notes, despite the hostility of officials like Randall, and despite the daunting obstacles and objections, it proved possible to initiate valuable humanitarian action to save Jews.[98]

The sincerity of Eleanor's personal feelings on the refugee problem were reinforced far more publicly in an article published in the *New Statesman and Nation* in April 1939:

> For forty years I have been successively in close touch with many forms of human maladjustment, destitution and injustice. But never – except perhaps over certain Indian questions – have I dwelt in such a Heartbreak House as the Refugee problem. It is just as though one stood hour after hour, day after day, with a small group of people outside bars behind which hordes of men, women and children were enduring every kind of deliberately inflicted physical and mental torture. We scrape at the bars with little files. A few victims are dragged painfully one by one through gaps. And all the time we are conscious that streams of people are passing behind us unaware of or indifferent to what is happening, who could if they united either push down the bars and rescue the victims, or – much more dangerously – stop the torturers.[99]

Like so much of Eleanor's writing and speeches, this was almost poetic in tone, and only the hardest heart could have failed to be moved by its poignancy. Her language was not insincere for she was passionate about the plight of refugees, and nor was it employed purely to engage her audience. Neither was it exaggerated, for she laid great emphasis upon supporting any claims with carefully researched facts and figures. Rather, the *New Statesman* piece was a well-crafted combination of rhetoric in which she argued about the practical politics of rescue and criticized the government's standpoint. The question of responsibility for the plight of the Jews was complex, but had as much to do with individuals as it had to do with the consequence of political actions. The Jews, she wrote, were not to blame for the persecution that was being heaped upon them for they, unlike political refugees who chose danger, 'had it thrust upon them as a consequence of their race'. Her readers, she argued, were the collective 'we', who were not responsible for creating 'anti-Semitism or Nazi-Fascism, except so far as these are the products of Versailles, of non-enforcement of the Minority Treaties, or of the abandonment of collective security'. But this same 'we' had brought about 'the destruction of Czechoslovakia through Munich, and of Spain through the hypocrisies of the Non-Intervention policy' and was 'most directly responsible for those [refugees] in or from Czechoslovakia or Spain'.[100] Her philosophical views on the nature of personal responsibility are worth recounting, for they reflect the various influences which shaped her ideology:

> As to responsibility, some people apparently feel it only for the evil they actually do: others feel guilty of every bit of evil in the world which they or their nations – with which they identify themselves – fail to prevent, provided it was possible to prevent or try to prevent it without creating a greater evil or neglecting a more important duty.[101]

Eleanor accepted her own measure of guilt, equating it to the principle inherent in Christian teaching concerning individual duty to one's neighbour. Once again, her writing was infused with references to the way in which her sense of pride in being British had been challenged, even seriously undermined. For despite its 'resources of wealth, land and influence', she was ashamed that her country could be so ungenerous in contributing towards a solution to the refugee crisis, accusing the nation of 'petty meanness'. The scorn she heaped upon government ministers, whose responses to questions in Parliament were a litany of rehearsed conciliatory statements, excuses and platitudes, was unrestrained. Of the 'serried row of rather uninspiring personalities upon the Treasury Bench' she wrote 'I am tempted to wish that they had indeed a collective soul, which could be condemned to spend eternity in seeing and feeling the torments which their policy has caused others to continue enduring, while their individual souls reposed blissfully in some insipid Paradise, listening to music played upon antiquated instruments'.[102] The only people to be exonerated from blame in this diatribe were 'the kindly, courteous, overworked officials of the government departments responsible for carrying out policy', amongst whom she included William Horace Montagu-Pollock, who briefly held the post of a first secretary at the Foreign Office until he was transferred to Stockholm in May 1939. He, in turn, wrote of how he found himself regarded as the 'guardian angel of refugees' who was 'inundated with (a) daily bunch of letters from Miss Rathbone MP'.[103] But her sound proposal of 'reasonably generous admission of those known to be in serious danger, for safe-keeping under supervision, coupled with the speeding up of arrangements for large-scale settlement overseas, financed by an international or colonial development loan' was clearly not going to figure on the British political agenda.[104]

Eleanor's approach to R.A. Butler was more successful. She stressed to him the urgency of her requests: 'they may seem trivial, but if you heard the tragic stories of suicides, men irrevocably lost to the Gestapo etc. which have already occurred through delays in the working of the British machinery, you would not think the matter trivial'.[105] He was asked for extra staff and office space to be provided in Prague to deal with the increased demand for visas and other documents, a request that was acted upon.[106] Eleanor's suggestion that representation be made to the Polish government, asking them not to hand Czech refugees over to the Germans, was also undertaken.[107] But it was a lengthy, impassioned letter from Miss Wellington, the only experienced refugee officer left working in Prague in April 1939, that precipitated an even more intense campaign. Her correspondence described the overwhelming workload, the miseries endured by the Jews at the hands of the Gestapo and the obstacles created by the Passport Control Office (PCO):

> which are almost greater than those created by the Gestapo … refusing visas on cards sans lists (even though it must be admitted that no one could have a card without being on some list), making obstructions over small mistakes in cards, refusing to recognise the possibility of a name on a card being spelt differently on a passport than on a card or HO list, and sending back passports not visaed [*sic*] time after time …

to say nothing of the interminable delays and, crucially, the lack of time left in which to save lives.[108] Following a small conference held between the PCR and representatives of the principal refugee organizations – including Miss Layton and Miss Warriner, who had intimate knowledge of the Czech refugee plight – Eleanor wrote again to Butler, with three further suggestions for improving the machinery affecting Czech refugees. She suggested that the PCO in Prague be empowered to grant visas to persons recommended by Miss Wellington, without necessarily waiting for a permit from the Home Office. There was Miss Warriner's suggestion that 'the British Consul in the Sudeten area should be empowered to grant a "travel document" to any woman on a list sent to him from the British Czech Committee in London'. And she urged that diplomatic bags be sent more frequently between Prague and London to minimize delays.[109] Much to the chagrin of Reginald Parkin, deputy head of the Passport Control Department, it seemed that a precedent for this course of action had been set by the PCO in Warsaw, strictly against Foreign Office regulations.[110]

Eleanor was also busy in other quarters, asking Osbert Peake, parliamentary undersecretary for home affairs, if he would authorize the PCO to grant up to five visas per week off his own bat. This question resulted in some extraordinary minuted notes between officials, whereby Eleanor was deliberately misled. She was to be told that unless the Czech committee sponsored the proposal it would be impossible for the Home Office to consider it. But in reality, as E.N. Cooper, an undersecretary in the Aliens Department dealing with refugee matters, reminded Randall in July 1939, 'As a matter of fact, the PCO has, as you know, a limited discretion with regard to the grant of visas, and the Home Office would not wish to oppose an arrangement of the kind contemplated in Miss Eleanor's letter if the PCO found no reasons against it'.[111]

NOTES

1. *Hansard* HC, vol. 276, cols 2761, 2763, 13 April 1933.
2. For this period of Nazi history, see M. Marrus, *The Holocaust in History* (London: Weidenfeld and Nicolson, 1988). There were some Jews who had already seen the writing on the wall and either left Germany before 1933, or, like Albert Einstein, decided not to return there from elsewhere in Europe. See S. Friedlander, *Nazi Germany and the Jews: The Years of Persecution 1933–39* (London: Weidenfeld and Nicolson, 1997).
3. EFR, 'Democracy's Fight for Life', *Manchester Guardian,* 2 May 1933, RP XIV.2 (6), University of Liverpool (ULL).
4. Letter of EFR to the Editor, *The Times*, 11 August 1933, RP XIV.2.6 (5), ULL.
5. Letter of EFR to the Editor, *The Times*, 11 August 1933, RP XIV.2.6 (5), ULL.
6. Report of the General Meeting of the Union of Jewish Women, 19 February 1934, UJW Papers, MS 129/ AJ161/16/4, USL.
7. Reply of EFR to Robert Fenn, 29 October 1935, RP XIV.2.6 (11), ULL.
8. Letter of M. Franklin to EFR, 7 February 1936, RP XIV.2.6 (16), ULL.

9. Letter of Rodgers to EFR, 5 February 1936, RP XIV.2.6 (16), ULL. M. Stocks, *Eleanor Rathbone: A Biography* (London: Victor Gollancz, 1949), p.227.
10. Notes by EFR on Commander Locker-Lampson's Letter, 6 February 1936, RP XIV.2.6 (12), ULL.
11. M.D. Peterson, 18 February 1935, NA FO 371/19676, W1370/356/98, f.13.
12. For the most comprehensive and incisive examination of the complexities and nuances of this situation, see L. London, *Whitehall and the Jews, 1933–1948: British Immigration Policy and the Holocaust* (Cambridge: Cambridge University Press, 2000), pp.58ff.
13. Minute of Mr Strang, 12 March 1938, NA FO 371/33287.
14. EFR, 'Great Britain and the Refugees: The Government's Niggardly Policy', *Manchester Guardian*, 23 May 1938, p.16.
15. *Hansard* HC, vol. 336, cols 834–6, 23 May 1938.
16. US Embassy, Memo, 24 March 1938, Nobel to A. Shillito, 28 March 1938, NA T160/842/F13577/01/1.
17. London, *Whitehall and the Jews*, pp.91–4.
18. EFR, 'A Personal View of the Refugee Problem', *The New Statesman and Nation*, 15 April 1939, p.569.
19. May 1938, NBKR 4/163, CAC.
20. Letters of EFR to Wickham-Steed, 3, 6 September 1938; Letters of Wickham-Steed to EFR, 6, 9 September 1938, RP XIV.2.15 (1), ULL.
21. *Hansard* HC, vol. 339, col. 47, 3 October 1938; London, *Whitehall and the Jews*, p.46.
22. Letter of EFR to Noel-Baker, 6 October 1938, NBKR 4/163, CAC.
23. Statement, 2 October 1938, NBKR 4/146/1, CAC.
24. Telegram of EFR to Cecil, 10 October 1938, BL, Add Mss 51141, Cecil Papers, f.278.
25. Letter of Senator Plaminkova to EFR, 28 October 1938, RP XIV.2.15 (5), ULL.
26. Interview of Miss Layton at Home Office, 19 January 1940, NA KV 2/2714/14a.
27. Phillips to Stopford, 31 October 1938, NA FO 371/21576, C13311/2320/12, f.56.
28. London, *Whitehall and the Jews*, pp.146–7.
29. *Hansard* HC, vol. 340, cols 369–70, 380, 3 November 1938.
30. Sir Walter Layton to Halifax, enclosing Memo, 'Emigration of refugees from Czecho-slovakia', 28 October 1938, NA T160/1324/F13577/05/1.
31. *Hansard* HC, vol. 340, col. 370, 3 November 1938.
32. Letter of Gabriel Carritt to the editor, *The Gownsman* (Cambridge), 19 November 1938, p.10, NA HO 294/53.
33. Special Branch Report, 5 November 1938, NA FO 371/21587/C14473, f.159.
34. Report on deputation, 16 November 1938, NA FO 371/21587/C14299.'
35. Letter of W. Gillies to Miss Layton, 10 November 1938, NA HO 294/53. Letter of EFR to Butler, 10 November 1938 and Letter of Butler to EFR, 11 November 1938, both NA FO 371/C13384/11896/12. Report on Deputation, 16 November 1938, NA FO 371/21587/C14299. Letter of Home Office to Makins, 21 November 1938 and Letter of Butler to EFR, 1 December 1938, both NA FO 371/21587/C14392. Minutes, P.L. Rose, 22 November 1938, NA FO 371/21587/14037.
36. Letter of EFR to BFUW, 2 November 1938, BFUW 27/2, WL.
37. EFR, 'Note on Situation in Prague', PCR, 20 January 1939, NA FO 371/24081, duplicated in NA HO 294/39.
38. *Hansard* HC, vol. 341, col. 505, 14 November 1938.
39. London, *Whitehall and the Jews*, p.100.
40. Cab.55 (38) 5, 16 November 1938, NA CAB 23/96.
41. *Hansard* HC, vol. 342, col. 3082, 22 December 1938; vol. 345, cols 2455–7, 3 April 1939.
42. Movement for the Care of Children from Germany: First Annual Report, 1938–1939, NA HO 213/302.
43. Letter of EFR to the Graduate Electors of the Combined English Universities, March 1939, RP XIV.3 (3), ULL.
44. Minutes of Refugee Committee, point 25, 28 November 1938, LNU5/53, BLPES.
45. Victor Cazalet, Diary Entry, n.d. but late 1938. By courtesy of Sir Edward Cazalet.
46. D. Cesarani, 'Mad Dogs and Englishmen: Towards a Taxonomy of Rescuers in a Bystander Country – Britain 1933–45', *The Journal of Holocaust Education*, 9, 2 and 3 (2000), pp.37–8.
47. Minutes of Refugee Committee, 18 January 1939, LNU5/53, BLPES.
48. Victor Cazalet, Diary Entry, 14 October 1942. By courtesy of Sir Edward Cazalet.
49. Correspondence relating to donations by Gestetner, from early 1939 can be found in CBF

Files, 113/3/44/56–7/100/106–7/110, Wiener Library.
50. WHI /10/3/17, PA.
51. WHI/10/2/21 and Minutes of meeting, 17 July 1940, WHI /10/3/9, PA.
52. Stocks, *Rathbone*, p.278.
53. Notes by Robert Stopford, n.d. but circa 1972, RJS 2/2, pp.15–16, RJS 04/14/9, IWM.
54. Ibid.
55. *Hansard* HC, vol. 342, cols 2904–5, 21 December 1938.
56. London, *Whitehall and the Jews*, p.46.
57. Sybil Oldfield, 'Doreen Warriner', *Oxford DNB*, http://www.oxforddnb.com/view/article/65817, Article 65817.
58. Letter of Miss Warriner to EFR, 9 January 1939, NA HO 294/53.
59. Letter of Miss Warriner to Miss Layton, 10 January 1939, NA HO 294/54.
60. Letter of Miss Warriner to EFR, 9 January 1939, NA HO 294/53.
61. RP XIV.4 (17–18), ULL. Masaryk was Czech ambassador in London from 1925 until his resignation in September 1938.
62. EFR may also have met Miss M. Hughes, an ex-Somervillian working with the Quakers and with refugees in Prague. Hughes knew Miss Warriner and expressed a wish to meet Rathbone about more refugee work. Letter of M. Hughes to EFR, 14 January 1939, RP XIV.2.15 (10).
63. Cazalet, Grenfell *et al.*, 'The Problem of the Refugees'.
64. Letter to Sir Hector Hetherington, 18 January 1939, RP XIV.2.15 (13).
65. D. Warriner, 'Winter in Prague', *Slavonic and East European Review*, 62 (April 1984), pp.220–1.
66. Notes on visit to Prague, 14–20 January 1939, RP XIV.2.15 (12), ULL.
67. M. Emanuel and V. Gissing, *Nicholas Winton and the Rescued Generation* (London: Vallentine Mitchell, 2002).
68. Author's telephone interview with Nicholas Winton, 19 January 2001. For the earlier loss of possessions, see Letter of EFR to Mr Hadow, 15 March 1937, RP XIV.2.9 (47), ULL.
69. F. Field, 'The Mother of Child Benefit', *Prospect* (May 2004), pp.77–8.
70. Sybil Oldfield found no evidence of Eleanor's role in child rescue. See S. Oldfield, '"It Is Usually She": British Women's Role in the Rescue and Care of the Kindertransport Kinder' in W. Benz, C. Curio and A. Hammel (eds), *Kindertransport*, *Shofar*, Special Edition, (Fall 2004). My thanks to Sybil Oldfield for alerting me to this article.
71. Article by Mrs Zena Herman, n.d. but circa 3 September 1948, Hadassah Archive, RG1, Box 30, Folder 221, American Jewish Historical Society (AJHS).
72. Author's telephone interview with Bertha Leverton, 15 January 2001. Letter of EFR to B. Engelhard, 28 June 1943, by kind permission of Bertha Leverton. She later went on to found the Kindertransport Reunion organization.
73. List of contributors, CBF files, Wiener Library.
74. Siegfried Taub (1876–1946), was secretary general of the Sudeten German Social Democratic Party from 1924. He emigrated to Sweden in 1939 and died in New York. See Warriner, 'Winter in Prague', p.211, n.7.
75. John Segrue died in October in a German prison camp after capture in 1941 while covering the war in Yugoslavia. He had served as a foreign correspondent for several British newspapers since before the First World War, covering the rise of Nazism in Germany until 1936, then reported from Vienna on the annexation of Austria to Germany in 1938.
76. John Munro Troutbeck entered the Foreign Office in 1920, and was First Secretary of the British Legation in Prague between 1937–39. See Warriner, 'Winter in Prague', p.211, n.5.
77. Eleanor refers to Sir John Maclay, but this person was actually Sir Ronald Macleay, (1870–1943), counsellor of the British Legation in Prague 1927–29 and chairman of the Lord Mayor's Committee for Czech Refugees, in Prague, 1938–39. See Warriner, 'Winter in Prague' p.212, n.9.
78. Notes on visit to Prague, 14–20 January 1939, RP XIV.2.15 (12), ULL.
79. Letter of M. Hughes to EFR, 14 January 1939, RP XIV.2.15 (10), ULL.
80. Letter of Doreen Warriner to Robert Stopford, 17 September 1972, 5/1. RJS 04/14/9/, IWM.
81. EFR, 'Note on Situation in Prague', 20 January 1939, NA FO 371/24081 and NA HO 294/39.
82. *Hansard* HC, vol. 343, col. 151, 31 January 1939; cols 827–8, 7 February 1939; cols 1200–1, 9 February 1939; vol. 345, col. 615, 16 March 1939; col. 888, 20 March 1939.
83. *Hansard* HC, vol. 343, cols 827–30, 7 February 1939.

84. *Hansard* HC, vol. 343, cols 1200–1, 9 February 1939.
85. *Hansard* HC, vol. 343, cols 1202–2, 9 February 1939.
86. London, *Whitehall and the Jews*, p.146.
87. Notes made by Robert Stopford, n.d. but circa 1972, RJS 2/2, 32, RJS 04/14/9, IWM.
88. EFR, Speech notes: Refugees, Sheffield University Union of Students Celebrity Lecture, 17 February 1939, RP XIV.3 (60), ULL.
89. *Hansard* HC, vol. 346, cols 340–1, 19 April 1939.
90. Letter of EFR to WSC, 18 April 1939, CHAR/2/374/66.
91. Warriner, 'Winter in Prague', p.228.
92. 19 March 1939, NA FO 371/24081.
93. Letter of EFR to Randall, 23 March 1939, NA FO 371/24081,W4984/520/48.
94. Ibid.
95. Eleanor had been told whilst in Prague that the PCO staff were 'completely aloof, uninterested and unhelpful over refugee questions'. See Letter of EFR to WSC, 18 April 1939, CHAR/2/374/66, CAC. For Warriner, see Stocks, *Rathbone*, p.261.
96. Notes of Randall, Minutes, Re: evacuation of refugees from Czechoslovakia, 28 March 1939, NA FO 371/24081,W4984/520/48.
97. Randall, Minutes, 15 July 1939, NA FO 371/24084. For an alternative view, see John Cornwell, *Hitler's Pope: The Secret History of Pius XII* (London: Viking, 1999).
98. Ibid. London, *Whitehall and the Jews*, pp.245–6.
99. EFR, 'Personal View', pp.568–9 and EFR, 'The British Government and Refugee Policy', *Manchester Guardian*, 6 April 1939.
100. EFR, 'Personal View', p.568. This is a rather curious reference to collective security, since no policy was ever adopted, so could hardly have been abandoned.
101. Ibid.
102. EFR, 'Personal View', p.569.
103. Letter of Montagu-Pollock to E.N. Cooper, 7 March 1939, NA FO 371/24153.
104. EFR, 'Personal View', p.569.
105. Letter of EFR to Butler, 17 May 1939, RP XIV.2.15 (19), ULL.
106. *Hansard* HC, vol. 345, cols 888–9, 20 March 1939 and Letter of EFR to Butler, 23 March 1939, NA FO 371/24081,W4984/520/48.
107. Letter of EFR to Butler, 18 April 1939; Minutes, Reilly, 21 April 1939; Letter of Butler to EFR, 26 April 1939, NA FO 371/24082,W6400/520/48. Also Minutes, Reilly, 18 April 1939, NA FO 371/24082,W5806/520/48.
108. Letter of Miss Wellington to Miss Courtney and Elizabeth, n.d. but circa April 1939, RP XIV.2.15 (16), and extracts from this letter, April 1939, RP XIV.2.15 (17), ULL. The letter was sent on to EFR by Miss Courtney on 28 April 1939, see RP XIV.2.15 (16), ULL.
109. Recommendation 2: Conference of PCR and Principal Refugee Organizations, 15 May 1939, RP XIV.2.15 (18), ULL. Letter of EFR to Butler, 17 May 1939, NA FO 371/24083,W8047. Mary Ormerod had made a similar request in respect of the diplomatic bags between London and Vienna in June and July 1938. See London, *Whitehall and the Jews*, p.68.
110. Letter of Randall to Cooper, 6 June 1939, NA FO 371/24083,W8047.
111. Letter of Cooper to Randall, 12 July 1939, NA FO 371/24084,W10698.

# 6

# *War Changes Everything: Internment at Home and Abroad*

By July 1939 the PCR, which, according to Victor Cazalet, was meeting almost daily,[1] comprised over 200 cross-party MPs.[2] Eleanor was now spearheading a vigorous campaign against the British government and the way it was handling the Czech loan, founded on her belief that Britain had a moral obligation to help the desperate Czech refugees. At the same time, funds, and the way they were handled, were undergoing change. The government agreement over refugee finance had died along with the Czech state following Hitler's occupation of the country on 15 March. To stop the German's appropriating the remaining funds – about one-seventh of the money had been withdrawn from the Bank of England to date – the balance was frozen, and a new law passed which restricted accessibility, which could only be authorized by the Treasury.[3] Well before then, the BCRC had exhausted the funds at their disposal, and at the beginning of May 1939 had made an application to the government for a grant of £1¾ million to cover liabilities made, or about to be incurred. A new organization was to take over from the BCRC, and the Home Office set about establishing the Czech Refugee Trust Fund (CRTF). Sir Henry Bunbury, a retired senior civil servant, whose background as an authority on public expenditure – he had been enlisted by the German Jewish Aid Committee to provide desperately needed administrative expertise – made him a suitable director-designate. In late July 1939 the BCRC was formally wound up and its liabilities and assets transferred to the new CRTF.[4]

Eleanor now had a case to put to Lord Winterton, the British representative at Evian and chairman of the IGCR, and she detailed 'the necessity for Governmental assistance ... towards the settlement of refugees'. She argued that almost every British expert on the refugee problem, excepting ministers, agreed that it was 'impossible for any large-scale, even partial, treatment of the problem without State assistance in the planning, financing and carrying out of schemes for the eventual settlement of refugees'. Once Eleanor began her campaign to save Jews from elsewhere in Nazi Europe after 1941 the scale of rescue plans was of great importance. Now the authority of Lord Lytton, Sir Neill Malcolm, former high commissioner for refugees from

Germany, and Sir Arthur Salter were invoked, as well as the observations of the prime minister and home secretary, in a Commons debate held months before on 25 November 1938.[5] Mr Culpin and the rest of the BCRC Trustees were given notice of the questions that Eleanor intended to put, pointing out that the 200 members of PCR Executive were very concerned about what they understood to be the financial position regarding Czech refugees. In an effort at helping, not hindering, the BCRC, she wanted to know if they were taking steps to raise the question of the unexpended portion of the £6,000,000 loan, which she calculated at the time to be £2,750,000. She got her answer more quickly than expected, for even before she had sent the letter to Mr Culpin and the others, or put the question to Sir John Simon in the House two days later, she had seen the reply to a written question put down on 13 July. She gathered that the government intended to recover for the Treasury the whole £6,000,000, and not merely the expended portion of £2,750,000.[6] This appalled Eleanor for it meant that,

> the British Treasury will make a nice little saving of six (or eight, including the intended addition) million pounds out of the destruction of the Republic whose frontiers we had guaranteed but were unable to protect. This will be done apparently at the cost of abandoning those unhappy refugees who failed to get out in time, many of them owing to the extremely slow and cautious action of the British Government during the winter months when they could easily have been got out.[7]

The response from Mr Culpin was equally speedy, and having explained that the trustees were trustees of the government, and not the BCRC, he let her know that the trust deed had just been signed between the home secretary, the chancellor of the Exchequer and the trustees. Their afternoon meeting with government representatives, Miss Layton and others was expected to last well into the night, for the immediate issue to be decided was 'whether they could continue to be represented in Prague at all, for they had just had a telegram to say that everything in Prague is to be closed down and their representatives are to leave at once'. Consideration had also to be given 'not only to the well-being of the refugees but also the Czech Government and their relations to the German Government. Some agreement with the German Government on this matter is necessary; otherwise the position of the Czech Government vis a vis the German Government will be weakened, which would prejudice the ultimate establishment of an independent Czechoslovakia.'[8]

Gathering support for her anti-government publicity campaign, she wrote personal letters to Dr Benes, whom she had met in Prague in

February 1937, and to Jan Masaryk, the exiled Czech leader.[9] Masaryk phoned Eleanor to thank her for her letter and all that she was doing and said he would consult Dr Benes the following day.

She also canvassed Hugh Seton-Watson, the scholar on Eastern Europe, Henry Wickham-Steed, Leo Amery, Unionist MP for the Sparksbrook (formerly South) division of Birmingham and Robert Boothby, MP for East Aberdeenshire.[10] Fellow refugee activist MPs Victor (now Captain) Cazalet and David Grenfell were sounded out on raising the question of finance and the Czech refugees in a Home Office debate, in case the debate on foreign affairs, which the Opposition wanted to have before the adjournment, did not take place.[11] As she concluded in her letters to Amery and Boothby, 'It will be too late by the time we re-assemble'.[12] At the same time she was disapproving of the CRTF for 'its extreme caution in financial matters and its poor publicity'.[13]

Trying to arrange for Sir John Simon to meet a PCR deputation proved difficult, but may not have surprised Eleanor, for her relationship with him was precarious. On many occasions in the past she had been critical of him,[14] and she found him to be quite insensitive to humanitarian considerations, showing little sympathy over Czechoslovakia.[15] In fact, by the time that he did meet them, on 2 August 1939, a final decision about funding had already been made.[16] For, at a meeting held on 29 July 1939, attended by Cooper, Bunbury, Margaret Layton, who, according to Randall, did not see 'eye-to-eye' with Eleanor,[17] and Captain V.C. Farrell, the passport control officer from Prague, it was agreed that 'no further financial assistance should be made, except under binding Settlements satisfactory to the government and the trustees'. The memorandum recorded how the 'new head of the Gestapo for refugee business, who was previously in charge of a similar position in Vienna, has announced his intention of procuring the emigration of at least 60,000 Jews in the twelve months or at the rate of, say, 200 a day'. This unnamed head was none other than Adolf Eichmann,[18] – and the question that remained unanswered for Cooper and the others was whether this forced migration would be 'orderly and conducted by tolerable methods or (as was the case in Austria) in a disorganized way by methods of persecution and terrorism'. They went further by asserting that Eleanor's campaign for extra money to finance another exodus was a grave mistake in strategy and would 'play into the hands of Gestapo and would be far more likely to encourage persecution and terror than avoid it'.[19] Bunbury undertook to discuss the subject at once with Sir Herbert Emerson, the director of the IGCR, and then to put Eleanor 'in possession of this point of view which, it was thought, she probably did not fully appreciate'. The fate of the refugees in Czechoslovakia was soon sealed: the CRTF pulled out of Prague as everything there was 'to be closed down and their representatives are to leave at once ... They have to consider not only the well-being of the refugees but also the Czech government and their relations to the German government'.[20]

All the while Eleanor had other refugee-related issues closer to home to deal with. There was the position of those who fell foul of the inadequate staffing levels at points of entry and who, despite holding visas, were likely to be refused admittance, and then sent back from whence they came.[21] Then there were pleas to the Home Office for them to adopt a more liberal policy in granting permits to married couples in domestic work, as well as allowing agricultural workers under the age of eighteen to stay in the country after training.[22] In the House she pressed strongly for a concession whereby elderly parents and relatives entering Palestine should be excluded from the immigration quota, imposed by the controversial White Paper of May 1939,[23] on the basis that those who could not work, and were not setting up a family, should be treated as a special class outside of the quota regulations.[24] Besides these concerns there was an urgent plea to the prime minister to expedite the passage of the British Nationality and Status of Aliens (Amendment) Act, so that British women would have the right restored to them to retain British nationality on their marriage to an alien.[25]

When the House resolved, on 4 August 1939, to adjourn for eight weeks, Eleanor was amongst those who voted with the Opposition, for she was of the same mind as Churchill that given the precarious political situation it was very odd for MPs to be taking two months holiday.[26] From the outset of the debate she was vociferous on a number of refugee issues, all of which were supported by her belief in Britain's obligation to help these refugees whose plight 'arose directly out of events of last March', a reference to Hitler's seizure of Prague in March 1939.[27] Mr MacDonald, the secretary of state for the colonies, was pressed on the possibility of refugees being admitted to Trinidad, and asked whether he had been able to organize asylum in Palestine, Cyprus or any other British colony for the 700 Czech refugees quarantined in Beirut. The latter group were, according to MacDonald, illegal immigrants: the British government could not accept responsibility for refugees outside of the regulated scheme, and his concerns over the impact of refugees on the local inhabitants in British colonies sat uneasily against his expressions of regret. Once again Eleanor made a plea that the £8 million loan promised to Czechoslovakia be used to assist refugees from that country,[28] but it was her final contribution to the debate which was the most emotive. In an impassioned speech she called for a more humane refugee policy, and rather than acting on government advice, which as Churchill cynically remarked, was 'to go away and play, taking our gas masks with us', she suggested to MPs:

> Let us take something else; the thought that while we are enjoying ourselves by sea or mountain, there are hundreds of thousands of men and women who are wondering about in the utmost destitution, many of them hiding by day, many of them already in the hands of the Gestapo and being beaten up daily in concentration camps and prisons.[29]

The next two weeks of August were, Eleanor wrote, 'desperately full of very urgent refugee questions'.[30] She was still, as Sir Henry Bunbury put it, 'on our trail',[31] pressing for the rescue of the one hundred or so women still in Prague, eighty-five of whom had British visas, but were still prevented from joining their husbands in Great Britain. The difficulties were great for there were no workers left in Prague willing to take on the task. Miss Warriner's activities as the BCRC representative had come to an abrupt end after the Gestapo found out she was giving cards (perhaps visas) to political refugees from Czechoslovakia, and for her own safety could not be asked to return there, even though she willing to take the risk, in the company of another worker.[32] Robert Stopford had refused to do anything as he had no official status any more. All Bunbury could do was wait for the permits to arrive for about twenty of the 'legal' women, a situation he described as 'disappointing'.[33]

Eleanor's summer holiday, and that of all MPs, was cut short by international events and she was in fighting spirit during the opening debate of the reassembled Parliament on 24 August 1939. Her strong appeal to the government 'before it is too late to strengthen their forces, and to make this a real National government' was reinforced by her call to 'form a government which really represents the people, the whole people and nothing but the people'.[34] A further nine months were to pass before a coalition government was formed, under the leadership of Winston Churchill.

When Eleanor wrote to Lord Reading on 30 August suggesting a meeting to discuss refugees, she was anticipating that war would be declared. Her concern was how best to safeguard them in wartime, and how their skills and manpower could be used in British national service, civilian or military, matters she understood that he had been talking to the Home Office about. Ideas that were discussed included Cazalet's suggestion of small single-nationality committees, including members of the Spanish International Brigades, each with a leading personality as advisor. This would be a valuable way of collecting information and 'vetting' the names, qualifications, and political reliability of those refugees willing to take up employment, data that could in turn be passed on to the government. Inevitably the matter of finance was raised. Eleanor took the view that anti-refugee feeling was much more likely to grow if the voluntary organizations had to continue begging for support, unless it could be made clear that it was to help refugees find work. It would be altogether more satisfactory if 'government financial provision were quietly made for this'.[35]

As prescient was Eleanor's conviction that, as far as security allowed, every MP should be in possession of detailed information concerning the war situation, regardless of their departmental affiliation. Wartime, she observed astutely, called for the adoption of special techniques so that Britain's democratically elected Parliament could continue to exercise its critical and constructive powers unhindered. To this end, the Emergency Powers (Defence) Acts 1939 and 1940 conferred the widest powers upon the government to deal with the wartime emergency. Eleanor's response, on 4 September 1939, the day after war was declared, following Germany's invasion of Poland, was to suggest the 'immediate formation of an informal group constituted without regard to party and chiefly of private members who have in recent years been working for similar objects and have found action through purely party machinery inadequate'.[36] Thus, at Eleanor's instigation, a circular letter of invitation went out to cross-party members from her Romney Street office, signed by David Grenfell, Graham White, Robert Boothby, Sir Arthur Salter and Harold Nicolson. Thus the All-Party Parliamentary Action Group was born, with the object of private discussion and action on problems arising out of the war, and by November 1939 there were more than fifty members. Eleanor took on much of the responsibility for the group, arranging meetings, inviting speakers and seeking the collaboration of David Lloyd George.[37] Besides gaining the support, once again, of reliable, eager and critical colleagues, there were also non-activists who were willing to help the defenceless, for Eleanor utilized the knowledge of anti-Nazi refugee experts[38] and refugee sources in the course of her work with the committee.[39]

Persecuted Jews in Nazi Europe were certainly not a British wartime priority, and this led to further changes in entry policy for refugees to the United Kingdom. First, any visas that had already been issued to enemy nationals were immediately cancelled, as it was assumed that anyone emigrating from German-controlled lands would have needed Nazi permission to leave and therefore was automatically suspect.[40] This prompted Eleanor to ask Captain Crookshank, the financial secretary to the Treasury, about money which had been deposited, by friends of would-be refugees from Czechoslovakia, with the Treasury through the CRTF, to fund their transit and other costs. With all visas cancelled, would he arrange for the release of money where requested, as these friends had been unable to recover the funds? Adamant that the Treasury had not received these deposits, Eleanor was advised to take the matter up with the CRTF.[41] At home, many refugees who had already settled into the country, and had already been subjected to the laborious pre-selection process, found themselves being encouraged by the Home Office to re-emigrate. The official excuse was that there were already far too many refugees in Britain, a situation that was complicated by the fact that the main Jewish organizations were no longer able to financially support them. In an extraordinary turn of events, government ministers were even able to persuade the Home Office to provide subsidies to help Jews re-emigrate. This prompted Sir Alexander Maxwell, parliamentary undersecretary at the Home Office, to remark that it would 'reverse the historic practice by which governments have borrowed money from Jews and will introduce a new procedure by which the government will lend some money to the Jews'.[42]

A new, Home Office-approved, non-sectarian body, the Central Committee for Refugees, was set up to distribute a monthly grant amongst the various organizations, but such was the desire of the Home Office to persuade as many Jews as possible to move elsewhere, that special subsidies, kept secret from the House of Commons, were made available to aid re-emigration and administration. Equally surreptitious was the extra funding loaned to the Jewish organizations by the Home Office in 1941.[43]

The onset of hostilities added a new and more intimate dimension as Eleanor became deeply involved with enemy aliens at home, and became personally involved with innumerable individuals. This was never going to be an easy course, for not only was she a woman in the male-dominated environment of politics and the House of Commons, but she was fighting for a cause which was seen by many as incompatible with the war effort. Her approach was such that junior ministers tried to avoid catching her eye in the Commons lobby lest she commandeered their help, and Harold Nicolson later referred to her as 'the Britomart of 1939'.[44]

This campaigning began in earnest on 4 September 1939, when Sir John Anderson, the newly appointed home secretary and minister of home security, announced the imposition of mobility restrictions on everyone from the Reich territories.[45] Most Jewish refugees, many of whom were stateless in fact or law, were now classified as enemy aliens, although Anderson did express the hope that there would be 'a general desire to avoid treating as enemies those who are friendly to the country which has offered them asylum'. Eschewing a strategy of mass internment in favour of a more liberal policy, he instigated a system of local tribunals to examine the cases of all enemy aliens, to categorize them according to the degree of risk they posed, and to establish whether the alien was friendly or hostile to Britain.[46] Of the 73,800 screened, less than 1 per cent were designated Category A and interned, 64,200 in Category C were exempt from any restrictions, and the remainder, classified as Category B, had restrictions imposed upon them.[47] The treatment of these enemy aliens struck at the heart of Eleanor's sense of justice, right and wrong, and severely challenged her belief in Britain's tradition of liberty, generosity and asylum, principles that, even in wartime, were of profound importance.

Henceforth it was Anderson who bore the brunt of her unrelenting questioning in the House of Commons as she challenged nearly every aspect of his refugee policies. Of specific concern was the categorizing of aliens and the problems they faced as a result of the tribunal system. She wanted a distinction drawn between Germans and Austrians, placing the latter in the same category as Czechs – who did not have to go before the tribunals – on the basis that they too had had their country forcibly taken from them. Anderson's response emphasized that 'security was paramount' and although he talked of showing 'sympathy for the kind of case you refer to' he informed her that 'sweeping distinctions ... automatically applied, would not be compatible with public interest'.[48]

The rhetoric of public versus national interest was to be reiterated time and time again over the next few years.[49] Now it was used as the main reason for not altering the restrictions on the mobility of aliens, which Eleanor argued had a severe effect on their work opportunities. There were, she argued, large numbers of friendly refugees whose services had been explicitly and personally applied for by employers who could not get British workers, but whose requests for permits were taking forever to be processed.[50] Her contention was that 'refugees who are idle, desperately hard up for money, and suffering from a burning sense of injustice (were) more likely than others to be suborned by the enemy; at least to become centres of anti-British propaganda'. And given the government's obsession with avoiding the financial maintenance of refugees, she tried appealing on the basis that 'financially they are a burden on refugee organisations and when refugee funds are exhausted must become a burden on the rates or the taxes'.[51]

Amidst this early campaigning against internment, Eleanor's concern for the safety of would-be immigrants from Czechoslovakia, some with relatives in Britain, others with British visas, all of whom were destitute and threatened with deportation, became even more urgent.[52] She had already asked Anderson in the House in early February 1940 if it was possible to grant a transit visa to a refugee, and had been told, not for the first time, that this was not possible.[53] Within days she wrote asking him to consider 'a small but important extension of the category of refugee immigrants admissible to Britain'. These were between 150 and 200 Czechs who already had a family member in the country under the care of the CRTF, and who were either in a neutral country where they could not safely stay, or were still in enemy territory but able to travel to a neutral county on a transit visa, providing the neutral country were assured the refugee could be passed on to Britain. Peake and Herbert Morrison, the Labour MP and minister of supply, were also urged to facilitate rescue by this minor modification in the law.[54] Anderson did agree to meet a PCR deputation, which had the additional presence of Sir Henry Bunbury as well as three of Eleanor's MP colleagues on the Advisory Committee to the CRTF – namely Victor (now Major) Cazalet, Harold Macmillan and Mr Geoffrey le M. Mander – but he could not be persuaded to help the endangered souls. His response to Eleanor, in March 1940, followed an established pattern, when he replied:

> it is my duty as Home Secretary to regard this problem from a more objective point of view, and considerations of sympathy with the unfortunate persons on whose behalf the deputation made their plea cannot be allowed to override considerations of what is best for the security of the country and for public interest. I do not think it would be in the best interest of the refugees themselves who are at present in this country to allow a further influx from territory under enemy jurisdiction. There is already considerable uneasiness about the number of aliens in this country, and fresh admissions would add to the public uneasiness and might do much to prejudice the position of refugees already here.[55]

His words demonstrated the government's perception, true or false, of the existence of anti-alien feeling within the country and the pressure that this was placing upon decisions in respect of immigration policy. It is difficult to be certain about the real level of unease in British society, for the first Mass-Observation of attitudes towards Jews did not take place until 1941,[56] but it is unlikely that the situation was as grave as Anderson implied.

All was not well, it seemed, within the CRTF, for a Special Branch report in late January 1940 referred to the present administration still being in a state of flux. This resulted in the formation of a London

Advisory Committee, with Elizabeth Macadam, 'who lives with Miss Rathbone', being appointed as one of the six members, all of whom were women.[57] Eleanor was clearly taking an interest in the running of the CRTF, for one of the committee members, who had recently left, had spent some considerable time with her on 21 February, discussing, amongst other matters, the poor way in which the Reigate and Derby hostels had been run. These hostels, like many others, had been set up by the Trust to provide temporary accommodation for the refugees, and before the outbreak of war, on the basis that they would be re-emigrating within months, once the necessary paperwork was completed. Local refugee committees were often involved in the running of the hostels, as were the various groups of Czech refugees. Miss Layton, reporting in early 1940, was very complimentary about the way the Czech refugees had established their groups, and of the great help they had been to the BCRC. With funds at a low ebb, the BCRC had come to rely heavily on the voluntary work undertaken by the refugees, who helped with many practical aspects including accommodation, welfare, employment and retraining issues. The CRTF was more than happy for the status quo to continue.[58] Having volunteers undertake much of the work was all very well, but Eleanor's correspondent had grave concerns over the Trust's expenditure, and the fact that despite Sir Henry Bunbury's projection, in May 1939, that about £17,000 was sufficient for the Trust Fund for one year, expenditure for administration for just four months was in excess of £15,000. It was still impossible to obtain figures relating to the number of refugees at any given place, or of costings, which made forward planning impossible. And the fact that German Jewish Medical Aid had been virtually financed by the CRTF since September 1939 – there was a grant of £500 for nine months of services rendered, free accommodation and the contribution of the staff, and rent-free use of the offices – really galled the author of the letter. It was, after all, the refugees who were suffering from this misuse of funds.[59] As to the concerns of the Special Branch, who were convinced that the CRTF was largely a Communist organization, Miss Mynatt reported to them, in January 1940, that it was a pre-condition of their (the refugees) admittance to the United Kingdom that they did not engage in political activities. This requirement was, she asserted, strictly adhered to.[60]

The rules of the game changed dramatically with the appointment of Winston Churchill as prime minister of the wartime coalition government on 10 May 1940. Whilst Anderson still thought internment 'unnecessary on security grounds and inexpedient on grounds of general policy',[61] the new prime minister was under pressure from the military leadership and the secret service who were determined upon this course of action. So too were the press, especially the *Sunday Express* and the *Daily Sketch*, which persisted in publishing unsubstantiated allegations about refugees acting as spies and saboteurs.[62] These, combined with public opinion and the fall of France, were enough reasons for Churchill to have no option but to introduce a policy of mass internment in the second week of May 1940.[63] The established categories were extended and in total some 27,000 aliens, including Jewish refugees, Italians, non-Jewish Germans and Austrians were interned.[64] Eleanor was once again on the attack, firing questions at Anderson, asking how soon he could review the cases of aliens who had recently been interned under a general order, especially where they were urgently needed in the labour force? And could he speed up the censorship of internees' letters?[65] Similarly Peake was subjected to a barrage of requests when he met a deputation, which included Emerson, Clare-Martin, Blanche Dugdale, Ernest Cove, Bunbury and Dorothy Buxton in June 1940.[66] When Sir Annesley Somerville, Conservative MP for Windsor, asked if it was right for interned aliens to be kept in 'luxurious idleness ... at a greater cost than the allowance paid to men with dependants', she accused him of cruelly insulting people 'who were longing to do active work in or out of internment', a point which she reiterated days later.[67]

Eleanor was so incensed by the futility of the policies that she produced a polemic piece, 'How British Policy towards Refugees Helps Hitler', with the rider that 'What follows is a one-sided presentment of the case ... Of course there is another side – that of the Military. But could not the two sides be reconciled by better planning and more use of expert heads of refugee organisations and their workers?' The general argument of the paper was summed up thus:

> Generally speaking, create such conditions of idleness and misery, such an atmosphere of uncertainty and fear as to the future, anxiety for wives and families, and embitterment among men and women who have believed the cause we are fighting for to be their own, that they will deteriorate in mind, body and character become permanently alienated from Great Britain, and – as their plight becomes known overseas – help to alienate the sympathies of the American and all other friendly people.[68]

In her usual fashion, Eleanor managed to engage simultaneously with the various strands of her refugee work. So, in June 1940, whilst her waking hours were consumed by the internment crisis at home, Germany's incursion into France threatened the lives of large numbers of refugees, opening the door for her to aid the rescue of some of them from war-torn Nazi Europe. With her reputation as a refugee activist well established, she was soon at the receiving end of numerous requests to assist in arranging a mission to evacuate foreign refugees who were considered to be in grave danger from German occupation. The first list, which included many world-famous distinguished scientists, academics and others, was sent to her on 23 June by Mr Sternfeld of the CRTF, and was followed the next day by a further list from Blanche Dugdale (a founding member of the League of Nations and a Gentile Zionist, Arthur Balfour's niece and a close friend of Chaim Weizmann). Yet a third list of over 100 names reached her from Richard Reitzner, deputy group leader of the Thomas Mann group of the CRT.[69] As she was to do time and again, Eleanor was prepared to pursue any chance of rescue, however slim, so she wrote to Butler on 24 June positing the notion of evacuating refugees by sea, 'if any ships are still in Bordeaux, or other port, possibly instructions could be sent to bring off these people'. In her heart of hearts she knew that it was unlikely that Butler could sanction such a scheme, for she added, 'I know it is only a 1–20 chance that you can do anything to save them, but one has to take 1–20 chances nowadays'.[70] Even though Butler had received a similar approach from the Labour Party, he replied that, 'Unhappily the speed of the German advance, and the appalling confusion at Bordeaux made the evacuation of such people on a large scale impossible'.[71] From Eleanor's point of view, and as later rescue proposals indicate, she would actually have been satisfied with a successful small-scale initiative, but she did not pursue this as an option at this time. This may well have been because she was well aware that Britain was in a precarious position itself, and was extremely apprehensive about the very real possibility of a German invasion.

But the main thrust of her parliamentary questions came on 10 July in the adjournment debate on refugees and other aliens, a session which lasted nearly six hours.[72] This debate, along with a further three concerning enemy aliens held before the end of December 1940, consumed a total of fourteen hours of parliamentary time: it was quite remarkable that the debate should have taken place at a time when Britain still faced the threat of invasion, a fact which undoubtedly reflected the pressure on, and concern felt by Parliament. Eleanor was more than prepared to do battle, having acquired and accumulated all the evidence and data she needed to argue against internment and its attendant policies. Much of this information came from Wilfred Israel, who played a unique and almost anonymous role on behalf of the refugees, being the main link between them and the various refugee organizations, including the PCR.[73]

Whilst Eleanor was only one of nineteen MPs to speak, the force of her arguments and the emotion with which she spoke marked her speech out as outstanding, a definite highlight in her oratorical career. But she had also, during the course of this debate, to deal with a great divergence of support from fellow MPs. On the one hand there was Victor Cazalet, her staunch supporter, who paid tribute to her by remarking that 'All refugees in this country, and indeed many refugees in other countries as well, owe her a deep debt of gratitude, and I am glad to have the opportunity to pay tribute to her work today'.[74] Conversely, there was the verbal attack made by Mrs Tate, Conservative MP for Frome, who accused Eleanor of being an MP 'who lost all sense of reason when the word "Jew" was mentioned'. In Mrs Tate's opinion, the material needs of fighting men came before the simple bare necessities of internees, all of whom she wanted rounded up. And to her way of thinking, Eleanor's appeal was a 'piteous and pathetic' one that could lead people to be carried away by sentiment.[75] But Eleanor was not seeking a response based on sentiment. She sought to awaken the individual conscience to what she perceived as the injustice of internment, and to the inhumane way in which the British government was treating individuals. Her speech hammered home every hardship suffered by the internees, from the case of young people whose studies were interrupted, to the sick, invalid and old. She decried the fund of ability wasting away in the camps, much of it previously involved in work of national importance, and she highlighted the case of the German professor of chemistry who committed suicide rather than face being interned.[76] At a more basic level, she complained bitterly about the lack of provision for schooling, to say nothing of the unfairness of internees being deprived of newspapers and wireless, books and personal musical instruments.[77]

One of the most palpable instances of the harsh reality of internment policies was the death of hundreds of internees being deported on the *Arandora Star*, which was torpedoed off the coast of Ireland en route for Canada on 2 July 1940. The refugee debate gave Eleanor the opportunity to air her concern over the very question of deportation, pointing out to Sir Edward Grigg, the joint undersecretary of state for war, the palpable sense of panic amongst internees and their families who had no idea whether they would be whisked overseas as some had already been. This parliamentary question was largely in response to a powerful letter sent to her by the camp representative at Huyton imploring her to submit an urgent plea to the government to halt compulsory transfers overseas, based on the refugee's 'sacred right of asylum in UK'.[78] With Eleanor trying to establish who was responsible for this decision-making, Peake was somewhat relieved to be able to deny Home Office culpability and to confirm that it was down to a Cabinet committee presided over by the Lord President of the Council, who was noticeable by his absence from the House. A week later Anderson was being asked if he knew that 7,500 male civilian internees had been sent overseas, including some who should not have been interned according to Home Office regulations. He assured Eleanor that steps were being taken to ensure that camp commandants were instructed not to send overseas internees who were apparently qualified for exemption until their release application had been considered.[79] In July 1940, the Commonwealth government agreed to accept 6,000 internees from the United Kingdom, and as the debate took place in the House of Commons, HMT (Hired Military Transport) *Dunera* was preparing to sail from Liverpool with her human cargo. Besides the 2,542 male German Jewish refugees, aged between 16 and 45, who had escaped from Nazi Germany, there were also on board 200 Italian POWs and 250 German Nazis. The conditions were appalling. Apart from overcrowding on the ship with the attendant problems of hygiene and harsh treatment by crew members, the journey was also made unpleasant by the fear of torpedo attacks, the uncertainty of the destination, and by tensions between Jewish refugees and German Nazi passengers. An official report, the *Dunera Memorandum*, written by the internees for the UK's high commissioner in Australia, described the search that the first group of internees who boarded the ship were subjected to:

> Everything carried in hand or loose in the pockets was taken off the internees. All less valuable effects like gloves, toilet utensils, eatables, pipes etc, were thrown disorderly on the ground. Valuables were stuffed into sacks or disappeared openly into the pockets of the soldiers. Soon rows of empty wallets were lying on the floor, the contents of emptied attaché cases were roughly thrown about, and the officially provided kitbags could be seen all over the place. Valuable documents, identity and emigration papers, testimonials of all kinds, were taken away, thrown on the ground or even ... torn up before the eyes of their very owners. No receipts were given, except by one single searching party. Appeals to the officers standing by were fruitless. Attempts of protest were roughly suppressed ... Of all the articles taken away on the landing stage, only a very few were ever seen again.[80]

The *Dunera* arrived in Australia on 27 August 1940, and those who disembarked in Sydney were transferred to Hay, located outside of the town in the Riverina district of southern New South Wales. Little did they know that Eleanor had questioned Peake in the House just two weeks before the *Dunera* landed, expressing her concern over the 250 or so wives and children who had been brought to London at the request of the Home Office, but who were still eagerly waiting for permission to join their husbands in Australia. Peake promised to see if he could expedite the next convoy, but no such convoy ever departed. For it was not long before reports began to arrive of the journey and of the dreadful conditions at Hay (see Plate 17). Eleanor was at the receiving end of a number of despairing letters and as a result of complaints by the PCR and others, the Home Office eventually sent Lt Colonel Julian Layton, a British-born Jew, out to Australia in November 1940, to inspect the conditions. As a result of his influence, the refugees were transferred to a camp where the climate and conditions were better.[81] Layton also assisted in obtaining compensation for those who suffered a loss during the *Dunera* scandal, in which three British soldiers were court-martialed for the brutal treatment and robbery of refugees. And as a lengthy letter sent to Eleanor from Quebec by Lord Marley, who had been at Evian, on 9 August reveals, she and the PCR were taking a very active interest in the way that the refugees in Canada were being treated, and what the chances were of them being released. Marley expressed his absolute amazement that the War Office had seen fit to send over fifteen officers from the Intelligence Branch of the War Office to 'regulate the status of the internees', as he doubted that they knew the difference between an anti-Nazi refugee and pro-Nazi spy. What he was able to say was that any releasable internee would not be set free in Canada, but would be repatriated to Britain, partly because there was so much anti-Semitic feeling in the country, and also because some men were thought to have taken on stolen identities to cover up their questionable backgrounds.[82]

Meanwhile, back at home, the 10 July debate provided some consolation to the internees with whom Eleanor corresponded, for, as she wrote, 'with two or three exceptions every speech (given by MPs) indicated strong sympathy with the position of refugees, and anxiety that everything possible should be done to alleviate the hardships and anxieties and sense of injustice from which they are suffering'.[83] Exactly how they felt about her pleas for patience and her request that they 'make allowances for the difficulties of those who are controlling you' remains unclear, but their appeal for an official visit was answered sooner than anyone, even Eleanor, could have expected.[84] Ten days after Sir Edward Grigg's, the joint undersecretary for war, surprise announcement that MPs could visit internment camps, Eleanor made the first of her many camp visits.[85] On 20 July she and Graham White travelled north to Huyton, an empty council estate which had been hastily surrounded by barbed wire, on the outskirts of her hometown of Liverpool. White's recollections of this experience deserve quoting at length for the insight they provide into the impact of Eleanor's presence:

> We went to the Huyton camp about ten days after the first aliens were brought there. There was practically no furniture – literally people had to sit on the bare steps or on the floors, and as one alien told us there was not even any toilet paper in the camp. On our arrival we saw the Commandant who was, in my judgment, an excellent man doing his best in nearly impossible circumstances ... We met the Committee, to the number of about a dozen, some of whom were distinguished scientists ...We had a long discussion with the Committee, mostly on the practical question as to what could be done to improve matters from an intellectual as well purely material point of view. Many of the people interned had been refugees from Austria from the time of the Anschluss, and others from Germany. Some of them had done, and after their release continued to do, valuable work for the Allied cause. When the discussions were over and we left the hut, we found to our surprise that word had got about that we were in the camp, and practically all the internees were gathered around the hut. It was a strangely moving experience to come out into the open and find oneself faced by a crowd of silent, anxious, unhappy people. They were all sorts for the net had brought in, promiscuously, unfortunates from Soho as well as people of great intellectual attainment. Looking at he crowd, I saw a hand waving to me and recognized H.W. Singer, who after his release worked in Manchester and contributed a number of articles under his own name to the *Manchester Guardian*. It was at once clear that something had to be said to these unhappy people. Eleanor spoke first. I have always regretted that I did not make notes at the time of what she said, but she spoke to them with moving sympathy of our concern for the state in which they were living and our anxiety to do everything that we could to improve conditions in every way possible. She then, as always, showed her keen sense of reality by asking them not to forget in the midst of their troubles that we were in a terrible crisis of the war and that from day to day we might be invaded. She assured them that the action from which they were suffering was foreign to the spirit of the British people. It was quite obvious that her speech had much encouraged and comforted these unfortunate people. I felt it was one of the most remarkable speeches that I had ever heard – made entirely without preparation ...[86] [See Plate 13.]

An internee later recollected the event in a letter to *The Times*:

> At Huyton, the large central camp for civilian internees, thousands of men are idling, deeply depressed and full of anxiety

> about their fate and that of their families, from whom they were taken without notice. Barbed wire all around reminds them of the Nazi concentration camps where most of them had suffered before. Wild rumours are spreading. Suddenly news is going round that two MPs are in the camp to talk to the Camp Father and perhaps to the internees. The Camp Father is patiently walking up and down in front of the hut that is almost besieged, well guarded by soldiers. In pouring rain he and the internees wait for a long time. Everybody keeps inside a small spark of hope that cannot be deadened by the rain. At last the doors open. A woman appears, behind her a man's face, both flanked by soldiers with fixed bayonets. The woman begins to address the men: 'You are not forgotten.' They hardly discern her words; many do not understand. But what they feel is: This is democracy! They feel the warmth of her motherly voice. The woman's face in the open door is beaten by the pouring rain. Her face, her voice are nursing the gleam of hope left in their hearts. Then they disperse and carry the message round among those thousands, most of whom have taken their part in the fight against Nazism; many are still taking it now.[87]

Yet another observer, Dolf Michaelis, an indefatigable worker for a number of organizations, including the Jewish Agency for Palestine, the Jewish National Fund and the Association of Jewish Refugees, who was interned at Huyton, never forgot Eleanor's words:

> I shall fight in the House the policy of indiscriminate internment. It is my considered opinion that some of those people who put you in here should themselves be interned and you should be let out. You are the last to be enemies of this country, and you are the first to have a good reason to fight Nazi Germany.[88]

But as Eleanor found on 10 August, conditions at Sutton Park, Sutton Coldfield were immeasurably worse than Huyton. For reasons best known to the War Office, the camp had hurriedly been transferred there from Kempton Park racecourse, and was totally unprepared to receive the seven hundred or so individuals. One internee wrote:

> Under canvas on peaty ground, very apt to be water logged ... elderly internees Category C (most of them between 45–69 years of age) we sleep on ground sheets without palliasses. These conditions as well as insufficient medical attention endanger health and life of already ailing people ... we are in desperate plight relying upon promises given to us in Parliament we ask your immediate help.[89]

Eleanor did respond, raising the matter with Eden ten days later. This, combined with the pressure already exerted by the PCR, resulted in the almost immediate closure of the Sutton Coldfield camp.[90] Another camp that was successfully 'given up' through Eleanor's efforts was Warth Mills camp, Bury, but up until August 1940, she had not been to any of the camps in Scotland. Following a very lengthy meeting with Philip Glass, the honorary secretary of the Glasgow Jewish Representative Council, she rectified this omission and went to Strachur camp with him just ten days later, on 15 August. Once again, and due to her influence, conditions improved markedly following her visit.[91] It is important to remember that Eleanor was not alone in denouncing the general policy of internment. In July 1940 John Maynard Keynes referred to the widespread outrage within government circles, claiming he had 'not met a single soul, inside or outside government departments who is not furious at what is going on'.[92] And Francois Lafitte's denunciatory and best-selling Penguin special study, *The Internment of Aliens*, compiled with the support of impartial civil servants, corroborated Eleanor's view that mass internment caused needless suffering and dislocation.[93] Samuel Hoare subsequently described the internment of refugee intellectuals and others as enemy aliens thus: 'Never was there a more obscurantist act, which tore scholars and scientists away from their work and deported them to the Isle of Man, Canada and Australia'.[94]

Another matter that arose out of the 10 July 1940 debate was the possibility of a single minister being put in charge of the whole refugee question, but this was a prospect that, at this juncture, really worried Eleanor. Her fear was that it might result in 'the Home Office, which does thoroughly understand, and is really sympathetic, being set aside and someone being appointed (for example Lord Swinton) who is quite new to the subject and far less progressively minded'. Lord Swinton's record was unlikely to endear him to Eleanor for he had supported a War Office idea to transport internees and prisoners-of-war overseas, and had warned the Cabinet, on behalf of the Home Defence (Security) Executive, about the danger of retaining aliens in the UK in view of the help they might render to invading forces.[95] She had voiced her concerns to the Labour Party leader, Clement Attlee, her acquaintance from the Settlement House movement decades earlier, and it was he who, the day after the debate, daringly raised the House's concerns over internment in Cabinet.[96] His subsequent suggestions closely echoed Eleanor's own, but his bold proposal, that the government abdicate responsibility for reviewing cases and finding work for internees, and hand the work over to a new 'really strong committee' made up of well-known refugee campaigners including Eleanor, the

Labour MP, Philip Noel-Baker, who was her fellow campaigner over Ethiopia's independence, and Graham White, was a step too far for the Cabinet.[97]

The redraft he was asked to prepare ensured that the Home Office retained control by the establishment of two new bodies: an Advisory Committee of three known as the 'Asquith (Internment) Committee' after its chairman, whose remit was to assist the home secretary in dealing with 'enemy aliens', and an Advisory Council on Aliens (COA), attached to the Refugee Department of the Foreign Office. Eleanor, Graham White, Noel-Baker, Emerson, Mr Willink, Sir Neill Malcolm, Lord Wolmer and Mr Latham were amongst those who were appointed members of the latter, under the chairmanship of Lord Lytton.[98] Their job was to advise on individual cases, and to make recommendations about the camps. What it was not to do, as Lord Swinton made clear to Anderson, was to concern itself with questions of security or the policy of internment.[99] These were matters for the Asquith committee, which is why Eleanor lost no time in sending them a detailed memorandum suggesting categories most suitable for early release. At the same time the PCR put together a plan to streamline applications by internees and their friends as well as employers wanting workers released, but this idea was put forward too late to be implemented.[100]

No account of Eleanor's work for interned aliens can ignore the relationship that developed between her and the Jewish community in Britain, represented by the Board of Deputies of British Jews (BDBJ). Both Professor Brodetsky, the Board's president, and the Executive Committee were keenly aware of, and immensely grateful to her for the pressure she brought to bear on government officials.[101] For example, Brodetsky wrote to her personally on 12 July 1940 thanking her for her part 'in initiating the debate on refugees in the House, and the fruitful results achieved thereby'.[102] Either Brodetsky or Adolf Brotman, the general secretary of the BDBJ, regularly attended Executive Committee meetings of the PCR, presenting their suggestions regarding subjects to be discussed.[103] Eleanor's role, and that of other MPs and Lords, was vital if the Board were to get questions put to the House in a hurry. But equally, they were aware of the onus of responsibility that she shouldered for, 'though willing to take on everything, they (Eleanor and Cazalet) must find it physically impossible to do all that they are required to do and intend to do'.[104] It was this assessment that precipitated the suggestion that personal contact with more MPs and lords be cultivated, thus providing more opportunities for parliamentary questions, and so ease the burden on Eleanor and Cazalet. The efficacy of the Board's activities in respect of refugees is hard to assess but it is fair to say that they were in a very difficult situation, constantly trying to balance the national interest against that of their brethren who were suffering at the hands of the Nazi regime. There was also the fear of raising the level of domestic anti-Semitism, so that having a Gentile activist like Eleanor helped deflect any criticism of self-interest.

Many of the eighty questions concerning internment that Eleanor put to the House[105] were precipitated by her liaison with the BDBJ, as in the case of Galician-born Jews interned as Austrians.[106] Then there was her outrage at the eighty or so aliens who had been imprisoned in Brixton prison for months without charge. Many had criminal records for very minor offences, such as pilfering, and posed no threat to security. They were denied the opportunity to plead their case for release at a tribunal, which Anderson claimed would not help them anyway.[107] In her capacity as a member of both the COA and the PCR, Eleanor had visited Brixton on Saturday 5 October 1940, and learnt at first hand how the British Fascist Party detainees – suspected enemies of the state – were receiving advantageous treatment over the aliens held there, who had no means of establishing the reasons for their prolonged detention, nor, it seemed, of improving their situation. In between this, and a visit to Liverpool prison the following weekend, she questioned Osbert Peake in the House, calling for the Asquith committee to be strengthened so that it could deal with these cases. Whilst the report she produced following the Brixton visit may have impressed the BDBJ for the way it 'summed up in a masterly way the whole situation concerning those aliens detained in prison',[108] the appointment of Herbert Morrison as home secretary in October 1940 did nothing to improve the situation. Eleanor was soon venting her anger to her friend and colleague, Philip Noel-Baker, asking how Morrison could 'justify the indefinite imprisonment of unconvicted men without any opportunity of self-defence?' And the analogies she drew were equally uncompromising: 'Are these not these exactly the methods of the Gestapo, of French *lettres de cachet* under the *Ancien Regime*, of banishment by administrative order under the *Czar*?' Noel-Baker held Eleanor in high esteem, crediting her with being 'really the only person in the country who understands the Refugee question and knows the facts', a compliment which she played down as 'an over-estimate' (see Plate 20).[109]

Eleanor was shocked at Peake's attitude towards the treatment of detainees, which seemed 'evasive and unimaginative, to put it mildly',[110] for even though there were promises to increase membership of the Asquith committee and hold more panel meetings,[111] she was not mollified.[112] In the House on 3 December 1940 she was again asking him about Asquith, but also whether he was aware that non-enemy aliens, detained under Article 12 (5A), and who still had no opportunity of self-defence, were now forbidden to write to MPs or make an appeal to the home secretary? His response was astonishing, for he accused Eleanor of making a 'statement without any foundation whatsoever', and denied ever having admitted the existence of the ban to her in correspondence. The spat that ensued brought Mr Shinwell, Mr Bevan and the Speaker into the fray, and Peake's about-turn, in which he admitted that there was a ban, but also that it had been withdrawn some weeks before, incensed Eleanor. How, she demanded, could she have known this, if he did not tell her? The verbal brawl only ended with the intervention of Sir Joseph Lamb, who remarked, 'In view of the fact that there is a war outside, may we not have armistice inside the House'.[113] Later that day, Eleanor had an opportunity of challenging Morrison on a number of issues, including the time it was going to take to deal with some 2,000 cases which were to come under a new category. Her sarcastic suggestion that this 'might take years' was met with an equally sarcastic reply from Morrison, who asked her if she enjoyed being pessimistic, followed by 'let us be as cheerful as we can and not talk about years when I think there is no need to do so'.[114]

Meanwhile, detainees were still prevented, by law, from writing to MPs, or appealing to the home secretary, a rule that, in her view damaged 'our country's reputation for humanity, justice and humane conditions', and which she wanted rescinded.[115] She herself had been so inundated with letters from individuals in prison, that she sent a representative sample of over thirty to Noel-Baker in December 1940.[116] Eleanor also found her own cunning solution to the official ban, by advising detainees to address their cases to Miss Craig, 'a lady who is interested in refugees, but who cannot, I think, be regarded as coming within the restriction'.[117] One refugee who was successful in getting released from internment as an enemy alien in Holloway Prison, through Eleanor's intervention, was a German woman, Gerda Dames, who was recommended to write to her by Manfred Vanson, in 1940. Vanson wrote and spoke to EFR, who eventually managed to get Dames released.[118] Nearly nine months later there were still detainees in Leeds prison, and in conditions which Eleanor told Peake were 'only suitable for convicted prisoners';[119] a further two months passed before he informed her that he had given instructions for these people to be moved to Brixton prison, which had been adapted for remand prisoners, whilst their case were under review.[120]

Whilst the day-to-day running of the PCR office was undertaken by Vera Craig and her volunteer assistants, Home Office files provide evidence of Eleanor's personal involvement with an unquantifiable number of individuals, including Alfred Richard Weyl, Feiwel Willner, Minna Specht and Gerasimos Stephanotos (Stefantos).[121] Weyl was born in Berlin in 1897, and arrived in Britain from Holland in September 1934, having been granted permission to stay for one month. He was eventually granted leave to remain, and established a light-aircraft business. He applied for naturalization in July 1939. His representations to Sir John Anderson, the home secretary, to get his case expedited 'as his services might be deemed useful in the case of an emergency' came to nothing, and by March 1940 his factory had been closed down and he was banned from working due to Air Ministry regulations. Internment followed in May 1940, and he was still interned in December 1940, when he wrote to Eleanor for her help. For, despite the intervention of the Royal Aeronautical Society, the eight applications that he had submitted to officials over the past six months had gone unanswered. Vera Craig, the PCR secretary, handled much of the correspondence and wrote to Mr Drinkwater in the Aliens Department of the Home Office in January 1941, complaining that 'this is one of the cases in which there has been a most unreasonable delay in dealing with application for release'. Drinkwater was not at all happy about the underlined paragraph, describing it as 'an improper remark, I think'.[122] Suggestions were made that Weyl was politically 'unreliable', and the security services kept blocking his release, despite the assertion of the PCR that he was 'strongly anti-Nazi and pro-Allied'.[123] Eleanor received numerous letters of support for Weyl from eminent aeronautical associates,[124] but the Home Office had to weigh this up against the impressions of others, including Otto Schiff, founder and chairman of the Jewish Refugees Committee, who had previously described Weyl as 'not the type of person I would recommend (for naturalisation) in any event'.[125] Vera Craig pursued the case throughout 1941 and 1942, but neither she nor the PCR got any thanks for their help. In April 1943 Weyl wrote of his 'disappointment with this committee, accusing them of 'repeatedly dissuading all sorts of people from doing steps in my favour', and singling out Craig as the least helpful.[126] Weyl was eventually released from internment on 18 November 1943, but as late as March 1946, was still barred from working in his area of aeronautical research.[127]

Another case, that of Gerasimos Stephanotos, a Greek national, was taken up by Eleanor in October 1940, and she used it to illustrate to Osbert Peake, parliamentary undersecretary at the Home Office, the 'hardship of chivying aliens around from one area to another as they become successively protected without – as far as I or they know – giving them any assistance towards the cost of removal; further, the question of whether holding Communist views is a legitimate reason for expulsion'.[128]

As for Dr Minna Specht, a lecturer in moral philosophy, Eleanor had met her on her first visit to Rushen, Isle of Man, in March 1941.[129] By the time she became involved, Specht had already written to Peake, applying for release from internment, to no avail. Eleanor's own correspondence to Peake, in May 1941 reasserted the release request, but also enquired whether Specht would be able to continue her work, as head of school in the camp, as a salaried employee after her (anticipated) release.[130] Home Office officials faced a chicken-and-egg dilemma – should they grapple with the release issue before the continued employment question, or vice versa?[131] Eleanor's interference does seem to have expedited matters, for Peake soon wrote to her confirming that Specht's case had been reconsidered, and her release from internment authorized. However, the question of her continuing work raised 'a number of (unspecified) difficulties' which needed careful consideration.[132]

Besides these cases, Eleanor was on the receiving end of innumerable letters from interned refugee scholars and scientists, and it was her fellow PCR member, A.V. Hill, who, in late July 1940, suggested that she contact Esther Simpson, secretary of the Society for the Protection of Science and Learning (SPSL), for advice on the question of the machinery required for securing their freedom.[133] The War Cabinet had recently issued a White Paper announcing enlarging the categories that were eligible for release, and Hill had just obtained a new concession from the home secretary whereby he agreed to interpret work of national importance to include 'contributions of significance to science and learning', which would allow recommended aliens who were free of any suspicion on personal grounds to be exempt or released from internment.[134] The working relationship that developed enabled them to share their concerns over aspects of the White Paper, especially appeals, and Eleanor wanted to establish a plan so that they avoided duplication, and thus complicating matters. Both the PCR and the SPSL were totally overwhelmed with cases by early August, and names and details of professional men passed backward and forwards between them at a rate of knots as they did their best on behalf of the internees.[135] The work involved with these cases was far from simple, and in many instances Esther Simpson acted as the go-between, forwarding case files that Eleanor sent her on to another agency, such as the German Emergency Committee, the Jewish Professional Committee, or in the case of a doctor, the Medical Department of the Council on Refugees at Bloomsbury House. Conversely, Eleanor was in a position to raise the issue of interned professionals in the House, asking Anderson, as on one occasion, if he knew that there were twenty-six doctors and approximately twenty-one dentists still detained in Huyton, and pointing out how much damage was caused to their practices and to hospital appointments by their internment.[136] She was also able to establish how many applications for release had been made since the issue of the White Paper. For once, Eleanor gave credit where it was due, albeit indirectly, for she wrote to Esther Simpson, who was very concerned about the release of her 'learned' internees, on 22 August saying, of the Home Office:

> I suspect the reason to be that the Home Office has given priority to urgent cases such as sickness, emigration and 'work of national importance' and I don't think that we can complain of that. They are, I know, making great efforts to hasten consideration and strengthening staff etc and I don't think the pace is too bad considering the difficulties; over 1700 releases in the first four to five weeks.[137]

Besides all the correspondence about individual scholars, the two activists became involved in a scheme that Hilda Oakeley, Eleanor's friend from Somerville days, and Lilian Bowes-Lyons, a first cousin of the Queen, wanted to operate, that of supplying expensive academic books to interned scholars. The benefits, as Eleanor explained to Mr Dybell at the Home Office, were twofold, for besides enabling internees to continue with their studies or research, it would 'provide occupation for a type of internee who appears to be particularly subject to depression and is difficult to cater for under ordinary schemes of employment and recreation'.[138] The Home Office response was not only favourable, pending a solution to the question of security, but it was suggested that the scheme be extended to benefit internees in Canada who were clamouring for books.[139]

Eleanor's work, and that of the PCR, continued unabated throughout 1941, and it was certainly a credit to the staff that they were able to undertake as much casework as they did, given the conditions they were working in. An 'obstinate time-bomb' had forced them out of the Marsham Street premises for two weeks, and on their return they had to manage in a half-wrecked building.[140] During the first three months of the year, Eleanor reflected carefully upon the domestic refugee situation.[141] Unable to personally attend the Refugee Conference held in London on 26–28 January, her report on the work of the PCR was presented on her behalf by the secretary. The report included details of the numbers of cases handled – some 3,000 during 1940 – and of the lengthy processes involved with each one, whether an alien was interned or not. There is no doubt that internment created an immense workload for Eleanor and the PCR, as is borne out by figures compiled by the committee for the period 15 July 1940 to 6 September 1941. Of 4,526 cases dealt with, 1,693 applications for release from internment were submitted to the Home Office: 1,069 of these were granted, 53 refused and 571 were still pending; 1,750 cases were passed on to other appropriate committees, and 1,083 cases were related to issues other than release from detention. Over 7,000 letters were sent, 8,500 telephone calls were taken and 3,500 made, whilst the office received 4,700 visitors.[142]

Eleanor also discussed the positive effect of the Committee's representations to government regarding the addition of extra 'alien' categories, the only note of disappointment being the failure to include one relating to the Pioneer Corps. Eleanor admitted that 'The value of the AMPC (Auxiliary Military Pioneer Corps) as affording a main outlet for the utilisation of young able-bodied who did not fit into any other categories had not at the time dawned upon us or the Home Office'. The main content of her presentation dealt with what she saw as the problems for the future, including the situation of internees in the Dominions, the need to further separate Nazis from anti-Nazis in the internment camps, the employment position and the establishment of a mixed camp, and greater cultural facilities within the camps. In conclusion, Eleanor first begged refugee organizations to ask refugees not to flood, and so overwhelm, the Home Office with separate letters and appeals, but to allow one organization to assemble information and submit it collectively. Warning of the danger of grievances being aired in the press, which, in her view, provided the enemy with propaganda material, she also urged refugees to remember 'the real difficulties that have and still beset the path of a Government engaged in a struggle for existence'. Lest anyone should challenge her loyalty to her country, Eleanor continued:

> There is one boast which I sometimes make to my refugee friends when I think they are in danger of forgetting the British side of the question. I don't believe that there is another country in the world which found itself in the position of extreme danger which this country was in in the midsummer of last year, where the sufferings of foreigners of enemy origin and injustice done to such foreigners would have aroused such a spontaneous uprising of protest from private citizens and from Members of Parliament of all parties and both Houses as took place during July and August of last year.[143]

One specific group of interned aliens who posed a problem in early 1941 were the Communists or suspected Communists at Huyton Camp, and when Eleanor met the home secretary on 12 February she expressed her concern that these people should not be detained in the same camp as 'strong Nazis'. Her suggestion that the otherwise excellent camp commandant 'had one defect in that he was not politically minded and did not appreciate how intensely a man with strong political opinions held his views' did not go down well. Even though the home secretary maintained, in minutes, that he did 'not know what Miss Rathbone is talking about' it was proposed that the pro-Germans or Nazi group be transferred from Huyton to Knapdale, rather confirming Eleanor's complaint.[144]

Another issue that she raised publicly in January 1941 was the situation of interned alien women who were anxious to do something to help Britain and who wanted an equivalent of the AMPC available to them. Wasted talent grieved Eleanor, for not only was it bad psychologically for internees but it was a valuable untapped resource. She wanted units set up which would fill in the gap in the Auxiliary Territorial Service (ATS). Her platform was the inaugural meeting of the International Women's Service Group, convened to establish a centre for the discussion of problems and the compiling of a register of foreign women labour.[145] The response to this was prompt, for just a week after *The Times* reported on Eleanor's speech, the COA were informed that the War Office had 'decided to accept for enrolment in to the ATS, alien women, at liberty or interned'.[146] There were also two cases concerning the re-naturalization of British-born women that she discussed with Richard Latham, a barrister and scholar working as a temporary clerk in the Foreign Office General Department Refugee Section, prior to bringing it to the attention of the COA. Even though Latham was very interested in the cases of Mrs Sander and Mrs Rosenmayer, agreeing that there were anomalies in the law, he was cautious in his response, asking Eleanor not to quote him 'by name as having taken this or that legal line as it is not my official job to comment on the law of the Home Office'.[147] The regular meetings of the COA were in fact an excellent additional forum where Eleanor could raise internment issues. At the February meetings she brought up the issue of the provision of family camps for married internees, and a few weeks later was urging that Nazis held in the Isle of Man camps were moved as quickly as possible, so as to bring an end to the friction caused by their presence.[148]

Generally speaking, she felt that the situation had improved immensely, and continued to do so steadily, but ultimately her aim was to get as many detainees released as quickly as possible. To this end she produced a lengthy memo in March 1941 summarizing the 'black spots' in the refugee situation, which were 'both urgent and immediately remediable, yet little known'.[149] Richard Latham commented that he found this to be 'a very sensible and useful memorandum' whilst his superior, Thomas Snow, who was head of the section, remarked that it was 'interesting, but does not call for any specific action of Foreign Office, except in respect of detention of non-enemy alien women in Holloway. We might ask the Home Office for numbers and for their observations on Eleanor Rathbone's remarks'.[150] The memo and suggestions were also discussed when the COA met on 9 April 1941, and both Lord Winterton and Emerson agreed that 'any steps on the lines proposed by Miss Rathbone might easily cause trouble' and that they could not ignore public opinion.

The utter confusion over the categorization of aliens was clearly demonstrated in April 1941 after Eleanor put a parliamentary question to Morrison concerning the Home Office interpretation of the A, B and C categories, and the distress caused to those Category B and C interned refugees of enemy extraction who had been reclassified as Category A. Although Morrison refused to be drawn, denying that there was any confusion over interpretation, Richard Latham noted that

> the Home Office in effect admit that there are but no intelligible criteria of classification into A, B & C category. They defend this situation by the marvellous argument that since nobody knows what it means to be in Category A, it cannot be an imputation on the character of a person so classified. The argument, though opportunist ... is sound.

He, like Eleanor, thought that by then there ought not to be any categories at all.[151]

Frank Newsam, a civil servant who was promoted to be the deputy undersecretary of state with special responsibility for security in April 1941, thought that her proposals for re-classification would cause confusion.[152] It was a shame that Philip Noel-Baker missed this particular meeting, for he would have given Eleanor some badly needed support against this officer, whom he described as 'that beast, Newsam'.[153] Much to Morrison's annoyance, Eleanor proceeded to raise these issues in the House. Amongst others, there were questions about the finer points of distinction between categories, and the inequitable situation that resulted, causing Morrison to retort sharply that 'I have already explained the distinction'.[154] Then there was his fury over her suggestion, supported by other evidence, that in one instance, a six-month delay over release was due to carelessness on the part of his department (see Plate 14).[155]

Other refugees whose cause Eleanor specifically championed were the very numerous fully qualified foreign doctors who had been cleared of posing any political danger, but who were either unemployed or doing manual work, and in some cases receiving public funds. She wanted to know why the government was arranging to bring over doctors from America before these people had been absorbed into the medical service. Like so many of Eleanor's parliamentary questions, this was a prelude to challenging the government on a specific case which she had raised several months before. Ernest Brown, the minister of health, did not like her suggestion that a particular refugee doctor was only offered a job after her question appeared on the order paper, even though the sequence of events pointed strongly to this.[156] And even though the government denied it, the British Medical Association demonstrated strong anti-alien hostility and resisted the employment of refugee doctors.[157] This was still the case in October 1941, when Eleanor was once again pursuing the minister of health.[158]

Nowhere was Morrison's lack of sympathy for detainees more evident than in his attitude towards refugees interned in Australia, the people she described as 'out of sight, out of mind'. Although Eleanor was glad that reports pointed to steadily improving conditions, there were certain aspects about which she was passionate. The Australian Commonwealth authorities had, from the outset, imposed a ban on internees sending cables, a regulation which Eleanor described as 'cruel'. Morrison tried to avoid becoming involved in this matter, referring to it as 'a long-distance business', but his contention that Eleanor was 'rather exaggerating the gravity of the situation' confirmed his lack of compassion and empathy.[159] Nor could he have been pleased to be reminded by Eleanor that the Canadian authorities had not found it necessary to impose such a prohibition. The ban was only one aspect of the Australian 'black spots' and even after Morrison told her, on 19 June 1941, that it had been lifted, Eleanor had still to fight for the release of these internees.[160] But this was never going to be easy, for besides being antagonistic towards Eleanor and her campaign, Morrison's stated aim was to ensure that as few refugees as possible were freed, either at home or abroad.[161] It is interesting that B. Donoughue, Morrison's official biographer, made no mention of Eleanor or the relationship between her and his subject. His limited references to Morrison and wartime detention present a picture of a benevolent home secretary who acted swiftly and generously, once appointed to release certain categories of internees. Had Donoughue been able to consult Home Office documents that have been opened since the compilation of his work he might have reached a rather different and more accurate conclusion.[162]

NOTES

1. This was according to Victor Cazalet. See Cazalet Diary 1938, n.d. but late 1938. By courtesy of Sir Edward Cazalet.
2. See Note submitted by the PCR, July 1939, RP XIV.2.15 (20), ULL.
3. Waley, Czech Claims, 11 September 1940, NA T 210/20.
4. Mr Culpin, Report on setting up the CRTF, 27 July 1939, NA HO 294/50.
5. Note submitted by the PCR to Lord Winterton, July 1939, RP XIV.2.15 (20), ULL.
6. Letter of EFR to Culpin (copied to all Trustees), 18 July 1939, RP XIV.2.15 (25), ULL. PQ 88, 20 July 1939, NA FO 371/24100,W10944/1873/48.
7. Letter of EFR, 'Refugees from Czechoslovakia; A Government Economy at their Expense', 20 July 1939, RP XIV.2.15 (29), ULL.
8. Note of phone conversation, 19 July 1939, RP XIV.2.15 (27), ULL.
9. Ibid. Letter of EFR to Dr Benes, 19 July 1939, RP XIV.2.15 (28), ULL.
10. Letters of EFR to Seton-Watson and Wickham-Steed, 21 July 1939, RP XIV.2.15 (34); Letter of EFR to Amery, 20 July 1939, RP XIV.2.15 (31); Letter of EFR to Boothby, 20 July 1939, RP XIV.2.15 (33), ULL.
11. Letter of EFR to Cazalet, 20 July 1939, RP XIV.2.15 (30); Letter of EFR to Grenfell, 20 July 1939, RP XIV.2.15 (32), ULL.
12. Letter of EFR to Amery, 20 July 1939, RP XIV.2.15 (31) and Letter of EFR to Boothby, 20 July 1939, RP XIV.2.15 (33), ULL.
13. Letter of EFR to Bunbury, 21 July 1939, RP XIV.2.15(35), ULL. For examples of those whom the CRTF helped, see T. Kushner and K. Knox, *Refugees in an Age of Genocide. Global, National and Local Perspectives during the Twentieth Century* (London: Frank Cass, 1999) pp.141–3.
14. Letter of EFR to Cazalet, 28 July 1939, RP XIV.2.15 (37), ULL.
15. Letter of EFR to Lord Balfour, 28 July 1939, RP XIV.2.15 (37), ULL.
16. Ibid. Letter of EFR to Sir John Simon, 14 July 1939, RP XIV.2.15 (23), ULL. For deputation, see 2 August 1939, NA T 172/1899.
17. Letter of Cooper to Randall, 12 July 1939, NA FO 371/24084,W10698.
18. For the most recent assessment of Eichmann, see D. Cesarani, *Eichmann: His Life and Crimes* (London: W. Heinemann, 2004).
19. Memo, 30 July 1939, NA HO 294/7, p.1.
20. Memo, 30 July 1939, NA HO 294/7, p.3.
21. Case cited was that of Mr Paul Wulkan who arrived at Croydon on 26 November 1938. Letter of Graham White to EFR, 13 January 1939, WHI /10/1/8, PA.
22. Recommendations II and III: Conference of PCR and Principal Refugee Organizations, 15 May 1939, RP XIV.2.15 (18), ULL.
23. Palestine: A Statement of Policy, Cmd 6019, May 1939.
24. *Hansard* HC, vol. 350, col. 1454 and reported in the *Jewish Chronicle*, 23 June 1939, p.24.
25. A British woman possessed this right up until 1870, and was a significant issue because of the current international situation. Letter to the prime minister, July 1939, WHI /10/1/12. PA.
26. Stocks, *Rathbone*, p.264.
27. *Hansard* HC, vol. 350, cols 2828–9, 4 August 1939.
28. NA FO 371/24100,W11673/1873/48. *Hansard* HC, vol. 350, cols 2892–906, 4 August 1939.
29. *Hansard* HC, vol. 350, cols 2893–6, 4 August 1939. For the longer draft of this speech see RP XIV.3 (62), ULL.
30. Letter of EFR to Elfrida, 19 August 1939, RP XIV.2.19 (2), ULL.
31. Letter of EFR to Sir Henry Bunbury, 9 August 1939, NA HO 294/54.
32. Letter of Kennard to Halifax, n.d. but before April 1939, NA FO 371/24083,W73358/5/39. Letter of EFR to Sir Henry Bunbury, 9 August 1939, NA HO 294/54.
33. Letter of Sir Henry Bunbury to Sir Malcolm Delevigne, 10 August 1939, NA HO 294/7.
34. *Hansard* HC, vol. 351, col. 35, 24 August 1939.
35. Letter of EFR to Lord Reading, 30 August 1939, CBF Files, 113/96, Wiener Library.
36. Letter of EFR, 4 September 1939, RP XIV.2.16 (1), ULL.
37. Letter of EFR to David Lloyd George, 16 September 1939, RP XIV.2.19, ULL.

38. Letter of EFR to Nicolson, 25 September 1939, RP XIV.2.19 (45), ULL. Minutes of meeting of APAG, 3 October 1939, RP XIV.2.19 (35), ULL. Letter of EFR to G. le M. Mander, 30 November 1939, and Mander, Notice of meeting, 6 December 1939, RP XIV.2.19 (63), ULL.
39. Letter of EFR to Vansittart, 18 September 1939, RP XIV.2.19 (45), ULL.
40. T. Kushner, *The Holocaust and the Liberal Imagination: A Social and Cultural History* (Oxford: Blackwell, 1994), p.151.
41. *Hansard* HC, vol. 352, col. 1203, 24 October 1939.
42. Memo from the home secretary, 22 September 1939, NA CAB 98/1, CRP (39) 17.
43. Correspondence, November 1939–January 1946, NA T 161/997/S45629/1.
44. H. Nicolson, 'Marginal Comment', *Spectator*, 11 January 1946. For the Britomart reference to Edmund Spenser's warrior queen, see H. Nicolson, 'People and Things', *Spectator*, 20 January 1939.
45. *Hansard* HC, vol. 351, cols 366–70, 4 September 1939.
46. Letter of Anderson to Lord Halifax, 7 November 1939, NA FO 371/22941.
47. P. and L. Gillman, *'Collar the Lot!' How Britain Interned and Expelled its Wartime Refugees* (London: Quartet, 1980), pp.45–6.
48. *Hansard* HC, vol. 351, col. 369, 4 September 1939.
49. Letter of Anderson to EFR, 15 November 1939, NA HO 213/1732.
50. *Hansard* HC, vol. 352, col. 1043, 19 October 1939.
51. Letter of EFR to Anderson, 29 November 1939, NA HO 213/1732.
52. EFR, Notes on divided families, 22 January 1940, RP XIV.2.15 (1), ULL. Report on Dependents in Czechoslovakia of Refugees already in the UK, February 1940, RP XIV.2.17 (6), ULL.
53. *Hansard* HC, vol. 356, col. 1269, 1 February 1940.
54. Letter of EFR to Anderson (and Peake), 3 February 1940, RP XIV.2.17 (3) and 7 February 1940, RP XIV.2.17 (5), ULL. Supplementary notes, 16 February 1940, RP XIV.2.17 (4), ULL. Letter of EFR to Bunbury, 17 February 1940, RP XIV.2.17 (6), ULL. Notes on Deputation to Home Secretary, 19 February 1940, RP XIV.2.17 (7), ULL.
55. Letter of Anderson to EFR, 6 March 1940, RP XIV.2.17 (8), p.1.
56. Mass Observation was the social research organization founded in 1937. A team of observers and a panel of volunteer writers were recruited to study the everyday lives of ordinary people in Britain. This original work continued until the early 1950s.
57. Special Branch Report, 28 January 1940, NA KV 2/2715, p.140.
58. M. Layton, The Group System, 9 January 1940, NA KV 2/2714/12a.
59. Letter to EFR (possibly from Mrs Noel-Baker), 27 February 1940, NBKR, 4X/7, File 2, CAC.
60. Report of M.B. Mynatt, 10 January 1940, NA KV 2/2714/11a.
61. Anderson, Memorandum, 'Control of Aliens', NA WP (G) (40) 115, 29 April 1940, PRP CAB 67/6.
62. F. Lafitte, *The Internment of Aliens* (Harmondsworth and New York: Allen Lane, 1940) pp.69–70.
63. For an overview of the pressure exerted upon Churchill by MPs and the military establishment, see R. Stent, *A Bespattered Page? The Internment of His Majesty's 'Most Loyal Enemy Aliens'* (London: Deutsch, 1980), pp.69–81.
64. Anderson, Memorandum, 'Control of Aliens', WP (G) (40) 115, 29 April 1940, NA CAB 67/6.
65. *Hansard* HC, vol. 361, cols 294–5, 23 May 1940.
66. Osbert Peake, Note of reception of PCR deputation, 24 June 1940, Acc 3121/C/2/3/5/1. BDBJ, LMA.
67. *Hansard* HC, vol. 361, col. 981, 6 June 1940 and col. 1114, 11 June 1940.
68. EFR, 'How British Policy towards refugees helps Hitler', 6 July 1940, RP XIV.2.17 (10), ULL.
69. Letter of W. Sternfeld to EFR, 23 June 1940; 3 letters of EFR to Butler, 24 June 1940, all NA FO 371/24326,C7400/7304/17.
70. Letter of EFR to Butler, 24 June 1940, NA FO 371/24326,C7400/7304/17.
71. Letter of Butler to EFR, 1 July 1940, NA FO 371/24326,C7400/7304/17.
72. *Hansard* HC, vol. 362, cols 1218–23, 10 July 1940.
73. N. Shepherd, *Wilfrid Israel: German Jewry's Secret Ambassador* (London: Weidenfeld and Nicolson, 1984), p.174.

74. *Hansard* HC, vol. 362, col. 1027, 10 July 1940.
75. *Hansard* HC, vol. 362, col. 1222, 10 July 1940. It seems likely that Mrs Tate was selected as a member of the parliamentary delegation that visited Buchenwald in 1945 because of her known scepticism about Nazi atrocities against Jews. Tragically she later committed suicide. *The Times*, 6 and 11 June 1947.
76. *Hansard* HC, vol. 362, col. 1215, 10 July 1940. Also 'Diary of an Austrian Refugee at Huyton Camp', July 1940, RP XIV.17 (16), ULL.
77. *Hansard* HC, vol. 362, col. 1216, 10 July 1940.
78. *Hansard* HC, vol. 362, cols 1217–20, 10 July 1940. Copy of Letter from Professor Wesissenberg to EFR, 7 July 1940, RP XIV. 2.17, ULL.
79. *Hansard* HC, vol. 363, cols 408–9, 18 July 1940.
80. www.thinkequal.com/page.cfm/ link=169.
81. M. Kochan, *Britain's Internees in the Second World War* (London: Macmillan, 1983), p.155.
82. Letter of Lord Marley to EFR, 9 August 1940, RP XIV.2.17 (18), ULL. *Hansard* HC, vol. 364, cols 983–4, 15 August 1940.
83. Letter of EFR to Weissenberg, 12 July 1940, RP XIV.2.17 (11), ULL.
84. Telegram of Weissenberg to PCR, 7 July 1940 and reply of EFR, 10 July 1940, RP XIV.2.17, ULL.
85. *Hansard* HC, vol. 362, cols 1269–70, 10 July 1940.
86. As cited in Stocks, *Rathbone*, pp.285–6.
87. Letter of H. Redditch, *The Times*, 14 October 1946 as cited in Stocks, *Rathbone*, p.286.
88. Dolf and Eva Michaelis, *Emissaries in Wartime London, 1938–1945* (Jerusalem: Hamaatik Press, 1989), p.7.
89. Telegram of H. Wedriner, Camp Leader to EFR, 10 August 1940, WHI /13/3/26, PA.
90. Letter of Graham White to Aline MacKinnon, 21 August 1940, WHI /13/3/30, PA.
91. Letter of Philip Cass to S. Salomon, 5 August 1940, Acc 3121/C/2/3/5/1, BDBJ, LMA.
92. John Maynard Keynes to Francis C. Scott, 23 July 1940, in D. Moggridge (ed.) *The Collected Writings of John Maynard Keynes,* vol. XXII, *Activities 1939–1945: Internal War Finance* (Cambridge: Cambridge University Press, 1978), pp.190–1.
93. Lafitte, *The Internment of Aliens.*
94. Viscount Templewood, *Nine Troubled Years* (London: Collins, 1954), p.241.
95. Letter of EFR to Graham White, 11 July 1940, WHI /10/3/8, PA. For Swinton's actions, see Stent, *A Bespattered Page?*, pp.95–6.
96. War Cabinet 200 (40), 11 July 1940, NA CAB 65/8.
97. War Cabinet, 'Aliens', Memorandum by the Lord Privy Seal, 16 July 1940, NA CAB 67/7.
98. War Cabinet 209 (40), 22 July 1940, NA CAB 65/8. Letter of W. Yaller to E.A. Seal, 24 July 1940, NA PREM 4 39/3.
99. Letter of Swinton to Anderson, 8 August 1940, NA HO 13/1769.
100. Letter of EFR to Weissenberg, 5 August 1940, RP XIV.2.17 (9), ULL. *Hansard* HC, vol. 365, col. 6, 5 September 1940.
101. Letter of secretary of BDBJ to EFR, 23 July 1940, Acc 3121/C/2/3/5/1, BDBJ, LMA.
102. Letter of Brodetsky to EFR, 12 July 1940, Acc 3121/C/2/3/5/2, BDBJ, LMA.
103. See, for example, Note on Executive Committee Meeting, PCR, 4 June 1940, Acc 3121/C/2/3/5/1, BDBJ, LMA.
104. Unsigned Letter to Brodetsky, 19 July 1940, Acc 3121/C/2/3/5/2, BDBJ, LMA.
105. R. Stent Papers, 80/6/1, Part 1, 56, IWM. Her parliamentary colleague, Wedgwood, put seventy-eight questions.
106. Letter of secretary of BDBJ to EFR, 19 July 1940, Acc 3121/C/2/3/5/2, BDBJ, LMA. Letter of secretary of BDBJ to Blanche Dugdale, 26 July 1940; Letter of Philip Glass to S. Salomon, 5 August 1940 and unsigned letter to Brodetsky, 7 August 1940, Acc 3121/C/2/3/5/1, BDBJ, LMA. The list of cases mentioned appears not to have survived. *Hansard* HC, vol. 365, col. 185, 19 September 1940.
107. Report on Visit to Brixton, 5 October 1940, RP XIV.2.17 (26), ULL. *Hansard* HC, vol. 364, col. 1439, 22 August 1940.
108. Meeting on Aliens in Prisons, 22 November 1940, Acc 3121/C/2/3/5, BDBJ, LMA.
109. Letter of Noel-Baker to EFR, 31 October 1940, NBKR, 4/581, CAC. Letter (reply) of EFR to Noel-Baker, 2 November 1940, NBKR, 4/580, CAC.
110. Ibid.
111. *Hansard* HC, vol. 365, col. 365, 9 October 1940, vol. 365, cols 586–7, 15 October 1940.

112. *Hansard* HC, vol. 367, cols 390–1, 3 December 1940; vol. 367, cols 853–4, 10 December 1940.
113. *Hansard* HC, vol. 367, cols 392–3, 3 December 1940.
114. *Hansard* HC, vol. 367, cols 452–3, 3 December 1940.
115. *Hansard* HC, vol. 367, col. 489, 3 December 1940.
116. Letter of EFR to Noel-Baker, 5 December 1940, NBKR 4/580, CAC.
117. EFR, 'Circular letter to internees in prison', 14 November 1940, RP XIV.2.17 (31), ULL.
118. Letter of M. Vanson to the author, 10 May 2001.
119. *Hansard* HC, vol. 373, col. 1021, 23 July 1941.
120. *Hansard* HC, vol. 374, col. 327, 11 September 1941.
121. CBF 113/51, Wiener Library.
122. Alfred Richard Weyl, NA HO 382,W1234; Feiwel Willner, NA HO 382,W2234; Minna Specht, NA HO 382,S4370; Gerasimos Stephanotos (Stefantos) NA HO 405,S39505.
123. Letter of V. Craig to Drinkwater, 21 December 1940, NA HO 382,W1234/7.
124. Letter of V. Craig to Prestige, 8 September 1941, NA HO 382,W1234.
125. Letter of Professor Eissner to EFR, 12 December 1941 and Letter of F. David to EFR, 1 June 1942, NA HO 382,W1234/9.
126. Letter of Denniston to Prestige, 3 September 1941, NA HO 382,W1234/9.
127. Letter of Weyl to Captain Pritchard, Royal Aeronautical Society, 10 April 1943, NA HO 382,W1234/9.
128. Letter of Denniston to Paterson, 24 July 1943 and Letter of C.F. Ryder, 5 March 1946, NAHO 382,W1234/9.
129. Letter of EFR to Peake, 28 October 1940, NA HO 405,S39505/5.
130. EFR, 'Black Spots on the Refugee Situation', March 1941, WHI/13/4/15/6, PA.
131. Letter of EFR to Peake (copied to Prestige and Sir John Moylan), 14 May 1941, NA HO 382 S4370/2.
132. Letter of Edmunds to Prestige, 30 May 1941, NA HO 382,S4370/2.
133. Letter of Peake to EFR, 7 June 1941, NA HO 382,S4370/2.
134. Letter of EFR to Esther Simpson, 29 July 1940, SPSL 120/2, f.244, BOD. Professor Hill was a co-founder of the Academic Assistance Council (later the SPSL) in 1933.
135. *Hansard* HC, vol. 363. col. 379, 18 July 1940.
136. SPSL 120/2 folios 245, 247, 257, 258–61, 262–4, 290, BOD.
137. *Hansard* HC, vol. 364, col. 431, 8 August 1940.
138. Letter of EFR to Esther Simpson, 12 September 1940, SPSL 120/2, f.266, BOD.
139. Letter of EFR to Mr Dybell, 30 September 1940, SPSL 120/2, f.278, BOD.
140. Reply of Mr Dybell to EFR, 2 October 1940, SPSL 120/2, f.277, BOD.
141. PCR Report up to March 1941, 24 March 1941, HC/LB/1/122, PA.
142. EFR, Report on the PCR, presented at the Refugee Conference, 26–28 January 1941 on her behalf, HC/LB/1/122, PA.
143. Refugee Conference, 26–28 January 1941, HC/LB/1/122, PA.
144. Memo of Miss Williams to Mr Kirk, 12 February 1941, NA HO 215/12.
145. 'Alien Women Anxious to Help Britain', *The Times*, 15 January 1941.
146. Letter of A. Piggott to COA, 22 January 1941, NA FO 371/29173.
147. Letter of EFR to Latham, 23 January 1941 and Letter of Latham to EFR, 29 January 1941, NA FO 371/29173.
148. COA Report, 28th meeting, 12 February 1941, and Report, 31st meeting, 26 March 1941, NA FO 371/29175.
149. EFR, Memo on 'Black Spots on the Refugee Situation', March 1941, WHI /13/4/15/4–5, PA.
150. Memo on Internment, 29 March 1941, NA FO 371/29176.
151. COA Report, April 1941, NA FO 371/29176.
152. Minutes of COA Meeting, 9 April 1941, NA HO 371/29176.
153. Letter of Noel-Baker to EFR, 16 April 1941 and Letter of Noel-Baker to Emerson, 6 February 1942, NBKR 4/581, CAC.
154. Point 4 in Memo, 'Black Spots'. *Hansard* HC, vol. 371, cols 243–5, 24 April 1941.
155. For the case of Felix Mayer (Meyer), see *Hansard* HC, vol. 369, col. 1406, 13 March 1941.
156. *Hansard* HC, vol. 371, cols 539–41, 1 May 1941.
157. Karola Decker, 'Divisions and Diversity: The Complexities of Medical Refuge in Britain, 1933–1948', *Bulletin of the History of Medicine*, 77, 4 (Winter 2003), pp.850–73.

158. *Hansard* HC, vol. 374, col. 700, 2 October 1941.
159. Point 5 in Memo, 'Black Spots'. *Hansard* HC, vol. 371, col. 1983, 24 April 1941; col. 1982, 29 May 1941.
160. *Hansard* HC, vol. 372, col. 804, 19 June 1941.
161. *Hansard* HC, vol. 373, col. 1516, 31 July 1941.
162. B. Donoughue, *Herbert Morrison. Portrait of a Politician* (London: Weidenfeld and Nicolson, 1973), pp.302–3, p.306.

# 7

# *Confronting the Holocaust*

Eleanor continued to deal with the urgent humanitarian concerns that arose from mass internment at home, as well as the deportation of detainees to Australia, mostly through the Parliamentary Committee on Refugees (PCR) and the Council on Aliens (COA). Unlike the PCR, which met very regularly, the COA only convened about once a month, and Eleanor rarely missed a meeting. She was simultaneously a joint president, with Graham White, of the Merseyside Council for Refugees, of which Tom Simey, the husband of her protégée Margaret, was chairman. Her Merseyside connection involved her in a number of individual cases, including that of a refugee lawyer, Dr Kurt Regner, an *Arandora Star* survivor who was interned in Australia and whom the Home Office would not release.[1] (see Plate 10, 11 and 12.) Over the weekend of Saturday and Sunday 12–13 July 1941, Eleanor, along with COA members Lord Winterton and Lady Reading, took an exhaustive tour around the internment camps – Hutchinson, Onchan, Granville, Port Erin, Port St Mary and Peel – on the Isle of Man (see Plates 10, 11 and 12).[2] The recommendations that came out of these visits were rather different from those made the previous year. There was less to note about the provision of basic needs, other than the 'hardship of internees who had to pay for medicines'; the observations were more about the quickest way of getting camps closed down, especially the three camps housing Italians which were surrounded by barbed wire.[3] Eleanor's ongoing concern over the many alien refugees who were anxious to take a full role in Civil Defence, but were thwarted by a lack of information as to what was possible, was aired in the House some months later.[4] And dissatisfied with the regular channels of information, she asked a German refugee friend to 'snoop' around and establish how well the employment exchanges were doing in respect of alien applicants.[5]

Funding all this work was a constant drain on resources, and as Eleanor explained, when writing to ask Sigmund Gestetner for a further donation, 'the remaining interned cases are chiefly more difficult and involve careful investigation and a lot of correspondence'.[6]

One person who voluntarily became involved in obtaining financial support at this time was A.V. Hill, a PCR member, a vice-president of the SPSL and, since 1940, Independent Conservative MP for

Cambridge University. He was shocked when he saw from the accounts that Eleanor was paying the committee's expenses herself, and with the help of Esther Simpson, the SPSL secretary, instigated a fund-raising drive amongst the scholars of Oxford and Cambridge. The response was magnificent, especially considering that many of the scholars were refugees themselves and had little cash to spare. One difficulty that arose, and which Professor Gilbert Murray highlighted, was the conception amongst many potential donors that the PCR was an official body and therefore the beneficiary of public funds.[7] Once the real status was explained – that it was purely voluntary – people were happy to make donations, large and small. Murray personally sent £20 immediately – the equivalent of about £1,200 by 2008 standards;[8] the SPSL allocated £60, and over £148 was collected from individual donors.[9] Such support was clear evidence of the esteem in which the refugees and their friends held the PCR, confirmation that they regarded their work as very useful.

The internees in Australia were a continuing source of concern, especially as there was a prevailing misapprehension amongst members of the general public there that these people were dangerous characters. Eleanor's plea to Morrison that he do something about correcting this impression brought a less than helpful response, for all he could say was that the Australian government had been reassured a year earlier about the character of internees and it was up to them to make this known. In an effort at redressing this situation Eleanor continually pressed the matter on Sir Herbert Emerson, and she drew on the confidential support of Lord Cranborne, secretary for the Dominions, who said that he would try and exercise some 'private and informal influence on the subject with the Australian High Commissioner'.[10] There was also her concern about the financial welfare of the wives who were left behind, and whether compensation money, promised to them by the financial secretary to the War Office, had been paid. Morrison was, no doubt, pleased to be exonerated from any responsibility and to pass this matter over to the secretary of state for war.[11]

Calls for help with individual cases kept coming Eleanor's way: for example, an actress, a Miss Woznianski was unable to get the Home Office to issue her with a work permit to appear at the Prince of Wales Theatre;[12] a chemist, Dr Reifenberg, could not get work in his field;[13] whilst Miss Rischowski, whom she had come across as an internee in Port Erin camp on the Isle of Man, was unable to obtain release owing to a complicated set of personal circumstances.[14] Of these, Irene Rischowski was subsequently freed and was then able to pursue the cases of fellow internees through Eleanor, Miss Craig and the PCR.[15]

Meanwhile, Eleanor kept a close eye on matters related to international rescue, for in the spring of 1941 she raised concerns with Emerson about the state of internees in Le Vernet camp in France.[16] This camp, in the department of Ariège near the Spanish border, had been established to hold Spanish Republicans who had fled into France when the Civil War ended. Eleanor had tried to involve John Winant, the US ambassador, in a move to improve the conditions, but even though he had referred the matter to Washington, the status quo, in October 1941, remained unchanged.[17] What is significant is that Eleanor had direct contact at a personal level with US officials, and was able to discuss refugee-related issues with them. This was to prove valuable in 1944, when President Franklin Roosevelt initiated the establishment of the US War Refugee Board (WRB), the only organization ever set up by any Allied government with the specific aim of rescuing Jews from the Nazis.

The opportunity of revitalizing the Le Vernet camp came about after she read *Scum of the Earth*, written by Arthur Koestler, who had arrived in Britain as a refugee in November 1940.[18] The book, a combination of reportage and autobiography, included Koestler's personal experiences of detention in Le Vernet, and those of his fellow internees, especially the International Brigaders (IBs). There were two aspects of the book that Eleanor identified as important. There was its propaganda value, which she considered 'could be used as a crowbar to prise into the consciences of people such as Winant, others in the USA, and the Vichy people if one could get it to them directly or making a loud stink in the Press'.[19] And there was the potential benefit of forging a stronger working relationship with Koestler himself. His wife, Dorothea, had written to Eleanor in 1937, in an effort to secure his release from prison in Seville, Spain, but the two did not meet until late 1940,[20] when they had discussed Eleanor's interest in the question of refugees with special qualifications serving in the Pioneer Corps.[21] Their recent meeting occurred whilst Koestler was on leave from his Pioneer Corps unit between 30 October and 6 November 1941, and now Eleanor made clear her support of his plan to rescue some of the eighty to one hundred thousand internees and stateless alien refugees in unoccupied France and French North Africa. Forty-five thousand of these, mostly Jews, were in internment camps. The scheme was dependent upon the United States agreeing to set up a quarantine camp for them on territory under their control for the rest of the war. Eleanor, in the company of Lady Violet Asquith,[22] Lady Cripps[23] and the journalist David Astor, attended several important meetings with Winant and Gustav Kullmann, a Swiss citizen and deputy high commissioner for refugees under Emerson, in the hope of persuading the US to take up the plan. Koestler kept in touch with Eleanor, and within days of his return to his company in Gloucestershire he sent her a lengthy memorandum in which he detailed the position of the refugees, the threat which they faced, and his suggestions for the next practical steps together with a proposed rescue scheme. The memo also went out to David Astor and Paul Sturge, the secretary of Friends Service Council, and as a way of publicizing the plan, Astor got Koestler to write an 800-word article for the *Observer*.[24] Official reaction from members of the Refugee Department to the plan was mixed: Lady Cheetham thought that the Washington embassy could be asked to enquire whether the Virgin Islands would be ready to take these refugees, but her colleague, Alan Walker, whose dislike of Eleanor and her campaigning was overt, described it as 'a somewhat utopian one, or in any case ambitious, more particularly at the present time as the States, like ourselves, have numerous other fish to fry'.[25]

Winant's initial reaction to this memo, which David Astor passed on to him, was rather more optimistic, and certainly encouraged the two campaigners,[26] but it was not long before Eleanor was the harbinger of bad news, as it became clear that the deterioration in relations between the US and Vichy France would prevent their scheme from being adopted.[27] Koestler's serious breakdown in health could hardly have been helped by the depressing letter that Eleanor sent him on 12 December 1941 for she had to concede that 'things were looking very badly for our project for obvious reasons. The U.S.A. authorities will be too taken up to consider anything except their own war anxieties; they will need their vacant islands etc. for their own internees; will be on worse relations than ever with Vichy etc.'[28] With Koestler incapacitated, it was left to Eleanor to try and persuade the US to take up the scheme, and in customary fashion she pursued every possible angle, involving as many sympathizers as possible. Miss Bertha Bracey, the Quaker interventionist and member of the National Council for Civil Liberties, wrote to her Society of Friends compatriots in the US, suggesting that they take the initiative in approaching Roosevelt, whilst Eleanor sent copies of Koestler's memo to Richard Law, the junior Foreign Office minister, and to Alec Randall, the head of the Refugee Department at the Foreign Office. Reporting to Koestler again in late December, she told him that since her last letter she had spoken to Randall about the scheme. The most serious obstacle seemed to be the difficulty with shipping, a problem that he and Winant confirmed, but this was not sufficient for Winant to want to drop the idea.[29] And it certainly did not deflect Eleanor from pursuing it, in the same way as she had with Butler in June 1940.

By the time she wrote to Koestler again in late January 1942, his health had improved sufficiently for her to anticipate his renewed involvement. She and David Astor had, meanwhile, met again with Lewis Einstein, an embassy official appointed by Winant. As far as Eleanor was concerned, the man was 'a newcomer to the refugee question (who) will need to be kept fed with information', and she and Astor had come away 'greatly discouraged and feeling that progress through that man was impossible'.[30] As the US were now belligerents, Astor and Einstein thought that the country would want Britain to share the responsibility of receiving the refugees for internment. Eleanor did not entirely agree with this argument, on the basis that Britain already had so many internees and was in a more immediately dangerous position than the US. Nevertheless she told Koestler of the strategic action she had taken in securing a meeting with Herbert Morrison, the home secretary and minister of home security.

The relationship between Eleanor and Morrison was already acrimonious, having deteriorated steadily since the internment crisis in 1940. His barely disguised lack of humanity towards refugees was to haunt her to the end of her days, and it must have required a supreme effort on her part to go cap-in-hand to him. But rescuing people was her principal aim, and she was prepared to use every means at her disposal to achieve this goal, adapting her approach to meet the situation. If being deferential was likely to be beneficial, then she tried to be so, and vice versa. As proactive as she was, she was a trustworthy confidante. Her hammering technique may have infuriated its recipients, but she was shameless in her pursuit of action and answers. Now she begged Morrison to consider giving some of the thousands of now-empty places in the Isle of Man camps to the refugees, but, in a deliberately shrewd move, suggested that the principal beneficiaries should be International Brigaders. This was on the grounds that 'they had suffered the longest and had the greatest moral claim on us through our part in the non-intervention scheme'. The argument was one she anticipated would appeal to Morrison and Jagger, his personal parliamentary secretary. It was important to get the principle of rescue accepted and a start made to pave the way for 'some of the more important politicals other than I.Bs to be slipped in'.[31]

Morrison's attitude may have appeared to be sympathetic, and his promise to really consider the whole matter genuine, but private notes that passed between Randall, Cheetham and Hutchinson of the Foreign Office after this meeting unequivocally rejected her rescue plan on numerous familiar grounds: it was too ambitious, impracticable even on a smaller scale, and would only be considered if the US led the way. Cheetham seemed more concerned about the possibility of typhus being introduced into the country.[32]

Eleanor continued to pursue the American angle, even coming up with a solution, approved by Koestler, to overcome the major obstacle of the apparent shipping difficulty. Her idea was to ask the Swiss government to provide an internment camp in Switzerland, with the costs of this, and of repatriation, met by the USA, the British government or donors. But Eleanor was shrewd enough to realize that 'the Swiss government may be wholly unwilling to consider such a proposal'. Cheetham had little hope that the Swiss would agree, and, not surprisingly, was certain 'that the Treasury would not readily agree to meet the expenditure' (see Plate 9).[33]

Eleanor was now totally immersed in the refugee catastrophe. When the Ministry of Information invited her to undertake a short lecturing tour in Sweden, aimed at promoting certain aspects of the British war effort, she refused because, as she wrote, 'it is a question of balancing the value of what I could hope to do in Sweden against the value of what I should leave undone in England'. Several of her current subjects were 'in crisis and ought not be deserted during the next few weeks'.[34] Amongst these was her anguish over the fate of the 769 Jewish refugees from Romania travelling on the *Struma*. The ship had left Constanza on 12 December 1941 en route for Palestine, but had become stranded in the sea off Istanbul. For two months Turkey refused leave for the passengers to land or for the ship to proceed, and the British government resolutely ignored pleas to authorize the refugees admission to Palestine. In late February 1942 the Turks towed the ship out into the Black Sea where it sank. All but two of the refugees on board drowned (see Plate 16).[35] Eleanor knew from Mr Linton of the Jewish Agency that these survivors were in imminent danger of being deported from Turkey, and on 19 March 1942, she was part of a deputation, which included Lord Melchett, Victor Cazalet and Wedgwood, which broached the subject with Lord Cranborne. Cranborne was, in fact, upset about the *Struma*, and in the course of conversation mentioned that the Jewish quota under the 1939 White Paper had been exhausted. It was inconceivable to Eleanor that this restriction had been adhered to in such extenuating humanitarian circumstances,[36] but lacking any figures, was unable to challenge Cranborne. She must have been even more disturbed to discover, days later, that the Jewish Joint Distribution Committee of America had actually offered £6,000 for the settlement of the 769 *Struma* refugees in Palestine, making them eligible for entry on the grounds of ensured maintenance alone.[37]

Eleanor was kept busy with regular COA meetings, innumerable individual internment and refugee cases, including her concern over the way that the Architects Registration Council was discriminating against alien architecture students,[38] another visit to the Isle of Man as well as parliamentary business. But as the demands of the internment crisis diminished, so the scale of horrors being perpetrated by the Nazis increased.[39] Information about atrocities against Jews in Nazi-occupied Europe was beginning to trickle through, and on 25 June 1942, the *Daily Telegraph* reported that 700,000 Polish Jews had been killed, some by mobile gas chambers.[40] Then there was news of the escalating crisis in France, for in July 1942 the Vichy regime agreed to hand over 10,000 Jews to the Germans, with thousands more French and foreign Jews fearing imminent death. Those who risked trying to escape to Switzerland were, in the main, thwarted, as the Swiss government closed its frontiers to most refugees, Jews especially, and stepped up military measures to prevent illegal entry.[41] More disturbing still was a report, passed on to the Foreign Office in August 1942 by a representative of the World Jewish Congress in Geneva, which indicated that Germany's leaders had plans for the wholesale extermination of European Jewry.[42] By late August 1942, it was clear to British officials that 'deportation to the east' was a euphemism for mass murder.[43]

It is difficult to pinpoint precisely when Eleanor realized that the Nazi policy towards Jews had changed, and that annihilation was their goal. However, given that she was in very close contact with William Temple, archbishop of Canterbury, in the summer of 1942, it is very likely that he would have told her about the reports he received from the YMCA representative in Geneva in August, September and October 1942, detailing the treatment of Jews in non-occupied France (see Plate 21).[44] Another likely source of information, but slightly later, was Jan Karski (Kowielski), a member of the Polish underground movement.[45] Karski had been asked by the Jewish leaders in the Warsaw ghetto to report to the government-in-exile on the plight of the Jews there and of the mass killings at Belzec extermination camp.[46] His mission in the West, and in London in late 1942, was to try and alert the government and activists to the fate of Polish Jewry.[47] Although Eleanor was not introduced to Karski until early 1943, Koestler first met him in November 1942, at around the time of his estranged wife's plight in occupied France. Given Eleanor's help in securing a transit visa for Dorothea to go to Portugal[48] and her subsequent contact with Koestler, it is reasonable to assume that she would have been apprised of Karski's information in late 1942.[49]

As the threat of Nazi policy towards the Jews increased, so the pressure from activists in Britain and the USA grew to such an extent that the British government had little option but to address the question of immigration into the country.[50] In a well-rehearsed fashion, Morrison's suggestions all reflected his intention, and that of the British government, to do as little as possible for refugees, whilst appearing to be generous.

He was initially of a mind to promote a scheme whereby children and old people were allowed into Britain, but Foreign Office minutes record the growing reluctance of officials to agree to a plan which seemed to involve 'giving priority in the grant of UK visas to Jews over all other categories of Allied nationals', which would 'be resented by the Allied governments'.[51]

The situation gained greater urgency after Pierre Laval, recently reappointed as the head of the Vichy government by Marshal Pétain, issued a public statement, on 10 September 1942, announcing his intention to 'cleanse France of its foreign Jewry', thus threatening the lives of some 100,000 people.[52] At a general level, this explicit warning did arouse a degree of sympathy in Britain, but more specifically, it had a very profound effect upon Eleanor, who was foremost amongst the active non-Jewish refugee sympathizers. The depth of her concern, which was driven as much by her personal humanitarianism as it was by her deeply held conviction that Britain should react to this crisis honourably, generously and with compassion, was evident in the correspondence, conversations and meetings between herself and numerous significant people including Bishop Bell of Chichester, William Temple, the archbishop of Canterbury, and Morrison (see Plate 22).

By the middle of October 1942, Eleanor was being fed with information about the refugees in France by Miss Bracey, whose source was, apparently, Bishop Bell. With the situation 'becoming more and more ghastly, more urgent', Bell mentioned the plight of French children in the Upper House of Convocation, but he was unable to attend the deputation to Morrison, which Eleanor arranged for the end of the month.[53] In preparation for this meeting she consulted Emerson, apprising him of the plan in view: to gain the support of the Central and South American governments and to appeal to Pétain to show mercy and allow the refugees to leave unoccupied France. Emerson had his reservations and was concerned that she should first ascertain whether such an approach might make matters worse, and even embarrass the American embassy at Vichy in the effort it was making, and he advised her to consult Winant before proceeding. But even if Winant's advice was against intervention, he could see no reason why these countries could not be invited to give visas.[54] Two days after Emerson wrote his memo, a large and influential deputation met Morrison, with Osbert Peake, Sir Alex Maxwell, Alec Randall, Sir John Stephenson of the Dominions Office and Mr Gent from the Colonial Office in attendance. On the refugee activist side there was Dr Temple, Victor Cazalet, the Moderator of the Free Churches, Miss Bracey, Mr Sorenson, Cardinal Hinsley, David Astor with Mary Sibthorp and Margaret Corbett Ashby, secretary and vice-chairman of the Friendly (subsequently Refugee) Aliens Protection Society respectively. The efforts of the latter committee were directed towards the protection of all friendly aliens, particularly those of foreign nationality, securing a recognized legal status for all refugees and the modification of the British government's internment policy.

A strategic decision was made that Archbishop William Temple, with whom Eleanor had a very close working relationship, should lead the group, even though he had to leave before the meeting concluded. Temple was deeply moved by the persecution of the Jews, and proved to be a valuable campaigner, renowned for his diplomacy. The fact that the majority of the deputation members were not Jewish was also significant, given Morrison's barely concealed dislike of Jews and open hostility towards refugees. These were not a group of Jews campaigning for the lives of their co-religionists, a cause which, the anti-alien lobby would argue, would create more domestic anti-Semitism and be perceived as conflicting with the war effort. Rather they were a group of humanitarian activists, from a wide section of the political and religious spectrum, united in their fight to rescue people in danger of annihilation.[55] But their many attributes were not enough to prevent the meeting deteriorating into an ideological and verbal battle between Eleanor and Morrison. She put it to the secretary of state that although Laval was not granting many exit permits, there was no reason why Britain should not be prepared to grant visas to larger numbers of children. And she urged the government not to count the cost, suggesting that Britain's generosity would bolster approaches to the South American states. But any hopes she may have harboured of a positive outcome for the French Jewish children were soon shattered, for, despite her eloquent representation, Morrison stood his ground, sticking to the government proposal to admit approximately 250 to 300 children with close relatives in the UK. Every member of the deputation was disappointed and dismayed by his reply. Cazalet wrote a short diary entry for 28 October 1942 saying, 'he refused any further concessions about children or parents from Vichy France. Eleanor very eloquent. Tremendous feeling engendered by Morrison's reply',[56] whilst Mary Sibthorp recorded in her 'notes from memory' of the meeting how his responses were full of the usual anti-alien rhetoric that asserted that Jewish refugees were not the only consideration, and that Britain could not, in wartime, 'open the door (to refugees) any wider ... the general body of opinion in this country was humanitarian, but there was also a body of opinion which is potentially anti-Semitic ... that Hitler could always make more victims than the country could absorb'.[57] In her subsequent report on the outcome to the archbishop, Sibthorp wrote of how the main points brought out in the interview were that 'the Home Secretary has apparently no grasp of the psychological results of the failure of Great Britain to take a lead in this matter or even assume equal responsibility with other powers'.[58] Margaret Corbett Ashby was equally distressed, bemoaning how 'in 40 years I have not seen a worse-handled deputation by any responsible Minister. No smallest concession was made'.[59] As for Eleanor, her initial reaction was to say that Morrison's reply was 'completely negative in substance and ungracious in form (some thought it offensive). He neither made nor held out any hopes of any concessions whatever'.[60]

Morrison's contention that admitting a few thousand refugee children and old people would heighten domestic anti-Semitism outraged Eleanor,[61] and although Archbishop Temple did express his own reservations concerning the 'introduction of a large number of Jewish refugees of working or fighting age (which) would make the prospect seriously worse', he could not imagine that children would have the same impact.[62] Nor were the deputation impressed by the home secretary's attempt to hide behind a spurious argument that Britain was already doing its share for refugees. Over and above all these excuses, Eleanor was appalled that he would think that 'public opinion would resent admitting a few thousand children and old people in danger of terrible death'.[63] What Eleanor did not know was that Morrison had already made up his mind a month earlier, in September 1942, not to admit more refugees, and was determined 'to resist any other appeals [other than for the few children with relatives in the UK] and refuse all further concessions'.[64] This information would have utterly depressed her and reinforced her view, and that of other campaigners, that Morrison was, without any shadow of doubt, an anti-Semite.

If Eleanor was perplexed as to what to do next, Temple was genuinely worried. There was the possibility of a House of Lords debate which Eleanor thought 'might do good in forcing Morrison to give further attention to the deputations request' and was, to her mind, a better option than a Commons debate, where she thought 'foolish speeches might be made. The Lords are easier to control.'[65] But it nevertheless presented a dilemma. If there was a Lords debate, Eleanor was keen that Temple refrain from mentioning the deputation's disappointment, and he agreed that 'nothing could be worse for the cause generally than to call public attention to the fact that our government is slow to move'. He was adamant that,

> we must not let it be said by either Vichy or Berlin that the feeling in England is not strong enough to carry the government. Of course the result is that the Home Secretary has us in a cleft stick

> because the only thing that would make a difference would be public action, which, for these people's sake, we must avoid.[66]

Not only did Eleanor eschew any public action, but she also refused to release any press reports, for she had agreed with Temple that this could jeopardise 'work' in France.[67] Considering how rashly she had responded to earlier confrontational situations, in India especially, her caution and sensitivity in this instance were uncharacteristic and no one could have been more surprised by the silence that followed Morrison's rejection than Randall. But it is clear that Eleanor had weighed up the pitfalls of pursuing the home secretary, for she confided in Mary Sibthorp, 'it is all rather difficult as we cannot publicly reproach the Home Secretary for doing so little for fear of injuring our efforts to persuade other people to do more'.[68] A week later she was still, albeit reluctantly, abstaining from press publicity, on the advice of Kullmann, Emerson and others who still 'urged caution for fear that protests in England might injure the work which Americans were doing for refugees in Vichy France'.[69]

Ultimately Morrison's attitude served to harden Eleanor's resolve to seek help elsewhere. Having sought advice on points from Emerson and Kullmann, and final approval from Temple,[70] she went ahead with the humanitarian appeal to the presidents of all the Latin American Republics that she had included in her proposals, begging them to issue visas and admit refugee children, mainly Jewish, threatened with persecution in unoccupied France. The telegram, sent to twenty Latin American presidents on 6 November 1942, was signed by distinguished signatories including the archbishop of Canterbury and Lloyd George, and this concerned Randall. He felt that the eminence of these people might lead the recipients to conclude that Her Majesty's government were behind the approach. So besides 'being deaf to all hints that the telegram should be sent *via* the Home Office' which would have given the missive official status, he quickly arranged to 'warn all HMs representatives abroad that this was a private enterprise'.[71] The same day minutes signed by Cheetham recorded that the president of Cuidad Trujillo had already offered refuge. More intriguing was the question of whether Eleanor should be told, in a 'confidential letter', of information contained within two further telegrams received by the Foreign Office, but since destroyed.[72]

Eleanor's correspondence with Temple continued as she tried to see Anthony Eden as 'the whole matter has become horribly urgent. I rather fear it will be forgotten by people at the top in view of their greater problems.'[73] This greater problem was the news on 9 November 1942 that the Germans had occupied the whole of France.

Amongst all this chaos there was a particular, individual victim of the occupation whom Eleanor tried to help. Koestler's estranged wife, Dorothea, a stateless Jew, was amongst those about to be rounded up in unoccupied France and deported to the 'East'. Whilst Koestler made approaches to Osbert Peake, parliamentary undersecretary at the Home Office, through Harold Nicolson, the National Labour MP, writer and journalist,[74] for a UK entry permit for Dorothea, Eleanor and the Relief Committee of the Friends Service Council successfully obtained a transit visa for her to go to Portugal.[75] But the visa came too late; not only was there no longer any chance of extricating Dorothea, but the whole refugee situation was dramatically altered.[76]

In a change of strategy, Eleanor drafted a confidential memorandum, dated 12 November 1942, which indicated 'points of immediate urgency resulting from German occupation' and sent it to the lord privy seal, Sir Stafford Cripps, Richard Law, Randall, Winant, Temple, as well as the heads of most of the principal refugee organizations in London. As the Spanish and Swiss frontiers still offered the best hope of escape for endangered Jewish, German-Austrian and Allied Nationalities refugees, she asked whether the Madrid embassy could be instructed to 'maintain and intensify its efforts for refugee immigrants, including Germans and Jews', whom they had hitherto neglected. Spain would be offered incentives in the form of concessions of food, petrol, and other necessities, but Eleanor questioned whether the Swiss would respond to an Allied governments' promise of money, food and financial support for illegal immigrants, and, in return, continue to intern them rather than send them back. Argentina and Chile remained possible places of refuge, especially as Eleanor believed that the Argentine ambassador had showed a 'marked interest and sympathy'. This was not a view that Philip Guedalla, the historian and essayist, shared. His opinion, which Esther Simpson, the secretary of the Society for the Protection of Science and Learning (SPSL), passed on to Eleanor, was that Argentinian goodwill should not be relied upon, and even though the Chileans might be better intentioned, they would be ignored by the enemy. Guedella nevertheless pointed out that it would be a simple matter to take up with the Chilean embassy in London, who were keen to 'stand well' with the United Nations.[77] Eleanor wanted to know whether the two countries could aid rescue by granting visas and obtaining exit permits,[78] and to consider the several thousand Jews in concentration camps in Morocco, the 900 or so International Brigaders in Camp Djelfa in South Algiers, and others for whom she sought relief.

Eleanor steeled herself to tackle Morrison again. The chance of saving the limited number of Jewish children for whom visas had eventually been procured was now completely lost and she made no effort to hide her anguish from him: she would have been more aggrieved had she known that this tragedy had caused consternation in some government circles, but for very different, and less humane reasons than hers. Official minutes note that Randall was concerned about the depressing publicity generated by the aborted rescue, and the difficulty Britain would have, in its wake, of adhering to a negative rescue policy.[79] As negative was Cheetham's private chastisement of Lord Cranborne for referring to Jews when discussing refugees in France and thought it 'a pity that it is now taken for granted that "refugees" are "Jews", especially when alluded to in France and Spain. There are Christian refugees too although doubtless they are a small minority.'[80]

The news in December 1942, of the mass extermination of Jews in Poland, overshadowed any other issues concerning refugees. On the same day that Temple wrote to Eden, demanding to know why the press was so silent about 'this abomination' when 'the knowledge ought to become public property now'[81] Eleanor wrote him an emotive and revealing letter, in which she discussed news of the 'reported horrors' of the extermination of Jews in Poland, and the validity of supporting evidence. Her belief in the information, which heralded the so-called 'Final Solution', was overwhelmingly clear, even though,

> obviously no cast iron proof of events in enemy occupied countries (is) available. But I think that the attached cable from Chaim Weizmann and the attached paragraph from the *Evening Standard* (2 Dec.) *are* justification for assuming – if not Hitler's alleged order for complete massacre by December 21st – at least massacre on a great scale. The *Zionist Review* for November 27th adds a great deal of detailed information from underground sources ...[82]

The content of the cable was unequivocal: 'Now have confirmation Hitler ordered to exterminate all Jews Nazi Occupied countries by Dec 31. [19]42. 2 million already massacred Sending you full report.'[83]

Eleanor expressed her anxiety that the governments concerned were 'taking the whole terrible question too coolly', evidenced by the lack of information passed on to the public. The British Broadcasting Corporation (BBC) was especially culpable, for even though most Britons viewed the Corporation as the most reliable source of news, it still failed to report on the atrocities.[84] As she wrote:

> One would think that the mass extermination of 'the chosen people' or a few millions of them was a quite minor incident, tragic but impossible to influence or entirely the responsibility of the German perpetrators ... Apart from the horror of it all, it is thoroughly bad

> for the morale of our own people to encourage them in such callous disregard of the sufferings of others.

There was more than a hint of the Victorian ideology of the deserving and undeserving poor within her remarks, only now it was the Jewish refugees, rather than the poor, who were worthy of help. This was evident in the following statement about the Jews, whom she thought 'suffer under such an inferiority complex that they are excessively timid about pressing their own grievances and seem to prefer others to take the initiative'.[85] Her empathy with the dilemma that the Jewish community in Britain faced was undeniable, but it is arguable whether she really understood the nature of their position. It is true that their leaders may have been cautious about exercising themselves in a more powerful political way, but this was because they felt insecure, rather than inadequate, within society. They were unwilling to raise their public profile partially for fear of arousing anti-Semitism. And if their behaviour was, at times, deferential, this was because they were fearful of creating the impression that the war was a Jewish rather than an international conflict.[86] The net result was that their 'moderate' and 'reasonable' demands were easily deflected.[87]

An urgent call for support from the Council of Christians and Jews prevented Temple aligning himself with Eleanor's plans for vigorous action. However, he had already written to Eden himself, wanting to know 'why the press was so silent about this abomination? ... the knowledge ought to become public property now', and he told Eleanor that he would try and see Eden.[88] Once again Eleanor approached Morrison, making an impassioned appeal to his elusive moral conscience: in the light of the situation which was 'at once more hopeless for the majority and more urgent for the few who could conceivably be rescued' she again begged, 'Has not the time come when our Government should modify its regulations and adopt a more generous policy? It cannot now be argued that this would lead to a great influx of refugees, or would merely encourage (as you suggested to the deputation) Hitler to unload his Jews upon us. His object now is extermination, not expulsion ...'.[89] The published words of the archbishop of Canterbury, that 'any Jews who were able to escape from the Nazis and make their way to British shores [should] be given a safe haven ... [since] in comparison with the monstrous evil confronting us, the reasons for hesitation usually advanced by officials have an air of irrelevance' were invoked to add weight to her plea. And in a conciliatory tone, she pandered to his ego by pointing out that she had seldom troubled him personally, realizing the weight of his duties and the '<u>relatively</u> [*sic*] small importance' of this matter in his eye.[90]

In the absence of a written reply, and having raised the matter of visas for refugees with Eden on 9 December, Eleanor put a short but very direct question about visas to aid rescue to Morrison in the House the following day:

> Whether in view of the situation brought about by the mass deportation and massacres of Jews in Poland and other Axis-controlled countries, he will revise the Regulations which have hitherto restricted the issue of visas and transit visas to certain very small and rigidly defined categories of refugees, so as to facilitate the rescue of the few (Jews) who do have a chance of escaping massacre?[91]

Morrison's response incensed her, for it was both patronizing and insulting: he told her that she was under a misapprehension in believing that a change in the policy concerning the issue of visas would have any substantial effect in saving lives. But Eleanor expressly referred to helping a few Jews, so that by rejecting what was, in fact, a very limited request, Morrison made it clear that neither he nor the Home Office were going to be influenced by humanitarian pleas. Nor was this the last time that he was to reject the possibility of small-scale rescue, for he refused to countenance the admission of any of the surviving Hungarian Jews into Britain in July 1944.[92] Thus, as far as Eleanor was concerned, Morrison's lack of humanity and overt animosity towards her and other rescue campaigners was an unequivocal manifestation of his prejudice towards Jews, and his explicit hostility towards refugees. This is further confirmed by evidence of his persistent intolerance of Jews in the post-war refugee policies that he promoted, and which Newsam, Morrison and others had begun to discuss as early as 1941.[93] All of these responses make it hard to conclude that he was not an anti-Semite. But this is a view with which William Rubinstein, in his study, *The Myth of Rescue*, would disagree, for according to him, Morrison was being realistic rather than xenophobic or inhumane in denying the issue of more visas, for the Jews whom Eleanor sought to help were, he argues, not refugees, but prisoners of the Nazis, and never had a chance of survival.[94] However, this ignores the fact that there were some Jews who managed to escape deportation to Auschwitz from Budapest in 1944, and for whom a transit visa was the key to safety.[95]

With evidence of the Nazi atrocities having reached officials and Eleanor by November 1942, her remonstrations became part of a much wider debate in Britain, and one that the government found increasingly difficult to ignore. The urgency of the situation had led the British section of the World Jewish Congress to launch a campaign for a United Nations Declaration on the Jews. The intention of the declaration was not to elicit sympathy but to stir the consciences of all civilized people, and to impel them and their governments into action.[96] The British government was to be asked not only to do its utmost to prevent further annihilation, but also to help the very limited numbers of surviving Jews find a place of refuge and safety.[97] It was a landmark victory when the British government finally succumbed to pressure from the pro-refugee lobby, including Eleanor, other Christians, Jews and particularly Polish campaigners, and reluctantly accepted the declaration. For the first and only occasion during the war, the fate of the Jews in Nazi Europe was explicitly emphasized, and hopes were raised amongst the campaigners that some lives might still be saved.

Such hopes were, however, brief, for the joint United Nations declaration that Eden read to the House on 17 December 1942 had been drawn up specifically to sidestep promises of rescue. Eden's rhetoric included condemnation of the Nazi 'bestial policy of cold blooded extermination'[98] and promises about post-war retribution for the perpetrators, but excluded any commitment to aid rescue or provide a safe haven for any victim who managed to escape Hitler's clutches.[99] The following day Eleanor was in correspondence with Bishop Bell again, articulating her thoughts on the atrocities in Poland and the Declaration:

> I rather fear that the results may be that people will feel that they have discharged their consciences and that nothing more is needed ... so I hope that Church leaders and everybody else will go on sticking pins into the consciences of the government and of everyone who can influence the government ... I have myself pestered Mr Eden and the other people concerned as much as I dare.[100]

In fact Eleanor anticipated and feared that the declaration would fail to offer any hopes of salvation, and had prepared a powerful speech for the expected post-declaration debate on the refugee question. But Eden denied MPs the chance of a discussion on the basis that he thought further dialogue of no value, and literally ignored her straightforward call for a debate.[101] What she did not know about was the correspondence between Randall and Mr Grey of the Foreign Office. Randall had hoped that Mr Law would be able to persuade Eleanor to give up the idea of a debate, on the grounds that it would be 'embarrassing and premature to raise the refugee question'. He considered that Eleanor was,

> so far as our intentions and actions are concerned, knocking at an open door ... It would also (although this is not for Miss Rathbone) involve the Home Office and perhaps produce a

> restatement of their Cabinet-approved policy with regard to the admission of aliens into the United Kingdom, with which Miss Rathbone so violently disagrees. As Sir Herbert Emerson is now pressing for a considered revision of our entire refugee policy, it might be unfortunate to force government into a reaffirmation of its practice and limitations hitherto.[102]

Eleanor's own comments on her draft speech notes bear testimony to her frustration at being excluded from speaking in the House, for it was marked, like others, 'one of many not given on this (the Jewish) question'.[103] What she did do was to include much of the speech text in a piece for the *New Statesman and Nation* entitled 'The Horror in Poland',[104] and in an article 'Let the Hunted Come in', published in the *News Chronicle* in late December 1942.[105] What the draft notes and articles show was Eleanor's remarkable grasp of the Jewish plight. She acknowledged that a large proportion of Europe's Jews had already been massacred, which confirmed the reliability of her informants, for it only became evident later that about three-quarters of the eventual total had already been annihilated.[106]

## NOTES

1. Letter of Merseyside Refugee Committee to Graham White, 8 July 1941, Parliamentary Archives (PA) WHI /13/5/9.
2. Report on visit, 12/13 July 1941. Council on Aliens Document 141, PA WHI /13/5/11.
3. Report of 39th Council on Aliens meeting, n.d. July 1941, NA FO 371/29178. Also Council on Aliens Document 141, 12/13 July 1941, PA WHI /13/5/11.
4. *Hansard* HC, vol. 374, cols 1129–30, 9 October 1941.
5. Letter of EFR to P. Brind, 20 October 1941, RP XIV.2.17 (57), University of Liverpool Library (ULL).
6. Letter of EFR to S. Gestetner, 8 October 1941, CBF 113/57, Wiener Library.
7. Letter of Gilbert Murray to Esther Simpson, 21 January 1942, SPSL 120/3, f. 357, Bodleian Library, Oxford (BOD).
8. Letter of Esther Simpson to Eleanor Rathbone, 26 January 1942, SPSL 120/3, f. 493, BOD.
9. Letter of Victor Cazalet to A.V. Hill, 20 October 1942, SPSL 120/3, f. 523, BOD.
10. *Hansard* HC, vol. 372, col. 806, 19 June 1941; vol. 373, col. 1519, 31 July 1941; vol. 374, cols 1480–2, 16 October 1941; vol. 376, col. 2052, 18 December 1941. Letter of EFR to R. Kidd, National Council for Civil Liberties, 26 July 1941, DCL/S/6, University of Hull Library. See also George Bell Papers, vol. 31, part 2, f. 313–24, LPL.
11. *Hansard* HC, vol. 370, col. 686, 27 March 1941; vol. 373, col. 435, 15 July 1941.
12. Letter of E.N. Cooper to EFR, 19 August 1941, RP XIV.2.17 (53), ULL.
13. Letter of Mr Scott (Ministry of Labour) to EFR, 30 August 1941, RP XIV.2.17 (54), ULL.
14. Letter of Ira Rischowski to EFR, 14 September 1941, Rishchowski Papers, 81/10/1, Imperial War Museum (IWM).
15. Letter of Ira Rischowski to Miss Craig, PCR, November 1941, 3 May 1942, Rishchowski Papers, 1/10/1, IWM.

16. Letter of EFR to Koestler, 14 October 1941, Koestler Archive, MS 2371/2/68, University of Edinburgh Library (UE).
17. D. Cesarani, *Arthur Koestler: The Homeless Mind* (London: Heinemann, 1999) p.157.
18. Cesarani, *Arthur Koestler*, p.170.
19. Letter of EFR to Koestler, 14 October 1941, Koestler Archive, MS 2371/2/68, UE.
20. Cesarani, *Arthur Koestler*, pp.128–35.
21. Letter of Koestler to EFR, 7 January 1941, Koestler Archive, MS 2372/1/156, UE.
22. Violet Bonham-Carter was H.H. Asquith's daughter and was a member of the wartime feminist lobby group known as the 'Woman Power Committee', with which Eleanor was briefly involved. Papers of the WPC, Coll. Misc. 548, British Library of Political and Economic Science, London School of Economics (BLPES). See also H. Smith, 'The Womanpower Problem in Britain during the Second World War', *Historical Journal*, 24, 4 (December 1984), pp.925–45.
23. Public servant and wife of Sir Stafford Cripps.
24. Cesarani, *Arthur Koestler*, p.185.
25. EFR, 'Scheme for the Rescue of Alien Refugees in Unoccupied France and French North Africa', 13 November 1941; Note by Cheetham, 5 December 1941; Note by Walker, 8 December 1941, all NA FO 371/29233, W14514.
26. Letter of Koestler to EFR, 9 November 1941, Koestler Archive, MS 2413/2, UE.
27. Letter of EFR to Koestler, 28 November 1941, Koestler Archive, MS 2371/2/139, UE.
28. Letter of EFR to Koestler, 12 December 1941, Koestler Archive, MS 2371/2/178, UE.
29. Letter of EFR to Koestler, 18 December 1941, Koestler Archive, MS 2371/2/178, UE.
30. Letter of EFR to Koestler, 24 January 1942, Koestler Archive, MS 2371/3/57–8, UE.
31. Ibid.
32. EFR, Notes on Internees in unoccupied France, 24 January 1942, NA FO 371/32654,W1204/107/48; NA FO 371/32654,W1204/107/.
33. Letter of EFR to US ambassador, 6 February 1942. NA FO371/32654,W2305/107/48.
34. Letter from Ministry of Information to EFR, 5 March 1942, RP XIV.2.19 (3); Letter of EFR to Bracken, 10 March 1942, RP XIV.2.19 (4), ULL.
35. B. Wasserstein, *Britain and the Jews of Europe 1939–1945*, 2nd edn (Oxford: Oxford University Press, 1988), pp.143–63, p.340.
36. One was a former passenger who had been allowed to leave the ship as she was pregnant; the other was David Stoliar. See Wasserstein, *Britain and the Jews*, pp.155–6. See Letter of J. Linton to the Political Department (of the Jewish Agency), 23 March 1942, Z4/14882, Central Zionist Archives, Jerusalem (CZA).
37. Letter of J. Linton to EFR, 26 March 1942, Z4/14882, CZA.
38. Letter of EFR to Esther Simpson, 18 July 1942, and Reply of Esther Simpson to EFR, 20 July 1942, SPSL 120/2, f. 299, 300, BOD.
39. For visit in August 1942, see 'Report of Activities of the PCR, January–September 1942', 14 October 1942, PA WHI /10/3/47.
40. S. Ward, 'Why the BBC ignored the Holocaust', *The Independent*, 22 August 1993.
41. For a detailed account of this episode, see Wasserstein, *Britain and the Jews*, pp.108–14.
42. L. London, *Whitehall and the Jews, 1933–1948. British Immigration Policy and the Holocaust* (Cambridge: Cambridge University Press, 2000), pp.198–9. See also S. Brodetsky, *Memoirs: From Ghetto to Israel* (London: Weidenfeld and Nicolson, 1960), p.218. For recent studies of this period, see C. Browning, *Fateful Months: Essays on the Emergence of the Final Solution* (New York: Holmes and Meier, 1985) and *The Origins of the Final Solution: The Evolution of Nazi Jewish Policy, September 1939–March 1942* (Lincoln, NE: University of Nebraska Press; Jerusalem, Yad Vashem, 2004).
43. Cooper, 'Memorandum on Post-War Problems', 29 August 1942, NA HO 213/1347, para.12.
44. The Reports to Temple in Temple Papers, 54/157–66, Lambeth Palace Library (LPL).
45. E. Thomas Wood and S.M. Jankowski, *Karski: How One Man Tried To Stop the Holocaust* (New York: Wiley, 1994).
46. 'Extermination of the Polish Jewry: What Happened in the Warsaw Ghetto', *Polish Fortnightly Review,* no.57, 1 December 1942, Papers of Baron Noel-Baker, 4/578, Churchill Archives Centre, Cambridge University (CAC).
47. Cesarani, *Arthur Koestler*, pp.202–3.
48. The visa came too late, for in November 1942 the Germans occupied the Free Zone and all chances of extricating Dorothea faded. See Cesarani, *Arthur Koestler*, pp.201–2.

49. Koestler introduced Eleanor and Gollancz to Karski at a party given by the Polish émigré artist, Feliks Topolski. See Cesarani, *Arthur Koestler*, pp.202–3.
50. Minute by Randall, 7 September 1942, NA FO 371/32683,W11681/4993/48.
51. Minutes by F.K. Roberts, R.L. Speight and Randall, 8 September 1942, NA FO 371/32683,W11681/4993/48.
52. Statement of Laval, quoted in A. Rhodes, *The Vatican in the Age of the Dictators 1922–45* (London: Hodder and Stoughton, 1973) p.316, in Wasserstein, *Britain and the Jews*, p.111.
53. Letter of EFR to Bell, 15 October 1942, Bell Papers, 31/2/476; Letter of EFR to White-Thomson, 15 October 1942, Bell Papers 31/2/477; Reply of Bell to EFR, 16 October 1942, Bell Papers, 31/2/478, LPL.
54. Memo of Emerson in advance of deputation, 26 October 1942, Temple Papers, 54/126, LPL.
55. Notes, written from memory, by M. Sibthorp, on deputation, 28 October 1942, MSS 2/1 Sibthorp Papers, MS 96/30/1, IWM; also in Temple Papers, 54/129–32, LPL and NA FO 371/32681,W14673/4555/48.
56. As noted by Cazalet in his diary entry for 28 October 1942. By courtesy of Sir Edward Cazalet.
57. M. Sibthorp, Notes written from memory on deputation, 28 October 1942, NA FO 371/32681,W14673/4555/48.
58. Letter of M. Sibthorp to 'His Grace', 3 November 1942, MSS 2/1, Sibthorp Papers, MS 96/30/1, IWM.
59. Letter of M. Corbett Ashby to Temple, 29 October 1942, Temple Papers, 54/135, LPL.
60. Handwritten letter of EFR to Temple, 29 October 1942, Temple Papers, 54/136, LPL.
61. Letter of Temple to EFR, 29 October 1942, Temple Papers, 54/134, LPL.
62. Letter of Temple to Sibthorp, 4 November 1942, Sibthorp Papers, MS 96/30/1, IWM.
63. Handwritten Letter of EFR to Temple, 29 October 1942, Temple Papers, 54/136, LPL.
64. War Cabinet Memo by Morrison, 23 September 1942, NA CAB 66/29,WP(42)427, and 28 September 1942, NA CAB 65/27,WM130 (42) 4.
65. Letter of EFR to Temple, 4 November 1942. Temple Papers, 54/142, LPL.
66. See also Letter of EFR to Bell, 16 November 1942, Bell Papers, 31/2/495, LPL.
67. Handwritten Letter of EFR to Temple, 29 October 1942, Temple Papers, 54/136, LPL.
68. Letter of EFR to Sibthorp, 9 November 1942, Sibthorp Papers, MS 96/30/1, IWM.
69. See also Letter of EFR to Bell, 16 November 1942, Bell Papers, 31/2/495, LPL. She also wrote to Esther Simpson, asking her that if the opportunity arose to interest influential people she should do so at her own discretion. See Letter of EFR to Esther Simpson, 17 November 1942, SPSL 120/2, f. 307, BOD.
70. Letter of EFR to Temple, 2 November 1942, Temple Papers, 54/140, LPL.
71. As noted in Minutes of Randall, 3 November 1942, NA FO 371/32681,W14915. For copy of Telegram, 3 November 1942, see Temple papers, 54/149, LPL.
72. Minutes, 7 November 1942, NA FO 371/32681,W14931; Telegram 131 (W11820) and Telegram 133 (W 12245) no longer exist.
73. Letter of EFR to Temple, 10 November 1942, Temple Papers, 54/154, LPL.
74. For Nicolson's life, see J. Lees-Milne, *Harold Nicolson: A Biography*, vol. 1, *1886–1929* (London: Chatto and Windus, 1980); vol. 2, *1930–1978* (London: Chatto and Windus, 1981); N. Nicolson (ed.), *Harold Nicolson: Diaries and Letters 1930–1939* (London: Collins, 1966); *1939 – 1945* (London: Collins, 1967), and for an overview of his refugee work, see D. Cesarani, 'Mad Dogs and Englishmen: Towards a Taxonomy of Rescuers in a 'Bystander' Country – Britain 1933–45', *Journal of Holocaust Education*, 9, 2 and 3 (2000), pp. 41–3.
75. Cesarani, *Arthur Koestler*, p.202.
76. Following the liberation of France, Koestler found out that Dorothea had managed to survive. See Cesarani, *Arthur Koestler*, p.234.
77. Letter of Esther Simpson to EFR, 2 December 1942, SPSL 120/2, f. 315, BOD.
78. PCR, 'Note by EFR on changes in refugee situation resulting from USA invasion of French North Africa', 10 November 1942, Temple Papers, 54/167, LPL. Confidential report of EFR, 12 November 1942, MSS 2/1 Sibthorp Papers, MS 96/30/1, IWM.
79. Notes of Randall, 9 September 1942, NA FO 371/32683.
80. November 1942, NA FO 371/32681/W14673.
81. Letter of Temple to Eden, 3 December 1942, Temple Papers, 54/181, LPL.
82. Letter of EFR to Temple, 3 December 1942, Temple Papers, 54/185–6, LPL.

83. Copy of cable signed by Stephen Wise and Chaim Weizmann, 1 December 1942, Temple Papers, 54/187, LPL.
84. S. Ward, 'Why the BBC ignored the Holocaust', *The Independent*, 22 August 1993. This is more incisively corroborated by Nicholas who stated 'the BBC News Department ended the war with the most enhanced report ... of any wartime BBC department', but further qualified this: 'although the motives for the BBC's role in playing down the Nazi extermination policies appear mixed (and indeed confused), the outcome remains a tragic blot on the BBC's wartime record'. S. Nicholas, *Echo of War: Home Front Propaganda and the Wartime BBC, 1939–45* (Manchester: Manchester University Press, 1996), p.159.
85. Letter of EFR to Temple, 3 December 1942, Temple Papers, 54/185–6, LPL.
86. For evaluations of the behaviour of the Anglo-Jewish community at this time, see T. Kushner, *The Holocaust and the Liberal Imagination: A Social and Cultural History* (Oxford: Blackwell, 1994), and R. Bolchover, *British Jewry and the Holocaust*, 2nd edn (Oxford: Littman Library of Jewish Civilization, 2003).
87. Kushner, *Liberal Imagination*, p.191.
88. Letter of Temple to Eden, Temple Papers 54/181, 3 December 1942, LPL; Letter of EFR to Temple, 3 December 1942, Temple Papers, 54/185–6, LPL. For deputation on 16 December 1942 by representatives of this council with Law, see Temple Papers, 54/197, LPL. There was a further deputation of British Jews with the foreign secretary on 17 December 1942. See Temple Papers, 54/219, LPL.
89. Letter of EFR to Morrison, 5 December 1942, NA HO 213/1827/470/12/64. The link between the wholesale murder of Jews and the overall intention of the Nazis had been established by December 1942, and was known to British officials. See London, *Whitehall and the Jews*, p.199, and Kushner, *Liberal Imagination*, pp.167–72.
90. Letter of EFR to Morrison, 5 December 1942, NA HO 213/1827/470/12/64.
91. *Hansard* HC, vol. 385, cols 1584–5, 9 December 1942; vol. 385, cols 1704–5, 10 December 1942.
92. Morrison, 1 July 1944, NA FO 371/42807/WR170, as quoted in Yehuda Bauer, *Jews For Sale? Nazi-Jewish Negotiations, 1933–1945* (New Haven, CONN and London: Yale University Press, 1994), p.188.
93. Post-war matters – policy. Note of Newsam, 2 August 1941; Newsam, 'British attitude and policy in relation to refugees and other foreigners after the war', 6 February 1942; Morrison to Peake and Maxwell, 6 March 1942, NA HO 213/1347.
94. W. Rubinstein, *The Myth of Rescue: Why the Democracies Could Not Have Saved More Jews from the Nazis* (London: Routledge, 1997), p.146.
95. Wasserstein, *Britain and the Jews*, pp.267–70.
96. Kushner, *Liberal Imagination*, p.169.
97. British section Memorandum, 4 December 1942, and Memorandum, December 1942, in C2/540, CZA, as cited in Kushner, *Liberal Imagination*, p.169.
98. *Hansard* HC, vol. 385, cols 2082–9, 17 December 1942. 'German Outrage on Humanity', *Sunday Times*, 20 December 1942 described how members of the House of Commons spontaneously rose to their feet to mark their appalled recognition of the mass murder of Jews.
99. Crozier, editor of the *Manchester Guardian,* later remarked to Eleanor that it was evident from Eden's speech that 'the attitude of the government had been entirely half-hearted'. Letter of Crozier to EFR, 17 May 1943, *Manchester Guardian* Archive, B/R45/4, John Rylands Library, University of Manchester (JRL).
100. Letter of EFR to Bell, 18 December 1942, Bell Papers 31/2/514, LPL.
101. *Hansard* HC, vol. 385, cols 208–29, 17 December 1942.
102. Minutes, Randall, 14 December 1942; Randall to Grey, 15 December 1942, NA FO 371/32682.
103. EFR, Speech Notes on the Jewish Question, 16 December 1942, RP XIV.3 (85), ULL.
104. EFR, 'The Horror in Poland', *New Statesman and Nation*, 17 December 1942.
105. EFR, 'Let the Hunted Come In', *News Chronicle*, 27 December 1942, p.2. The House of Commons did not finally debate the refugee question until 19 May 1943.
106. Raoul Hilberg, who suggests a final total of 5.1 million, provides an estimate of Jewish deaths by year. He posits that 2.7 million Jews were killed in 1942, giving a cumulative figure of 3.9 million dead by 1 January 1943. See R. Hilberg, *The Destruction of the European Jews*, vol. 3, revised and definitive edition (New York and London: Holmes and Meier, 1985), p.1120, as cited in Kushner, *Liberal Imagination*, p.321, f.2.

# 8

# *Rescuing the Perishing*

Anyone reading Eleanor's articles could not have missed her deep disappointment at the government's apathetic record on rescue, but conversely would have been impressed by her spirit of generosity and hope. In a totally pragmatic way, she was prepared to put the past behind, provided Britain faced up to her 'more direct and immediate responsibility'. The question she posed, 'What can we do as a Nation and in union with other nations?' was answered with her call for a concerted plan in which the most significant feature was the crucial role that the Balkan states of Hungary, Romania and Bulgaria would have in providing a safe haven for Jews. Unlike the government, Eleanor was not prepared to assume that 'Hitler's unwilling Allies' were immune to external influence, even though these countries had an appalling record when it came to the treatment of Jews. In notes for the speech which she had been thwarted from giving, she had written:

> By this time they [Hungary, Romania, Bulgaria] must know in their hearts that the United Nations are going to win the War. They must be haunted by fear of retribution. If the Voice of Christianity, of compassion for tortured humanity, appeals to them in vain – and there are men and women in every country to whom it will appeal – they may listen to a voice which tell [*sic*] them that before it is too late, they had better buy off some of the vengeance that will otherwise overtake them, by showing a reluctance to participate in this last and worst of Nazi crimes – the extermination of a whole people.

But if the Balkan states were to be convinced of the benefits of rescue, Britain would have to demonstrate that 'we and our Allies *really care* – care passionately, care to the extent of being willing to make great efforts and sacrifices ourselves'. Testimony to Britain's failure in this regard was what Eleanor described as the prevailing 'Conspiracy of Silence about this dreadful tragedy – silence in the Press, silence in Parliament. *That must end*.'[1]

Her text also reinforced the ideological gulf that existed between Eleanor and the government concerning rescue. She did not consider rescue and the war effort to be incompatible aims: indeed in her opinion the benefits that Britain would accrue from setting an example to other nations by implementing schemes of rescue were legion. Not only would others be inclined to follow suit, but also Britain's reputation as a humanitarian, liberal state, which Eleanor perceived as badly tarnished, could be redeemed. But the government adhered to its view that winning the war would resolve the crisis, and that rescue was incompatible with this aim. In any case they would not accept that wide-scale rescue schemes were possible, either because they feared the consequences of raising hopes unrealistically, or because they feared the anti-Semitic backlash generated by an influx of refugees. Eleanor had, in fact, a far more realistic view of the status quo, for by late 1942 she knew that the remaining numbers who could possibly be rescued were small; as she wrote, 'The best we can do now will be too little too late. Let us see that even that little is not left undone.' And of the oft-repeated official concern about domestic anti-Semitism, she had this to say:

> It would be an insult indeed to suggest that there is anything to fear from anti-Semitic [*sic*] influence here. Anti-semitism [*sic*] is an ugly infectious disease, like scabies or leprousy [*sic*], born of dirt. But our people, even the anti-semites [*sic*] amongst them are not so callous that they would rather let Jewish men and women and children be tortured to death than see them admitted here. Until recently they have been kept in ignorance of the terrible facts. They are not to blame if they seemed indifferent.

Such statements demonstrate Eleanor's greater faith in the basic humanity of the population than was revealed by government attitudes.[2] Once again Eleanor was correct, for Mass-Observation surveys carried out in 1941 and 1943 indicated that domestic hostility towards Jews had declined from twenty-six per cent to thirteen per cent and continued to decline during the remaining war years.[3]

Although Eleanor invoked the 'Voice of Christianity' in her December draft speech notes, she was not a practising Christian, but was nevertheless imbued with the importance of the Christmas message of peace and hope, using a Christian discourse to put her point across. To reinforce her view that Britain's war aims and the rescue of Jews were not incompatible she argued that it would be a mockery to ring church bells at Christmas, a sign of joy, when the very nation who gave the Bible to mankind were being exterminated.[4] She was no killjoy, but she could not understand how British people, particularly the older ones, with any heart or sense of right and wrong could celebrate with a clear conscience. She wrote poignantly of the difficulty people would have in expiating their shame: 'If peace came tomorrow, we could not forget the millions for whom it would come too late, nor wash our hands of the stain of blood'. Nor was she able to hide her shame at Britain's myopia, for she was convinced that with 'greater foresight, courage [*sic*] there would have been no war, and if our policy towards refugees had been less miserably cautious, selfish and unimaginative, 1,000s of those already dead or in danger of death, might now be free and happy, contributing from their rich store of talent and industry to the welfare of mankind'.[5]

This statement was a direct reference to her belief in collective security as a means of preventing war, as well as her earlier work on behalf of refugees, policies that the government had eschewed. It was also a tribute to the talents, skills and enterprise of Jews that she so admired, and confirmation that these were people who, in her view, deserved to be saved.

Here, as on other occasions, Eleanor adopted a tactic that government officials disliked, by exemplifying personal cases. It was far easier for civil servants to argue against responsibility for a group of faceless individuals, but she hoped to strengthen her case against the harshness of official regulations by personalizing the refugees and giving names. An important aspect of this tactic, and a further evidence of her humanity, was the way in which this technique gave people the dignity of recognition, the very commodity that the Nuremberg laws and Nazi persecution were systematically destroying.[6]

Having spoken at a public meeting held by the BDBJ on 20 December 1942,[7] Eleanor then spent Christmas Eve writing to her colleague, Graham White, expressing her fears and outlining her plans. One fear was that her reputation, which she described as being 'tainted with the refugee brush', was an impediment to the rescue cause.[8] That she was viewed, in certain quarters, as polluted by her contact with Jewish refugees, was a depressing reflection of the claim being widely disseminated in Nazi Germany, that Jews were contaminated and could infect other people, and therefore could be eliminated. And it was for this reason that she suggested that MPs with a lower 'refugee profile' should exert pressure on the government.[9] From this evolved her conclusion that a specific pressure group or committee, devoted to 'salvage work', was required. To this end, she and Professor A.V. Hill, the physiologist, MP and founder member of the SPSL, convened an initial meeting of interested parties at the Royal Institution on 7 January 1943. Amongst those who attended were Violet Bonham-Carter, Sir George Jones, Josiah Wedgwood MP, Leonard Stein, Mr Bert Locker, Norman Bentwich, Professor Brodetsky, Lord Perth, Lord

Farringdon, Simon Marks, a founder of Marks and Spencer, and Adolf Brotman, General Secretary of the BDBJ and Rabbi Dr Solomon Schonfeld. It was Rabbi Schonfeld who, apparently, suggested that a special parliamentary committee keep a watch on the situation, but Eleanor was against this, on the basis that the one parliamentary committee was enough. The PCR was dealing with domestic refugee issues and she felt that a second would only lead to confusion.[10] She circulated a document for discussion, 'Jewish Massacres: the case for an offer to Hitler', which looked at the possibility of the British government approaching Germany and other enemy countries and asking them to allow Jews to emigrate, but the idea of any such approach was dismissed by many of the members as inadvisable or impractical.[11]

Alongside this, Eleanor and her fellow refugee campaigners had become outraged by the failure of the UN declaration to offer any hope of rescue, and became more determined than ever to force the government's hand. The only feasible option left was to embarrass the government by mustering public support in favour of action. Thus a publicity campaign was launched to 'arouse increasing concern in the public mind'. Victor Gollancz, Eleanor's close friend and ally, in his capacity as a writer and publicist, initiated the propaganda drive, with the publication of his speedily compiled polemic, *Let My People Go*,[12] in which the central theme was his denunciation of the government-held view that the only way to help the Jews was to win the war. The booklet was produced within a week of the declaration in December 1942, and had a powerful and immediate impact upon society in general. The first print run of 10,000 sold out within days, a further 50,000 copies were purchased by the end of January 1943, and a total of a quarter of a million copies were sold within three months.[13] Gollancz's appeal for public support resulted in a deluge of donations of money and food, as well as offers of accommodation, on the doorsteps of MPs and the Foreign Office.[14] And so Eleanor and the other refugee activists kept up the pressure.

Private meetings to discuss the establishment of a new committee continued in early 1943, whilst Eleanor persisted, both in and out of the House, to raise refugee concerns with the foreign secretary, Anthony Eden,[15] and Morrison.[16] On one occasion Eleanor was involved in questioning Eden about the Vatican's attitude towards the German barbarities, and pressed him to elicit more than the very mild reference made by His Holiness in his Christmas Eve broadcast.[17]

Officials kept resisting requests to receive deputations, until Eden finally agreed to receive an all-party deputation which consisted of Melchett, Eleanor, Quintin Hogg, A.V. Hill, Mr Silverman, Graham White and Mr Holdsworth on 28 January 1943 to discuss the question of help for Jews in enemy-occupied territory.[18] Morrison and Colonel Oliver Stanley, the secretary of state for the colonies, were also present. The outcome was depressingly unproductive, and would have been even more so had Eleanor and her colleagues known that a secret War Cabinet Committee on the Reception and Accommodation of Jewish Refugees (WCC) had been recently established, and had predetermined the line to be taken by the three officials, that of encouraging the defence of the British policy of inaction.[19] Eleanor's previous suggestion to Morrison, that Jews in Germany might be exchanged for Belgian or Dutch internees, or Germans waiting to be repatriated from the Isle of Man, was not well received. If such a scheme were possible, she was told that priority would be given to some of the thousands of British and Allied nationals left in great hardship in Germany. And the WCC wanted it emphasized 'to the utmost degree' that any activist asking for large-scale action to rescue refugees would 'be asking for the diversion of shipping and other resources from the war effort'. In an all too familiar way, the rhetoric of such action prolonging the war was invoked, but it was the final phrase in this sentence which was so extraordinary, for the WCC asserted that neither 'refugees or the suffering peoples of Europe' would desire this.[20] Their attitude towards Jews, and their reluctance to acknowledge the Jewish dimension of Nazi atrocities, became all too obvious in early January 1943, when the word 'Jewish' was erased from the title, in line with the official view that 'it is not the policy of HMG to regard the Jews as belonging to a separate category. It is felt that discrimination of this kind savors too strongly of the Nazi attitude towards Jews.'[21]

Nowhere was Eleanor's despondency more palpable than in a letter she sent to her close colleague and PCR chairman, Victor Cazalet, in early February 1943. 'Dear Victor', she wrote, 'It is good you are back as I want your help and advice badly'.[22] The advice she sought was related to her paper, 'The Nazi Massacres of Jews and Poles: What rescue measures are practically possible?' which she had distributed widely, along with other documents on the subject of rescue, to government officials and others.[23] The key problem, which she discussed with Noel-Baker, a critic of government inactivity, and now minister of war transport, was conveying Jews, an aspect that he had told her he was thinking about. But Eleanor was wise enough to admit that it was useless to put 'totally impracticable suggestions' to government, and she looked to Noel-Baker for feasible ideas, on the basis that he was 'the one Minister – probably with Lord Selborne – who combines the expert knowledge with the keen sympathy necessary'.[24] One specific proposal, which, in the light of the current climate, Eleanor concluded was 'the key to the whole matter', was that a new minister (or high commissioner) be appointed to deal specifically with the refugee problem.[25] This was not her idea, but had been put to her by several people. One, she thought, was General Sir Neill Malcolm, but he flatly denied this, and wrote to Eleanor repudiating her claim 'in the strongest terms'.[26] In fact Noel-Baker himself seems to have been responsible for the idea, for Eleanor wrote to him on 12 February 1943, saying that she was 'increasingly in love with your suggestion as to a High Commissioner who could visit the neutral states for negotiations'.[27] Noel-Baker had already sent Law a list of practical proposals for help to be given to European Jews by the United Nations a month earlier, and had suggested the appointment of a new high commissioner to put these into effect. Eleanor had discussed the idea with numerous people, including Temple, who commented, 'it holds out some prospect of getting past the block caused by the multitude of departments which at present have to do with the Jewish question'. The Bishop of Chichester was also consulted, and agreed that 'I am sure that until you get a man of high authority charged with the responsibility, nothing will be done'. He suggested Sir Hubert Young, who had great experience in Palestine, Iraq and as governor of Nyasaland, North Rhodesia and Trinidad. In fact Eleanor told Noel Baker that she thought 'High Commissioner' might be a tactless title because people would say that there was one already in the person of Emerson, and, as she remarked 'he is obviously not the right man'.[28] She also wanted to establish informal contacts with several of the relevant ambassadors and ministers of Allies and neutral states, and was hoping to make a return visit with Cazalet to see the Argentine ambassador, and also to make contact with the Swiss, Swedish and various other legations, including Panama.[29] Sir Wyndham Deedes had already taken her to see the Turkish ambassador, whose main suggestion was a ferry service by neutral ships, maybe supplied by Panama or Sweden, and this was no doubt why she was keen to contact their legation.[30]

Eden's 'disappointing' answers to parliamentary questions concerning the 'Jewish massacres' in mid-February 1943 prompted Eleanor to write to him again. She was especially perturbed by his 'disparaging reference to the proposal for "a new Nansen"', a reference to the League of Nations first high commissioner for refugees whose humanitarianism earned him the Nobel Peace Prize in 1922.[31] As she wrote to Eden, 'most of us feel that the latter proposal is the key step to effective action. My memo previously sent to you states the case and I think shows we do not underrate the difficulties. How can these be overcome by the slow channels of diplomatic correspondence?' She also challenged him again about visas for the United Kingdom, since his intimation, given weeks before, that Home Office restrictions would be relaxed, had come to nothing.[32] Her view was that the test for entry was still one of self-interest on the part of government – only those who could make an outstanding contribution to the war effort and pose no burden on the public purse would be considered – those in the most desperate danger, even with familial ties with Britain, didn't stand a chance of obtaining a visa. And she concluded by saying 'In the face of the Home Office attitude, how can it be truthfully be said that "the government is doing everything possible?"'[33] Morrison was evidently a party to this letter, for he responded in terms which left her in no doubt as to his views. Her assertion of Britain's self-interest in respect of the issue of visas was considered by him to be 'nothing less than a perversion of the facts and shows a disregard of statements made in the House and elsewhere of which you must be cognisant'. His closing remarks reiterated the view constantly reasserted by the government of 'the desire for an Allied victory and the concentration of all efforts to this end in order to save the lives and liberties of all oppressed peoples of Europe'.[34] But what Eleanor and the other refugee activists wanted was an Allied victory and a tangible effort at rescue.

The 'icy flow of discouraging answers' that Eleanor received from Randall were on her mind when she wrote to Viscount Cecil and Temple in late February and early March 1943, giving them advance notice of a private meeting of refugee activists. She told Cecil that 'unless the government adopts the "new Nansen idea" I don't see any hope that our agitation will have saved a single Jewish life', whilst Temple received these despairing words from her, 'I don't believe all our efforts have resulted in the rescue of a single Jew – man, woman or child'.[35] The Refugee Department at the Foreign Office, under Randall, was one of the 'multitude of departments' that Temple felt was obstructing rescue, and her memo certainly stirred up a hornets nest.

Emerson, in a letter to Randall, talked of Eleanor's memo, 'with its confusion of ideas' but nevertheless conceded that it

> does seem to me very strongly to emphasise the point which I made when Kullmann and I met you last Monday, namely that there should be a discussion at an early date on the motion made by the MPs – that there should be a clear statement of the issues and of the action which the UN are able and willing to take.[36]

Similarly, Randall's response to Eleanor's paper, 'The Nazi Massacres of Jews and Poles: What rescue measures are practically possible?', gives an insight into his attitude towards her. She had sent him a copy of this in late February 1943, having already circulated it to the executive of the PCR. Desperate situations called for desperate measures, and she offered no apology for adding to the volume of letters and correspondence which Randall had, no doubt, received on the subject. Rather there was statement of fact and an acknowledgment that 'I suspect that you think us pestering busybodies who had much better leave the matter to be dealt with by the government departments concerned. But that is not the way democracy works, and I think you must admit that we have good reason for anxiety, considering the slow progress that is being made.'[37] What choice did she and fellow activists have but to continue 'prodding' in an attempt at finding out more of what was going on 'behind the scenes?' Cheetham, who had sight of the letter, was quite infuriated and disagreed entirely, saying, 'Miss R ought to keep her "prodding" for the House of Commons. It is <u>not</u> the way democracy works to prod officials in government departments who are carrying out a policy agreed by the government, to make them admit refugees in categories unsanctioned by the government. She should know better.'[38] Randall was less vehement but preferred not to answer in writing. Instead he wrote in private minutes of how he would like to tell her that his department did not resent prodding, that they worked under ministerial instructions, and that if Eleanor wanted a 'peep behind the scenes' he could provide her with a recent example of Foreign Office involvement with Polish refugees being rescued from Persia.[39] In fact, days before, Colonel Stanley had proudly reported the safe arrival, in Palestine, of over 1,200 Polish Jewish refugee men, women and children from Persia, undertaken with the goodwill and efforts of the British government, and under the protection of the Royal Navy. This still left Eleanor asking, unsuccessfully, for news about the 4,000 children and 500 adults from Bulgaria whose transmission was promised to MPs.[40]

Meanwhile Randall, in response to this same paper, described Eleanor, in minutes, as,

> the impatient idealist who cannot bear to think that there is not a ready solution for a particular human problem on which she feels so passionately. But she really must not claim a monopoly or imply that Minister [*sic*] and Government officials are too busy or too indifferent or inefficient to deal with the practical problems of which she knows very little. The Jewish disaster is only part of the vast human problem of Europe under Nazi control; other parts are starving children, the deliberate extinction of Polish and Czech intelligentsia (sic), forced labour and the spiritual perversion of youth. Will Miss Rathbone suggest that it is still callousness to hold that an Allied victory is the only effective way of ending these horrors. Why therefore

> insinuate callousness or at least indifference over the refugee problem?[41]

He gave three small instances of her incomplete information, which might be mentioned confidentially but were not to be discussed with her. These were the lack of room for any more refugees on Cyprus, which was bursting with Greek refugees, the refusal of the Turkish government to act as a country of refuge for European Jews, and of Eire's refusal to take adult refugees.[42] Only later, in 1944, did the American War Refugee Board (WRB) have a measure of success in regard to Turkey.[43]

But most disturbing was Randall's belief that she would have a better chance of success if she shed the illusion demonstrated in her paragraph 12:

> This unreal talk of the problem of millions, or hundreds of thousands at the present juncture of the war is simply not justified by the facts and persisting in it either irritates opinion by unjustly insinuating that the Authorities are indifferent to the lives of vast numbers of people or cruelly raises hope that a) Hitler will release people if we ask for them (he has refused to release even children), or b) that food, shipping, housing, willingness of Governments to receive an indiscriminate mass of people all make the rest of the problem easy.[44]

This last statement shows the grave difficulty that Eleanor and other refugee activists faced, for despite the rapid growth of knowledge of the atrocities by early 1943 which they and others worked hard at disseminating, officials like Randall were unwilling to believe the scale of destruction.[45] If he had been less biased, and accepted the veracity of the evidence, he may have measured his words more carefully when he subsequently asserted that 'The Jewish disaster is only part of the vast human problem of Europe under Nazi control'. Certainly there were, as he wrote 'starving children, the deliberate extinction of Polish and Czech intelligenzia [*sic*], forced labour, the spiritual perversion of youth' to be considered, but the difference was that Jews were deliberately and systematically being exterminated. He could not believe one of her 'chief allusions' that 'any government in the world would be willing to add to its food and other difficulties by receiving an indiscriminate mass of Jewish refugees who, no doubt, through no fault of their own (for Hitler could be relied on only to throw out persons of no use as man-power), would have to be maintained indefinitely'. But his assertion that, 'no doubt there will be a vast refugee problem when the war ends and there will be special refugee problems as the countries of Europe are liberated' was not as he envisaged. For by then, according to Hilberg's figures, over 3.9 million Jews had already been murdered.[46]

Eleanor continued to put questions to Eden in the House: the specific issues she wanted answers to included whether his information on Nazi massacres coincided with recent reports from the World Jewish Congress, and whether the proposed Ottawa meeting – where British and US officials were to meet to start exploring rescue proposals – could not be expedited and held urgently in London, where most of the exiled governments were resident. Behind all of these, and many other questions, was the fact that she was acutely aware that time was of the essence and that exploratory talks would only lead to further delays and prevarication.[47] Early March 1943 also found her asking Colonel Oliver Stanley, the secretary of state for the colonies, whether any of the 4,000 children and 500 adults involved in an emigration scheme from Bulgaria had arrived in Palestine. It seems that Eleanor had not given notice of this question, for Stanley refused to answer, and it was not long before she was in contact with Mr Linton of the Jewish Agency, seeking up-to-date information. His reply was depressing, for not a single child had arrived, Britain had still not simplified the procedures for granting Palestine visas, the situation in Bulgaria had deteriorated, and there was no way of knowing how long the route via Turkey, which was essential to the mission, would remain open. His representative in Turkey had cabled on 16 March, 'Situation unbearable as till now no definite arrangements makeable'.[48] Beyond this, as Stanley subsequently wrote to Eleanor, the transport difficulties were enormous, involving negotiations through diplomatic channels with the Turkish and Bulgarian governments. But he did assure her that it was his 'most earnest desire that everything possible should be done to give effect to these immigration schemes with promptitude and alacrity'.[49] The visa procedure was, in fact, simplified and settled by 31 March, but the shipping difficulties, enumerated in an aide memoire dated 29 March, remained.[50]

Against a background of governmental intransigence and the increasing awareness of the cost in human life, a further conference of refugee activists was held at the House of Commons on 9 March 1943, nearly two months after the Royal Institution meeting called by Eleanor and A.V. Hill. The gathering was strictly private which, as Eleanor stressed in her opening remarks, allowed those present to speak 'off the record'. The participants were to discuss establishing a non-political, non-sectarian pressure committee which would, in Emerson's words, 'co-ordinate the work of organizations and individuals working for or interested in the rescue of those threatened by Nazi persecution of whatever race or religion'. Notwithstanding the archbishop of

Canterbury's view that the newly constituted Council of Christians and Jews could undertake the job, the outcome was the founding of the National Committee for Rescue from Nazi Terror (NCRNT) which contained many notable names amongst the thirty-five vice-presidents. These included the chief rabbi, the archbishops of Canterbury and York, and Sir William Beveridge, as well as stalwarts like Victor Gollancz, Victor Cazalet and David Grenfell. Mary Sibthorp was appointed honorary secretary. Whilst the committee was under the nominal presidency of the Marquess of Crewe, there is no doubt that Eleanor was the driving force behind the new group.[51] The most compelling reason for her disguising her leadership role was so the group could be distanced from the accusation that she was 'tainted with the refugee brush'. However, it is doubtful whether this attempt at adopting a more discrete role made any difference to those in government, for there were many who were hostile to the notion of rescue, irrespective of the leadership (see Plate 28).[52]

In an effort at gaining Cabinet support, Eleanor wrote to Winston Churchill. She sensed that he would have a more sympathetic ear, although she knew that he might not wish to discuss a matter of Cabinet policy with an individual MP:

> for many months my work has been mainly concentrated on this terrible problem. I am in close touch with all the Jewish and other bodies chiefly concerned with it; have discussed it with most of the Ministers principally involved and – informally – with representatives of the Allied governments. I think I know the subject as a whole better than any other MP and perhaps as well as anyone in London. So I don't underrate the enormous difficulties in the way of substantial rescue measures. But I am convinced that there are some things that could and should be done and would rescue a good many thousands, without the slightest damage to the war effort. Also that these things will not be done unless there is both a changed spirit and an improved administrative machinery, such as only you can bring about.

It was Colonel Harvie-Watt, Churchill's parliamentary private secretary, who informed Eleanor, 'with the utmost civility', that this was not a matter that the prime minister could discuss.[53]

The committee, which was initially funded by Gollancz and run from his offices, embodied all of Eleanor's cherished principles and ideals, her belief in British humanity, honour and justice. It was no coincidence that it sought, through its work, to restore what she believed was Britain's reputation for liberalism by rescuing endangered Jews.[54] It had, as its stated aims:

> To act as a medium for co-operation between the various organisations, groups and individuals in the United Kingdom interested in saving victims of Axis persecution of whatever race or religion. To consider what practical measures can be taken to this end.
>
> To establish and maintain relations with non-official organisations and groups in other countries working for the same purpose.[55]

Eleanor's imprint was very evident in the *Twelve Point Programme for Immediate Rescue Measures for Jews of Europe*, which the NCRNT formally presented in early April 1943.[56] The document crystallized the proposals she had been campaigning for over many months, and she was eager that it be presented at the forthcoming Bermuda Conference, the private and informal UN conference at which Britain and the USA were due to discuss the refugee question. She was on her feet in the House on 7 April quizzing Eden about the date of the conference, still to be announced, and the terms of reference of the meeting – was it to be merely exploratory or would immediate relief measures be put into operation? Eden said in his reply, that it would 'naturally include any measures for the relief of refugees in addition to those already in operation', and thought that this answered her question, but it did not. Randall had plenty to say in minutes the following day regarding her question:

> Until we get firm replies to our two chief questions to the US government, namely 1) names of delegates and 2) date, we cannot answer all these queries. In any case I should have thought an announcement about dates was inadvisable for security reasons, and we have asked the Americans to synchronise publicity with us. We can however, give terms of reference and say that while the discussion will be exploratory, it will not exclude further immediate measures for the relief of refugees.

But it was his last sentence which was the most damning: 'It is time that the idea of "measures of rescue" (i.e. actually removing people from Hitler's clutches) was shown up as illusory', leaving little doubt that rescue was never going to be a consideration.[57]

Eleanor's entreaties to Eden, who had further delayed the House of Commons debate on refugees until after Bermuda,[58] to meet a pre-Bermuda deputation of NCRNT representatives, were rejected, on the grounds that 'I do not think that if I were to receive a deputation we could really cover any new ground. Let Mr Law do whatever he can at the conference and after that we could, if necessary, have a meeting.'[59] His refusal must have pleased Morrison, for he doubted there was any point in a meeting before Bermuda, and if there were, he emphasized that he would decidedly not want to be there. Nor did he want Eden, who was more susceptible to humanitarian pleas, to 'commit the Home Office'. As to the Twelve-Point Plan, a copy of which had been sent with the request for a meeting, Walker advised Eden that:

> in devising a reply we should, I feel, avoid argument on points of detail as far as possible, since in present circumstances i.e. while the conversations are going on, it is neither possible nor expedient to do otherwise. As a sop, however, to Miss Rathbone, I think we can communicate the twelve-point programme to Bermuda, and so inform her.[60]

But of course, transmission did not guarantee that the plan would receive consideration.

Eleanor sent Eden another letter before the Bermuda conference, reminding him of other refugee matters which were of concern to her, but which were not in the plan, including relaxing British visa regulations, the provision of new refugee camps and the appointment of a travelling high commissioner. She was unapologetic for being so persistent, writing, 'Meantime, what can we all do but go on making ourselves a nuisance to you and everyone else in authority? We recognise the disadvantages of publicity. But nothing here seems to happen without.'[61]

Meanwhile, the early momentum of public sympathy for the victims of persecution, precipitated by the UN Declaration in December 1942, waned in the face of government inactivity,[62] and the need for a revitalized domestic propaganda campaign became a matter of great urgency.[63] One strand of this was for the NCRNT to call a press conference in advance of Peake's statement on Bermuda, at which journalists were urged to give the refugee question as much publicity as possible before and after the debate. Notes that Eleanor prepared for the press conference highlighted the dire situation and drew attention to Goebbels' article in which the extermination of between six and eight million Jews was predicted; she also drew attention to the increasing horrors since Eden's pronouncement on 17 December, to the 'cruel' British visa regulations which could have been relaxed, and more besides. Eleanor and her committee were very discouraged by the poor attendance at this press briefing,[64] but enlisting the support of the *Manchester Guardian* was not difficult, for she had a very good working relationship with the editor, William Crozier. She was not afraid to confide in him at this difficult time, and revealed her deep concern, that 'if the government hasn't succeeded up till now in finding shipping even to evacuate refugees already in Spain and Portugal and for those from the Balkans to

Palestine, what hope is there that they will find it when a second front in Europe has begun?'[65]

The admission of refugees to Great Britain continued to elicit questions in the House, and, not surprisingly, brought Eleanor into conflict again with Morrison. The suggestion of introducing a block visa system was raised by Commander Locker-Lampson on 1 April 1943, and was abruptly dismissed by Morrison on the grounds that it 'would not be of any assistance in helping refugees to escape from enemy or enemy-occupied territory', nor, he maintained, would it help those who had escaped already to neutral territory. Eleanor was quick to challenge this negative response, asking 'does the Home Secretary seriously maintain that if neutral countries know that blocks of visas are available for refugees to enter this country from enemy-occupied countries, that will not encourage them to admit more refugees?' But Morrison stuck to his original response and refused to discuss the matter any further.[66] NCRNT meetings were called at short notice, urgent letters transmitted, and Cazalet undertook, at Eleanor's suggestion, to see the British representative to the Vatican whilst in London. But it was also agreed that Winant should not be approached at present.

Eleanor's personal contribution to breaking the 'conspiracy of silence' was her pamphlet, *Rescue the Perishing*,[67] published under the auspices of the NCRNT in late April 1943. The first print run was 10,000 copies, paid for by Eleanor, and by June 1943, 25,000 copies had been circulated. Here she set out to answer all the well-rehearsed anti-refugee arguments and, using statistics, to show how little the government had really done in respect of rescue (see Plate 24).[68] But beyond this, she reaffirmed her unswerving loyalty to her country, a loyalty that her determined opponents still considered incompatible with her rescue mission, when she wrote 'I have been accused of belittling the record of my own country, and no English woman likes to do that, even justly' (see Plates 25 and 26).[69]

The unequivocal support which the pamphlet received from Crozier, who described it as 'excellent, and supplementing Gollancz, should be very useful',[70] contrasted sharply with that of Peake, who directed a vindictive attack against the content and Eleanor's integrity during the much-delayed, post-Bermuda Conference debate on the refugee question in the House of Commons on 19 May 1943. Having been given notice of Eleanor's intention to speak, he pre-empted her and criticized many of her proposals, before launching a tirade against *Rescue the Perishing*. First he questioned the validity of her case evidence, and when she tried to defend herself, he refused to be drawn into a dispute over his answers. His challenge may well have been justified, but she was left waiting, no doubt seething, before she could defend herself. He then continued to discuss issues including visas, the admission of children, propaganda and rescue measures, wherever possible destroying suggestions made by Eleanor and the NCRNT.

When Eleanor was able to get to her feet again, she was quick to point out that MPs had been given almost no information as to the outcome of Bermuda, and what Britain and the USA proposed. This, she said, was a matter of grave concern:

> It is clearly difficult for me to follow my right hon. Friend, because there has been so much that he has not been able to tell us and so much which he hinted it would be dangerous to discuss in public. We feel like the schoolboy who was asked to write an essay on snakes in Ireland, and who could only say that there were no snakes in Ireland. There is so much we are debarred from saying, and so much it would be imprudent to say.[71]

And in an overt moment of cynicism, she added that the only pleasurable emotion she felt on the subject at that moment was that the delegates had returned safely, 'because all journeys are dangerous nowadays', and adding, 'My right hon. Friend's whole speech seemed to be a plea for gratitude for what the Government have done in the past and for what they vaguely foreshadow may be done under the decisions of the Bermuda Conference. That is to ask for gratitude for small mercies.'[72] (See Plate 18.)

She must have been very displeased with Peake's assessment of her pamphlet, which he regarded as sensationalist and full of 'more inaccuracies' than he could enumerate, and that it disseminated rescue suggestions that were 'fantastic'. Before long she was challenging him privately to explain what he meant, and was mystified by his reply:

> He explained that he was referring not to inaccuracies of fact but of opinion; that he disagreed with the whole presentation of the case in my pamphlet. I thought that a strange explanation. An opinion may be justified or erroneous; it cannot surely be 'inaccurate.' Mr Peake is entitled to his opinions and I to mine. Readers can judge between us.[73]

The matter did not rest there for a week later Peake wrote a lengthy and detailed letter, as he thought he ought to 'supplement what passed between us on the telephone by some further observations'. In the first instance he qualified his accusation, maintaining that he 'would not think of attributing to you any deliberate mis-statements. What I deplore is not so much inaccuracies of detail as the misleading character of the general picture you present of the situation, and of the action which has been, or might be taken by the Government.' He went on to criticize the name of the committee as well as the title of her pamphlet, maintaining that 'they convey the impression that you know of, or are advocating measures which the Government could adopt for rescuing those who are under the Nazi terror in imminent danger of "perishing", i.e. the Jews whom Hitler is deporting and massacring.'[74] In Eleanor's defence, Sir Austin Hudson, MP for Hackney North, had already tried to allay Peake's suspicion over the name of the committee, stating that 'It was set up for a very simple reason. We found that a large number of organizations and members of this House were interested, and were all wanting to do something and an endeavour was made to bring all those people together in one organization.'[75]

Peake regretted that she was, in his opinion, at such pains to 'decry and discredit this country's record in regard to refugees' and that she found the home secretary's claim that 'we have done more for refugees than any other country', an astonishing one. Where, he asked, was the argument or facts to support Sir John Hope-Simpson's words, included in her pamphlet, that 'Great Britain has ceased to be a country of asylum?' And what use was there in directing readers to Hope-Simpson's book when the content was woefully out of date, and lacked any admission figures post-November 1938, when the usual visa procedure was suspended and some 73,000 refugees, adults and children, were admitted? What he failed to mention was that, by his own admission, a mere 260 Germans and Austrians had been admitted as war refugees between 12 May 1940 and 31 March 1943. So Peake's three-page diatribe went on, ending with a riposte which laid the blame for the content squarely on Eleanor's shoulders. 'I refuse to believe that the Vice-Presidents of your committee desire to commend this sort of thing to the public as a contribution to the study of the subject, and I can only conclude that they have not read your pamphlet.'[76] In fact, an executive meeting in April 1943 had agreed that the pamphlet would have the backing of the NCRNT, and that future publications would be proof read by Cazalet and Gollancz.[77] But some of Peake's criticism may have been valid: the views expressed were stated as 'entirely those of the author', Eleanor met all the production costs, and she very quickly produced an addendum which dealt with the two points at issue between Peake and herself.[78] Then, when she came to rewrite the pamphlet in January 1944, she commented to Brodetsky of the BDBJ that she was 'much dissatisfied' with the original, and thought it 'dull, ill-arranged, and quite out-of-date'. Eleanor's prospective audiences were, in her words,

> only a limited public; mainly the few thousand names on our mailing list of people already in full sympathy ... who needed the kind of material that will enable them to meet the doubts and difficulties

> which they hear raised by others. I have tried to remember in writing it that anything issued in the name of such a committee as ours must be both strictly accurate and very cautious to avoid overstatement or polemical matter not bearing on our issue.[79]

But even so, there was no merit in her producing literature which was obsolete.

There is no doubt that Eleanor's assessment of Peake had diminished significantly since the outbreak of war: whereas in 1939 she had described him as 'a particularly nice and humane man, who has always paid my requests great attention',[80] she now viewed him with animus, not least because of his fatalistic attitude towards the rescue of Jews. In his speech Peake called upon MPs to 'recognise that these people are for the present mostly beyond the possibility of rescue' even though, as Eleanor argued, the timing was critical, for the Mediterranean had become relatively safe for shipping, prior to the beginning of the second front movements.[81] Nor was his argument that 'the rate of extermination is such that no measures of rescue or relief, however large a scale, could be commensurate with the problem',[82] any consolation, for Eleanor had repeatedly proposed small-scale initiatives that could feasibly have saved even a few lives. In a veiled attack on Eleanor, Peake talked about dispelling a few illusions 'in regard to the grant or refusal of visas' and that it was 'a misunderstanding which would be pitiful if it were not so mischievous' to regard a visa as giving an assurance of safe conduct to Britain. When he claimed that 'he could not send visas direct into enemy territory and that it might endanger refugees if he communicated with them', Eleanor had a sharp riposte:

> Does he believe I need telling that? For months past every letter I have written to refugees has reminded them of these two facts. Does the Under-Secretary really mean to deny that refugees do not sometimes have secret ways of communication with their relatives in enemy territory? I do not know how they do it, but they do it through one channel or another, through neutral channels. But whether that is so or not in any particular case, does he tell me that it does not make a difference when a refugee arrives at the border if the authorities of that country have been informed beforehand that a visa is awaiting the refugee? It is common sense that it makes a difference.[83]

Peake's rhetoric, repeated by Colonel Sir A. Lambert Ward, MP for Kingston-upon-Hull, North West, rehearsed the fear of an influx of refugees precipitating an anti-Semitic backlash, which Eleanor vociferously refuted, stating, 'It is an insult to the British people to suppose that even those who "don't like Jews" would rather leave them to be massacred than find asylum for a few more thousand of them'.[84] This was not, as a Gallup poll conducted in late February 1943 showed, at all the case.

Francis Meynell, a temporary civil servant at the Board of Trade, and husband of Alix Kilroy, later Dame Alix Meynell, the first woman principal in the Board of Trade, was so shocked by the content of Gollancz's pamphlet, *Let My People Go*, that he had convened a private meeting of concerned individuals. The group, which included a number of senior civil servants who had demonstrated a sympathetic attitude towards Jewish refugees before the war, resolved to shake up the government inertia, establish what measures could best be taken to aid refugees, and decide how to persuade the government to adopt these policies. Based on Britain's long tradition of asylum – of which Eleanor was a whole-hearted advocate – the group, which included Eleanor, Tom Driberg MP and Victor Gollancz, decided to campaign publicly for a 'full open-door policy'. The government were to be asked to provide temporary shelter for any Jews who could escape, to establish reception centres over which Britain had jurisdiction, and to encourage other countries to follow their example. And so as to prove to the British government that the population was, in fact, supportive of such humanitarian measures, the NCRNT sponsored a Gallup poll, which Meynell organized and financially supported.[85] The response was unequivocal and showed a significant amount of public sympathy towards the admission of threatened Jews: seventy-eight per cent of those questioned supported admission, the total made up of forty per cent who specified asylum only until another place of refuge could be found, twenty-eight per cent who approved of admission until the end of the war, and ten per cent for an indefinite time.[86] Nor was this the full extent of support, for the Foreign Office was inundated with letters demanding action and offering money from across the spectrum of the British population. This deluge of correspondence prompted Randall to briefly consider a standard letter of reply before deciding to abandon replying at all.[87] Inevitably, Peake rehearsed the firmly held government opinion that 'victory ... will contribute more to their salvation than any diversion of our war efforts in measures of relief, even if such measures could be put into effect'.[88]

With the relationship between Eleanor and Peake at an all-time low, her feelings towards Morrison, the home secretary, were equally bitter, as she made patently clear in her criticism of him during the debate:

> I must say that in one respect this country excels. There is no other country where public opinion favours a strong and generous

> policy. Yet when we approach the Home Secretary we are made to feel that pressure from public opinion has not merely helped but has hardened his attitude. It seems that he wants to show that he is a strong man by refusing to make even the smallest concession and that his attitude has been influenced sometimes less by the merits of the case than by his dislike of yielding anything to his critics. He has made some concessions today, and I will say no more about that, but why does he always make us feel in his Parliamentary answers, and even in our approaches to him privately, as if the whole question of refugees was becoming a bore and an irritation to him and that he was transferring to refugees the dislike which he quite openly feels for ourselves?[89]

It was no wonder that she reasserted her call for a special Ministry for Refugees to be appointed to deal with the problem, as proposed in her pamphlet, and as discussed with Noel-Baker and others months previously.[90] Towards the end of this debate, Eden's chastisement of Eleanor for what he considered her unfair accusation that the government had tried to buy off criticism by 'a few concessions now and again' landed her in further trouble. She did not, she told Eden, doubt his good will, but she could not say the same for some of his colleagues, and their apparent lack of any sense of urgency. Eden's sharp riposte, that 'the hon. Lady must not differentiate among the excellencies of the various ministers. Our decisions are taken together. We are a band of brothers and there is no distinction', closed the door on any further comments.[91]

However depressed Eleanor may have been by Peake, Morrison and Eden that day, she did have her supporters in the House: Mr Mack, MP for Newcastle-under-Lyme rose to his feet with 'nothing less than a generous tribute of appreciation and profound respect ... to the hon. Lady who opened this discussion for the fine sentiments, the truly Christian sentiments, which were embodied in her remarks'. Cazalet was equally generous when he said, 'I have been associated with her for over 10 years in this problem of refugees, and it is impossible to exaggerate the complete disinterestedness, the great personal generosity and the unquenchable importunity which she has shown in matters dealing with it'.[92] And A.V. Hill, in his capacity as junior member for Cambridge University, paid tribute to Cazalet and Eleanor, dubbing her 'the patron saint of refugees'.[93]

The closing of the very heated debate was by no means the end of the accusations and counter-accusations between Peake and Eleanor, for neither would concede defeat and the spat continued outside the House.[94] Lord Winterton added his support for Peake and Eden alongside his public denunciation of Eleanor's remedies in the columns of the *Daily Telegraph*, calling them 'either impracticable or beside the point'.[95] It was Harold Nicolson who sprang to her defence, arguing that 'some of them may, in truth, not be feasible, but others might at least be attempted'.[96] Only later did Peake reveal that Eleanor had been 'the bane of his official life as under-secretary at the Home Office for nearly five years'.[97]

From the Jewish perspective the outcome of Bermuda was far from encouraging, for the delegates failed to reach agreement upon immediate relief measures.[98] At a regular meeting of the COA on 27 May 1943, Eleanor mentioned that she intended to raise one matter in the House, the question of the exchange of Jews in Hitler's hands against Germans in Allied hands, and also to ask the secretary of state to consider this scheme when she next saw him. But as Cheetham reported in Foreign Office minutes, 'the scheme was considered and emphatically rejected by British and American delegates at the Bermuda Conference'.[99]

The informal deputation, headed by Eleanor, that Eden agreed to receive on 1 June 1943, was postponed, but minutes make it clear that he had already decided that 'conversation was to be limited to the foreign aspects of the refugee problem'.[100] The delay gave Eleanor time to consult Randall about her most urgent point, that a stern official warning be given to Bulgaria to stop the deportation of Jews, and that if they did not, they would be behaving as inhumanely as the Nazis.[101] In minutes, Randall reported that he had refrained from reminding Eleanor that when the government had given such a public warning on 17 December 1942, she and her friends had treated it with contempt because it had not been followed up by any practical schemes of rescue. But as she was likely to raise the matter again, further consultation might be useful. This precipitated a considerable amount of correspondence between Randall, Mr Scarlett of the Southern Department, Mr Hendriks, Lord Perth and others, before a decision was made. Randall's problem was whether a promise of retribution would do the Jews good or harm, and whilst there was still a vague hope of rescuing some Bulgarian children, he wanted to tread carefully. It was left to Lord Perth to privately convey Randall's alternative plan which both the Central and Southern Departments accepted as the best course of action – to ask the British wireless services in Bulgarian and other South-Eastern European languages to carry a summary of a report published by *The Times* on 1 June with a comment on the negative outcome for the Bulgarian government in the face of the inevitable Allied victory. Perth was also deputed to persuade her that the government were 'not indifferent to the refugee problem, had not failed to take action along lines desired by her and the NCRNT, and were prevented from taking measures of alleviation by circumstances not under their control'.[102]

A rescue scheme proposed by Salomon Adler-Rudel, the accredited representative of the Jewish Agency in London, had offered the possibility of a safe haven in Sweden for up to 20,000 Jewish children. The proposal looked highly promising when it was first discussed with Jan Karski in Eleanor's flat in May 1943, prior to the major debate in the House on refugees, but it failed to materialize.[103] Indeed, when Adler-Rudel was trying to speed up negotiations at the end of July 1943, it was Eleanor who introduced him to John Winant.[104] Eleanor's entreaties at the end of June to Sir W. Battershill, the permanent under-secretary of state at the Colonial Office, concerning the threatened deportation of Jews from Italy, brought little comfort. The difficulties posed by sea transport were given as the main stumbling block, so that immigration certificates for Palestine were of no use, and not a solution. An approach to the Vatican to intervene urgently to stop the deportations had been made, as had an approach to the Swiss government to give asylum to refugees, but success could only be hoped for.[105] Weeks later, in September 1943, Eleanor was complaining to Randall that no provision had been made in the terms of the Italian armistice for the rescue of refugees. She wanted to hammer home her belief that the Foreign Office had a responsibility to address German persecution, and to respond to the threat faced by Jews in German-occupied areas of Italy. Whilst Sir William Malkin and Randall were immediately concerned with how to deal with a possible exodus of refugees, Randall did suggest that other armistice arrangements might, in fact, have some reference to refugees in general.[106]

Still full of gloom, Eleanor led a deputation to Law on 30 June, accompanied by Lord Perth, Lord Samuel, David Grenfell and Quintin Hogg. She had evidently written to Eden twice before this meeting, on 24 and 25 June, but both of these letters have been destroyed 'under statute'. It seems that there was a question mark over whether she should be told about bringing in the US government in an approach to the Swiss to aid the rescue of Jews from Italy, but as the idea had been turned down, there was no need to mention it to her. By 15 July 1943, Henderson of the Foreign Office was reporting back on a conversation between Eleanor and Randall, when Eleanor said that 'it is now too late to do anything for the Jews of Italy' and that this was 'just another example of delay by departments until any opportunity of rescuing them had passed'.[107]

During the hour and half the deputation spent with Law, progress was only made on minor issues, whilst on the whole 'the position continued to be unsatisfactory'.[108] On the matter of permits for entry into

Palestine, which was only applicable to children, the deputation felt very keenly that if the 'children scheme' broke down, the permits ought to be transferred to adults. This was, as Law pointed out, something that only the Colonial Office could deal with, and within days Eleanor had written to Colonel Stanley, asking him to meet her and three or four all-party MPs – Mr Hammersley, Lord Samuel and Quintin Hogg were named – to discuss the Palestine immigration issue as well as the Jews under threat in Italy, the Balkans and the exchange of Germans in British hands and wives and children of Palestinians in enemy hands. She not only wanted his views on what line to take in the House, but also what advice to give those who consulted her.[109] Stanley deferred meeting Eleanor until after he had met with representatives of the Jewish Agency, but it remains unclear whether the deputation ever took place. Nevertheless it was agreed at an NCRNT executive meeting in August, that on all questions relating to Palestine, the Jewish Agency had priority of interest.[110]

In the wake of Eleanor's debacle with Peake in May 1943, she had become totally dispirited by the apparent stalemate between the government and the pro-rescue lobby, having noted, with a degree of sarcasm, how during the debate Eden had 'reproached them [the NCRNT] for implying that the government cared less about the matter than we did'.[111] She concluded at this time that 'the government has little sense of urgency over the whole matter, very little hope of doing anything for rescue except on a small scale, and a strong desire to avoid pressure'.[112] As Crozier observed in a letter to her in August 1943, 'most of the rescue schemes are bound to come to nothing unless the Government, or some enterprising person in it or nominated by it, treats the whole thing as though it were our own people who were concerned. We should have a lot of refugees out by this time!'[113]

The single victory around this time was the successful outcome of Eleanor's campaign to have a large sum of money transferred to Spain through official channels for the relief of refugees,[114] even though it had involved her being sent on 'a wild goose chase' by Randall and Eden, which she very much resented.[115] Although surviving letters relating to this matter are scant, this plan was, as Louise London describes, part of a much bigger scheme that the British government, and the Ministry of Economic Warfare in particular, had been involved with since early 1943.[116] What Eleanor's correspondence does demonstrate, once more, is the extent of her contacts, in this case her regular communication with Sir Samuel Hoare, the ambassador to Spain, and R.A.B. Mynors, of the Treasury Department.[117] On a less happy note, in 1943 she had to deal with the temporary loss of support of Victor Gollancz, who had suffered a nervous breakdown,[118] and more grievously, the coincidental deaths of two staunch allies. Victor Cazalet was killed in an air crash off the coast of Gibraltar on 3 July,[119] followed by Josiah Wedgwood's death on 26 July.

NOTES

1. EFR, Speech Notes on the Jewish Question, 16 December 1942, RP XIV.3.85, ULL.
2. Ibid.
3. Kushner, *Liberal Imagination*, pp.187–8.
4. The question of church bells being rung was raised in the house in December 1942. See *Hansard* HC, vol. 385, col. 1695, 10 December 1942.
5. EFR, Speech Notes on the Jewish Question, 16 December 1942, RP XIV.3.85, ULL.
6. Ibid.
7. The Jewish community held a week of mourning and prayer from 13–20 December 1942. See Brodetsky, *Memoirs*, p.220. The foreign secretary also met a deputation from the Board of Deputies on 22 December 1942, when he was urged to do his utmost to allow escaped Jews into the UK, NA CAB 65/27,WM172 (42) 5.
8. Letter of EFR to Graham White, 24 December 1942, PA WHI /10/3/52.
9. Ibid.
10. Letter of Schonfeld to Brodetsky, 12 January 1943, and Memo, 19 January 1943, Acc 3121/C/2/2/5/3, Board of Deputies of British Jews (BDBJ), London Metropolitan Archives (LMA); Letter of Schonfeld to Dr Hertz, January 1943, Schonfeld Papers, MS 183/3/4, University of Southampton Library (USL).
11. Memo by EFR, 'Jewish Massacres: The Case for an Offer to Hitler', 7 January 1943, MSS2/1 Sibthorp Papers, MS 96/30/1, IWM; Report of meeting held at the Royal Institution, London, 7 January 1943, Acc 3121/E1/74, BDBJ, LMA.
12. V. Gollancz, *Let My People Go* (London: Victor Gollancz, 1942/43); also Ruth Dudley-Edwards, *Victor Gollancz* (London: Gollancz, 1987), pp.374–6.
13. Dudley-Edwards, *Victor Gollancz*, p.375.
14. Kushner, *Liberal Imagination*, p.177.
15. *Hansard* HC, vol. 386, cols 184–5, 20 January 1943.
16. *Hansard* HC, vol. 386, cols 289–91, 21 January 1943; cols 863–7, 3 February 1943; cols 1446–7, 11 February 1943; cRuth ol. 1927, 18 February 1943; vol. 387, cols 284–5, 25 February 1943; vol. 387, cols 638–40, 654–5, 10 March 1943; vol.387, cols 846–49, 11 March 1943; vol. 387, cols 1319–20, 1343, 18 March 1943; vol. 388, cols. 189–90, 31 March 1943; vol. 388, cols 319–21, 1 April 1943; Letter of EFR to Morrison, 25 January 1943 in which she suggested that over seventy civilian internees on the Isle of Man might possibly be exchanged for endangered Jews on the Continent, Acc 3121/C/2/2/5, BDBJ, LMA.
17. *Hansard* HC, vol. 386, cols 184–5, 20 January 1943.
18. *The Times*, 28, 29 January 1943; NA FO 371/36651,W2215/49/48.
19. Minutes of third meeting of WCC, 27 January 1943, NA CAB 95/15; Eden mentioned the Cabinet Committee during the course of the debate on 19 May 1943, see *Hansard* HC, vol. 389, col. 1198.
20. Letter of Eden, 21 January 1943, NA FO 371/36651,W2339/49/48.
21. For the change in the title see Eden, Note, 9 January 1943, JR 43(4).NA CAB 95/15.
22. Letter of EFR to Cazalet, 13 February 1943, Vol. 'Annex to Israeli Supreme Court Opening, 1992', Cazalet Papers. By kind permission of Sir Edward Cazalet.
23. EFR, 12 February 1943 in MSS 2/1, Sibthorp Papers, MS 96/30/1, IWM; PA WHI /10/3/58. Other papers included 'Nazi mass murders – what you can do about it', 'Nazi Massacres of Jews', Draft, 14 January 1943, Acc 3121/C/2/2/5, BDBJ, LMA; Amendments to 'Suggested steps etc.', 19 January 1943, Acc 3121/C3/536, 19 January 1943, BDBJ, LMA; 'Note, with examples, of the harsh working of Home Office regulations regarding the issue of visas to refugees', EFR, 24 February 1943, Parkes Papers, MS 60 15/57/1, USL.
24. Letter of EFR to Noel-Baker, 8 February 1943, Papers of Baron Noel-Baker, 4/578, CAC.
25. Letter of EFR to Cazalet, 13 February 1943, Cazalet Papers. By kind permission of Sir Edward Cazalet.

26. Letter of Emerson to Randall, 22 February 1943 NA FO 371/36653,W3321/49/48.
27. Letter of EFR to Noel-Baker, 12 February 1943, Papers of Baron Noel-Baker, 4/581, CAC; Letter of Noel-Baker to Law, 8 January 1943, Papers of Baron Noel-Baker, 4/578, CAC; Letter of Parkes to Temple, 25 January 1942, Temple Papers, 54/59, LPL.
28. Letter of EFR to Temple, 13 February 1943, Temple Papers, 54/252, LPL; Letter of Bell to EFR, 16 February 1943, Bell Papers, 32/24, LPL. Eleanor dismissed Emerson as a candidate: Letter of EFR to Noel-Baker, 12 February 1943, Papers of Baron Noel-Baker, 4/581, CAC.
29. Letter of EFR to Victor Gollancz, 13 February 1943, Vol. 'Annex to Israeli Supreme Court Opening 1992', Cazalet Papers. By kind permission of Sir Edward Cazalet.
30. Letter of EFR to Noel-Baker, 12 February 1943, Papers of Baron Noel-Baker, 4/581, CAC.
31. Christian A.R. Christensen, *Fridtjof Nansen: A Life in the Service of Science and Humanity* (Geneva: UN High Commissioner for Refugees, 1961).
32. *Hansard* HC, vol. 386, col. 1927, 18 February 1943.
33. Letter of EFR to Eden, 25 February 1943, NA FO 371/36653.
34. Letter of Morrison to EFR, 9 March 1943, NA FO 371/366.
35. Letter of EFR to Randall, 27 February 1943, NA FO 371/36653,W3465; Letter of EFR to Temple, 2 March 1943, Temple Papers, 54/281, LPL; Letter of EFR to Cecil, 28 February 1943, Cecil Papers, Add MSS 51141, f. 303, BL.
36. Letter of Emerson to Randall, 24 February 1943, NA FO 371/36653,W3321/49/48.
37. Letter of EFR to Randall, 27 February 1943, NA FO 371/36653,W3465.
38. Minutes, Cheetham and Randall, 15 March 1943, NA FO 371/36653,W3465/49/48.
39. Minutes, Cheetham and Randall, 15 March 1943, NA FO 371/36653,W3465/49/48.
40. *Hansard* HC, vol. 387, cols 654–5, 10 March 1943.
41. Minutes of Randall, 22 February 1943, NA FO 371/36653,W3321/49/48, also WO 95/1499.
42. Ibid.
43. Letter of Pehle to EFR, 8 April 1944, NCRNT file, War Refugee Board Papers, Box 17, Franklin D. Roosevelt Library, New York (WRB Archive).
44. Minutes of Randall, 22 February 1943, NA FO 371/36653,W3321/49/48, also WO 95/1499.
45. A. Bunting, 'Representing Rescue: The National Committee for Rescue from Nazi Terror, the British and the Rescue of Jews from Nazism', *Journal of Holocaust Education*, 9, 1 (2000), pp.65–84.
46. Minutes of Randall, 22 February 1943, NA FO 371/36653,W3321/49/48, also WO 95/1499. See R. Hilberg, *The Destruction of the European Jews*, vol. 3, p.1120, as cited in Kushner, *Liberal Imagination*, p.321, f.2.
47. *Hansard* HC, vol. 387, cols 638–40, 10 March 1943.
48. Letter of Linton to EFR, 24 March 1943, CZA Z4/14882.
49. Letter of O. Stanley to EFR, 29 March 1943, CZA Z4/14882.
50. Aide memoire, 29 March 1943, Acc 3121/C/2/2/5, LMA; Letter of Linton to EFR, 2 April 1943, CZA Z4/14882.
51. Letter of EFR to Graham White, 24 December 1942, PA WHI /10/3/52.
52. Minutes of meeting, 9 March 1943, Acc 3121/3/536/1, BDBJ, LMA.
53. Letter of EFR to Winston Churchill, 29 March 1943, and Note of Churchill to Harvie-Watt, 1 April 1943, NA PREM/51/8.
54. General meeting of NCRNT, 7 April 1943, MS 60/15/57, f. 1.
55. National Committee for Rescue from Nazi Terror, n.d. but circa March 1943, Sibthorp papers 96/30/1, MSS 2/1, IWM.
56. First draft, 5 April 1943; re-draft, 6 April 1943, Acc 3121/3/536/1, BDBJ, LMA.
57. *Hansard* HC, vol. 388, col. 588, 7 April 1943; Randall, Minutes, 7–9 April 1943, NA FO371/36658,W5559/49/48.
58. The question of a debate before Easter was put by Mr Arthur Greenwood, MP. *Hansard* HC, vol. 388, col. 813, 8 April 1943.
59. Letter of EFR to Eden and Reply of Eden to EFR, 9 April 1943, NA FO 371/36658,W5673/49/48.
60. Walker, Minutes, 14 April 1943, NA FO 371/36658,W5673/49/48.
61. Letter of EFR to Eden, 10 April 1943, NA FO 371/36658,W5673/49/48.
62. As noted by Gollancz, NCRNT meeting, 13 April 1943, Acc 3121/C3/536/1, BDBJ, LMA.
63. Minutes of General Meeting of NCRNT, 7 April 1943, Acc 3121/E3/536/1, BDBJ, LMA.

64. Letter of Sibthorp to Brodetsky, 14 May 1943, Acc 3121/3/536/1, BDBJ, LMA.
65. Letter of EFR to Crozier, 13 May 1943, *Manchester Guardian* Archive, B/R45/3, JRL.
66. *Hansard* HC, vol. 388, cols 319–21, 1 April 1943.
67. Minutes of executive meeting, NCRNT, 29 April 1943; Report, 16 June 1943, Acc 3121/E3/536/1, BDBJ, LMA.
68. An updated version of *Rescue the Perishing*, which incorporated the 'Ten-Point Programme for Measures of Rescue from Nazi Terror', was produced in January 1944.
69. EFR, *Rescue the Perishing*, p.10.
70. Letter of Crozier to EFR, 17 May 1943, *Manchester Guardian* Archive, B/R45/4, JRL. Crozier was referring to Gollancz's pamphlet, *Let My People Go*, published in December 1942.
71. *Hansard* HC, vol. 389, cols 1132–3, 19 May 1943. St Patrick was supposed to have banished all the snakes from Ireland, although in fact there were never any on the island.
72. *Hansard* HC, vol. 389, col. 1133, 19 May 1943.
73. *Rescue the Perishing*, Addendum, 20 May 1943, p.2, PA WHI /10/3/68.
74. *Hansard* HC, vol. 388, col. 189, 31 March 1943.
75. *Hansard* HC, vol. 389, col. 1167–8, 19 May 1943.
76. Letter of Peake to EFR, 25 May 1943, NA FO 371/36662.
77. Minutes of NCRNT executive meeting, 29 April 1943, Acc 3121/C3/536/1, BDBJ, LMA.
78. Minutes of NCRNT executive meeting, 20 May 1943, Acc 3121/E3/536/1, BDBJ, LMA.
79. Letter of EFR to Brodetsky, 27 January 1944, Acc 3121/C3/536/1, BDBJ, LMA.
80. This was in connection with a report about Women Patrols that EFR sent on to Peake. See Letter of EFR to Elfrida, 19 August 1939, RP XIV.2.19 (2), ULL.
81. Letter of Crozier to EFR, 17 May 1943, *Manchester Guardian* Archive, B/R45/4, JRL.
82. *Hansard* HC, vol. 389, col. 1120, 19 May 1943.
83. *Hansard* HC, vol. 389, col. 1140, 19 May 1943.
84. *Hansard* HC, vol. 389, col. 1146, 19 May 1943; EFR, Replies to objections, 'Twelve Point Programme', *Rescue the Perishing*, p.3.
85. Copy of Notes of meeting, 3 February 1943, Sir Francis Meynell Papers, XVII Folder F, CUL. The NCRNT sponsored this poll. Those present included EFR, Gollancz, Francis Meynell, Dennis Cohen, Alan Sainsbury, Sydney Bernstein, Tom Driberg, Evelyn Sharp, Alix Kilroy (later Alix Meynell) and Mrs Reginald McKenna. See A. Meynell, *Public Servant, Private Woman* (London: Gollancz, 1988), pp.201–3.
86. *News Chronicle*, 26 March 1943.
87. Cheetham, Minute, 19 January 1943, NA FO 371/36649; Randall, Minute, 13 January 1943, NA FO 371/36649; correspondence, 20 January–4 February 1943, NA FO 371/36651.
88. *Hansard* HC, vol. 389, col. 1118, 19 May 1943. Peake's: supporters in the debate included Mr Herbert Butcher, MP for Holland with Boston, Colonel Sir A. Lambert-Ward, MP for Kingston-upon-Hull, North-West and Earl Winterton, MP for Horsham and Worthing.
89. *Hansard* HC, vol. 389, col. 1141, 19 May 1943.
90. *Hansard* HC, vol. 389, cols 1137–8, 19 May 1943.
91. *Hansard* HC, vol. 389, col. 1200, 19 May 1943.
92. *Hansard* HC, vol. 389, col. 1156, 19 May 1943.
93. *Hansard* HC, vol. 389, col. 1183, 19 May 1943.
94. EFR, Addendum to *Rescue the Perishing*, 20 May 1943, PA WHI /10/3/68; Letter of Peake to Eleanor, 25 May 1943, NA FO 371/36662.
95. *Daily Telegraph*, 24 May 1943.
96. H. Nicolson, 'Marginal Comment', *The Spectator*, 28 May 1943.
97. M. Stocks, *Eleanor Rathbone: A Biography* (London: Victor Gollancz, 1949), p.288.
98. Kushner, *Liberal Imagination*, pp.180–2.
99. Cheetham, Minutes, 28 May 1943, NA FO 371/36662,W7956.
100. Minutes, 10 June 1943, NA FO 371/36662,W8621/49/48.
101. Suggestions for discussion with Mr Eden at informal deputation on Tuesday 1 June 1943, 29 May 1943, PA WHI /10/3/69.
102. Suggestions for discussion at informal discussion on Tuesday June 1 st 1943, NA FO 371/36662,W8192/49/48.
103. Notes of discussion at EFR's flat on 5 May 1943. Temple Papers, 55/7–8; Letter of Temple to Eden, and copy to Selborne, 7 May 1943, Temple Papers, 55/9; Reply of Eden to Temple, Temple Papers, 21 May 1943, LPL. For Sweden's role during the Holocaust,

see P. Levine, *From Indifference to Activism: Swedish Diplomacy and the Holocaust, 1938–1944* (Stockholm: Uppsala University Library, 1998).

104. S.Adler-Rudel, 'A Chronicle of Rescue Efforts', *Leo Baeck Institute Year Book*, XI (1966), pp.213–41.
105. 29 June 1943, NA CO 733/446/13.
106. Memo of Randall, 28 September 1943, NA FO 371/36666,W13938/49/48.
107. Memo, July 1943, NA CO 733/446/1376021/45/42.
108. 29 June 1943, NA CO 733/446/13. Executive meeting, NCRNT, 1 July 1943, Acc 3121/E3/536, BDBJ, LMA.
109. Letter of EFR to Stanley, 6 July 1943, NA CO 733/446/13.
110. Minutes of executive meeting, NRNT, 19 August 1943, Acc 3121/E3/536/1, BDBJ, LMA.
111. Confidential Note by EFR, 28 June 1943, Acc 3121/E3/536/1, BDBJ, LMA.
112. Ibid.
113. Letter of Crozier to EFR, 1 August 1943, *Manchester Guardian* Archive, B/R45/5, JRL.
114. Letter of Bell to finance officer, FO, 30 July 1943, Bell Papers, 32/76, LPL.
115. Letters of EFR to Bell, 2 and 11 June 1943, Bell Papers, 32/68, LPL.
116. London, *Whitehall and the Jews*, pp.192–7.
117. Letter of EFR to Bell, 2 June 1943, Bell Papers, 32/68, LPL.
118. Dudley-Edwards, *Victor Gollancz*, pp.378–83.
119. Cazalet and General Sikorski, head of the Polish government in exile, were killed on 3 July 1943.

15. Refugees from the Sudetenland, following its annexation by Germany, arrive in Prague. Prague, Czechoslovakia, c. October 1938. Courtesy of United States Holocaust Memorial Museum, New York.

16. 'View of the Struma in the Istanbul harbor [*sic*], February 1942'. Photograph 09115. United States Holocaust Memorial Museum, New York. Courtesy of David Stoliar.

17. Hay Internment Camp, Australia, August 1940. Accession RW78/58-59. Unknown Photographer. Courtesy of Charles Sturt University Regional Archives, Australia.

18. British and American delegates in Bermuda attending the Bermuda Conference on Refugees, late April 1943. From left to right: George Hall, financial secretary to the Admiralty; Harold W. Dodds, president of Princeton University; Richard Law, minister of state at the Foreign Office and head of the British delegation; Congressman Sol Bloom; Osbert Peake, Home Office under secretary of state. © Press Association Images.

19. Sir Victor Gollancz (1893–1967). © Getty Images.

20. Philip J. Noel-Baker (L) talking with Herbert Morrison at the Labour Conference, 31 December 1944. © Getty Images.

21. William Temple, 1943. Photograph by Yousuf Karsh, Camera Press, London.

22. Bishop Bell at Kemsley House, 19 January 1943. Bell Papers, 357, folio 187. By courtesy of Lambeth Palace Library.

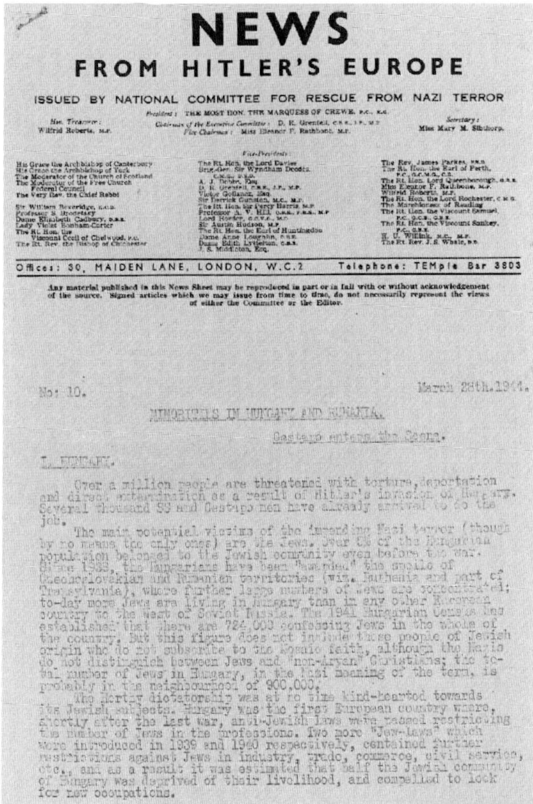

# NEWS
## FROM HITLER'S EUROPE

ISSUED BY NATIONAL COMMITTEE FOR RESCUE FROM NAZI TERROR



Offices: 30, MAIDEN LANE, LONDON, W.C.2 Telephone: TEMple Bar 3803



No: 10. March 28th.1944.

MINORITIES IN HUNGARY AND RUMANIA.

Gestapo enters the Scene.

I. HUNGARY.

Over a million people are threatened with torture, deportation and direct extermination as a result of Hitler's invasion of Hungary. Several thousand SS and Gestapo men have already arrived to do the job.

The main potential victims of the impending Nazi terror (though by no means the only ones) are the Jews. Over [illegible] of the Hungarian population belonged to the Jewish community even before the war. Since 1938, the Hungarians have been "awarded" the spoils of Czechoslovakian and Rumanian territories (viz. Ruthenia and part of Transylvania), where further large numbers of Jews are concentrated; to-day more Jews are living in Hungary than in any other European country to the west of Soviet Russia. The 1941 Hungarian Census has established that there are 724,000 confessing Jews in the whole of the country. But this figure does not include those people of Jewish origin who do not subscribe to the Mosaic faith, although the Nazis do not distinguish between Jews and "non-Aryan" Christians; the total number of Jews in Hungary, in the Nazi meaning of the term, is probably in the neighbourhood of 900,000.

The Horthy dictatorship was at no time kind-hearted towards its Jewish subjects. Hungary was the first European country where, shortly after the last war, anti-Jewish laws were passed restricting the number of Jews in the professions. Two more "Jew-laws" which were introduced in 1939 and 1940 respectively, contained further restrictions against Jews in industry, trade, commerce, civil service, etc., and as a result it was estimated that half the Jewish community of Hungary was deprived of their livelihood, and compelled to look for new occupations.

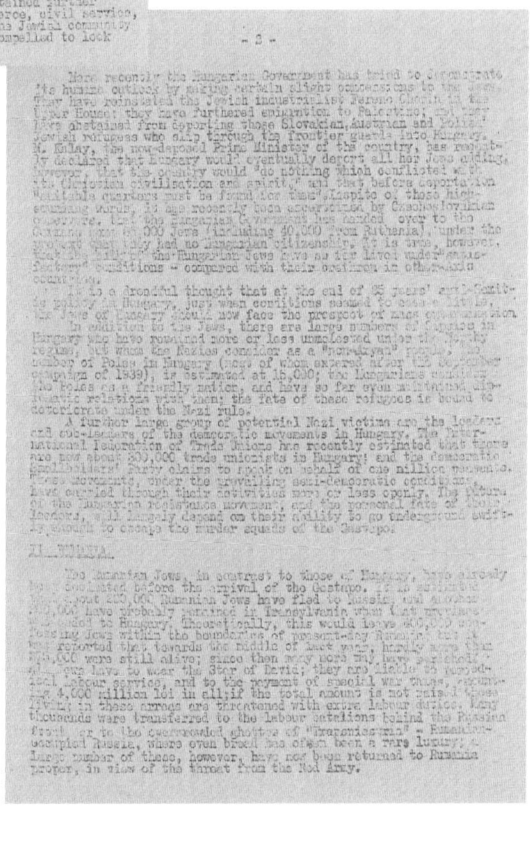

- 2 -

More recently the Hungarian Government has tried to demonstrate its humane outlook by making certain slight concessions to the Jews. They have reinstated the Jewish industrialist Ferenc Chorin in the Upper House; they have furthered emigration to Palestine; and they have abstained from deporting those Slovakian, Austrian and Polish Jewish refugees who slip through the frontier guards into Hungary. M. Kallay, the now-deposed Prime Minister of the country, has repeatedly declared that Hungary would eventually deport all her Jews adding, however, that the country would "do nothing which conflicted with its Christian civilisation and spirit," and that before deportation "suitable quarters must be found for them". Inspite of these high-sounding words, it has recently been ascertained by Czechoslovakian [illegible], that the Hungarian Government has handed over to the [illegible] [illegible],000 Jews (including 40,000 from Ruthenia), under the pretext that they had no Hungarian citizenship. It is true, however, that [illegible] the Hungarian Jews have so far lived under "satisfactory" conditions - compared with their brethren in other Axis countries.

It is a dreadful thought that at the end of [illegible] years' anti-Semitic policy in Hungary, just when conditions seemed to ease a little, the Jews of Hungary should now face the prospect of mass extermination.

In addition to the Jews, there are large numbers of [illegible] in Hungary who have remained more or less unmolested under the [illegible] regime, but whom the Nazies consider as a "non-Aryan" people. The number of Poles in Hungary (most of whom entered after the September campaign of 1939), is estimated at 15,000; the Hungarians [illegible] the Poles as a friendly nation, and have so far even maintained diplomatic relations with them; the fate of these refugees is bound to deteriorate under the Nazi rule.

A further large group of potential Nazi victims are the leaders and sub-leaders of the democratic movements in Hungary. The International Federation of Trade Unions has recently estimated that there are now about 300,000 trade unionists in Hungary; and the democratic Smallholders' Party claims to speak on behalf of one million peasants. These movements, under the prevailing semi-democratic conditions, have carried through their activities more or less openly. The future of the Hungarian resistance movement, and the personal fate of their leaders, will largely depend on their ability to go underground swiftly enough to escape the murder squads of the Gestapo.

II. RUMANIA.

The Rumanian Jews, in contrast to those of Hungary, have already been decimated before the arrival of the Gestapo. It is estimated that about 200,000 Rumanian Jews have fled to Russia, and another [illegible],000 have probably remained in Transylvania when that province was ceded to Hungary. Theoretically, this would leave 400,000 confessing Jews within the boundaries of present-day Rumania; but it was reported that towards the middle of last year, hardly more than [illegible],000 were still alive; since then many more may have perished. All Jews have to wear the Star of David; they are liable to [illegible] labour service, and to the payment of special war taxes, amounting 4,000 million lei in all; if the total amount is not raised those living in these arrears are threatened with extra labour duties. Many thousands were transferred to the labour battalions behind the Russian front, or to the overcrowded ghettos of "Transnistria" - Rumanian-occupied Russia, where even bread has often been a rare luxury; a large number of these, however, have now been returned to Rumania proper, in view of the threat from the Red Army.

23. *News from Hitler's Europe*, No.10, 28 March 1944, pp.1, 2. Papers of Miss M. Sibthorp, MMS 4, 96.30.1. Courtesy of Imperial War Museum, London.

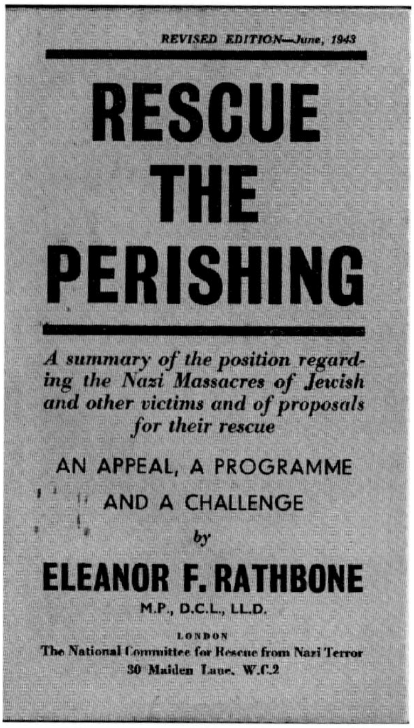

REVISED EDITION—June, 1943

# RESCUE THE PERISHING

*A summary of the position regarding the Nazi Massacres of Jewish and other victims and of proposals for their rescue*

AN APPEAL, A PROGRAMME AND A CHALLENGE

*by*

**ELEANOR F. RATHBONE**

M.P., D.C.L., LL.D.

LONDON
The National Committee for Rescue from Nazi Terror
30 Maiden Lane, W.C.2

24. Front cover of *Rescue the Perishing* (Victor Gollancz, 1943). Courtesy of The Wiener Library, London.

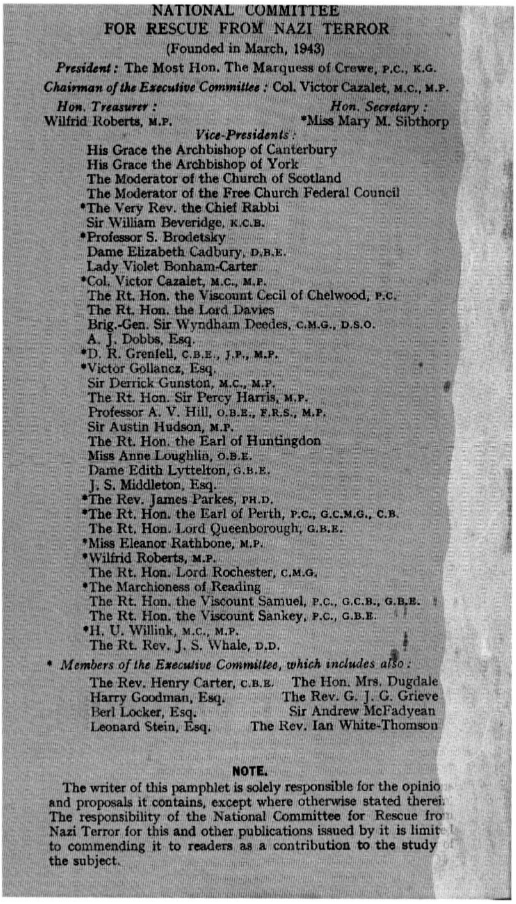

NATIONAL COMMITTEE
FOR RESCUE FROM NAZI TERROR
(Founded in March, 1943)

*President:* The Most Hon. The Marquess of Crewe, P.C., K.G.
*Chairman of the Executive Committee:* Col. Victor Cazalet, M.C., M.P.
*Hon. Treasurer:* Wilfrid Roberts, M.P.
*Hon. Secretary:* *Miss Mary M. Sibthorp

*Vice-Presidents:*
His Grace the Archbishop of Canterbury
His Grace the Archbishop of York
The Moderator of the Church of Scotland
The Moderator of the Free Church Federal Council
*The Very Rev. the Chief Rabbi
Sir William Beveridge, K.C.B.
*Professor S. Brodetsky
Dame Elizabeth Cadbury, D.B.E.
Lady Violet Bonham-Carter
*Col. Victor Cazalet, M.C., M.P.
The Rt. Hon. the Viscount Cecil of Chelwood, P.C.
The Rt. Hon. the Lord Davies
Brig.-Gen. Sir Wyndham Deedes, C.M.G., D.S.O.
A. J. Dobbs, Esq.
*D. R. Grenfell, C.B.E., J.P., M.P.
*Victor Gollancz, Esq.
Sir Derrick Gunston, M.C., M.P.
The Rt. Hon. Sir Percy Harris, M.P.
Professor A. V. Hill, O.B.E., F.R.S., M.P.
Sir Austin Hudson, M.P.
The Rt. Hon. the Earl of Huntingdon
Miss Anne Loughlin, O.B.E.
Dame Edith Lyttelton, G.B.E.
J. S. Middleton, Esq.
*The Rev. James Parkes, PH.D.
*The Rt. Hon. the Earl of Perth, P.C., G.C.M.G., C.B.
The Rt. Hon. Lord Queenborough, G.B.E.
*Miss Eleanor Rathbone, M.P.
*Wilfrid Roberts, M.P.
The Rt. Hon. Lord Rochester, C.M.G.
*The Marchioness of Reading
The Rt. Hon. the Viscount Samuel, P.C., G.C.B., G.B.E.
The Rt. Hon. the Viscount Sankey, P.C., G.B.E.
*H. U. Willink, M.C., M.P.
The Rt. Rev. J. S. Whale, D.D.

* *Members of the Executive Committee, which includes also:*

| | |
|---|---|
| The Rev. Henry Carter, C.B.E. | The Hon. Mrs. Dugdale |
| Harry Goodman, Esq. | The Rev. G. J. G. Grieve |
| Berl Locker, Esq. | Sir Andrew McFadyean |
| Leonard Stein, Esq. | The Rev. Ian White-Thomson |

**NOTE.**

The writer of this pamphlet is solely responsible for the opinio[ns] and proposals it contains, except where otherwise stated therei[n]. The responsibility of the National Committee for Rescue fro[m] Nazi Terror for this and other publications issued by it is limit[ed] to commending it to readers as a contribution to the study [of] the subject.

25. Inside cover page of *Rescue the Perishing*, listing all the members of the committee (Victor Gollancz, 1943). Courtesy of The Wiener Library, London.

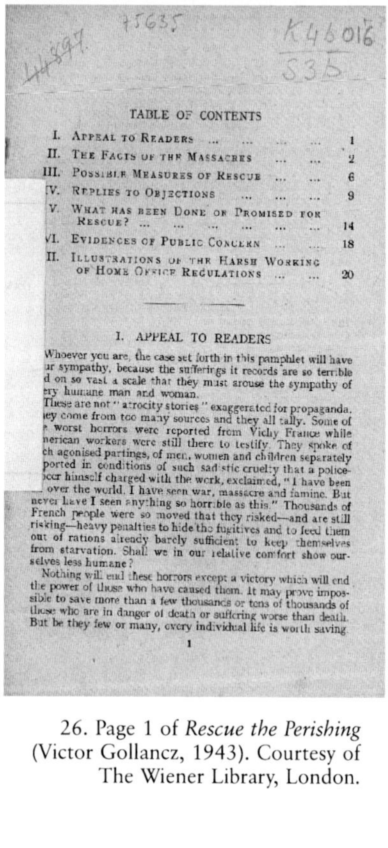



TABLE OF CONTENTS



I. APPEAL TO READERS

Whoever you are, the case set forth in this pamphlet will have [yo]ur sympathy, because the sufferings it records are so terrible [an]d on so vast a scale that they must arouse the sympathy of [ev]ery humane man and woman.

These are not "atrocity stories" exaggerated for propaganda. [Th]ey come from too many sources and they all tally. Some of [th]e worst horrors were reported from Vichy France while [Am]erican workers were still there to testify. They spoke of [su]ch agonised partings, of men, women and children separately [de]ported in conditions of such sadistic cruelty that a police-[off]icer himself charged with the work, exclaimed, "I have been [all] over the world. I have seen war, massacre and famine. But never have I seen anything so horrible as this." Thousands of French people were so moved that they risked—and are still risking—heavy penalties to hide the fugitives and to feed them out of rations already barely sufficient to keep themselves from starvation. Shall we in our relative comfort show ourselves less humane?

Nothing will end these horrors except a victory which will end the power of those who have caused them. It may prove impossible to save more than a few thousands or tens of thousands of those who are in danger of death or suffering worse than death. But be they few or many, every individual life is worth saving.

1

26. Page 1 of *Rescue the Perishing* (Victor Gollancz, 1943). Courtesy of The Wiener Library, London.

## TEN-POINT PROGRAMME
## FOR MEASURES OF RESCUE FROM NAZI TERROR

*January, 1944.*

1. **RESCUE IN LANDS COMING UNDER ALLIED CONTROL.** Instructions should be given to all Allied Commanders wherever operating, and requests made to chiefs of Guerilla Forces, to do everything possible, without hindering military operations, to rescue Jews and political prisoners. These should be transferred with the minimum of formality to countries of safety.

   Similarly, immediate arrangements should be made to ensure that wherever there is a landing in Europe, military commanders should regard it is an urgent duty to do everything practicable to rescue those likely otherwise to be massacred.

   To facilitate evacuation of those rescued, there should be extended provision of refuge camps and use of those already available, in places easily accessible under Allied control, for the temporary disposal of refugees collected from enemy-occupied or neutral countries.

2. **ENCOURAGEMENT TO NEUTRAL STATES TO ADMIT MORE REFUGEES,** by

   (a) Gifts of and/or facilities for obtaining food, clothing, fuel, etc.; and/or financial aid now or after victory.

   (b) Guarantees by the United Nations, or those willing to co-operate, that the refugees will, to an extent defined by numbers or date of reception, be evacuated after victory or sooner where practicable; such guarantees to be formally conveyed to the Neutral Governments.

   (c) H.M.'s Government to take the initiative by promising to find homes post-war for a substantial number of those refugees who prove to be non-repatriable and to invite the Dominions to do the same.*

3. **RECONSIDERATION OF REGULATIONS FOR UNITED KINGDOM VISAS** in order to include:

   (a) Greater liberality in the admission of refugees. The present strictly utilitarian tests of usefulness for the war effort should be supplemented by the humanitarian tests of rescue from Nazi terror, both subject to precautions for security.

   (b) Removal of the present rule that a visa cannot be promised for any refugee while still in enemy-occupied territory, in cases where there is reason to believe that the promise would facilitate the refugee's escape or admission to a neutral country.

4. **WORKERS EXPERIENCED IN DEALING WITH REFUGEES,** with the appropriate linguistic and other qualifications, should be sent to assist the British Authorities in all countries where such assistance may be needed.

   Supplementary Passport Control Officers should be appointed to Consulates in Neutral countries, to relieve the greatly overworked officials.

5. **INCREASED TRANSPORT FACILITIES FOR EVACUATING REFUGEES,** including:

   (a) The use of neutral or other ships as ferry boats between ports in neutral or enemy countries where refugees could be congregated and ports under British or Allied control.

   (b) The use of ships which have brought troops, supplies, etc., to Allied ports or food to Greece, for taking refugees to places of safety on their homeward journey.

6. **THE ADMISSION OF JEWISH REFUGEES TO PALESTINE** should be facilitated by:

   (a) The removal of the restriction, announced by the Colonial Secretary but unjustified by the terms of the White Paper of May, 1939, that the 34,000 certificates still available under the immigration quota of the White Paper must be used mainly for children.

   (b) The supply of unnamed certificates to the British representatives at Ankara, to be filled up on nomination by the representative of the Jewish Agency for Palestine, for refugees whether already in neutral territory or to facilitate their escape thereto.

   (c) Extended arrangements if permitted by the Turkish Government, for the accommodation within their territories, without expense to them, of refugees in transit, and for facilities for transport.

7. **CONTINUED PRESSURE ON GERMANY AND ITS SATELLITES** (including Vichy) to refrain from cruelties and deportations and to let their victims go; making it clear that those responsible for these cruelties will be considered as war criminals.

8. **FREQUENT APPEALS, THROUGH RADIO AND LEAFLETS, TO THE PEOPLES OF ENEMY AND ENEMY-OCCUPIED LANDS,** making known the facts and urging them to resist deportations and cruelties politically and by succouring the victims.

9. **RECOGNITION OF THE EXTREME URGENCY AND IMPORTANCE OF THE PROBLEM.** The position should be frequently reviewed by the Cabinet. Parliament should be kept fully informed of the activities of the Inter-Governmental Committee and of U.N.R.R.A. The British representatives on these bodies should take the initiative in proposing all possible measures of rescue.

10. **Adoption of the principle that, whatever other Nations may do or leave undone, the British Contribution to the work of Rescue should be the speediest and most generous possible without delaying victory.**

* The above assurances should be given publicly or privately, as discretion requires. The contributions promised would necessarily vary with the circumstances both of the States giving and the States receiving the assurances. Their purpose is to encourage the Neutral States not only to continue to receive escaping refugees but to offer to receive large numbers from the Enemy Powers. Their response may become increasingly favourable as our victory approaches. The willingness of the Neutral States to make offers may depend on how far they can count on the necessary aid. Assurances have already been officially given of help both in maintenance and in evacuation. (See the Foreign Office statement issued December 10th.) The task will, we gather, be shared between U.N.R.R.A. and the Inter-Governmental Committee on Refugees, the former being concerned chiefly with post-war maintenance and the repatriation of those who can return to their home-lands, the latter assuming responsibility for finding homes for those who cannot return. The numbers of these non-repatriables may be very large, owing to racial and political difficulties and the fear of being permanently encumbered with them may deter the Neutral States from making large offers. Hence the importance of Point 2(c).

27. The National Committee for Rescue from Nazi Terror: Ten-Point Programme, January 1944. Courtesy of Imperial War Museum, London.

## NATIONAL COMMITTEE FOR RESCUE FROM NAZI TERROR

*President:* THE MOST HON. THE MARQUESS OF CREWE, P.C., K.G.

*Vice-Presidents:*

His Grace the Archbishop of Canterbury
His Grace the Archbishop of York
The Moderator of the Church of Scotland
The Moderator of the Free Church Federal Council
†The Very Rev. the Chief Rabbi
Sir William Beveridge, K.C.B.
†Professor S. Brodetsky
Dame Elizabeth Cadbury, D.B.E.
†Lady Violet Bonham-Carter
The Rt. Hon. the Viscount Cecil of Chelwood, P.C.
The Rt. Rev. the Bishop of Chichester
†The Rt. Hon. the Lord Davies
†Brig.-Gen. Sir Wyndham Deedes, C.M.G., D.S.O.
A. J. Dobbs, Esq.
†D. R. Grenfell, C.B.E., J.P., M.P.
†Victor Gollancz, Esq.
Sir Derrick Gunston, M.C., M.P.
The Rt. Hon. Sir Percy Harris, M.P.
Professor A. V. Hill, O.B.E., F.R.S., M.P.
Lord Horder, G.C.V.O., M.D.
Sir Austin Hudson, M.P.
The Rt. Hon. the Earl of Huntingdon
Dame Anne Loughlin, O.B.E.
†J. S. Middleton, Esq.
†The Rev. James Parkes, PH.D.
†The Rt. Hon. the Earl of Perth, P.C., G.C.M.G., C.B.
The Rt. Hon. Lord Queenborough, G.B.E.
†Miss Eleanor F. Rathbone, M.P.
†Wilfrid Roberts, M.P.
The Rt. Hon. the Lord Rochester, C.M.G.
†The Marchioness of Reading
The Rt. Hon. the Viscount Samuel, P.C., G.C.B., G.B.E.
The Rt. Hon. the Viscount Sankey, P.C., G.B.E.
The Rt. Rev. J. S. Whale, D.D.

† Also Members of the Executive Committee.

*Executive Committee:*

The Rev. Henry Carter, C.B.E.
Harry Goodman, Esq.
Capt. The Hon. Quintin Hogg, M.P.
Ilse Locker, Esq.
The Hon. Harold Nicolson, C.M.G., M.P.
The Hon. Frank Pakenham
The Hon. Mrs. Edgar Dugdale
The Rev. G. J. G. Grieve
Mrs. Cazalet Keir, M.P.
Sir Andrew McFadyean
The Rev. Ian White-Thomson
Leonard Stein, Esq.

*Hon. Treasurer:* Wilfrid Roberts, M.P.
*Chairman of the Executive Committee:* D. R. Grenfell, C.B.E., J.P., M.P.
*Vice-Chairman:* Miss Eleanor F. Rathbone, M.P.
*Secretary:* Miss Mary M. Sibthorp.

## HUMAN LIVES CAN BE SAVED

The Committee was founded in March, 1943, to act as a medium for co-operation between the various organisations, groups and individuals in the U.K. interested in saving victims of Axis persecution of whatever race or religion.

We cannot do our work efficiently unless we have a large and determined body of public opinion behind us.

Please read the 10-point programme overleaf.

We are anxious to enrol as corresponding Members of the National Committee both individuals and organisations so that we may send them our literature and keep them in touch with the course of events.

The minimum Annual Subscription is 10/6.

PLEASE HELP US! PLEASE FILL IN THE FORM BELOW!

---

*I wish to become a corresponding member of the
*My organisation wishes to become a corresponding member of the

NATIONAL COMMITTEE FOR RESCUE FROM NAZI TERROR
30, MAIDEN LANE, LONDON, W.C.2.

I enclose a subscription of £ : :
*I wish to help with the organisation of a local Committee.

Name ..............................
Address ..............................
Occupation ..............................
Organisation ..............................

★ Cross out which is inapplicable.

28. The National Committee for Rescue from Nazi Terror: Lists of members and application form. Courtesy of Imperial War Museum, London.

29. Dedication ceremony of the Eleanor Rathbone School at Magdiel, 19 October 1949, with Bertha Schoolman speaking. Courtesy of Hadassah Archives at the American Jewish Historical Society, New York.

30. The Eleanor Rathbone Building, Magdiel, Israel, 19 October 1949. Youth Aliyah Collection at the American Jewish Historical Society. Reproduced courtesy of Central Zionist Archives, Jerusalem, Israel.

# 9

# *The National Committee for Rescue from Nazi Terror*

Neither Eleanor nor the NCRNT had high expectations of the revived Intergovernmental Committee on Refugees (IGCR), first established in July 1938 following the Evian Conference. The appointment of Lord Winterton as chairman did not bode well, for he had already made his feelings quite clear about Eleanor's rescue plans. Besides this, he was known for his social antipathy towards Jews and for his anti-Zionist views.[1] There was also the Committee's post-Evian record to consider, but the NCRNT nevertheless gave it some support, on the basis that every door to rescue ought to be kept open.[2] Eleanor would have been more optimistic had she been appointed as a 'kind of assessor' on the committee, a suggestion that Lord Perth first mooted, informally, to Randall in early June 1943. He thought this would 'blunt all the intense criticism of HMG'.[3] Perth's argument for Eleanor's inclusion was presented in such a way as to make it appear that the government would be the main beneficiaries. He put it that, as an insider, she would gain confidence in, and become less suspicious of the IGCR's activities, and this would, in turn 'blunt all the intense criticism of HMG (and) if she were on the inside I do not think that she would raise difficulties unnecessarily'.[4] There was the added 'unanswerable value' that might ensue from the vital sources of information that she had access to, through her contact with various societies and individuals.[5] His suggestion then received the added backing of the Marquess of Crewe, who wrote at length to Law in late August.[6] Another supporter, but from a different viewpoint, was Lady Cheetham, who saw the appointment as a way of controlling Eleanor's activities:

> Collaboration from the 'Terror' committee and realization that we feel the sufferings of the persecuted and are trying to help them just as much as they, would be very welcome. At present their antagonistic attitude is disheartening. I agree with Lord Perth that it would be useful to appoint Miss Eleanor to some official post on the IGCR where her sympathy with the refugees might find practical expression and she would come up against some of the main difficulties of the problem and realise that a

> block of visas is no magic carpet which will automatically carry away the persecuted from Nazi occupied Europe.[7]

Cheetham's colleague, Walker, whilst admitting to having no knowledge of the assessor system, was of the same mind and thought that 'it seems a good idea to draw the dragons teeth by taking it into our confidence'.[8] Yet another champion of the idea was Violet Bonham-Carter, who commended her to her friend Eden because 'she has fought the battle for refugees with such splendid courage and, as you know, no one has more detailed knowledge and experience of the problems involved'.[9]

Officials continued to vacillate over the advisability of Eleanor's appointment, and at one point Eden seemed sorely tempted by the notion.[10] But Emerson was adamantly against this and would only consider consultation with appointed representatives of voluntary organizations.[11] This was not an option that Eleanor would accept, for it would have left her and the NCRNT ignorant of the subjects discussed or decisions reached.[12] Of course the two were inextricably linked, but Walker's remarks on possible collaboration between Eleanor, the NCRNT and the IGCR highlight the extent to which Eleanor and the committee were seen as synonymous, and the degree of hostility which existed between Eleanor, Emerson and Lord Winterton:

> If by collaboration is meant collaboration with Miss Eleanor there is the personal factor, which may be termed lack of esteem between Sir Herbert Emerson and Miss Eleanor on the one hand and Lord Winterton and Miss Eleanor on the other which is not conducive to the smooth conduct of affairs.[13]

Emerson wasted no time in dismissing the notion of Eleanor as an assessor,[14] and any chance of her representing the interest of refugees on the IGCR was destroyed in a contemptuous Foreign Office memo of 3 September 1943, signed by Law:

> The reconstitution of the IGC [*sic*] is very important though Miss Rathbone still complains about personalities and her chief complaint that there was no one with sole interest in refugees was now answered ... refugee enthusiasts can now be turned to Sir Herbert Emerson and his vice-director, Mr Patrick Malin, of whom we have formed an excellent impression ... We are being pressed to get Jews and enthusiasts like Miss Rathbone appointed to the Committee. The Americans oppose this but Sir Herbert Emerson is working out a scheme which would allow a certain co-operation on the part of the voluntary organizations ... I'm convinced that we can't use Miss Eleanor or any of her kidney as 'assessors'.

> Assessors are concerned with facts. Miss Eleanor is interested in policies, (and) would just sit there trying to force her particular views down the throats of the others. Anyway, the Americans won't have her.[15]

The resentment towards Eleanor was more than evident here, and was particularly insulting, for since her earliest days of social work in Liverpool she had always been exceptionally concerned with establishing facts. And it was these facts, gleaned from her wide variety of sources, which drove the need for rescue policies. She produced a regular stream of documents which examined, for example, 'Specific Rescue Measures for Victims of Nazi Persecution' and 'The Position up-to-date of the rescue Movement for Victims of Nazi Terror'. She was particularly perplexed by a number of issues, including the position of the Italian Jews, Jews vetted for Palestine who were still held in Spain, the danger that Switzerland might close down on all other refugees because of the large number of war prisoners escaping there from Italy, and much more. As far as the IGCR was concerned, it was sixteen months since the policies of deportation and massacre had become known, nine and a half months since the UN Declaration promising retribution, and five months since the Bermuda Conference referred the question of rescue and postwar settlement to the IGCR. And the full committee had still to meet. Eleanor could not understand why, of the forty-five states approached, only six so far – the same six as were chosen for the Evian conference – were represented, especially Argentina, which was still in full diplomatic and commercial relations with Germany. Conversely, many countries directly concerned with victims, for example Czechoslovakia, Poland and Belgium, or places of rescue, such as Sweden and Switzerland, were not represented.

Her overriding concern was the effect that all this could have on world opinion and on the chances of rescue.[16] More NCRNT executive meetings took place where the IGCR was again discussed, and where Eleanor reported on the USA, the Emergency Conference for the Rescue of European Jews and Congressman Will Rogers's visit to Britain. Rogers was an active agitator on Capitol Hill in favour of American efforts to rescue the Jews in Europe and was a member of Peter Bergson's Emergency Committee to Save the Jewish People of Europe, a pressure group that played a role in Roosevelt's decision to establish the War Refugee Board. In August 1943 he undertook a five-week, unofficial, self-financed mission to the United Kingdom, and was a keynote speaker at the opening conference in London of Bergson's emergency committee. Eleanor entered into negotiations with him during this visit, putting the position to him quite frankly, verbally and in writing, that it 'was desirable that an American Committee be formed on the same broad basis as our own' and that 'the composition of the Bergson Committee' would not fit in with this.[17] Bergson's committee had a very different profile to the NCRNT and it was inevitable that no liaison was set up between the two groups. Instead, Gollancz wrote privately to Isaiah Berlin, and the offer of assistance from Norman Angell, the prominent liberal humanitarian and author, on his return to the USA, was accepted.[18]

Simultaneously, the work of the PCR continued, with Eleanor pursuing Ernest Bevin over the employment – or not – of alien dentists. In spite of the desperate shortage of dentists for both general work and school work, the behaviour of the dental profession, which she described as 'jealous and exclusive', had prevented a Temporary Register being set up, with the result that her committee alone had details of some fifty to sixty professionals with German or Austrian qualifications and who were not employed in their field.[19]

By November 1943 Eleanor and Lord Perth had decided not to press Emerson any further for the appointment of assessors.[20] Describing the IGCR as 'a most unwieldy and unsuitable committee', Eleanor had become increasingly frustrated by the slow pace at which it operated.[21] The Treasury did not complete the financial arrangements to enable the IGCR to begin functioning until December 1943,[22] although they were not quite as inactive as Eleanor insinuated, for Emerson was doing his best to persuade more countries to join the committee.[23] Behind the scenes the Refugee Department resented her persistent questioning in the House.[24] In minutes on 29 October 1943, Randall wrote that 'MPs are entitled to ask Questions regarding HMGs participation in the Committee, but clearly Miss Rathbone's Question is intended as an indirect criticism of the Committee and should be handled accordingly'. To this end, he withheld the information that seven governments had already replied, and that Emerson was 'trying to get more in, and [the] Secretary of State in Moscow [was] trying to secure membership of [the] Soviet government. Instead, he submitted a draft reply that was intended 'at once to conciliate her and to foil her attempt to fasten on us responsibility for answering Questions about the IGC [*sic*] which the Committee should deal with'.[25] Hot on his heels was Walker, whose minuted response recorded 'This nagging at the committee through the medium of Parliament is hardly likely to prevail upon the governments who have been invited to join the committee to do so more expeditiously'. It was also thought that her questioning was, perhaps, a ploy to lead the government into supplying information that it was not up to them to disclose.[26] Eleanor was equally perturbed by the negative discussions she was having with Foreign Office officials,[27] exacerbated by Law, George Hall and Randall's rejection of her calls for a Debate on the Address, on the grounds that, first, the UK was doing more than it could disclose and had to be more vague than the real facts justified, and second, protest by the British government and Parliament stimulated rather than deterred Nazi persecution. In the draft of a strictly confidential letter to Hall on 24 November 1943 – the same day as the NCRNT held an executive meeting – Eleanor wrote:

> We felt perplexed and uneasy ... Recognise strength of objections and that whether justified or not. A Ministerial reply refusing assurances we press for might harm and not help our course. But fears to ignore the subject in the Debate on the Address – the biggest annual opportunity for the discussion of important issues – gives the impression that the UK government and Parliament has lost interest in the subject and were influenced by growing anti-Semitism [*sic*] as Goebbels has implied.[28]

Whilst her remarks were loaded with cynicism, her impression of official indifference was not altogether wrong, for unbeknown to her, the WCC, which had only been set up in early 1943, had not met since late June 1943, and did not, in fact, convene again until 14 March 1944.[29] Nor had Randall seen the need to respond to the US government's call for a joint statement of action taken since Bermuda, on the grounds that 'there is not much straw for this particular piece of brick-making'.[30]

The second letter that went to Hall on 26 November embodied points which Brodetsky had passed on to Eleanor through his office, a reminder of the extent to which the BDBJ relied upon her to act as a conduit between themselves and government officials. More than that, the Board did, from time to time, make small donations to the NCRNT, but the committee's financial situation, which was reliant on gifts of money, was so grave in October 1944, that there was a real possibility that they would have to cease their activities.[31] One issue over which she raised grave concerns was what she understood to be Randall's position, that the vast majority of refugees could be repatriated after the war. She felt that not only did he completely underestimate the numbers involved, but that there were many thousands of Germans, Poles and perhaps Romanians 'who can never reasonably be expected to return to countries where anti-Semitism is deeply rooted, the countries in ruin, families massacred'. But she did compromise on a number of points: these included agreeing to not tabling an amendment or staging a full debate, and not pressing the government on difficult points, in return for which the government would make a short statement in general terms and she could anticipate two or three of her supporters following with short speeches.[32] Hall wrote that he was very keen that Eleanor, rather than any other activist, should be the speaker, on the basis that she 'knew the whole case and the Government's difficulties', and Eleanor accepted this. Whether she detected Hall's duplicity in complimenting her is questionable, for she told Graham White that 'I think that this is the best we can hope for, and pretty good'.[33] On 13 December, Eleanor reported, in a confidential memo, of her meeting with Emerson three days earlier. A declaration was likely to be made shortly on behalf of the UN (or certain members of the organization), but this did not calm her fears. She made no apologies for being blunt when she said, 'I regard both the proposed declaration and the published statement as wholly unsatisfactory as they fail to reassure Neutrals as to the future of the one section of refugees they are likely to be worried about, and this impedes the Neutrals from offering to receive further large numbers.'[34]

The debate on the war situation and foreign affairs took place, as promised, on 14 December 1943. Eleanor had already sent a note to Hall, assuring him that she would be 'much less outspoken in the House if called to speak, though I hope to say something on the main point of the note' (which she had sent Eden). This had infuriated Randall, who pencilled in his own undisguised contempt on Eleanor's letter, 'This is an ill-informed note and the insinuation in the final para. Seems to me really offensive. So much of Miss R's case has already been discussed, but we might, I suppose, do it again.'[35]

Eleanor did get her chance to speak and she was uncompromising in her attack on the Declaration for, in her words, and as she predicted, it

> failed to deal with the crucial question of what was to happen to the refugees who could not be repatriated and what are we going to do to make it easier for the neutral states to offer them hospitality. I beseech my right hon. Friend and through him the Cabinet to give further thought to this matter. Do not let them be content with urging our Allies to repatriate their own nationals ... Let them say plainly that what we are prepared to do ourselves and to ask our Dominions and the United States what they are prepared to do ...

And when she asked Eden directly, 'Cannot our own country and the United States do what the smaller countries cannot do, and undertake to provide for the settlement of those who may not be repatriated after the war?' his answer was non-committal. Beyond being unable to give a pledge, he maintained that he was not familiar enough with the matter and would have to look into it before communicating further with her.[36] It was Hall who subsequently responded, asking her to re-read the answer to her very question in a letter from Law to Crewe on 26 November. If his letter indicated a certain loss of patience with her, Eleanor seemed not to notice, for she subsequently thanked him for going into the matter so fully, and for providing her with useful additional information. But the long and the short of it was that the IGCR – in whom Eleanor had little faith – were to be directly responsible for the resettlement and repatriation of refugees, so releasing the Government from any obligation.[37] This was not, it should be said, because she thought Emerson to be in any way incompetent. Rather, she held him and his three colleagues in the highest esteem, but the machinery with which they had to work was, as far as she was concerned, cumbersome and slow.[38]

The anniversary of the 17 December 1942 declaration was looming, and Eleanor had readily agreed to write an article for the *Manchester Guardian*, reminding readers of, as Crozier put it, 'what has and has not been done within the twelve months on behalf of the refugees ... the leisurely stages of action and point out how little at the finish it all amounts to'. And in a revealing finale to her reply to Crozier, Eleanor concluded, 'it is the most heartbreaking subject I ever worked at. We get nowhere and there is an air of "hush-hush" and it is very hard to estimate at the real value'.[39]

The lack of an official lead, combined with the diminution of press coverage, had certainly dented public interest in the subject of refugees and rescue, and the NCRNT, upon whom the burden of public and private campaigning depended, had already agreed upon a domestic propaganda campaign. The emphasis now was not limited to trying to reinforce evidence of the extent of the atrocities against Jews, facts that the general public found increasingly difficult to assimilate, but included countering anti-Semitism at home, in the hope that it would promote renewed pressure on government with regard to rescue. Crewe was to write to the prime minister to stress two points, the most important being the question of guarantees and the emphasis on British responsibility in Palestine, for Eleanor was adamant that the Palestine White Paper of 1939 was responsible for the 'non-saving of thousands of Jewish lives'.[40] And in the fallout from the recent debate, a sub-committee was appointed to handle this campaign.[41]

Eleanor herself set about producing a number of pamphlets, including one entitled *Continuing Terror: How to Rescue Hitler's Victims*, another, *Falsehoods and Facts about the Jews*, all of which were utilized in the campaign. The latter differed markedly from *Continuing Terror* for it was compiled as a Jewish defence document to counter domestic anti-Semitism, which, according to government officials, was a valid reason for not allowing more Jewish refugees into the country. Whereas government officials had been the harshest critics of *Rescue the Perishing*, Eleanor now faced the fury of her friend and colleague, Victor Gollancz,[42] who by now was addressing her as 'My dear Eleanor'. Whether this implied a less formal relationship, or was Gollancz being a touch patronizing, is uncertain. He maintained, not unreasonably, that anti-Semitism defied logic or reason, so that to attempt an approach that owed everything to logical arguments was flawed. Gollancz did not question Eleanor's basic liberalism and universalism but he feared that her pamphlet would give the wrong impression: 'You will forgive me for saying that if I had not known you I should have said "Here is a terrifically humanitarian woman who loathes any form of persecution and has an extremely strong sense of decency and justice: but it's perfectly clear that in her heart of hearts she really dislikes the Jews, and finds them objectionable."'[43] Presenting a Gentile readership with well-rehearsed anti-Semitic stereotypes of Jews upset him the most. Thus he asked:

> I would put it to you: apart from what you have heard, how many Jews have you actually come across to whom any of these things apply? It is the same with the legend of the 'noisiness' and 'loudness' of Jews ... The trouble, as a matter of fact, with the majority of well-established Jews in England is that they tend to reproduce somewhat to excess the British reserve ...[44]

The irony of this was that Gollancz personally exhibited many of the very characteristic stereotypes he so derided. For, as his biographer, Ruth Dudley Edwards has described, he was noisy, and prone to public displays of ostentation. Ironically, the 'clannishness' – Jewish family loyalty – that he claimed to despise, was the very thing that had supported him, and provided the starting capital for his own business. And as a well-established Jew himself, he was far from reserved. On the contrary, he had a reputation amongst some British Jews for being extrovert to the point of embarrassment.[45] At worst, Eleanor made an error of judgment in the apologist tone of the pamphlet, but equally, as has been argued, Gollancz's criticism of it was ill-conceived. There is also Pedersen's assessment of *Falsehoods and Facts* to be considered. She has deduced that Eleanor's responses to questions involving Jews, specifically those in this pamphlet, were all informed (or inflected, as she writes) by her own identification with Jews, and 'not simply humanitarian universalism'.[46] It is true that Eleanor came to identify with Jews in many ways, and confessed how much she admired their enterprise, tenacity, culture and values. But to claim, as Pedersen does, that as 'the daughter of a provincial merchant dynasty', Eleanor would have seen nothing wrong in the accusation of being 'clannish' or 'tight-fisted', is misguided, for it demonstrates a lack of understanding of the prevailing nature of anti-Semitism in Britain. Anti-Semites used these terms in a derogatory fashion, intending to demean and malign Jews, a discourse in which Eleanor would never have engaged. She was undoubtedly a proponent of family loyalty, but not in the way that Pedersen, or Gollancz, understood it. Besides this, Pedersen has ignored a far more significant aspect of the pamphlet, namely Eleanor's implicit references to the calumnies of the *Protocols of the Elders of Zion*. Here she countered claims, albeit briefly, that 'the Jews control the Press' and 'the Jews control the Banks and the Stock Exchange'.[47] As to the success of her pamphlet, the only tangible form of evidence are the sales figures, which indicate that about 30,000 copies were printed, an insignificant quantity in comparison with Gollancz's own pamphlet, *Let my People Go*.[48] It therefore seems likely that Eleanor's pamphlet did not reach the wide audience she may have anticipated, and that in terms of an anti-defamation campaign, it proved quite useless.

Gollancz was not the only person to castigate Eleanor, and given the antagonism in government circles towards her campaigning activities, it was not entirely surprising that her pamphlets were censured by the usual coterie of officials. Cheetham was scathing in her attack on *Continuing Terror*, claiming that 'there was nothing new in this pamphlet' and that the sub-title was

> very misleading since it implies that schemes are set out by which Jews could be rescued: it is furthermore implied on p.18 that if there were a front rank statesman with energy and conviction these schemes could be carried out. Miss Rathbone must know quite well that we have no means of getting unfortunate Jews in Hitler's clutches out of them and it is dishonest to say that energy and conviction could bring such measures about.[49]

Randall was equally critical:

> This is the old pamphlet, toned down, in its reference to HMG but containing the same old central fallacy on p.18. I think Miss Rathbone should have this pointed out to her with perfect frankness: a combination of Gladstone and Nansen, in the middle of a desperate war, would avail little so long as Germany will not allow even Jewish children to leave, and to suggest the contrary is a cruel policy towards refugees who have succeeded in getting to safety.[50]

As for Walker, his blatant dislike of Eleanor was undisguised, nowhere more so than in minutes he wrote in connection with the WRB plan to set up a refugee camp in Tripolitania to rescue Jews via Turkey and the Black Sea:

> In view of the continued opposition of the military authorities I can only suggest that another attempt be made to secure a camp or camps in Syria. We are under great and increasing pressure from the Americans, not to mention the 'perishing' Miss Rathbone. Extra accommodation must be found, if only as 'eye-wash'. It could then be placed under UNRRA, the more international flavour of which might reassure the Arabs who fear what they hold to be the pro-Jewish policy of HMG.

Ultimately, the camp which Britain gave approval to in June 1944 never materialized.[51]

All the remarks made by Walker, Randall and Cheetham, as well as so many made by Peake and Morrison, are significant for they are characteristic of the obstacles that Eleanor was up against: her campaigning was regarded in official circles with increasing disdain, her persistence was an irritant, responses to her proposals were often tailored to placate her and she was only tolerated because of her political status.[52] Nor was there ever any question of her or her parliamentary colleagues, male or female, being involved in decision making.

Apart from Eleanor and Gollancz's contributions, the regular cyclostyled bulletin, *News From Hitler's Europe*, which was produced by the NCRNT from October 1943 until late 1945, proved to be a much more important initiative of the renewed publicity campaign. Whilst Eva Hubback played down the value of the publication, describing it as a 'small and unpretentious bulletin' (see Plate 23),[53] it contained immensely detailed information about the progress of the war, gleaned from a wide variety of sources as diverse as underground representatives and foreign newspapers.[54] In this respect it exonerated Eleanor from the charge made by Cheetham, Walker and other officials, and more recently Rubinstein, that she lacked real knowledge about the refugee situation in Europe, and that neither she, Gollancz, nor the committee members understood 'the diabolical evil they were attempting to ameliorate'.[55] On the contrary, both she and the NCRNT probably had a far more realistic understanding of the enormity and gravity of the crisis than the government.

Eleanor's reputation for having up-to-date knowledge of refugee-related matters and contacts in the USA was quite evident when, in late January 1944, Crozier wrote to her asking if she had 'any information about this new War Refugee Board' which the *Zionist Review* had written about, and which they suggested was 'important'.[56] The *Manchester Guardian*'s question was answered with Eden's announcement in the House on 9 February, that Roosevelt had established a WRB consisting of the secretary of state, the secretary of the Treasury and secretary of war. Outlining the objectives of the Board, that of the rescue and relief of refugees, he re-affirmed HMG's 'earnest desire and practical intention of associating themselves with the WRB, in particular endeavouring to carry out the aims which the President has set before it'.[57] He was adamant, in the face of questioning by Mr Lipson, the Independent Conservative MP for Cheltenham, that the government's body was as effective. But Eleanor went further, asking him bluntly whether he could claim that 'a strictly private Cabinet Committee is at all equivalent to this American Board, with its carefully defined position, its frequent access to the President and its executive director? Will he consider appointing somebody analogous to that board?' But this was not to be, as Eden made clear when he replied that 'I have considered it. The hon. Lady knows our machinery perhaps better than anyone, and knows that this War Cabinet Committee has a responsibility to the Foreign Office. We think that, on the whole, that is the best way.'[58] Cheetham was delighted when, some days later, Lord Halifax had to correct the impression of one member of the WRB who thought that the British WCC was the same as the Cabinet. She thought his answer, that it was 'a specialised body, to deal with this (refugee) problem' was very good, and could be 'made use of in reply to Miss Rathbone'.[59]

The WCC was not, in any respect, comparable to the WRB. In the first instance the British committee had been inactive for the six months prior to the establishment of the WRB and was only reactivated because of the new situation. Even Law and Emerson agreed, in private, that the British committee was not by any means the same as the WRB, for the latter had a specific commitment, governmental support and financial foundation, as well as the speed of its actions. But the most fundamental difference was in its philosophy on rescue, for the WRB's first loyalty was to the Jews of Europe, and not to either 'Anglo-American cooperation or to the British conception of a financial blockade'.[60] Ultimately, Eden's intransigence over the matter of a British equivalent of the WRB enabled the government to contain their rescue policies within established and limited parameters. The day following Eden's announcement of the establishment of the WRB, Eleanor gave a short report at a general meeting of the NCRNT, and told members that the Executive Committee had drafted an agreed addendum to the Ten-Point Programme, calling, yet again, for the British government 'to establish an organ with a full-time Executive director in order to maintain contact with the newly established WRB' (see Plate 27).[61] The call was repeated in an article in *The Times* on 22 February 1944, in advance of a big public NCRNT meeting on 29 February at Central Hall, Westminster, intended to launch a new campaign. Emerson had been invited to attend, and had sought Randall's advice before accepting. Randall in turn reported to Law: he had persuaded Emerson that, as he thought the committee were intending to 'set aside the IGC [*sic*] and might also, quite well, attack the policy of HMG', it would be very difficult for him to be present. He was clearly very concerned about what might be said at the meeting, which he thought was likely to 'hold up America as a shining example to HMG. It would seem advisable to prevent such misleading and unjust comparison', and he wanted to silence Eleanor and her colleagues. He was also angered by the rumour that 'Miss Rathbone and her friends are going around saying that the War Refugee Board is going really to rescue Jews from Europe by secret means and that HMG should be urged to do likewise'.[62] He considered that 'any public mention of this would be extremely unfortunate' mainly because it might jeopardise the 'secret lanes' being used to get British prisoners, mainly RAF personnel, out, but also because quite a few refugees from France and Spain had apparently used this secret route. Kullmann had hinted that the Swiss government had hopes of getting 1,500 Jewish children out of France into Switzerland by secret means, provided there was no publicity. Randall dismissed Eleanor's views and aims on the question of rescue as 'quite unreal (and) based on ignorance of the true situation and what is worst of all may do real harm to such efforts as are being made to assist refugees'.[63] Her response to the WRB was, in fact, a mixture of disappointment and relief.[64] Much of her frustration emanated from the way in which officials of her own government had repeatedly rejected her demands for the establishment of a British equivalent of the WRB.

From Eleanor's perspective, it must have been a source of deep dismay to her, and her national pride, that it was the Americans, and not the British, who had responded so readily to this humanitarian crisis. For what was at stake here were not only rescuing human lives, but also rescuing the liberal identity of Britain, and her sense of honour and justice. Conversely, she must have been relieved to know, that, at last, there was an organization in place, albeit in the US, whose philosophy on the rescue of Jews mirrored her own. Nor did the similarity end there, for Roosevelt's executive order of 22 January 1944 that established the WRB had much in common with the NCRNT programme, to the extent that it could be argued that, indirectly, the committee had acted as a model for the American Board.[65] In any event, the very existence of the WRB was problematic for it served to reinforce the ideological gulf between the two nations.[66] Eleanor was undeterred by this and eager to move on with aiding the rescue of refugees, and thus established a personal rapport with the American organization. Interestingly, neither Mary Stocks nor Susan Pedersen have made any reference to Eleanor's liaison with the WRB, and it must be assumed that neither was aware of this significant connection. It is also important to reflect upon Eleanor's position as an Independent MP, for whilst Pamela Shatzkes has suggested that her lack of support from any party machinery was a disadvantage,[67] the fact that she had no party line to tow, and was not answerable to a party leader, was a distinct advantage. Any party affiliation would surely have militated against her pursuing her own goals and may have prevented her making direct contact with the WRB.

Eleanor's first letter to John Pehle, the 33-year-old Gentile executive director of the WRB, was sent in early March 1944.[68] She had been directed to him by Norman Angell[69] and made contact through Lauren Casady, the American Treasury representative in London. Casady was subsequently empowered by Pehle to meet Eleanor and 'discuss more fully the Board's activities' with her. Besides including a copy of the NCRNT's Ten-Point Programme, she set out some additional questions that were causing her the greatest anxiety at the time. She suggested that the US president and the prime minister send authoritative statements warning Germany and its satellites of British and world attitudes towards the persecution of Jews, the punishment of war criminals and the post-war situation, rather than the current warnings given by nameless voices. In a direct approach to Eden, Eleanor only agreed to postpone asking the prime minister in the House if he had or would warn the enemy satellites because, as she wrote,

> I fear that enough has already been said over the radio, by Mr Law in the House, and by Government people in the USA to make the Gestapo to put pressure on the Satellites, but not enough to convince either Germany or the Satellites that the British and USA Governments really do mean business by their warnings and will implement them. A warning by the Prime Minister, or by him and the President jointly would have this effect, even if it were made privately to the Satellites through diplomatic channels.[70]

She also made a plea for more financial aid for refugees in occupied countries, saying, 'We gather that many more might escape, especially from France into Spain or Switzerland, more doubtfully from Poland and elsewhere, if funds could be conveyed to them to pay for their maintenance in hiding or guides when escaping',[71] a reminder of her contacts with innumerable underground sources and escaped refugees. As to funding, the WRB had in fact licensed $100,000 to the International Red Cross to spend on goods for Jews in enemy territory, an action that provoked an open display of hostility by Randall, not only towards the WRB, but also to the principle of rescue itself.[72]

Eleanor's other concern was the matter of Turkey, and the limit imposed by the government on the number of transit visas they were issuing, for 'the Turkish authorities seem very unfriendly on this point'.[73] Besides raising this issue with Pehle, and asking his view as to whether stronger pressure from the USA and its government could not be used, she also pressed Randall and Eden over the apparent lack of cooperation of the Turkish government.[74] Randall, in minutes, had already expressed his view that it was inadvisable to criticize Turkey or to make them appear indifferent or anti-Jewish, as the Foreign and Colonial Office were discussing plans that would, he claimed, result in larger numbers being admitted.[75] In her letter to Eden on the subject Eleanor accepted that Law might be right and that the Turks were 'touchy about outside interference' but Eden could still, she argued, let them know, in the politest terms, that their lack of generosity and anti-Semitism made MPs feel unfriendly towards them.[76] When she did put down her question on 27 March 1944, Eden's reply did not reflect what she knew to be the Turkish attitude. Instead he maintained that the Turks had been cooperating in efforts to save refugees and that their scope was limited due to the number of exit permits being issued.[77] Pehle's letter to her in early April held out more hope, for it seemed that the WRB representative in Turkey, with the full cooperation of the American ambassador, had succeeded in 'gaining a measure of cooperation by the Turkish government as a result of which a number of lives have been saved'.[78]

Coincidental to this, Eleanor also met Nahum Goldmann, the chairman of the World Jewish Congress, on his official visit to London in March 1944 to promote the American WRB, and to try and persuade the British government and the governments-in-exile to set up their own WRBs.[79] The British government's lack of enthusiasm was explicit in Goldmann's memo when he wrote that 'Some attempt was made, unofficially, in British circles to whittle down the impression (of the WRB) by characterizing it as window-dressing and a political manoever [*sic*] in an election year'. His impression of Eleanor and the committee was unequivocally favourable, 'Wide sections of Parliament, especially the committee to save the victims of the Nazi terror, of which Miss Eleanor Rathbone, MP, is the leading member, were ready to renew their campaign in order to get the British Government to adopt policies similar to those of the War Refugee Board'.[80]

The contrast in her dealings with Pehle and British officials could not have been more marked, for instead of her proposals being dismissed with a raft of well-rehearsed excuses, she found herself in the unique position of being encouraged by Goldmann to send 'any further comments or suggestions' that she might have to the WRB.[81] It was a novelty for her to be told that one particular suggestion of hers, whereby 'uniformed trained staff be attached to Supreme headquarters with the specific task of organizing the relief and rescue of European Jews, and that these staff would enter large metropolitan areas such as Paris before the American troops'[82] was considered a very valuable idea that warranted immediate effect. Eleanor had great faith in the ability of the WRB to rescue thousands of Jews from Nazi Europe, but the extent of their success remains uncertain, and has been the subject of academic scrutiny. For whilst David Wyman has assessed that the organization helped save approximately 200,000 Jews, William Rubinstein has challenged this, not only reducing the figure to around 20,000, but also suggesting that the WRB may not have actually saved a single life.[83] This is an extreme view that should be treated with caution, especially as it is not founded on any original critical research. Equally questionable is Rubinstein's unequivocal denunciation of the NCRNT's activities, and his assertion that their proposals were 'every bit as useless and misguided as their American counterparts'.[84]

Juxtaposed against Eleanor's personal dealings with the WRB in mid-1944 was her involvement with yet another refugee crisis. It should be borne in mind that she was now nearly 70 years old and in poor health,[85] but she nevertheless approached the desperate plight of Hungary's Jews, the last major group of victims of Nazi annihilation, with tenacity and compassion. When the Nazis invaded Hungary on 19 March 1944, the Jewish population numbered around 750,000. Ghettos were created with extraordinary speed, and in late May deportations began to Auschwitz, Poland and the gas chambers, organized with ruthless efficiency by Adolf Eichmann, and in full view of the world.[86]

Eleanor was at the forefront of the refugee activists when they held a conference to consider the position of their co-religionists in Hungary, asking Randall for information or suggestions, neither of which he could provide. But he held out some hope when she pressed him, again, about warnings to the satellite nations, for he told her in confidence, that the Foreign Office had 'under consideration, a new message which might be useful with the satellites'.[87] In minutes a week later, Randall conceded that 'It would be useful to warn the satellites publicly against assisting Germany in a policy of exterminating the Jews and others', but this decision was reached in the knowledge that President

Roosevelt was about to publish such a warning. The government was so concerned about public opinion, and how they would be viewed in comparison with America, that the British press and the BBC were being advised to 'comment on the President's statement when it appears, associating HMG sympathetically with it'.[88]

Following Eden's warning statement to the satellite nations in the House of Commons on 30 March, Eleanor continued to pursue the matter, urging Randall to try again for concurrent action by the USSR and for the warning to be distributed abroad by leaflets. There was also the question of whether it was conceivable for HMG to suggest that the Vatican intervene, in view of the Roman Catholic population in the country. How much influence Eleanor's suggestion had is uncertain, but a telegram was sent from the Home Office to the Holy See on 30 March 1944, in the hope of gaining the support of the cardinal secretary of state, so that Vatican influence might be exerted.[89] Weeks went by without Randall sending a formal reply, for which he apologized. But by this time, as he surmised, Eleanor knew, from Walker, that following their appeal, the Pope had taken action at Bucharest and Budapest – but did not elaborate on what form this action took – and that the Turkish authorities had promised to grant visas to applicants who presented themselves at Turkish consulates with Palestine immigration certificates.[90] In fact when Randall sent this letter, Eleanor was already in Westminster Hospital in London, having damaged a previously injured shin. A two-week stay proved insufficient to heal the wound, and she spent another seven weeks there before being discharged on 1 July 1944. To add insult to injury, this was the same day that a V2 rocket landed in Tufton Street, near enough to her home at 5 Tufton Court to blast its doors and windows, and create a havoc of debris and dust inside. With her flat out of commission, Eleanor decamped to her friend Eva Hubback's house in Golders Green to convalesce.[91]

During her weeks of hospitalization, Eleanor continued with as much work as possible, with her screened-off cubicle doubling up as an office. In her absence, the NCRNT met regularly and above all emphasized the need to keep the liaison between the Foreign Office and the IGCR alive. To this end Grenfell, Nicolson and Roberts made up a small committee for this express purpose.[92] Even though the NCRNT had not, as part of their remit, considered the question of refugees in Mauritius before now, Eleanor had personally conducted a lot of correspondence about this matter. She now asked Graham White if he would put down a question about the numbers of Jewish refugees, mostly from Austria and Czechoslovakia, who had been interned there since 1942, following their unsuccessful attempt to enter Palestine.[93]

She had previously received a 'spiteful answer' from the home secretary which she said was 'obviously intended to throw discredit on the Mauritius refugees', and to move the limelight away from the government's failure to release them from detention.[94] Back in harness in August, Eleanor took up the issue again with Colonel Stanley, pointing out how harsh it was that later 'illegal immigrants' had been admitted to Palestine, yet these people who were equally 'flying from persecution' should have been held indefinitely.[95] Another six months were to pass before Colonel Stanley, the secretary of state for the colonies, was able to report that these refugees were, at last, to be allowed to enter Palestine, with the caveat of transport and conditions permitting.[96]

The massacres of Hungary's Jews were at the top of Eleanor's political agenda in early July 1944. *News From Hitler's Europe* had already reminded readers of the unmitigated reign of terror in Hungary and that the WRB were reporting that about 500,000 Hungarian Jews being 'threatened with deportation to an "unknown destination"'.[97] She was in no doubt that these were 'going so rapidly that there will be few Hungarian Jews left to save unless something can be done at once', and her suggestion to Eden, that he urgently consider whether he, or better still the prime minister, could approach Stalin, and induce him to threaten the Hungarian government unless they stopped the massacres, was well received. Before she met Randall on 18 July, Eden had written to her, telling her that her suggestion had been adopted.[98] But it was Randall who felt compelled to warn her, in the strictest confidence, that whilst an approach 'in this sense' had been made, 'the Russians were in a very hard and realistic frame of mind and might quite well reply that they did not believe in words'.[99] Complex international discussions were already in progress in connection with Admiral Horthy, the Hungarian regent, and his offer to let certain categories of Hungarian Jews go.[100]

A lot of preparation now went into the points that the NCRNT deputation would put to Eden on 26 July 1944. Particular emphasis was to be made of the 'extremely small results' and the impression that 'the spirit in which the matter is being tackled is one of extreme caution, the pace of action too slow through conventional diplomatic channels with not enough gate crashing'. A major point was Eleanor's call for Britain to enter into urgent negotiations with Horthy to accept and, if possible, extend his offer to include all Hungarian Jews. Besides this, there were calls to set up reception camps for refugees in North Africa and elsewhere, including Britain. An easing of the rigid restriction on visas into Britain was called for, so that Britain could be seen to be as generous as other countries were being urged to be: fundamentally, a humanitarian approach was being called for, one that put lives and not political agendas first.[101]

Being told that the transportations of Jews beyond the Hungarian borders had ceased was, of course, welcome news, but the responses of Hall, the parliamentary undersecretary, to the NCRNT proposals, were less encouraging.[102] Eleanor and her fellow activists were told that there would not be any negotiation with an enemy government, and only Switzerland, as the protecting power, could do this. On the question of entry into Palestine, it was easy for the Foreign Office to 'pass the buck' by saying that this was a matter for the Colonial Office, but the truth is that they were fearful of a flood of refugees. Similarly, to claim, as Hall did, that 'no refugee had been refused sanctuary in the United Kingdom once he or she arrived' omitted to mention that, beyond the improbability of escaping, obtaining a visa in the first place was fraught with obstacles.

Eleanor was in no doubt that time was of the essence, and her frustration at the lack of action was evident in a letter to Eden on 31 July 1944, in which she remarked, 'All this is very perturbing. It means that although Horthy's offer was published in the press some two and a half weeks ago, no one in Hungary has yet been told of our Government's determination to find transport and accommodation for all who could get out'.[103] A central aspect of the delay was communication with the Americans concerning Britain's request for an agreement of collaboration. Exactly who was responsible for the delay is unclear, for the WRB noted in their weekly report for 29 May–3 June 1944 that, 'While assurances of "warmest support and sympathy" have not been lacking, we have received little active co-operation to date from the British in connection with refugee rescues and relief'.[104] As far as Eleanor was concerned, she could not see why it was necessary to await US cooperation and, in an attempt at impressing upon Eden the urgency of the situation, she reminded him, in a direct reference to the Adler-Rudel scheme for rescue which had been discussed in her flat a year previously, 'A promising opportunity a year ago, in Sweden, was lost because of their delays; but this is a far greater opportunity'.[105]

Eleanor's concern was heightened by information, passed to her by Hall, that Horthy had moved the goalpost and had added the condition that Germany must give its consent to the release of 8,000 Jews to Palestine before they could leave Hungary. Now her fear was that 'Horthy may have yielded to Gestapo or internal anti-semitic [*sic*] pressure partly because no definite assurance has yet been sent to him (so Hall admitted) of the desire of our government to take full advantage of the offer and facilitate it in every possible way'. She concluded by begging that 'action be speeded up. It may be already too late.'[106] And despite Eden's confidential reply to her, on 16 August 1944, which included his assurance that 'we have taken action as rapidly as possible',[107]

Eleanor's remarks proved prophetic. It was indeed too late, for only days before the two governments finally declared their intention to help Hungary's Jews, the deportations to certain death had recommenced.[108] Besides Hall's hollow promise that 'we would accept anybody who could get out' was the disturbing fact, unbeknown to Eleanor, that there had never been any question of these refugees being admitted to Britain. Morrison had already made it clear to Eden that, in respect of Hungarian Jews, he looked upon it as 'essential that we do nothing at all which involves the risk that the further reception of refugees here might be the ultimate outcome'.[109] As in the case of the French children denied admittance in 1942, Morrison once again displayed his true colours, and his overt hostility towards Jewish refugees. Added to his view was that of Newsam, another of Eleanor's opponents, whom Philip Noel-Baker had referred to as 'that beast' in 1941. His concern over Sir Clifford Heathcote-Smith's proposal that 'the Prime Minister and the President should declare all Jews and others in Axis hands who had been deprived of their nationality to be under the provisional protection of the USA and the UK until the conclusion of hostilities or the signature of peace' was unequivocal: 'Protection, once given, is difficult to withdraw and we could not contemplate with equanimity the possibility that this heterogeneous collection of Stateless persons might, at the end of hostilities, expect the Powers which have afforded them protection to accord them hospitality,' citing, for example, how 'a shortage of housing would prevent us from welcoming any considerable increase in our population'.[110]

Not surprisingly, as soon as Eleanor and the NCRNT got wind of press reports that the satellite countries were taking soundings as to the terms which the Allies would agree to end hostilities, they wasted no time in communicating with Eden again. If the reports were true they urged to him to call for the persecution of the Jews to end, and for all anti-Semitic legislation and discrimination to be abrogated.[111] It was not until towards the end of September 1944 that Eleanor noted the latest information from Sweden, which reported that the deportations had finally been halted.[112] A total of between 500,000 and 600,000 Hungarian Jews perished during the war, most of them from May to September 1944.[113]

Given the pressure that Eleanor was under, it is hardly surprising that she declined an invitation from Mrs Epstein, the president of the Hadassah Women's Zionist Organization in America, to undertake a two-month speaking tour 'to further Palestine work and cement Anglo American relations'.[114] As she rightly observed, the 'Palestine issue' had mainly to be decided in Britain, and was a matter to which she kept returning in Parliament and beyond.

The PCR was still operating throughout this period, and whilst much of the day-to-day work was dealt with by Vera Craig, Mary Sibthorp and others, Eleanor maintained a close involvement. This was especially so when there were difficult matters to deal with concerning the remaining internees, and the cases cited here give a flavour of the nature and extent of the work in 1944, and the relationship between Morrison and the PCR. Reporting to Graham White on a forthcoming meeting of the COA in September 1944, Eleanor wanted to tackle the rights of camp commandants to make recommendations about the release of internees, and whilst she was sure Emerson would help, she did not expect to get any co-operation from Morrison. Yet again, she wrote of his dislike of her, saying,

> I think it best for my points not to be mentioned on the Agenda, but raised by me because H. Morrison and all his subordinates have become so persistently hostile to me, to the extent of refusing releases of cases which I have seemed to champion. (This may seem inconceivable but the evidence is really irresistible. See my summary of the case of three 'Petty Criminals' for whom I asked reconsideration; refused to me and subsequently to Vera Craig.) Hence the more the case can be explained by Emerson and yourself, the better the chances are of success.[115]

Vera Craig went even further in her correspondence with Graham White, talking of the 'gross scandal' of these continued detentions. She wrote of the vindictiveness of the Home Office, and how 'she would give him details of half-a-dozen more cases if you would consider waving a fiery sword in the face of the Home Secretary'.[116]

The cases that Eleanor was concerned with in this instance were all men detained under Regulation 12 (5A) of the Public Order Act on the grounds of previous offences against the criminal law which would normally have resulted in deportation. Sazja Rosenbaum, Leon Tauman, Max Grebler, Arnold Kleinberger and Leo Friedberg were all Polish Jews, skilled men who had nevertheless committed minor offences of theft, and for which they had served short prison sentences. They, and several others including a Mr Blumenstein, had all been 'nominally detained' since 1940/41, pending deportation to Poland, if, as Eleanor commented, this were ever possible. Her complaint was that the release of similar offenders seemed to have happened in an arbitrary fashion, and in some cases the offenders had far worse criminal records. Was Vera Craig correct in her view that Eleanor's championing of these cases was probably the reason why they were still detained?[117] The Friedberg case alone generated a huge amount of correspondence and Eleanor had what was described as 'a voluminous file of her own'. It was difficult to do anything for him as an individual case, so Eleanor was treating a collection of such cases. And to encourage him, she wrote, 'I think I can only beg you to keep up your heart ... (we) will continue to do all we can about it', assuring him that all cases were reviewed at intervals.[118]

From the tone of Eleanor's remarks in letters and speeches it is evident that she felt utterly despondent by what she perceived as her failure to save more Jews from extermination. And it was not only her political and moral conscience that was troubled, for she felt personally responsible for the British nation's conscience. New ways of assuaging her self-imposed guilt included her active campaigning on behalf of Poles facing deportation,[119] which brought her into contact with Ignacy Schwartzbart of the Polish government-in-exile, whom, it seems, she had met some months previously.[120] As Eleanor remarked, the deportations were not due to Nazi persecution, and were thus beyond the remit of the NCRNT. However, Schwartzbart's remarks about her serve as a reminder of the universality of her compassion, for he commended this 'good hearted old woman ... for looking after anyone in need'. Schwartzbart, a strong Zionist,[121] was interested in her involvement, but was really eager to discuss two crucial Jewish issues with her. The first concerned the current situation of Jews still in concentration camps in Poland, and he asked her if she could find out more information from the British mission, who, apparently, knew more than the Czech government in exile. The other was an urgent request for funds needed to save 300 Jews in Bergen-Belsen. He wanted her to help transfer 200,000 Swiss francs, or the equivalent, for their rescue, but she had to inform him of the difficulties of moving money to Switzerland, and in an effort at helping, put him in touch with Mr Mason, Randall's replacement at the Foreign Office.[122]

His suspicion, that 'she didn't have much political influence anymore' is noteworthy, for it suggests that he, at least, believed that her persistent campaigning for refugees had influenced government in the past.[123] In reality the British government were never going to accede to any rescue proposals which conflicted with their objectives, for they stuck to the universalist belief that winning the war would solve the Jewish question, and that any relaxation in immigration policies would increase anti-Semitism and not be in the best national interest. Eleanor's real power was vested in her ability to apply pressure and act as the moral and humanitarian conscience of the nation, a crucial role that few were willing to undertake, and that none pursued with her degree of passion and tenacity.

Despite the financial difficulties which continued to plague the NCRNT, a decision was made, in late January 1945, to continue the work of the committee. It seemed likely to be needed until at least after the end of the war in Europe, and maybe beyond, 'as long as the danger of future racial or political persecution continues and the welfare of those threatened needs safeguarding'.[124] News of yet more massacres of Jews continued to reach Eleanor, including a lengthy bulletin issued by the Joint Committee of the Jewish Agency in Palestine,[125] and prompted Eleanor, on behalf of the Committee, to send a telegram to Dr Max Huber, the president of the International Committee of the Red Cross (ICRC), pledging support in the efforts they were making 'to induce the German authorities to allow your delegate free access to and permission to relieve necessities of all civilians, including Jews who are now interned and excluded from privileges extended to other civilian internees under International Convention'. She knew from Mr Kubowitzki, the head of the rescue department of the World Jewish Congress, who was on a short visit to London, that the ICRC were trying to persuade the German Government to allow them free access to camps in Germany and German-occupied countries. But she also heard from him, after sending the telegram, that the 'massacres of interned Jews are being speeded up everywhere, and that even the so-called privileged camp of Theresienstadt was likely to be threatened'. A further letter from the ICRC, dated 6 March 1945, brought little comfort, despite the assurance that 'the International Committee attach the greatest importance to this question and your Committee may rest assured that they are giving the matter their most careful and unfailing attention'.[126]

In late March 1945 Eleanor finished putting together a new, lengthy and comprehensive document, 'Facts about Refugees',[127] which included evidence that the British government was far more interested in finding ways of removing as many domestic refugees post-war than it was in offering help to European victims of Nazism. Sections were devoted to numerous aspects of the subject, including the provision of statistical information on the actual numbers of refugees in the country – smaller than the public believed – and to the demography of these souls, mainly very old and very young, due to the admission restrictions imposed by the British government in the months before the outbreak of war. It considered what percentage would want to stay in Britain, whether refugees were 'dangerous', and their legal position, which was far from rosy.[128]

Apart from the NCRNT, she became involved with Gollancz and other humanitarian activists, in his 'Save Europe Now' campaign, which aimed to both publicize and mobilize support for the freeing of British resources to aid famine relief in Europe. German refugees were being expelled from Poland and Czechoslovakia and were in a desperate condition, and Eleanor was amongst the numerous eminent signatories to Gollancz's 'daring, disarming and eye-catching proposal that ordinary people at home took a cut in rations to "Save Europe"'.[129] Besides this, in 1943 she had become the first president of the organization known as German Educational Reconstruction, a group of people with widely differing political and religious convictions who worked to assist German refugee educationalists prepare for their eventual return to their own country.[130]

A disturbing repercussion of the publication of the atrocities committed in the camps was the way in which the British public mixed up Jewish refugees with German nationals, towards whom a genocidal attitude had developed. This prompted the Association of Jewish Refugees to write to Eleanor in April 1945, reasserting 'the suffering undergone by Jews in concentration camps between 1933 and the outbreak of war. This association has always made it clear that no bonds are left between Jewish refugees and Germany, but it seems necessary to show once again that the Jews were Hitler's first victims in the concentration camps as they were anywhere else.'[131] The twenty-page bulletin published by the Joint Rescue Committee of the Jewish Agency for Palestine that accompanied the AJR letter was a catalogue of the human tragedy of Nazi actions. And it is worth noting that even in 1945, a major Jewish refugee organization was still euphemistically referring to 'concentration' camps, when in fact many of the camps were used for the extermination of prisoners.

Gollancz's response to the atrocities committed in Buchenwald, revealed after the Americans liberated the camp in April 1945, was a propaganda pamphlet, *What Buchenwald Really Means*, intended to counter the growing anti-German hate campaign at home, which was so badly affecting German Jews. Eleanor, who had tried in September 1944 to get the government to denounce Hitler and his genocidal intentions, had then sought the advice of Temple regarding a letter to *The Times* on the massacre at Buchenwald. The suggestion had come from some German refugees in London who had approached Eleanor, very distressed that the British were doing nothing to protest, and believing that this would be interpreted by anti-Nazis in Germany as indifference to crimes against Germans. Temple not only sent Eleanor a letter in response, but as if to make certain that she knew his view, he telegraphed her to say he could not head the signatories, nor write a message himself, as he did not think it would do any good. Harold Nicholson was of the same mind, and, on this occasion, Eleanor took note of her advisers and did not proceed.[132]

Now, in the aftermath of the liberation, and following the end of the war in Europe in May 1945, Eleanor added her own thoughts to those of Gollancz in a 'letter to the Editor' of the *Manchester Guardian*, in which she commended his pamphlet and explored, publicly, the notions of collective guilt and personal responsibility:

> I believe that the greater burden of guilt must rest on the nation which from 1933–45 failed to overthrow its government and in which the great majority during the war fought or laboured as they were bidden. But I ask myself, as Gollancz does, what would I have done if I had been an Anti-Nazi during those years? Would I have protested or actively resisted, knowing that it would mean a concentration camp and probably death by torture for myself and the utter ruin of those nearest to me? Or would I have reflected 'the time is not yet. I had better wait until I can join hands with other resisters with some chance of overthrowing these criminal?' That was the course actually taken by those who tried to kill Hitler last year ... others practised undetected resistance and did what they could to mitigate cruelties and to rescue Jews and other victims.

Readers needed to remember and realize these things, for how else 'could we expect European nations who have suffered even more than ourselves from German aggression and cruelty to remember?' Significantly, in a spirit of forgiveness and reconciliation, she reasserted her pride in the British people's finest tradition:

> their love of justice, their sense of fair play even for hated enemies. It would be a disaster if we forsook this tradition in our hour of victory, when the future of the world may depend on whether justice and stern punishment can be meted out to the guilty, without encouraging a spirit of hatred and revenge which may not only destroy many innocent people but may so embitter future relations as to sow the seeds of another war.[133]

Meanwhile, there were difficulties within the NCRNT itself, for Mary Sibthorp felt that she had lost Eleanor's confidence and had been supplanted by Mr Hirsch, a German Jew who was assistant secretary of the NCRNT. Despite Eleanor's assurance of her faith in Mary Sibthorp, the latter tendered her resignation in June, but subsequently agreed to stay on until after the general election.[134] By then, the PCR and the NCRNT were working on more or less the same problems, and at an executive meeting held on 24 July, Eleanor suggested that Mr Hirsch and David Tait act as joint secretaries on a trial basis for the next three months. Once the election results were announced, it was planned to take up, as a matter of urgency, the issue of British visas and transport for the liberated with the home secretary, and to try and obtain permission from the Home Office for Hirsch to visit Germany and Switzerland. Eleanor also wanted to restart the campaign for generous action in regard to naturalization, especially for those who had served in the armed forces, done valuable work in industry or for learning. There was also the question of whether to change the name of the NCRNT, preferably omitting the word Nazi from the title, thus enabling them to deal with questions related to 'displaced persons' who were non-repatriable on political or humanitarian grounds.[135] Eleanor saw Emerson in advance of the planned committee meeting in July 1945, and it was his view that publicity needed to be very specific, and concentrate on enlightening public opinion and stressing the value of the refugee contribution to the war effort. He was very much against a general press campaign supporting mass naturalization, which, he asserted, would be opposed on the grounds of a housing shortage, the need for jobs to be given to ex-service men, and, because since persecution had ended, the belief that it was safe for refugees to go home.[136] The notion that Jews, in particular, would want to return to countries from which they had escaped near-certain death, and in which many had lost all their family members, was quite beyond the pale, and Eleanor and her committee were vociferous in their opposition to the compulsory repatriation of these souls. The NCRNT passed a resolution in early August 1945, calling for Her Majesty's government to 'contribute constructively towards the solution of the problem of the rehabilitation and permanent settlement of those displaced or stateless persons who are unwilling to return to or remain in their countries of origin'.[137]

Morrison was, characteristically, against providing aliens, whether of good conduct, members of the armed forces, or even the highly successful industrialists whose expertise the Department of Overseas Trade might want to harness, any assurance that they could stay in Britain. Nor would he give an assurance that they might not be randomly expelled. Exhibiting a total absence of humanity, he advised ministers to treat with caution claims that Jewish refugees 'would be in terror of returning to Germany: It was possible that post-war Germany would abandon anti-Semitism altogether. If the Jews were allowed to remain here they might be an explosive element in the country, especially if the economic situation deteriorated.' He also had his own views about where the Jews should go, for at the same Cabinet meeting, he said that he was 'seriously alarmed regarding the possibility of anti-Semitism in this country. If, arising out of the war settlement, territory other than Palestine became available for colonization by refugees, the best solution would be to send them there.'[138]

But as his post as home secretary was about to end, with Churchill replacing Labour ministers in the government, the decision was one his replacement would have to make. With a caretaker government in place, and R.G. Somervell as home secretary, the position of refugees in Britain was still very uncertain. Somervell rehearsed the frequently used domestic anti-Semitism argument, as well as expounding the financial and social implications of maintaining refugees, as reasons for not allowing refugees to stay, and so a political decision was still left in abeyance.[139]

Eleanor found waiting for a reply to her request for a deputation intolerable, and wrote frankly of her concern to Norman Bentwich, even though he was on holiday. She had read a letter in *The Times* on the Palestine question which had given her an idea, and although she had 'fired off a letter' in response, she had qualms about sending it without his consent, as much of the information had been passed on to her by him, for confidential use only. But the fact that she had gathered so much corroborative material from various other quarters including the *Zionist Review*, *Palcon* and from Dr Alexander of the German-Jewish Refugees organization, rather dispelled her reservations:

> I feel so strongly at the way the liberated Jews etc. are being treated that I think something more ought to be done about it then [*sic*] to wait till we succeed – if we ever do – in rousing the interest of these pre-occupied Ministers ... I think myself that the situation is too bad to observe excessive caution about it, the one main point of limiting liberated German Jews to the same rations as other Germans comes out in all the reports from everyone and it is quite intolerable.[140]

The Palestine case was at the core of an impassioned speech which she gave during the course of the debate on European conditions on 20 August 1945, several months after the liberation of the extermination camps in Eastern Europe. Even though she limited her contribution to three closely related subjects – the food situation in Europe, the position of displaced persons in Europe who could not be returned to their homelands, and, above all 'the position of the largest and most tragically situated group of those persons, the survivors of the Nazi concentration camps, the Jewish survivors who have nothing they consider home but Palestine, and who find the door barred against them',[141] her speech provided the most comprehensive picture of her view of the Palestine problem. Palestine, had, since her visit there in 1934, earned an increasingly special place in her heart and mind, and was, as far as Eleanor was concerned, the place where the Jewish refugees could, and should, find the refuge they deserved. She had no qualms about stating that the British nation had a special responsibility for the Jews, for it was the 'iniquitous' Palestine White Paper of 1939 which had

> closed the gates of Palestine against Jewish immigrants, except on an extremely limited scale and by so doing, in effect, condemned hundreds of thousands of men, women and children to unspeakable suffering, and eventually death. They could have been got out in time. They could have lived safely and happily during the war years with their kindred in their promised national home, but the door was shut in their faces. The past is irremediable. The dead cannot be brought back to life. But what of the living? What of the poor surviving remnant of European Jewry? Shall we not incur a terrible responsibility if they are left to perish – as they probably will perish if they have to endure the rigor of a European winter under their present conditions?[142]

Posing a challenge to the newly elected Labour Party, which had, in opposition in 1939, voted against the White Paper, Eleanor asked the government to now 'show the sincerity of their professions of sympathy with the Jewish claims' – or had they, at the time, merely been angling for the Jewish vote? Would the policy on Palestine, when it was announced, 'be in accordance with the principles previously enunciated by the Labour Party?' Siding with the Zionist claim for a Jewish State as part of the British Commonwealth of Nations mirrored views she had expressed in 1934 following her visit to Palestine. Here she was forcefully reasserting her admiration for the Jews and enunciating their contribution to religion, philosophy, science and culture throughout the ages, and praising them for the part they had played in supporting the Allied cause during the war. Showing a distinct racial preference, she condemned the Palestine Arabs for their 'grudging, half-hearted and often insincere (war) efforts'. Her recognition that a long-term solution to the Palestine problem would take time, was, with the benefit of hindsight, a gross understatement. But at the time she talked of a solution that gave 'full justice to the real rights of the Arabs', and one that satisfied Arab nationalistic aspirations provided they had a basis in justice and common sense. As in 1934, she alluded to the Jews in Palestine acting as a 'civilizing force' in a backward region when she said 'It would be enormously to the economic benefit of the Arabs in Palestine and equally to the Arabs everywhere because it would show what can be done with undeveloped lands, when developed as the Jews would do it'. In the strongest terms she called for a solution to the immediate problem, which was to 'open the gates of Palestine and let the Jews come in'.[143]

Her unequivocal support for a Jewish homeland, in which refugees who had survived the Nazi terror could make a new life, strengthened her connections with, and increased the admiration that the Jewish community in Britain felt for her. An ardent supporter of the Zionist cause, she was determined to help them bring home the case for a Jewish homeland to the British people, as notes of a talk she had with Mr Samuel Landman, a member of the BDBJ, following her contribution to the Debate on the Address in the House on 20 August 1945, shows. Her advice was for the Board to

> Keep on hammering the main facts of your case. Don't suppose because it is familiar to you it is equally familiar to British people in their own domestic problems. But our people are very sensitive on the point of honour. They profoundly dislike the charge of breaking faith. Keep on reminding them of all that was said at the time of the Balfour Declaration and in the debates on the White Paper in 1939. Remind them of the famous sayings by Mr Winston Churchill, Mr Amery and their Conservative supporters, by Sir Archibald Sinclair and, above all, by the Labour leaders who were then in the Opposition but are now responsible for the British Government. Remind them that almost the entire Labour Party then voted against the White Paper as a breach of a plain obligation. But whilst in this matter you must practise the pertinacity of the importunate widow, you must also practise the patience and perseverance of Bruce's spider, who climbed up fifty times and dropped down again before it reached its goal. Don't expect a quick and complete success. Take everything that is offered you and keep on clamouring for more until you get something really satisfactory ... you may have to reconcile yourselves to the 'inevitability of gradualness'. But if you practise perseverance and patience you will get there in the end.[144]

Her concern was subsequently reiterated in a private letter to the editor of the *Manchester Guardian*, to whom she wrote, 'the position of the Jews on the Continent (and as to that I have made a pretty close study) is really desperately bad'.[145] Even though she was on holiday in Scotland in September 1945, Eleanor was busy writing to Hall at the Colonial Office, articulating her worries over unconfirmed rumours concerning the provisions of the 1939 White Paper. If, as the Reuter's London message said, Jewish immigration was to be restricted to 1,500 monthly, rather than the immediate 100,000 asked for by the Jewish Agency, and apparently supported by President Truman, it would be 'too bad to be true'.[146] In the continued absence of a statement on Palestine in late October, Eleanor was determined to exert pressure on Clement Attlee, seeking an assurance that 'no irrevocable decisions will be made without the House having the opportunity of a full Debate'. As she knew, and as he pointed out, he had given such an assurance on 9 October, but as far as Eleanor was concerned, regular reminders did no harm, and she had no intention of letting sleeping dogs lie.[147]

Meanwhile, the autumn of 1945 brought changes within the PCR. David Tait had been appointed secretary in the September, and in October, Eleanor was considering the reconstruction of the committee, the admission of new members and, most importantly, the appointment of a new chairman. The naturalization issue was still there, and official reconsideration of visas for those who failed to get out of Germany, but who had been granted visas pre-war, was due, but Tait feared the worst.[148] James Chuter Ede, the secretary of state for the Home Department in Clement Attlee's new Labour government, was under pressure from Eleanor and others to make a speedy declaration of policy regarding the admission to Britain of concentration camp survivors with relatives here. How many applications had been granted, how many still awaited a decision, and 'in view of the humanitarian considerations involved, would he make a declaration of policy in this matter and expedite decisions on the applications still pending?' Ede would not accept Eleanor's assertion that 'the numbers involved are not very great', and she and her fellow MPs dismissed his reference to the 300 or more children from concentration camps to whom his predecessor, Morrison, had granted entry, as a diversion and irrelevant to the question asked.[149] Hirsch's visit to Switzerland and Germany had to be cancelled as the French transit visa did not arrive in time. Eleanor had only received interim replies to her questions on visas for concentration camp survivors, and awaited the home secretary's statement in the House.[150] The question over naturalization did move forward, for Ede's announcement, on 15 November 1945, that the suspension on the investigation of applicants for naturalization, imposed in 20 November 1940, was to be lifted, was good news. And even though there was a backlog of about 6,500 cases, these were to be dealt with alongside new applicants on a priority basis. There was some confusion over who would be considered a priority, and Eleanor voiced her own concerns, asking Ede for clarification as to whether those who had served in the armed forces included 'the Armed Forces of our Allies? He will remember that the previous Prime Minster held out, especially to Poles, the prospect that they would be given naturalization if they did not wish to return to their own country. Would that also apply to other Allies?'[151] His reply, which referred her to a previous answer, did nothing more than elicit a promise of keeping it in mind.

Eleanor's published letters seem to have precipitated a flurry of invitations to speak and write on the Jewish question. Amongst these, the BDBJ asked her to lead a proposed deputation to the prime minister.[152]

Her distinguished reputation for supporting refugees, and the fact that she was a 'local', made her the ideal person to draw in to fight an anti-alien petition in Hampstead, London in October 1945.[153] She and Elizabeth had moved to Hampstead Lane, Highgate in North London in April 1945, and coincidental to the anti-alien campaign, they became a place of safety for Friedl and Ernst Lustig, two Jewish refugees from Germany. The couple had met and married in England, and were expecting their first child when Eleanor offered them accommodation until they were able to get settled permanently. In the event their daughter, Harriet, was born whilst they were still living in Eleanor's house.[154]

Eleanor's long experience with refugee issues and her deeply held interest in Palestine as a homeland for the displaced Jews of Europe persuaded her to put her name forward as a member of the proposed Anglo-American Committee of Enquiry into the Palestine question.[155] In her letter to Ernest Bevin on 22 November she made it clear that she had only pursued this course of action once or twice during her sixteen years in Parliament, but that

> this time it is a very important body and I well recognize that I may be considered quite unacceptable, even if, as I rather assume, you want at least one or two women members ... My work for refugees, those both inside and outside this country, has led to my giving perhaps half or more of my working time to study of the whole subject of both short-term and long-term measures of rescue and of settlement, whether in Palestine or elsewhere. Hence I have some knowledge though in parts very sketchy, of both sides of the problem to be submitted to the committee – the European and the Palestinian side. I will only add that I reckon myself a Zionist, though of so realistic and compromising a type that I doubt whether the Zionist leaders would so regard me. It is very distasteful to me to put forward ones name in this way, but as a pure Independent, I have no natural intermediary, and it seems simpler and more straightforward not to seek one.

Bevin's brief reply, on 25 November, thanked her for her 'public spirited offer to serve upon the Palestine Committee' and an assurance that he would let her have a further answer in due course.[156]

Meanwhile, the situation in Palestine continued to worsen and Eleanor persisted in asking parliamentary questions,[157] but her anger at being denied a debate on Palestine in December 1945 was obvious in a memo sent to 'Members believed to be sympathetic to the Jewish side of the Palestinian problem'. She wrote of how 'the subject is to be smothered as much as possible' and, as an alternative strategy, to adopt a questioning campaign:

> I have put down a few questions which struck me as useful, but there may be other and better ones. Could you have a word with me in the Lobby to let me know what you think of the idea (of a campaign) and are willing to take part. There are only four or five days left as possible under the regulations before we adjourn. But even if we cannot get in all we want, it would be worth putting in questions for reply on the first appropriate day after we reassemble on January 22nd (1946). That would show the Government, the Jewish bodies, and any MPs sufficiently interested, that the problem is not being ignored.[158]

Eleanor's popularity with government officials was not enhanced at this time as she took up the complex case of one particular detainee, a Polish Jew named Willner who was, in December 1945, being held at Beltane School, Wimbledon, and in danger of being repatriated. He inundated her with begging and fawning letters, describing her as 'the best Samaritan of the country ... a person gifted with a high sense of proportion, full understanding and the adequate interpretation of human rights and justice'.[159] Rathbone subsequently wrote a number of letters to G.H. Oliver, parliamentary undersecretary at the Home Office, remarking, 'Here is another case, one of three sent you today of a man who wants me to intervene in his repatriation ... I know nothing of the case, but in view of the fact that 1) he is a Jew and 2) all his relatives were murdered in Poland, it would seem a peculiarly cruel form of repatriation.'[160] As the details of the case emerged Eleanor had to concede that the man was 'a bad lot', but she nevertheless stuck by her view that 'even criminals have their rights'. These 'rights' related to his assertion that he was not a Pole, having been born in Austria in 1909, and therefore could not be deported to Poland.[161] If he was in fact stateless, which she thought was 'pretty clear'[162] then, according to Dr Kullmann, Sir Herbert Emerson's deputy, the Home Office had no right to forcibly remove him. Eleanor proceeded to ask the home secretary 'to define what he does claim as his rights of deportation', adding 'and (I) may try for a supplementary about the particular case'.[163] Oliver took a very dim view of Willner, whom he described in minutes as 'a horrible fellow who seems to be a flagellation pervert in addition to a swindler, preying on refugees, should be got rid of at the earliest possible moment'.[164] And the Home Office was equally displeased by Eleanor's pursuit of the case. Minutes noted that as she had put down a question, 'it hardly seems desirable to send her any detailed reply to the letter (of 12 December)'. Their attitude towards her persistence was even more overtly demonstrated in this note:

> It is not for the Secretary of State to embrace (with the uncritical

> enthusiasm displayed by Miss Rathbone for any protest however ill-founded which will frustrate the administration of the Aliens Order) an eleventh hour plea that he (Willner) has lost Polish nationality unless some evidence is produced.[165]

Nor could they see any reason to receive the deputation Eleanor had proposed, adding 'as Miss Rathbone will be told in reply to her Question, no alien can be deported except to a territory whose government recognize him or is willing to admit him.'[166] As far as Eleanor's involvement with this case was concerned, she approached it through the prism of humanitarianism, which prevented her from taking an objective view of it. But nevertheless, her persistence did put the general question of deportation and forced repatriation firmly on the political agenda, and, in late December 1945, Eden did agree to meet a deputation in the New Year to discuss the issues.

But ultimately this meeting was cancelled, Eleanor never received another letter from Bevin, nor was she able to put down any further questions on Palestine, for she died suddenly, at her home in Highgate, on 2 January 1946.

The Family Allowance Act of 1945, for which Eleanor campaigned for so long, came into operation in August 1946.

NOTES

1. As Tony Kushner notes, Winterton was rejected as Lord Moyne's replacement in Cairo in 1944 because, in the words of Churchill's advisor, he was 'chairman of the Antisemitic [*sic*] League'. See Kushner, *Liberal Imagination*, p.199.
2. Letter of Perth to Randall, 15 June 1943, NA FO 371/36726,W8828/6731/48.
3. Minutes, Randall, 9 June 1943, NA FO 371/366662,W8192/49/48.
4. Letter of Perth to Randall, 15 June 1943, NA FO 371/36726,W8828/6731/48.
5. Ibid.
6. Letter of Crewe (for NCRNT) to Law, 26 August 1943, NA FO 371/36728,W12497.
7. Minutes of Cheetham, 17 June 1943, NA FO 371/36726,W8828/6731/48.
8. Note added to minutes of Cheetham, 17 June 1943, NA FO 371/36726,W8828/6731/48.
9. Letter of Lady Bonham-Carter to Eden, 21 July 1943; Eden to Churchill (in which he put forward her suggestion), 2 August 1943, NA FO 371/36727,W11245/6731/48. See also Letter of Irene Ward (Woman Power Committee) to Law, July 1943, and reply of Law to Ward, 26 July 1943, NA FO 371/36727,W10921/6731/48.
10. Prime minister's personal minute, serial no. M53713, 29 July 1943, and Eden to Churchill, 2 August 1943, NA FO 371/36727,W11245.
11. Draft memo by Emerson, 9 August 1943, NA FO 371/36727,W11589.
12. Confidential meeting of NCRNT, 1 September 1943, Acc 3121/E3/536/1, BDBJ, LMA.
13. Note by Walker, 12 August 1943, NA FO 371/371/36665,W11961.
14. Draft memo by Emerson, 9 August 1943, NA FO 371/36727,W11589.
15. Memo on the refugee situation, 3 September 1943, NA FO 371/3666,W12842/49/48.
16. Note by EFR, 1 October 1943, Acc 3121/E3/536/1, BDBJ, LMA.
17. Executive meeting NCRNT, 6 October 1943, Acc 3121/E3/5361/2, BDBJ, LMA.
18. A. Hurwitz, 'The Struggle over the Creation of the War Refugee Board', *Holocaust and*

*Genocide Studies* (London: Pergamon Press, 1991), Vol. 6 (1): pp.17–31. NCRNT general meeting, 4 November 1943, Acc 3121/E3/536/2, BDBJ, LMA.
19. Letter of EFR to Bevin, 26 October 1943, PA WHI /10/3/76. For the 'blackballing' of refugee dentists, see J.S. Zamet, 'Aliens or Colleagues? Refugees from Nazi Oppression 1933–45', *British Dental Journal* (2006) p.201, pp.397–437.
20. Notes of general meeting of NCRNT, 4 November 1943, Acc 3121/E3/536/2, BDBJ, LMA.
21. See letter of EFR to Crozier, 13 August 1943, *Manchester Guardian* Archive, B/R45/6, JRL.
22. London, *Whitehall and the Jews*, p.233.
23. The plenary session of the IGCR began on 15 August 1944, and Mary Sibthorp, the secretary of the NCRNT, attended as an observer. Letter of EFR and D. Grenfell for the NCRNT to ambassadors, (8) August 1944, MSS 157/3/SE/1/28, Gollancz Papers, MRC.
24. For PQs, see Letter of EFR to Hall, 11 October 1943 (re: her PQ for 13 October 1943), NA FO 371/36729,W14460/6731/48, and *Hansard* HC, vol. 393, cols 638–9, 3 November 1943. Hall was Parliamentary Under-Secretary of State for Foreign Affairs.
25. Note by Randall, 29 October 1943, NA FO 371/36729,W15384/6731/48.
26. Walker, Minutes, 26 October 1943, NA FO 371/36729,W15384/6731/48.
27. In December 1943, Eleanor obtained Eden's agreement for him to meet a small deputation in January 1944. This was to be the first such meeting since early 1943. See letters of EFR to Eden, 28 December 1943 and 7 January 1944, NA FO 371/42751,W544/83/48. For report on deputation, see Report, 27 January 1944, NA FO 371/42751.
28. Draft Letter of EFR to Hall, 24 November 1943, Acc 3121/E3/536/2, BDBJ, LMA.
29. JR (44) 1st meeting, 14 March 1944, NA CAB 95/15.
30. Note by Randall, 29 November 1943, NA FO 371/36669,W16144. Note by the minister of state, 3 December 1943, NA CAB 95/15 JR (43) 26.
31. A 'further' donation of £100 was made on 21 February 1944, and another grant of £200 on 7 June 1944, Acc 3121/E3/5361/1. For the financial crisis see Minutes of the Anglo-Jewish Association, 11 October 1944, AJA Records, 37/4/5, USL.
32. Letter of EFR to Brodetsky, 30 November 1943, Acc 3121/E3/536/1, and Letter of EFR to Hall, 26 November 1943, Acc 3121/E3/536/2, BDBJ, LMA.
33. Letter of EFR to Graham White, 7 December 1943, PA WHI /10/3/80.
34. Notes on NCRNT meeting, 13 December 1943, Acc 3121/E3/536/1, BDBJ, LMA.
35. Letter of EFR to Hall, 4 December 1943, NA FO 371/42752,W543/83/48.
36. *Hansard* HC, vol. 395, cols 1473, 1646, 14 December 1943.
37. Letter of Hall to EFR, 7 January 1944; Letter of EFR to Hall, 10 January 1944, NA FO 371/42751,W543/83/48.
38. *Hansard* HC, vol. 397, col. 1470, 1 March 1944.
39. Letter of Crozier to EFR, 29 November 1943 and Reply of EFR to Crozier, 3 December 1943, *Manchester Guardian* Archive, B/R45/8–9, JRL.
40. Letter of Crewe to Churchill, 10 November 1943, Acc 3121/C/2/2/5. Minutes of executive meeting, NCRNT, 9 November 1943, Acc 3121/E3/536/2, BDBJ, LMA.
41. Notes on proposed campaign, 23 November 1943, Acc 3121/E3/536/1, BDBJ, LMA.
42. Besides Gollancz's censure, there were other critics whose opinion Eleanor valued, including the Reverend W.W. Simpson, of the Council of Christians and Jews, and the Reverend James Parkes who pointed out that titles purporting to state the truth while identifying the others as liars always create 'a suspicion of [the] objectivity of the author'. See Simpson to members of the publications sub-committee, 1 January 1944; Parkes, 'Some comments on Miss Eleanor's proposed pamphlet', January 1944; Simpson to Parkes, 13 June 1944, Parkes Papers, MS 60, USL.
43. Letter of Gollancz to EFR, 22 August 1944, Author File, The Orion Archive, Orion Publishing Group, London.
44. Ibid.
45. Dudley-Edwards, *Victor Gollancz*, p.391.
46. Pedersen, *Politics of Conscience*, p.358.
47. E.F. Rathbone, *Falsehoods and Facts* (London: Victor Gollancz, 1944), pp.v–vi.
48. Dudley-Edwards, *Victor Gollancz*, p.391.
49. Cheetham, Minutes, 25 February 1944, NA FO 371/42751,W2859/83/48.
50. Randall, Minutes, 25 February 1944, NA FO 371/42751,W2859/83/48.
51. Minute of Walker, 29 February 1944, NA FO 371/42727,W2971/16/48. For the agreement, see US embassy to Randall, 16 June 1944, NA FO 371/42370,W9775/16/48.
52. Cheetham was equally obstructive towards the BDBJ, and on one occasion in 1944 wrote in

an internal memo, 'Mr Brotman had been told that the memo of the Board of Deputies would be given due consideration. Perhaps it is not necessary to inform him that time was not available for it to be considered by the Commonwealth Prime Ministers.' See NA FO 371/42751.
53. *News From Hitler's Europe*, Issue 2, 22 October 1943, Sibthorp Papers, MS96/30/1, IWM.
54. For some examples, see Bunting, *Representing Rescue*, pp.81–2.
55. Rubinstein, *Myth of Rescue*, p.136.
56. Letter of Crozier to EFR, 31 January 1944, *Manchester Guardian* Archive, B/R45/12, JRL.
57. Eden, Note on the WRB, JR 44 (1) in NA CAB 95/15. *Hansard* HC, vol. 396, cols 1741–2, 9 February 1944.
58. *Hansard* HC, vol. 396, col. 1742, 9 February 1944.
59. Minutes, 19 and 29 February 1944, NA FO 371/42727,W3012/116/48.
60. Kushner, *Liberal Imagination*, p.196.
61. Minutes of general meeting, NCRNT, 10 February 1944, Acc 3121/E3/536/1, BDBJ, LMA.
62. Minutes of Law to Randall, 22 February 1944, NA FO 371/42727,W3201/16/48. Letter from NCRNT, *The Times*, 10 April 1944.
63. Minutes of Law to Randall, 22 February 1944, NA FO 371/42727,W3201/16/48.
64. Speech of EFR, 29 February 1944, Sibthorp Papers, 96/30/1, Mss 2/1, IWM. Also Note of Sibthorp (for the NCRNT) to Eden, 14 June 1944, NA FO 371/42730,W9635/16/48.
65. Ibid., p.191.
66. For reports on cooperation with Britain in early 1944, see D. Wyman (ed.), *America and the Holocaust: War Refugee Board 'Weekly Reports'*, vol. II (New York and London: Garland, 1989), pp.13, 21–2, 38, 45.
67. P. Shatzkes, *Holocaust and Rescue: Impotent or Indifferent Anglo-Jewry 1938–1945*, (Basingstoke: Palgrave, 2002), pp.227–8.
68. Letter of EFR, for NCRNT, to Pehle, 10 March 1944, NCRNT file, WRB Archive, Box 17.
69. Telegram of Angell to EFR, n.d. but probably post-8 March 1944. Also Letter of Angell to EFR, 8 March 1944, Angell Collection, Ball State University Archives and Special Collections.
70. Letter of EFR to Eden, 4 March 1944, NA FO 371/42751/3567/83/48.
71. Letter of EFR to Pehle, 10 March 1944, NCRNT file, WRB Archive, Box 17.
72. London, *Whitehall and the Jews*, p.231.
73. Letter of EFR to Pehle, 10 March 1944, NCRNT file, WRB Archive, Box 17.
74. Letter of EFR to Randall, 1 Apr 1944, NA FO 371/42723,W5134/15/48.
75. NA FO 371/42727,W3201/16/48.
76. Letter of EFR to Eden, 4 March 1944, NA FO 371/42751/3567/83/48.
77. Letter of Pehle to EFR, 8 April 1944, NCRNT file, WRB Archive, Box 17.
78. Memo of Goldmann, 23 March 1944, WJC file, WRB Archive, Box 29.
79. Memo of Goldmann, 23 March 1944, WJC file, WRB Archive, Box 29.
80. Letter of Pehle to EFR, 8 April 1944, NCRNT file, WRB Archive, Box 17.
81. Letter of Casady to Pehle, 30 June 1944, NCRNT File, WRB Archive, Box 17.
82. Rubinstein, *Myth of Rescue*, pp.182–97.
83. Rubinstein, *Myth of Rescue*, p.135.
84. Letter of EFR to Graham White, 7 June 1944, PA WHI /10/3/92.
85. D. Cesarani, *Eichmann: His Life and Crimes* (London: Heinemann, 2004).
86. Randall, Minutes, 21 March 1944, NA FO 371/42723,W4586/15/48.
87. Randall, Minutes, 29 March 1944, NA FO 371/42728,W4807/15/48.
88. Randall, Minutes, 30 March 1944, NA FO 371/42723,W4586/15/48.
89. Letter of EFR to Randall, NA FO 371/42723,W5134/15/48.
90. Letter of Randall to EFR, 15 May 1944, NA FO 371/42723,W5134/15/48. *Hansard* HC, 21 February 1945, vol. 408, cols 802–3.
91. Stocks, *Rathbone*, pp.293–4.
92. NCRNT Meeting, 18 May 1944, Acc 3121/E1/74, BDBJ. LMA.
93. Notes for talk with Colonel Stanley, 8 August 1944, NA FO 371/42814,WR685/3/48.
94. Letter of EFR to Graham White, 7 June 1944, PA WHI /10/3/92.
95. Notes for Talk with the colonial secretary, 8 August 1944, NA FO 371/42814,WR685/3/48.
96. *Hansard* HC, 21 February 1945, vol. 408, cols 802–3.
97. *News From Hitler's Europe*, 20 June 1944.
98. Letter of EFR to Eden, 6 July 1994; Reply of Eden to EFR, 7 July 1944, NA FO 371/42808.
99. Notes on Randall interview with EFR, 18 July 1944. NA FO 371/42810/WR363/3/48.

100. See, for example, Randolph Braham, *The Politics of Genocide: The Holocaust in Hungary*, vol. 2, (New York and Guildford: Columbia University Press, 1981).
101. Notes on points for deputation, 24 July 1944, Acc 3121/E3/5361/2, BDBJ, LMA.
102. Record of NCRNT meeting on 26 July 1944, NA FO 371/42814.
103. Letter of EFR to Eden, 31 July 1944, NA FO 371/42814.
104. As cited in Kushner and Knox, *Age of Genocide*, p.202.
105. Letter of EFR to Eden, 31 July 1944, NA FO 371/42814 and Acc 3121/E3/536/2, BDBJ, LMA. On Sweden, see Temple Papers, 55/7–8, LPL.
106. Letter of EFR to Eden, 9 August 1944, NA FO 371/42815,WR752/3/48.
107. Letter of Eden to EFR, 16 August 1944, NA FO 371/42815,WR752/3/48.
108. Braham, *Politics of Genocide*, pp.791–7.
109. Morrison to Eden, 1 July 1944, NA FO 371/42808,WR170/3/48.
110. Letter of Newsam to Mason, 19 September 1944, NA T161/Box 1441 51823/3.
111. Letter of NCRNT, signed by EFR, Temple, Grenfell, Perth and Roberts, to Eden, 19 August 1944, Temple Papers, 55/199, LPL. For this and Eden's reply, dated 31 August 1944, that 'careful note taken of suggestions', see NA FO 371/42815,WR 811/3/48.
112. Report of EFR on meeting with Emerson, James Mann, special representative WRB, and Mr Mason, who replaced Randall at the FO, 25 September 1944, Acc 3121/E3/536/2.
113. Braham, *Politics of Genocide*, and D. Cesarani (ed.), *Genocide and Rescue: The Holocaust in Hungary, 1944*, (Oxford and New York: Berg, 1997) as cited in Kushner and Knox, *Age of Genocide*, p.201.
114. Telegram from Epstein to EFR, 2 September 1944, RP XIV.2.19 (6–8), ULL.
115. Letter of EFR to Graham White, 18 September 1944, PA WHI /10/3/97.
116. Letter of V. Craig to Graham White, 16 November 1944, PA WHI /10/2/20.
117. Ibid.
118. Letter of D. Tait to Graham White, 18 January 1945, PA WHI /10/2/29.
119. The papers relating to the deportation of Poles into the USSR are to be found in RP XIV.2.18 (1–40). Included are some papers concerning anti-Semitism in the Polish Army. See also Letter to the editor, 'Return of the Poles', *Manchester Guardian*, 19 July 1945, which refers to Eleanor's speech in the House of Commons, 15 December 1944. For her private correspondence with the *Manchester Guardian* on the subject, see *Manchester Guardian* Archive, B/R45/15–18, JRL.
120. Notes of meeting with Eleanor, 5 February 1945 in Schwartzbart Diaries, Yad Vashem Institute Archives. I am grateful to Tony Kushner for alerting me to this document. There is some confusion as to when the two first met, but Schwartzbart said he had last seen Eleanor 9 or 10 months previously. However, an earlier diary entry says he met her on 29 January 1945. For questions concerning anti-Semitism in the Polish army, see *Hansard* HC, vol. 398, col. 2012, 5 April 1944, and cols 2273–5, 6 April 1944. Schwartzbart was certainly present at an NCRNT meeting on 20 July 1943. See MS 60/15/57/f2, USL.
121. As noted on a letter of EFR to Wilfrid Roberts, 1 May 1944. This note is not in Eleanor's handwriting. RP XIV.2.18 (7), ULL.
122. Notes of meeting with Eleanor, 5 February 1945, in Schwartzbart Diaries, Yad Vashem Institute Archives. I am grateful to Tony Kushner for alerting me to this entry. For an overview of her concern over the Polish question see Stocks, *Eleanor Rathbone*, pp.304–7, and EFR, Speech notes, 28 February 1944, RP XIV.3 (77), ULL.
123. In an earlier entry he said, 'Unfortunately her influence is only a moral one, which in political life is tantamount to no influence'. 29 January 1945, Schwartzbart Diaries, Yad Vashem Institute Archives.
124. Circular letter, 22 February 1945, Acc 3121/E3/5361/2, BDBJ, LMA.
125. Bulletin, February 1945, JRCJAP, RP XIV.2.17 (64), LPL.
126. Reply of ICRC to EFR's letter of 20 January 1945 and NCRNT telegram of 18 January 1945, 6 March 1945, G 59/4, Archives of the International Committee of the Red Cross, Geneva.
127. NCRNT, 30 March 1945, 96/30/1 Sibthorp Papers, MSS 2/1, IWM.
128. See NA HO 213/1009 as cited in Kushner, *Liberal Imagination*, p.200. Also 'Facts About Refugees', NCRNT, 30 March 1945, which refers to an article in the *Daily Express*, 21 March 1945, in which it was reported that the government intended to allow only one third of the refugees already in Britain to stay. Sibthorp Papers 96/30/1, MSS 2/1, IWM.
129. For Gollancz's 'Save Europe Now' campaign, see M. Frank, *Expelling the Germans: British Opinion and Post-1945 Population Transfer in Context* (Oxford: Oxford

University Press, 2007).
130. J. Anderson, 'GER: A Voluntary Anglo-German Contribution' in A. Hearnden (ed.), *The British in Germany: Educational Reconstruction after 1945* (London: Hamilton, 1978).
131. Letter of AJR to EFR, 30 April 1945, RP XIV.2.17 (65) and (64), ULL.
132. Letter of EFR to Temple, 21 September 1944. Telegram and letter to EFR from Temple, Temple Papers, 55/201–04, LPL.
133. EFR, Letter to the editor, 'The Significance of Buchenwald', *Manchester Guardian*, 22 May 1945, p.4.
134. Letter of Sibthorp to Brodetsky, 7 June 1945, Acc 3121/E3/536/2, BDBJ, LMA.
135. EFR, Notes for NCRNT Meeting, 24 July 1945, Acc 3121/E3/536/2, BDBJ, LMA.
136. NCRNT Exec. meeting, 24 July 1945, Acc 3121/E3/536/1, BDBJ, LMA.
137. Suggested resolution for NCRNT meeting, 2 August 1945, Acc 3121/E3/536/2, BDBJ, LMA.
138. JR (45) 2nd meeting, 16 May 1945, NA CAB 95/15.
139. CM 16 (45)2, 20 July 1945, NA CAB 65/53; CP (45)82, 17 July 1945 NA CAB 66/67.
140. Letter of EFR to Bentwich, 15 August 1945, A255/617, CZA.
141. *Hansard* HC, vol. 413, col. 361, 20 August 1945.
142. Ibid., cols 363–4.
143. Ibid., cols 364–5.
144. Notes of talk between EFR and Samuel Landman, 27 August 1945, RP XIV.6 (13), ULL.
145. Letter of EFR to the editor, 26 September 1945, *Manchester Guardian* Archive, B/R45/19, JRL.
146. Letter of EFR to Hall, 25 September 1945, Z 4/14882, CZA.
147. *Hansard* HC, vol. 414, col. 22, 9 October 1945, and vol. 415, cols 232–3, 30 October 1945.
148. Letter of D. Tait to Dr Skemp (SPSL), 19 October 1945, MSS SPSL 120/2, f. 208, BOD.
149. *Hansard* HC, vol. 414, cols 1339–43, 18 October 1945.
150. NCRNT Minutes, 9 November 1945, BDBJ, Acc 3121/E3/536/2, LMA.
151. *Hansard* HC, vol. 415, cols 2305–10, 15 November 1945.
152. Letter of BDBJ to EFR, 27 September 1945, RP XIV.6 (13), ULL.
153. For a study of this petition, see G. Macklin, '"A Quite Natural and Moderate Defensive Action?" The 1945 Hampstead "Anti-alien" Petition', *Patterns of Prejudice*, 37, 3 (2003), pp.277–300. One of the organizers of the petition, Margaret Crabtree, had written to Eleanor the year before, complaining about the German Jews in Hampstead, and of Eleanor's support for them. See letter of M. Crabtree to EFR, 25 January 1944, RP XIV.2.17 (62), and EFR, Notes of speech, 22 October 1945, RP XIV.3 (80), ULL.
154. Author's telephone interview with Mrs Harriet Hagan, 22 July 2001.
155. *Hansard* HC, vol. 415, cols 1928–34, 13 November 1945. Letter of EFR to Bevin, 22 November 1945, RP XIV.6 (13), ULL.
156. Letter of EFR to Bevin, 22 November 1945, RP XIV.6.13,ULL. Letter of Bevin to EFR, 25 November 1945, RP XIV.6.13, ULL.
157. *Hansard* HC, vol. 415, cols 322–3, 30 October 1945; vol. 415, cols 1927–34, 13 November 1945; vol. 417, col. 634, 13 December 1945.
158. Memo of EFR to MPs, 10 December 1945, RP XIV.6 (13), ULL.
159. Letter of F. Willner to EFR, 25 November 1944, NA HO 405 W2234.
160. Letter of EFR to G. Oliver, 21 October 1945, NA HO 405 W2234/4.
161. Letter of F. Willner to EFR, November 1945, NA HO 405 W2234/2.
162. Letter of EFR to Oliver, 14 December 1945, NA HO 405 W2234/4.
163. Letters of EFR to Oliver, 12 and 14 December 1945, NA HO 405 W2234/4.
164. Draft for Mr Oliver to EFR, November 1945, NA HO 405 W2234/2.
165. Undersecretary of state case, Minutes, 14 December 1945, NA HO 405 W2234/4.
166. Letters EFR to Oliver, 12, 14 and 21 December 1945, NA HO 405 W2234/4.

# 10

# *Conclusion*

> *'With gratitude to the memory of Eleanor Rathbone, Member of Parliament 1929–1946 ... who strove for tolerance, understanding and open doors.'*[1]

Eleanor Rathbone's commitment to the cause of refugees, most of them Jewish, fleeing persecution in Nazi-occupied Europe before and during the Second World War came towards the end of her long career as a humanitarian activist. By any standards, her deeds and actions marked her out as a remarkable individual, for she selflessly devoted the whole of her working life to championing the cause of the disadvantaged, the impoverished and the under-represented in British society, in the imperial colonies as well as in Europe. What changed over the decades was the focal point of her attention, and it was her conscience and acute awareness of the needs of people outside of her own privileged circle that determined the causes she embraced, rather than a commitment to a particular movement or gendered issue.

Eleanor was a shining example of the Rathbone family principle, 'what ought to be done, could be done', and at no time during her years as a Member of Parliament did the refugees, especially Jews, who were either trying to escape from Nazi-occupied Europe or who had found refuge in Britain, have a more passionate and devoted advocate. She exhibited a unique fortitude and mindset which kept her focused on the refugee question, a cause that was arguably the most challenging, and certainly the most heartbreaking of any she confronted.

The rise of Fascism and Nazism, and their insidious threat to the lives and freedom of individuals, was more than she could bear, and her dedication to alleviating the plight of the innocent victims of this human tragedy ultimately eclipsed all other concerns. The refugee issue grieved Eleanor more than any other, for it tested her cherished ideals, her deeply rooted sense of patriotism, and her faith in Britain's tradition of democracy, liberty, asylum and generosity. Her strong sense of decency, and of right and wrong, were challenged by the policy of appeasement and the later Munich Agreement, which represented the antithesis of these beliefs, and made her ashamed to be British. It led her to accuse British politicians of being 'short-sighted, selfish and ungenerous',[2] charges that illuminate her relationship with government officials. This was frequently acrimonious, and the discourses in which she was engaged revealed the prejudice, both covert and overt, of many of them towards Jews. Even when the intransigence of these public servants in respect of the impending human disaster is considered in its historical context, it is hard to avoid the conclusion that some were indeed anti-Semitic.

It was a constant source of anguish to her that the British government did not consider the plight of the Jews in the same way as she did. For, unlike many officials with whom she battled, she saw saving the lives of refugees, especially Jews, as a national and personal responsibility that should, and could, be undertaken without undermining the defence of Britain and the objective of defeating the enemy.

Eleanor can perhaps best be described as unconventional, for she defied the norms of conventional society by supporting the unpopular cause of Jewish refugees. And even though her actions may have been viewed as nonconformist, this did not diminish her ability to influence people from all walks of life to back her campaigning activities. That she had the unswerving loyalty of a network of supporters from a broad spectrum of society is an acknowledgement of the power of her influence and of the respect that she and her cause commanded.

She was, regrettably, correct when she predicted that victory would come too late to save the majority of Europe's Jews, and it was the anticipation of impending catastrophe, and her own conscience, which drove her to relentlessly pursue her campaign. In contrast to others at the time, she never doubted the gravity of the crisis or the veracity of the dreadful news that was passed on to her. Her independence, politically, economically and socially, allowed her to pursue her goals, unfettered by the opinion of others. She was answerable to no one but herself and her conscience, and she maintained an innate belief that her actions would make a difference, and were worth any amount of effort. Her motives were unquestionably genuine and her compassion boundless. Nowhere was this better expressed than in the tribute that her friend and co-activist, Victor Gollancz, wrote after her death:

> No one who did not have the privilege of working daily with Eleanor Rathbone can have any conception of what she did for refugees in general and Jewish refugees in particular. It wasn't merely that she gave every single case the most careful consideration: it was that she never ceased to *think* 'How can I best help these people? How can I carry on the work a stage further? What is the next thing to do?' She once told me that she did her best thinking in the small hours of the morning ... to that nightly

> thinking some Jews owe their lives: many more owe to it a little hope and a little faith in human goodness. Eleanor Rathbone was truly humble, and would have quite genuinely desired no epitaph: but if she had been told that she must have one, I believe that she would have desired that it should be 'If a few people are a little happier because of me, my life has not wholely [*sic*] failed.[3]

Eleanor Rathbone was an exceptional human being who defies categorization, sociologically or historically. The path she chose, to help refugees fleeing Nazi persecution was brave, remarkable and unique, for no other refugee activist in the non-Christian world succeeded in crossing the boundaries, and no one, not even the Reverend James Parkes,[4] who was widely acclaimed for his devotion to persecuted Jewry, committed themselves so wholeheartedly to the cause.

Whether lives were saved as a direct result of her actions is uncertain, but ultimately what was important was that she dared to put her head above the parapet, and cared enough to speak out and to act. Eleanor fought long and hard to awaken the consciences of her fellow citizens, and to restore Britain's reputation as a generous and humane society through her campaigning. For that, she deserves to be remembered and is owed a very great debt.

*To Eleanor Rathbone who knew, cared and acted.*[5]

NOTES

1. Dedication in W. Mosse, *Second Chance. Two Centuries of German-speaking Jews in the United Kingdom* (Tübingen: Mohr, 1991).
2. M. Stocks, *Eleanor Rathbone: A Biography* (London: Victor Gollancz, 1949), p.340.
3. V. Gollancz, 'Eleanor Rathbone', *AJR Information* (February 1946), p.13.
4. J. Parkes, *Voyage of Discoveries* (London: Victor Gollancz, 1969). Parkes died in 1981; for his life, see Haim Chertok, *He Also Spoke as a Jew: The Life of James Parkes* (London: Vallentine Mitchell, 2006) and Colin Richmond, *Campaigner Against Anti-Semitism: The Reverend James Parkes 1896–1981* (London: Vallentine Mitchell, 2005).
5. Dedication in T. Kushner, *The Holocaust and the Liberal Imagination: A Social and Cultural History* (Oxford: Blackwell, 1994).

# *Postscript: Tributes to Eleanor Rathbone*

## ELEANOR'S PERSONAL TRIBUTE

Beyond Eleanor's campaigning, her strong sense of personal responsibility towards the Czech refugees and her concern for their well-being were demonstrated tangibly in December 1940, when she added a codicil to her will. She included a legacy of £7,500 for 'the benefit of refugees from any country, chiefly but not necessarily exclusively political refugees from the country Protectorate or area prior to 1939 known as Czechoslovakia'. After her death in January 1946, the Eleanor Rathbone Trust worked in conjunction with the Czech Refugee Trust Fund and in August 1946 a notice in the *News Chronicle* brought forth some applications for money from a number of refugees.[1] Other refugees were to benefit from Eleanor's legacy, for in September 1946, Victor Gollancz approached Elizabeth Macadam, one of the trustees, seeking financial help for an initiative being organized by the Countess Karolyi, on behalf of children, mostly orphaned, in Hungary. He was sure that this was 'a work of rescue' into which Eleanor would have 'thrown herself heart and soul if she had known the circumstances'.[2] By October 1946, the trustees had agreed to make a donation of £200 to the Countess's Children's Fund, which was establishing a children's home in Hungary.[3]

## INTERNATIONAL TRIBUTES

Within a month of Eleanor's death, Elizabeth Macadam had been approached by the Children and Youth Aliyah Committee in Great Britain, proposing a permanent memorial for Eleanor in Palestine.[4] On the one hand they wanted tangible recognition of the deep interest that Eleanor had expressed on her visit to Palestine in 1934, when she had met Henrietta Szold and seen the work being done by the organization for children, and the educational and agricultural systems being used. But they also wanted to make an enduring tribute and expression of gratitude for her work for persecuted Jewry.[5]

A few months later, in November 1946, the *Manchester Guardian* reported that there were plans for a memorial to Eleanor. An appeal was subsequently launched, in conjunction with the London Rathbone Memorial Committee, to raise funds for a school in Israel.[6] The Association of Jewish Refugees were represented on the appeal committee as they felt that 'Jewish refugees owe a special obligation to contribute to this project as an expression of their gratitude to Eleanor Rathbone'.[7] The cornerstone for the school, designed by Tel-Aviv architects Averbuch and Baron, was laid on 3 September 1948.[8]

The Eleanor Rathbone School (House) at the Youth Aliyah Farming Institute in Magdiel, near Tel Aviv, was finally opened by Dr Vera Weizmann, Chaim Weizmann's wife, on 19 October 1949. The building had four classrooms, laboratories, a concert hall, library, reading room and offices.[9] Eleanor's fellow MP and refugee activist, David Grenfell, had travelled, with Dr Israel Feldman, a fellow member of the London Committee of the Rathbone Memorial Institute in Palestine and chairman of the British Youth Aliyah Committee, from London for the ceremony, and he presented a picture of Eleanor to the Institute.[10] Dr Feldman had this to say:

> After the death in London on January 2nd 1946, of Miss Eleanor Rathbone, a representative committee was formed in Great Britain with a view to arranging for a fitting permanent memorial to this great social worker. With no hesitation whatever this committee accepted the proposal conveyed through the Youth Aliyah Committee of Great Britain that an institution for the comprehensive rehabilitation of Jewish children in Israel would be a most suitable memorial to Eleanor Rathbone and one of a type that she herself would have wished ... In the sphere of humanity Eleanor Rathbone recognised no boundaries, and it is in that spirit that I now formally ask the Governors of this institution on behalf of the Committee in Great Britain and of Youth Aliyah to accept this great trust. We are confident that through your work within these walls, and in a wider sphere, the cherished memory of this great Christian lady, Eleanor Rathbone, will remain fresh and fragrant and that generations of Israeli children will throughout the years learn to bless her work.[11]

The foreign minister, Moishe Sharrett, paid tribute to Eleanor, whom he had met in London in 1944 in connection with the Jews of Hungary, describing her as 'a unique British woman who devoted her life to fighting for causes which she considered just. She had fought relentlessly to save European Jews, and especially the children.'[12] The London committee under the patronage of Lord Horder and chairmanship of Mrs Barbara Ayrton-Gould MP had contributed 10,000 IL towards the total building costs which totalled 24,000 IL. The following day, 22 October 1949, David Grenfell gave a most moving speech that was broadcast on Kol Israel. The Eleanor Rathbone School still stands today, immortalizing her spirit, courage and compassion (see Plates 29 and 30).

## CLOSER TO HOME: LIVING MEMORIALS

In 1964, and as a result of a joint project between the Association of Jewish Refugees and the Central British Fund for World Jewish Relief, the then recipient of West German reparation funds, a strikingly modern thirteen-storey block of studio flats, originally intended to provide sheltered accommodation for elderly Jewish refugees, was opened in Highgate, North London, not far from Eleanor's last home. As a tribute to the woman who had fought so hard on behalf of refugees fleeing Nazi persecution, the building was named Eleanor Rathbone House, and remained so until its closure in the late 1990s. The building was sold at auction in July 2003 for £5.7 million.[13]

Amongst the other tributes paid to Eleanor, in March 1986, a blue plaque was placed outside Tufton Court, Tufton Street, London SW1, the place where she had lived for many years. And on 29 July 2001 a blue plaque was installed at Greenbank House, Mossley Hill Liverpool, to commemorate the house where she and her father William, both social reformers, had resided.

## NOTES

1. 28 August 1946, NA HO 294/7.
2. Letter of V. Gollancz to E. Macadam, 3 September 1946, Victor Gollancz Papers, MSS 157/3/RA/1/4, Modern Records Centre (MRC).
3. Letters connected with this donation in the Victor Gollancz Papers, MSS 157/3/RA/1/1–21, MRC.
4. Letter of E. Macadam to V. Gollancz, 27 February 1946, Victor Gollancz Papers, MSS 157/3/RA/1/2, MRC.
5. Eleanor Rathbone Memorial Scheme, Victor Gollancz Papers, MSS 1578/3/ RA/1/3, MRC.
6. *Manchester Guardian,* 23 November 1946; 'Eleanor Rathbone Memorial', *AJR Information* (12 December 1946), p.96.
7. 'Eleanor Rathbone Memorial', *AJR Information* (12 December 1946), p.94.
8. Letter of Eva Michaelis to Mrs Kramarsky, 10 October 1948, Hadassah Archive, RG1, Box 30, Folder 221. Also Report, 'Opening of the ER Memorial Building at Magdiel (Israel) on October 19, 1949', Hadassah Archive, RG1, Box 30, Folder 221, American Jewish Historical Society (AJHS).
9. *Palestine Post*, 20 October 1949, pp.2, 3; 21 October 1949, p.4. *Jewish Chronicle*, 21 October 1949.
10. *Child and Youth Aliyah Facts and Figures* (1 November 1949), pp.2–3, Hadassah Archive, RG1, Box 29, Folder 215, AJHS.
11. *Informative Bulletin* (19 October 1949), Hadassah Archive, RG1, Box 30, Folder 221, AJHS.
12. Ibid.
13. Ruth Rothenberg, 'End of an Era at Eleanor Rathbone House', *AJR Journal* (October 2003).

# *Bibliography*

This bibliography lists unpublished sources consulted, though not necessarily cited. It also includes a select list of published sources consulted, though not necessarily cited.

UNPUBLISHED DOCUMENTARY SOURCES

*United Kingdom*

1. Government Papers (all National Archives, Kew)

Record classes consulted (in the notes all citations are given the prefix NA)

*Cabinet Office*

CAB 23 Cabinet Minutes to 1939, 1916–39
CAB 65 Cabinet Minutes 1939–45
CAB 66 Cabinet Memoranda WP and CP Series, 1939–45
CAB 67 Cabinet Memoranda WP (G) Series 1939–41
CAB 95 Committees on the Middle East and Africa, 1939–45
CAB 98 Miscellaneous Committees, 1939–47

*Colonial Office*

CO 733 Palestine Original Correspondence, 1921–45
CO 793 Palestine: Registers of Correspondence, 1921–48

*Foreign Office*

FO 371 Foreign Office – General Correspondence: Political, 1906–57

*Home Office*

HO 13 Home Office: Criminal Entry Books
HO 45 Home Office: Registered Papers 1839–1979
HO 213 Home Office: Aliens Department: General (GEN) Files and Aliens' Naturalization and Nationality Files (ALN and NTY Symbol Series) Files, 1920–61
HO 214 Internees: Personal Files, 1940–9
HO 215 Internment: General Files, 1940–51

HO 294 Czechoslovak Refugee Trust: Records, 1938–79
HO 382 Home Office: Aliens Department: Aliens Personal Files, 1895–1992
HO 405 Home Office: Aliens Department and successors: Aliens Personal Files, Applications for Naturalization, 1906–96

*Prime Minister's Files*
PREM 1 Prime Minister's Office: Correspondence and Papers, 1916–40
PREM 4 Confidential Papers, 1939–46

*Security Service*
KV 2: Security Service Personal (PF Series) Files 1913–79

*Treasury*
T 160 Treasury: Registered Files: Finance Files (F Series) 1887–1948
T 161 Supply Files, 1905–51
T 172 Chancellor of the Exchequer's Office: Miscellaneous papers 1792–1962

PRIVATE PAPERS

Listed by location

*BBC Written Archives*
Margery Fry file
Eleanor Rathbone file

*British Library, London*
Cecil of Chelwood
Sir R.F. Harrod
Society of Authors
Marie Stopes

*British Library, Oriental and India Office, London*
Cornelia Sorabji
Samuel Hoare (Templewood collection)
John Simon

*British Library of Political and Economic Science, London*
Lord Beveridge (Academic Assistance Council)
League of Nations Union

G. Wallas
Women Power Committee

*Cambridge University Library*
Crewe (Robert Offley Ashburton Crewe-Milnes)
Committee For Intellectual Liberty
Walter Layton
Sir Francis Meynell
Viscount Templewood (Sir Samuel Hoare)

*Churchill Archives Centre, Churchill College, Cambridge*
Winston Spencer Churchill
Professor Archibald Vivian Hill
Lord Philip Noel-Baker
Viscount Thurso

*Contemporary Medical Archives, Wellcome Library, London*
Eugenics Society

*Imperial War Museum*
Julian Layton
Mrs I. Rischowski
Mary Sibthorp
Ronald Stent
Robert Stopford

*Institute of Education, University of London*
German Educational Reconstruction

*John Rylands University Library of Manchester*
Labour History Archive: William Gillies papers
*Manchester Guardian*

*Lambeth Palace, London*
George Bell
William Temple

*Lancashire Record Office, Preston, Lancs.*
Cooper Papers

*London Metropolitan Archives*
Board of Deputies of British Jews

*Modern Records Centre, University of Warwick*
Wilfrid Roberts
Victor Gollancz

*National Archives of Scotland*
Lord Lothian

*National Library of Wales*
New Commonwealth Collection, Lord Davies of Llandinam

*New Bodleian Library, Oxford*
Autograph Papers
John Lawrence Le Breton Hammond
Francis Sydney Marvin
Gilbert Murray
Society for the Protection of Science and Learning
Sidgwick and Jackson
E.J. Thompson

*Parkes Library, University of Southampton*
Cissy B. Rosenfelder
Rabbi Solomon Schonfeld
Union of Jewish Women
Rabbi Joseph H. Hertz
James Parkes

*Parliamentary Archive, London*
Lloyd George
Parliamentary Committee on Refugees
Viscount Samuel
H. Graham White

*Library of Religious Society of Friends, London*
India Conciliation Group

*Somerville College, Oxford*
Minute books of the Associated Prigs Society 1894–99
College meetings, Minutes I. Michaelmas Term 1894–Hilary Term 1901
Annual Reports of Somerville Students Association 1898 onwards
Reports of Collections, Somerville Hall, October 1891

*Sydney Jones Library, University of Liverpool*
Eleanor Rathbone (RP XIV)

*Trinity College Library, Cambridge University*
R.A. Butler

*University of Birmingham*
Oliver Lodge

*University of Edinburgh*
Arthur Koestler

*University of Hull*
National Council for Civil Liberties

*University of Reading*
Nancy Astor

*Women's Library, London Guildhall University*
Eleanor Rathbone
Margaret Corbett Ashby
International Alliance of Women
Kathleen Courtney
Six Point Group
Open Door Council
British Federation of University Women
St Joan International Alliance

*Weiner Library, London*
Central British Fund for World Jewish Relief (microfilm)

PRIVATE COLLECTIONS

Papers of Margery Fry
Papers of Victor Cazalet (by courtesy of Sir Edward Cazalet)
Orion Archive

*Israel*
Central Zionist Archives, Jerusalem
Henrietta Szold
Norman Bentwich
Schwartzbart Diaries, Yad Vashem Institute Archives

The Zionist Organization
The Jewish Agency for Palestine/Israel, Central Office, London Papers
Weizmann Archives, Weizmann Institute of Science, Jerusalem
World Jewish Congress
Youth Aliyah

*Switzerland*
International Committee of the Red Cross, Geneva
National Committee for the Rescue from Nazi Terror Papers

*United States of America*
Hadassah Archive (Youth Aliyah), American Jewish Historical Society, New York
Katherine Mayo, Beinecke Library, Yale University
Norman Angell collection, Ball State University Archives and Special Collections, Indiana
Records of the War Refugee Board, Franklin D. Roosevelt Presidential Library, Hyde Park, New York

ORAL TESTIMONY

*Personal Interviews by the Author*
Vera Schaerli, Sussex, 22 February 2000
Joan Gibson, Southgate, London, 31 March 2000
Helga Wolff, Wembley, 23 May 2000
Margaret Simey, Liverpool, 5 June 2000
Tim Rathbone, London, 5 July 2000
Siggy Nissel, Barnet, Herts., 12 November 2000
Ernst and Janet Sondheimer, Highgate, 20 December 2000
Arieh Handler, St John's Wood, 11 April 2003

*Telephone Interviews by the Author*
Herbert Anderson, 1 April 2000
Willi Usher, 14 November 2000
Noreen Rathbone, 21 November 2000
Livia Gollancz, 9 January 2001
Vera Gissing, 14 January 2001
Bertha Leverton, 15 January 2001
Dorothy Rainford, 16 January 2001
Nicholas Winton, 19 January 2001
Cyril Goldstein, 24 March 2001
Ilse Eton, 6 April 2001

Nan McKean, 16 June 2001
Harriet Hagen, 22 July 2001

UNPUBLISHED THESES AND PAPERS

Cohen, S., 'Eleanor Rathbone and the Refugees' (PhD diss., University of Southampton, 2005).

Gooptu, S., 'Cornelia Sorabji 1866–1954: A Woman's Biography' (D.Phil. diss., Oxford University, 1997).

Humphreys, R., 'The Poor Law and Charity: The Charity Organisation Society in the Provinces 1870–1890' (PhD diss., University of London, 1991).

London, L., 'British Immigration Control Procedures and Jewish Refugees 1939–42' (PhD diss., University of London, 1992).

Okkenhaug, I.M., 'The Quality of Heroic Living, of High Endeavour and Adventure: Anglican Mission, Women and Education in Palestine 1888–1948' (D.Art. diss., University of Bergen, 1999).

Simoni, M., '"Germs Know No Racial Lines". Health Policies in British Palestine (1930–1939)' (PhD diss., University of London, 2001).

Williams, B., 'History of Liverpool's Jewish Community'. Paper presented to Manchester Jewish Museum, June 1987.

RADIO PROGRAMMES

Transcript of BBC Home Service (Schools) programme given by Margery Fry, 'For the Fourteens. "Eleanor Rathbone"', 18 March 1952.

PUBLISHED WORKS

Adams, P., *Somerville for Women: An Oxford College 1879–1993* (Oxford: Oxford University Press, 1996).

Adler-Rudel, S., 'A Chronicle of Rescue Efforts', *Leo Baeck Institute Year Book*, XI (1966), pp.213–41.

Alberti, J., *Eleanor Rathbone* (London: Sage, 1996).

Barker, P. (ed.), *Founders of the Welfare State* (London: Heinemann, 1984).

Bauer, Y., *Jews For Sale? Nazi-Jewish Negotiations, 1933–1945* (New Haven, CONN and London: Yale University Press, 1994).

Bentwich, N., *England in Palestine* (London: Kegan Paul, 1932).

—— *They Found Refuge: An Account of British Jewry's Work for Victims of Nazi Oppression* (London: Cresset, 1956).

—— *My 77 Years: An Account of my Life and Times 1883–1960* (London: Routledge and Kegan Paul, 1962).

Bernstein, D. (ed.), *Pioneers and Homemakers: Jewish Women in Pre-State Israel* (Albany, NY: State University of New York, 1992).

Birn, D., *The League of Nations Union 1918–1945* (Oxford: Clarendon Press, 1981).

Bolchover, R., *British Jewry and the Holocaust*, 2nd edn (Oxford: Littman Library of Jewish Civilization, 2003).

Braham, R., *The Politics of Genocide: The Holocaust in Hungary*, vol. 2 (New York and Guildford: Columbia University Press, 1981).

Brittain, V., *The Women at Oxford* (London: Harrap, 1960).

Brodetsky, S., *Memoirs: From Ghetto to Israel* (London: Weidenfeld and Nicolson, 1960).

Brookes, P., *Women at Westminster: An Account of Women in the British Parliament 1918–1966* (London: Peter Davies, 1967).

Bruley, S., 'Women Against War and Fascism: Communism, Feminism and the People's Front', in J. Fyrth (ed.), *Britain, Fascism and the Popular Front* (London: Laurence and Wishart, 1985), pp.135–56.

Browning, C., *Fateful Months: Essays on the Emergence of the Final Solution* (New York: Holmes and Meier, 1985).

—— *The Origins of the Final Solution: The Evolution of Nazi Jewish Policy, September 1939–March 1942* (Lincoln, NE: University of Nebraska Press; Jerusalem: Yad Vashem, 2004).

Bunting, A., 'Representing Rescue: The National Committee for Rescue from Nazi Terror, the British and the Rescue of Jews from Nazism', *The Journal of Holocaust Education*, 9, 1 (2000), pp.65–84.

Burton, A., *Burdens of History: British Feminists, Indian Women and Imperial Culture 1865–1915* (Chapel Hill, NC and London: University of North Carolina, 1994).

—— *At the Heart of the Empire: Indians and the Colonial Encounter in Late-Victorian Britain* (Berkeley, CA and London: University of California Press, 1998).

Candy, C., 'Competing Transnational Representations of the 1930s Indian Franchise Question', in I. Fletcher, L. Mayhall and P. Levine (eds), *Women's Suffrage in the British Empire: Citizenship, Nation and Race* (London: Routledge, 2000), pp.191–206.

Carsten, F., 'German Refugees in Great Britain 1933–1945', in G. Hirshfeld (ed.), *Exile in Britain: Refugees from Hitler's Germany* (Leamington Spa: Berg for the German Historical Institute, 1984), pp.11–28.

Ceadel, M., *Semi-Detached Idealists: The British Peace Movement and International Relations 1854–1945* (Oxford: Oxford University Press, 2000).

Cesarani, D., *Arthur Koestler: The Homeless Mind* (London: Heinemann, 1999).
—— 'Mad Dogs and Englishmen: Towards a Taxonomy of Rescuers in a Bystander Country – Britain 1933–45', *The Journal of Holocaust Education*, 9, 2 and 3 (2000), pp.28–56.
—— *Eichmann: His Life and Crimes* (London: W. Heinemann, 2004).
—— (ed.), *The Final Solution* (London: Routledge, 1993).
—— (ed.), *The Internment of Aliens in Twentieth-Century Britain* (London and Portland, OR: Frank Cass, 1993).
—— (ed.), *Genocide and Rescue: The Holocaust in Hungary 1944* (Oxford and New York: Berg, 1997).
Chertok, H., *He Also Spoke as a Jew: The Life of James Parkes* (London: Vallentine Mitchell, 2006).
Christensen, C.A.R., *Fridtjof Nansen: A Life in the Service of Science and Humanity* (Geneva: UN High Commissioner for Refugees, 1961).
Cohen, M., *Churchill and the Jews* (London: Frank Cass, 1985).
Cooper, R.M. (ed.), *Refugee Scholars: Conversations with Tessa Simpson* (Leeds: Moorland, 1992).
Dawidowicz, L., *The War against the Jews, 1933–1945*, 10th edn (Harmondsworth: Penguin, 1987).
Decker, K., 'Divisions and Diversity: The Complexities of Medical Refuge in Britain, 1933–1948', *Bulletin of the History of Medicine*, 77, 4 (Winter 2003), pp.850–73.
Donoughue, B., *Herbert Morrison: Portrait of a Politician* (London: Weidenfeld and Nicolson, 1973).
Emanuel, M. and V. Gissing, *Nicholas Winton and the Rescued Generation* (London: Vallentine Mitchell, 2002).
Engel, D., *In the Shadow of Auschwitz: The Polish Government in Exile 1939–42* (Chapel Hill, NC and London: University of North Carolina Press, 1987).
—— *Facing a Holocaust: The Polish Government in Exile 1943–45* (Chapel Hill, NC and London: University of North Carolina Press, 1993).
Feingold, H., *The Politics of Rescue: The Roosevelt Administration and the Holocaust, 1938–45* (New Brunswick, NJ: Rutgers University Press, 1970).
Fogelman, E., *Conscience and Courage: Rescuers of Jews during the Holocaust* (London: Cassell, 1993).
Frank, M., *Expelling the Germans: British Opinion and Post-1945 Population Transfer in Context* (Oxford: Oxford University Press, 2007).
Friedlander, S., *Nazi Germany and the Jews: The Years of Persecution 1933–39* (London: Weidenfeld and Nicolson, 1997).

Fyrth, J., *The Signal Was Spain: The Aid Spain Movement in Britain 1936–39* (London: Laurence and Wishart, 1986).
Gilbert, M., *Britain, Palestine and the Jews 1891–1939* (Oxford: Oxford Centre for Postgraduate Hebrew Studies, 1977).
—— *Auschwitz and the Allies* (London: Joseph, 1981).
—— *Churchill and the Jews* (London: Simon and Schuster, 2007).
Gillman, P. and L. Gillman, *'Collar the Lot!' How Britain Interned and Expelled its Wartime Refugees* (London: Quartet, 1980).
Gollancz, V., *Let My People Go* (London: Victor Gollancz, 1942/43).
—— 'Eleanor Rathbone', *AJR Information* (February 1946), p.13.
Gottlieb, A.Z., *Men of Vision: Anglo-Jewry's Aid to Victims of the Nazi Regime, 1939–45* (London: Weidenfeld and Nicolson, 1998).
Harris, M.J. and D. Oppenheimer (eds), *Into the Arms of Strangers: Stories of the Kindertransport* (London: Bloomsbury, 2000).
Harrison, B., *Prudent Revolutionaries: Portraits of British Feminists between the Wars* (Oxford: Clarendon Press, 1987).
Hilberg, R., *The Destruction of the European Jews*, vol. 3, 2nd edn (New York and London: Holmes and Meier, 1985).
Holmes, C., *John Bull's Island: Immigration and British Society 1871–1971* (Basingstoke: Macmillan, 1988).
Hyamson, A., *Palestine under the Mandate 1920–1948* (London: Methuen, 1950).
Kacewicz, G., *Great Britain, the Soviet Union and the Polish Government in Exile, 1939–1945* (The Hague and London: Nijhoff, 1979).
Kapp, Y. and M. Mynatt, *British Policy and the Refugees 1933–1941* (London: Frank Cass, 1997).
Kochan, M., *Britain's Internees in the Second World War* (London: Macmillan, 1983).
Kushner, T., *The Persistence of Prejudice: Antisemitism in British Society during the Second World War* (Manchester: Manchester University Press, 1989).
—— *The Holocaust and the Liberal Imagination: A Social and Cultural History* (Oxford: Blackwell, 1994).
—— '"Pissing in the Wind"? The Search for Nuance in the Study of Holocaust "Bystanders"', *The Journal of Holocaust Education*, 9, 2 and 3 (2000), pp.57–76.
Kushner, T. and K. Knox, *Refugees in an Age of Genocide: Global, National and Local Perspectives during the Twentieth Century* (London: Frank Cass, 1999).
Kushner, T. and K. Lunn (eds), *The Politics of Marginality: Race, the Radical Right and Minorities in Twentieth-Century Britain* (London: Frank Cass, 1990).

Lafitte, F., *The Internment of Aliens* (Harmondsworth and New York: Allen Lane, 1940).
Leverton, B. and S. Lowensohn, *I Came Alone* (Lewes: Book Guild, 1990).
Levine, P., *From Indifference to Activism: Swedish Diplomacy and the Holocaust, 1938–1944* (Stockholm: Uppsala University Library, 1998).
London, L., *Whitehall and the Jews, 1933–1948. British Immigration Policy and the Holocaust* (Cambridge: Cambridge University Press, 2000).
Macklin, G. '"A Quite Natural and Moderate Defensive Action?" The 1945 Hampstead "Anti-alien" Petition', *Patterns of Prejudice*, 37, 3 (2003), pp.277–300.
Marrus, M., *The Unwanted: European Refugees and the Twentieth Century* (New York and Oxford: Oxford University Press, 1985).
—— *The Holocaust in History* (London: Weidenfeld and Nicolson, 1988).
Mayo, K. (edited and with an introduction by M. Sinha), *Selections from Mother India* (Ann Arbor, MI: University of Michigan Press, 2000).
Medawar, J. and D. Pyke, *Hitler's Gift: Scientists who Fled Nazi Germany* (London: Richard Cohen Books, 2000).
Michaelis, D. and E. Michaelis, *Emissaries in Wartime London, 1938–1945* (Jerusalem: Hamaatik Press, 1989).
Mosse, W., *Second Chance: Two Centuries of German-speaking Jews in the United Kingdom* (Tübingen: Mohr, 1991).
Newman, A., *The Board of Deputies of British Jews 1760–1985* (London: Vallentine Mitchell, 1987).
Nicholas, S., *Echo of War: Home Front Propaganda and the Wartime BBC, 1939–45* (Manchester: Manchester University Press, 1996).
Oldfield, S., *Women Humanitarians: A Biographical Dictionary of British Women Active between 1900–1950* (London: Continuum, 2001).
—— '"It Is Usually She": British Women's Role in the Rescue and Care of the Kindertransport Kinder', in W. Benz, C. Curio and A. Hammel (eds), *Kindertransport*, *Shofar*, Special Edition (Fall 2004), pp.57–70.
Oliner, S. and P., *The Altruistic Personality: Rescuers of Jews in Nazi Europe* (New York: Free Press; London: Collier Macmillan, 1988).
Parkes, J., *Voyage of Discoveries* (London: Victor Gollancz, 1969).
Pedersen, S., 'National Bodies, Unspeakable Acts: The Sexual Politics of Colonial Policy-making', *Journal of Modern History*, 63 (1991), pp.647–80.

—— *Eleanor Rathbone and the Politics of Conscience* (London: Yale University Press, 2004).

Pedersen S. and P. Mandler (eds), *After the Victorians: Private Conscience and Public Duty in Modern Britain* (London: Routledge, 1994).

Penkower, M.N., *The Jews Were Expendable: Free World Diplomacy and the Holocaust* (Urbana, IL: University of Illinois Press, 1983).

Ramusack, B., 'Catalysts or Helpers? British Feminists, Indian Women's Rights and Indian Independence', in G. Minault (ed.), *The Extended Family: Women and Political Participation in India and Pakistan* (Delhi: Chanakya Publications, 1981), pp.109–50.

—— 'Cultural Missionaries, Maternal Imperialists, Feminist Allies: British Women Activists in India 1865–1945', *Women's Studies International Forum*, 13, 4 (1990), pp.309–21.

Rathbone, E.F., *William Rathbone: A Memoir* (London: Macmillan, 1905).

—— *Child Marriage: The Indian Minotaur. An Object Lesson from the Past to the Future* (London: George Allen and Unwin, 1934).

—— *War Can be Averted* (London: Gollancz, 1938).

—— *Rescue the Perishing* (London: Gollancz, 1943).

—— *Falsehoods and Facts about the Jews* (London: Gollancz, 1944).

Richmond, C., *Campaigner Against Anti-Semitism: The Reverend James Parkes 1896–1981* (London: Vallentine Mitchell, 2005).

Richter, M., *The Politics of Conscience: T.H. Green and His Age* (London: Weidenfeld and Nicolson, 1964).

Roseman, M., *The Villa, the Lake, the Meeting: Wansee and the Final Solution* (London: Allen Lane/Penguin, 2002).

Rubinstein, W., *The Myth of Rescue: Why the Democracies Could Not Have Saved More Jews from the Nazis* (London: Routledge, 1997).

Searle, G., *Eugenics and Politics in Britain, 1910–1914* (Leyden: Noordhoff International Publishing, 1976).

Segev, T., *One Palestine, Complete: Jews and Arabs under the British Mandate* (London: Little, Brown, 2000).

Seller, M., *We Built Up Our Lives: Jewish Refugees Interned by Great Britain in World War II* (Westport, CT and London: Greenwood Press, 2001).

Shatzkes, P., *Holocaust and Rescue: Impotent or Indifferent Anglo-Jewry 1938–1945* (Basingstoke: Palgrave, 2002).

Shepherd, N., *Wilfrid Israel: German Jewry's Secret Ambassador* (London: Weidenfeld and Nicolson, 1984).

—— *Ploughing Sand: British Rule in Palestine 1917–1948* (London: John Murray, 1999).

Sherman, A.J., *Island Refuge: Britain and Refugees from the Third Reich*

*1933–39*, 2nd edn (Ilford: Frank Cass, 1994).
—— *Mandate Days: British Lives in Palestine 1918–1948* (London: Thames and Hudson, 1997).
Simey, M., *Eleanor Rathbone 1872–1946, A Centenary Tribute* (Liverpool: Liverpool University Press, 1974).
—— *Charity Rediscovered: A Study of Philanthropic Effort in Nineteenth-Century Liverpool* (Liverpool: Liverpool University Press, 1992).
—— *The Disinherited Society: A Personal View of Social Responsibility in Liverpool during the Twentieth Century* (Liverpool: Liverpool University Press, 1996).
Sinha, M., 'Reading Mother India: Empire, Nation and the Female Voice', *Journal of Women's History*, 6, 2 (Summer 1994), pp.1527–2036.
—— 'Suffragism and Internationalism: The Enfranchisement of British and Indian Women under an Imperial State', in I. Fletcher, L. Mayhall and P. Levine (eds), *Women's Suffrage in the British Empire: Citizenship, Nation and Race* (London: Routledge, 2000), pp.224–39.
Sompolinsky, M., *Britain and the Holocaust: The Failure of Anglo-Jewish Leadership?* (Brighton: Sussex Academic Press, 1999).
Stent, R., *A Bespattered Page? The Internment of His Majesty's 'Most Loyal Enemy Aliens'*, (London: Deutsch, 1980).
Stocks, M., *Eleanor Rathbone: A Biography* (London: Victor Gollancz, 1949).
Stone, D., *Breeding Superman: Nietzsche, Race and Eugenics in Edwardian and Interwar Britain* (Liverpool: Liverpool University Press, 2002).
Taylor, A.J.P., *The Trouble Makers: Dissent over Foreign Policy, 1792–1939* (Harmondsworth: Penguin, 1957).
Templewood, Viscount, *Nine Troubled Years* (London: Collins, 1954).
Thompson, N., *The Anti-Appeasers: Conservative Opposition to Appeasement in the 1930s* (Oxford: Clarendon Press, 1971).
Tuchman, B., *Bible and Sword: England and Palestine from the Bronze Age to Balfour* (London: Phoenix, 2001).
Warriner, D., 'Winter in Prague', *Slavonic and East European Review*, 62 (April 1984), pp.209–40.
Wasserstein, B., *Britain and the Jews of Europe 1939–1945*, 2nd edn (Oxford: Oxford University Press, 1988).
Wood, E. Thomas and S.M. Jankowski, *Karski: How One Man Tried To Stop the Holocaust* (New York: Wiley, 1994).
Wyman, D. (ed.), *America and the Holocaust: War Refugee Board 'Weekly Reports'*, vol. II (New York and London: Garland, 1989).

—— *The Abandonment of the Jews: America and the Holocaust 1941–45* (New York: Pantheon, 1984).

Zamet, J.S., 'Aliens or Colleagues? Refugees from Nazi Oppression 1933–45', *British Dental Journal* (2006), pp.397–407.

Zweig, R., *Britain and Palestine during the Second World War* (Woodbridge: Boydell for the Royal Historical Society, 1986).

# *Index*

E



F

I

N

O



P

T